Forces in

Modern

British

Literature

1885–1956

Forces in

WILLIAM
YORK
TINDALL

Modern

British

Literature

VINTAGE BOOKS
1956
NEW YORK

1885–1956

© WILLIAM YORK TINDALL, 1956
PUBLISHED BY VINTAGE BOOKS, INC.
REPRINTED BY ARRANGEMENT WITH ALFRED A. KNOPF, INC.
FIRST EDITION, 1947. REPRINTED TWICE.

FIRST VINTAGE EDITION

PREFACE:

*T*HIS account of contemporary literature in the British Isles was published for the first time in 1947. The present edition differs in several particulars from the first. Bringing it more or less up to date, I added many things —but left more out; for time changes values, and not only selection but compression proved necessary again. 1885 still seemed a good beginning because at that time naturalism and symbolism began to shape British literature; around that time Yeats, Shaw, and Moore commenced their work, and Hopkins was in full career; and shortly before that time Joyce and Virginia Woolf were born. Since almost everything in current literature is implicit in the literature of the 1880's, I have treated the intervening period as a unit. Developments within its complexity determine my chapters. Their patterns are various, at their simplest chronological, suggesting causes and effects; but such patterns are conveniences. My concern has been not only with history, but also with meanings and values.

The labyrinth of contemporary British literature is part of a greater design that involves the literatures of America and the Continent. It is foolish to isolate part of this whole, yet impossible in a book of this size to do justice to the whole. By way of compromise I have tried, while considering the part, to preserve a sense of the whole by pointing to connections between British and other literatures, especially French, and between British literature and foreign ideas. Hence the brief accounts of Baudelaire,

Zola, Henry James, Bergson, Freud, Kafka, the surrealists, and many others. The footnotes, chiefly bibliographical, will guide those who care to follow additional clues.

Although literature since 1885 constitutes a whole, there is little reason but convenience for separating it from earlier literature. The literature of our time belongs to the great romantic movement with which we associate Wordsworth and Rousseau. Labels like "romantic," at once tiresome and useful, help us to understand the character of a period and of its individual works. But when one says "romantic," one must define, for nothing is more confusing than romanticism and nothing more complex. Because of this complexity the many definers of romanticism, missing the whole, identify one or more of its parts. Like my predecessors, I shall content myself with isolating what I consider some of the principal qualities of romanticism: the transcendental, the exploratory, and the bourgeois.

Since the Renaissance, humanism and science have conspired to break the "chain of being" that, uniting the upper regions of reality with the lower, had unified all things. Seeking the lost spiritual half of reality, some romantics tried to join it with matter again through religion or symbol. Symbolist poetry, Methodist enthusiasm, the Oxford Movement, and synthetic orientalism are typical results. Others tried to find spiritual satisfaction in secular objects—in flowers, mountains, ruins, savages, heroes, and the past. Shelley, Thoreau, Carlyle, Rimbaud, Dostoyevsky, Shaw, and D. H. Lawrence come easily to mind. For the eighteenth-century conviction that churches were churches and flowers flowers, these transcendentalists, trying to find meaning in a meaningless world, substituted wonder. In *Science and the Modern World* Whitehead calls romanticism the rediscovery of value.

Classicism is making the most of limitations. The eighteenth century, having fixed the limits of reality, achieved perfection within them. In poetry the couplet was the type and symbol of limitation and perfection. Jane Austen, perfect in her province, chose to ignore what lay beyond it. But some of her contemporaries, impatient with limits, began to explore regions above, behind, and below her reality. For later artists reality included all nature from the material to the immaterial, all kinds and classes of men, all levels of consciousness. With the aid of science, symbol, and myth these explorers continually penetrated new areas of experience and, at whatever cost to perfection, enriched the arts.

Such enrichment coincided with the emergence of the present ruling class. Limitation was aristocratic. As capital replaced land, the revolt against limits became bourgeois. Rapid technical change, so characteristic of bourgeois industry, became characteristic of bourgeois art. Romanticism, becoming an expression of the middle class, became the triumph of middle-class taste. That many romantic artists have been enemies of the middle class is unimportant; for, since a ruling class determines its enemies, our artists and their arts are unmistakably bourgeois. Whether or not we like romanticism and the middle class, we too are middle-class romantics. Contemporary literature excites us not only because it is important, wonderful, and expansive, but also because it is our expression.

For the revision of this book I am indebted to James Gilvarry, Leo Hamalian, Stuart Hampshire, Daniel Hoffman, Lincoln Reis, and Jacob Schwartz, who offered information or advice; but my principal debts are to David Daiches, Geoffrey Wagner, and the librarians of Columbia University, who helped me catch up with the times.

                                                             W.Y.T.

Columbia University
November 17, 1955

ACKNOWLEDGMENTS:

I am indebted to Dodd, Mead & Company for permission to quote from *The Simpleton of the Unexpected Isles* by Bernard Shaw, copyright, 1936, by Bernard Shaw; to Harcourt, Brace and Company, Inc., for permission to quote from *To the Lighthouse* and *The Common Reader* by Virginia Woolf; to Henry Holt and Company, Inc., for a passage reprinted from "The Listeners" included in *Collected Poems* by Walter de la Mare, copyright, 1920, by Henry Holt and Company; to Brandt & Brandt for permission to quote from Max Beerbohm's *Seven Men*, published by Alfred A. Knopf, Inc., copyright, 1920, by Max Beerbohm; to The Macmillan Company for permission to quote from *The Dynasts* by Thomas Hardy and from *Autobiography, Essays,* and *Collected Poems* by W. B. Yeats; to New Directions for permission to quote from *The Collected Poems of Dylan Thomas;* to Charles Scribner's Sons for permission to quote from *Plays* by August Strindberg; to The Viking Press for permission to quote from *A Portrait of the Artist as a Young Man* by James Joyce; to the family of Gerard Manley Hopkins and to the Oxford University Press for permission to quote from *The Letters of Gerard Manley Hopkins to Robert Bridges.*

I am indebted to the late Dylan Thomas for permission to quote from a letter printed in *New Verse.*

CONTENTS:

I   *Exile*   PAGE   3

II   *Left*   27

III   *Right*   52

IV   *Disenchantment*   92

V   *The Troughs of Zolaism*   120

VI   *The Hunt for a Father*   154

VII   *The Stream of Consciousness*   187

VIII   *The Unconscious*   212

IX   *The Forest of Symbols*   246

X   *Myth and the Natural Man*   296

Index   FOLLOWS PAGE 316

Forces in

Modern

British

Literature

1885–1956

CHAPTER ONE: *Exile*

*T*HE artist's exile from middle-class society accounts in part for the character of our literature. Causes, if not effects, of this exile are easy to understand. More people than ever before could read, but, while literacy spread, its level fell and fewer could follow what they read. Moral and utilitarian, the ruling class had little tolerance for beauty, which, at best, seemed useless or disreputable. In effect, readers and the ruling class, like republican Plato before them, led the artist to the gates of the city and sent him along.

Accustomed to expressing feelings and ideas shared with a literate audience, poets slowly realized their disinclination or inability to express feelings so much coarser than their own or to celebrate the growing ugliness around them. Byron and Shelley abandoned England, while Carlyle and Arnold scolded on the shore. And on the French coast, looking out of his window, Baudelaire was filled with the "immense nausea of billboards."

Poets occupied their exile with poems and with theories about them. By example and reason they announced the independence of art, its freedom not only from society and moral convention but from nature itself. Some were content to shock the Philistines. Others, retreating into ivory towers, privately pursued naked beauty up the stairs. Pure literature became impure and, after a while, difficult. The enemies of the people, satisfying themselves, left the satisfaction of common taste to journalists and commercial artists.

This situation is the subject of George Gissing's *New Grub Street* (1891). Edwin Reardon, the hero, is kept by refinement, neurosis, and poverty from supplying "good, coarse, marketable stuff for the world's vulgar." By temperament he is unable to curry favor with editors, reviewers, and the literary gang, who, praising friends, damning enemies, tell the ignorant what is what. Jasper Milvain, however, knowing literature a trade, reasonably maintains that "we people of brains are justified in supplying the mob with the food it likes." As his field he takes the "upper middle-class of intellect, the people who like to feel that what they are reading has some special cleverness, but who can't distinguish between stones and paste." Whelpdale descends further than this middle-brow, planning a paper for "the quarter-educated; that is to say, the great new generation that is being turned out by the Board Schools." Adapting themselves to reality, Milvain and Whelpdale are suitably rewarded, but Reardon miserably expires. This novel, Gissing's best, is the best picture of audience and writer in our time.

As if to prove the soundness of Gissing, Arnold Bennett confessed with disconcerting honesty in *The Truth about an Author* (1903) to sentiments identical with Milvain's; and in his *Journals* (1932) he called himself an artist "with strong mercantile interests." Seeing the nature of his audience, he indefatigably supplied it with trash: sensational novels, absurd plays, "pocket philosophies," books on how to do this or that. With consequent wealth he bought a yacht, supported a mistress, and expired amidst comforts. But Bennett was an artist as well as a commercial artist. To satisfy himself he sometimes wrote a "serious" work for which he expected no reward. That these works, surprisingly, were as acceptable as the trash he wrote is to be explained perhaps by his acceptance of the world. No artist of our time was less an exile.[1]

[1] *A Great Man* (1904) is a cynical picture of the popular novelist and his public. Cf. Virginia Woolf on the "Middlebrow," *The Death of the Moth* (1942).

I

About the middle of the last century the doctrine of
art for art's sake began to encourage the exiled. Affirming
the separation of art from middle-class society, art for art's
sake implies the autonomy of art and artist, the rejection
of didactic aim, and the refusal to subject art to moral or
social judgments.[2] A work of art, the exiles said, must be
judged by beauty alone. This doctrine, said Tennyson, is
"the way to Hell."

An art remote from common life, intolerably pursuing ideals opposite to those of society, may seem evasive.
But ivory towers in suburbs are commentaries upon them.
Given ugliness and limited morality, and the pursuit of
beauty becomes as inevitable and useful as the antimacas-
sar. If this art is to be justified by beauty alone, its position
becomes less sure. But many of the works produced in the
name of beauty are equal in beauty to those of Tennyson.

Art for the sake of art, which flowered during the
eighties and nineties in the work of Wilde, Moore, and
Symons and later in the work of Joyce, had many roots in
the past. Its ultimate origins were in the German romantic
philosophers and in Keats and Poe. Rossetti, isolated from
society, revived Keats and offered an art without moral
or social purpose. Morris, desolated by the ugliness around
him, tried to restore beauty to useful things. Gautier in
Mademoiselle de Maupin (1834), Baudelaire in his poems
and in his preface to Poe, and Flaubert in his novels illustrated or recommended art for art's sake. Getting the doctrine from them, Whistler brought it to Swinburne, whose
essays pugnaciously defended *Poems and Ballads* (1866)
from his middle-class critics. While Swinburne inflamed
the young, Walter Pater seduced them. In the famous conclusion to his *Renaissance* (1873), where gemlike flames
consumed them as they discriminated moments for the
moments' sake, Pater summarized his German, French,

[2] Albert J. Farmer: *Le Mouvement esthétique et "décadent" en
Angleterre* (1931). Louise Rosenblatt: "*L'Idée de l'art pour l'art dans
la littérature anglaise pendant la période victorienne* (1931). William
Gaunt: *The Aesthetic Adventure* (1945).

and English predecessors in a prose that was itself the best argument for the cause of art. *Marius the Epicurean* (1885), tempered by Pater's almost religious asceticism, proved almost as seductive. Young men read these books, exaggerated what they read, and painted the nineties yellow.

Young Oscar Wilde discovered beauty at Oxford, where amid his fabulous blue china he read Swinburne, Rossetti, Baudelaire, and Pater, whose *Renaissance* became his "golden book." [3] Upon his graduation Wilde became apostle of beauty to the Philistines. Basing his conduct upon that of Swinburne and Baudelaire, his beautiful costume of velveteen shorts and silk stockings upon what he thought Rossetti meant, Wilde astounded Piccadilly. He was extravagant but shrewd. His shocking presence was designed not only to dramatize the ideas of the æsthetic philosophers but to make himself known. Consequently his *Poems* (1881) went through five editions. In these mediocre verses, which, anticipating Eliot's, summarize the past by theft and allusion, Wilde urged the Spirit of Beauty to elevate the "cheating merchants." Seeing little harm as yet in this eccentric, they caricatured his poppy and his lily in *Punch*. In *Patience* (1881) W. S. Gilbert, cleverly reflecting popular judgment, presented Wilde as an æsthetic sham, whose anti-Philistine excesses might be attributed to Rossetti and Swinburne. But America had never heard of Wilde. That *Patience* might have point, D'Oyly Carte, the producer, hired Wilde in 1882 to make a lecture tour of the States. He consented to this Philistine plan because it gave him further publicity and the chance to spread his gospel. A cartoon by Max Beerbohm shows the apostle of beauty confronting bearded farmers.

[3] Hesketh Pearson: *The Life of Oscar Wilde* (1946). Arthur Ransome: *Oscar Wilde* (1912). André Gide: *Si le grain ne meurt* (1920). Vincent O'Sullivan: *Aspects of Wilde* (1936). Frank Harris: *Oscar Wilde* (1916). Robert Sherard: *Bernard Shaw, Frank Harris and Oscar Wilde* (1936). Patrick Byrne: *The Wildes of Merrion Square* (1953). Vyvyan Holland: *Son of Oscar Wilde* (1954).

In *De Profundis* Wilde refers to *The Renaissance* as "that book which has had such strange influence over my life." See T. S. Eliot's attack on Pater in *The Eighteen-eighties* (1930), edited by Walter de la Mare.

He exhorted them to abandon morality for beauty, to liberate art from didactic purpose, to beautify dress, furniture,
and pots.[4] He told them of Rossetti, Swinburne, and
Whistler. Of the sunflower and the lily he observed: "We
love these flowers in spite of what Mr. Gilbert may tell
you, not for any vegetable fashion at all, but because they
are elegant in design."

Whistler, who had brought the word to Swinburne,
now brought it in his Chelsea studio to Wilde and sharpened his wit. Annoyed with Wilde's vulgarization of
beauty, Whistler said in *Ten O'Clock* (1885) that art is so
far beyond the understanding of the public, who judge it
by its subject and its morality, that the attempt of amateur æsthetes to make it popular is absurd. Art is superior
not only to Wilde and the public, but to nature. This brilliant statement of art for the artist's sake annoyed Wilde,
who, defending the æsthetic movement in the *Pall Mall
Gazette,* affirmed that poets, not painters, were the proper
judges of art.[5]

Abandoning his æsthetic costume and his attempt to
vulgarize beauty, he adopted, like Whistler, the deportment
of the dandy and proceeded to justify Whistler's charge of
unoriginality by using *Intentions* (1891) to make Whistler's extreme position more extreme. Art, says Wilde in
these essays, is so independent of common morality that
it is immoral, so superior to nature that it is artificial, so
remote from subject matter that it expresses nothing but
itself. The names of Gautier, Baudelaire, Pater, and Swinburne, cited to support this extravagance, reveal his other
sources. His originality is his style, which with paradox,
reversal of popular saying, and epigram gave new point
to old doctrine. "Nothing," he said, "succeeds like excess."

This manifesto was only the beginning. Wilde shocked
the public more with immoral, witty art. In *The Picture of*

[4] In America Wilde delivered lectures on "The English Renaissance" and "Decorative Art in America." Lloyd Lewis and Henry Smith:
Oscar Wilde Discovers America (1936).

[5] For the controversy, see Whistler: *The Gentle Art of Making
Enemies* (1890). "The Soul of Man under Socialism," Wilde's plea for
anarchism, is his most comprehensive statement of the conflict of artist
and public.

Dorian Gray (1891) Lord Henry, a dandy who despises the ugly middle class, expounds to innocent Dorian the New Hedonism, a mixture of Huysmans and Pater. The search for new experiences, each more exquisite than the last, leads Dorian, like a depraved Marius, to varieties of sin. Cautiously reviewing this story in the *Bookman,* Pater called Dorian's career "an unsuccessful experiment in Epicureanism, in life as a fine art." The public was less moderate. Angry journalists found Wilde intolerable. In his prefatory epigrams Wilde told these moralists that "all art is quite useless"; in letters to the press he found his book too moral to be good; and in private he called it "vicious but perfect."

Although Wilde amused and flattered them in his harmless plays, respectable men, seeing him as their enemy, bided their time. His strange amours, which proved that artists as well as art are above received morality, gave the respectable their chance. Wilde's imprisonment in 1895 was a penalty more severe perhaps than one deserved whose principal, if not his capital, sin was imprudence. But his punishment was less the punishment of particular misdemeanors than the symbolic revenge of a class upon artists and their arts.

George Moore's amours were prudent or fictive. Hence his safety among Philistines; but Moore incurred, if not the penalty of their laws, their censure. They blamed him for seeing life whole in novels he wrote according to the methods of Zola and Flaubert. The circulating libraries, which could make or break an author, banned his books. In *Confessions of a Young Man* (1888) Moore attacks those who would subject all literature to the requirements of young ladies. Using the arguments of Swinburne and Gautier, he proclaims the freedom of the artist and of art, which he illustrates as shockingly as possible. He would gladly sacrifice the virtue of innumerable models, he boasts, for one glorious picture. A pagan in evening dress, he describes his horrid pleasures. In *Modern Painting* (1893), essays on the French, he repeats Whistler's views on the unimportance of subject and morality.

But Pater was Moore's principal model and his philosopher. In 1885 he read *Marius* and found that English, no less than French, was capable of style. This book became his "Bible"; he praised Pater in his *Confessions* and sent him a copy. In 1889 he met Pater, whose British reserve, tried by Moore's Irish impulsiveness, sought refuge in Oxford. But Moore persisted in his devotion and under Pater's spell discovered the sentence, the paragraph, and finally, to Wilde's amusement, style.

To Moore, literature, already separated from society, became style, separated from substance. Decreasingly interested in what he said and increasingly in how he said it, he experimented in memoir and novel with pure, then purer style. The full effects of this development were not obvious until *The Brook Kerith* (1916) and *Héloïse and Abélard* (1921), which may be read for style alone, but if read for substance are less readable. In *Pure Poetry* (1924), an anthology, inspired by Abbé Brémond, of poetry separated from intellectual, social, or moral substance, Moore applied to poetry the principles he had applied so well to prose. Art for art's sake and the school of Pater and Flaubert could expect no further triumph.[6]

Pure poetry and the cult of Pater were also the ideals of the Rhymers' Club, founded in 1891 by William Butler Yeats, Ernest Rhys, and T. W. Rolleston. Of the ten or twelve members Arthur Symons, Ernest Dowson, and Lionel Johnson, besides the founders, were the chief. At the Cheshire Cheese they read to one another the poems they published in two anthologies. They considered Dowson the best poet, Johnson, the second, and Yeats the third. Apart from society in the Cheshire Cheese, their Latin Quarter, they pursued beauty as far as decorum allowed. In this refuge from confusion and the times, they breathed the atmosphere of Pater, which was too thin for life. Yeats and Rhys adapted themselves to external reality; the others succumbed, falling off stools in pubs, collapsing in gutters,

[6] See Moore's remarks on style in *Avowals* (1919), and *Conversations in Ebury Street* (1924). Charles Morgan: *Epitaph on George Moore* (1935), analyzes the style.

jumping off cliffs, or going mad. Their lives, according to Yeats, reflect the disparity between world and ideal, their verses all that is opposite to their lives.[7]

The poems of Dowson fix fine sensations and moods, finding in purity of form a vehicle that is its own end. Fastidious in diction, deliberate in craft, they celebrate the fleeting moment. Perfect, minor, "Neobule" and "Villanelle of Sunset" attenuate the tradition of Swinburne, Poe, and Flaubert. Dowson's most famous poem, *"Non sum qualis eram bonæ sub regno Cynaræ,"* symbolizes the conflict between Pater's ideal and reality. Flinging roses, crying for madder music, stronger wine, Dowson follows the course of Dorian Gray and all the students of sensation.[8]

Johnson wrote ascetic, marmoreal verse, says Yeats, to subdue disorder, his age's and his own. A traditionalist like Dowson, he sought refuge in the manner of Dryden and Gray. Yet this all but classical verse reflects the other side of Pater, his religious austerity. In an essay on Pater, Johnson, who had been Pater's student at Oxford, condemns those who, misinterpreting the master, "live for a succession of exquisite emotions, the gifts of beauty in nature and in art." Pater, his true follower proclaims, had no followers; and reading Johnson's excellent, cold poem "By the Statue of King Charles at Charing Cross," one finds it hard to disagree.[9]

The verses of Arthur Symons, devoted to exquisite emotions, each more exquisite, owe almost as much to

[7] The best accounts of the group are in Yeats: *Autobiography*, Ernest Rhys: *Everyman Remembers* (1931), John Davidson: *Earl Lavender* (1895). Anthologies: *The Book of the Rhymers' Club* (1892), *The Second Book of the Rhymers' Club* (1894).

For the æsthetic nineties see Holbrook Jackson: *The Eighteen Nineties* (1913); Osbert Burdett: *The Beardsley Period* (1925); William Rothenstein: *Men and Memories* (Vol. I, 1931); B. I. Evans: *English Poetry in the Later Nineteenth Century* (1933). Anthologies: A. J. A. Symons: *An Anthology of Nineties Verse* (1929); Donald Davidson: *British Poetry of the Eighteen-nineties* (1937).

[8] *The Poetical Works of Dowson* (1934), edited by Desmond Flower. *Verses* (1896). *Decorations* (1899). Mark Longaker: *Ernest Dowson* (1944).

[9] *Poetical Works* (1915), edited by Ezra Pound; *Poems* (1895); *Ireland* (1897); *Post Liminium* (1912), essays. Arthur Patrick: *Lionel Johnson* (1939).

Pater as to Baudelaire. From the *Renaissance* and from a
visit to the master, Symons learned that life and prose
could be fine arts. Burning with a hard gemlike flame must
have held for adolescent Welsh Methodists like Symons
an attractiveness that staggers the imagination.[1]

Contemplating his contemporaries in *The Works of
Max Beerbohm* (1896), Max Beerbohm devoted one essay
to Wilde and the cult of Rossetti, another to Pater. These
essays constitute the obituary of æstheticism by an aloof,
eminently reasonable young man on whom, Wilde said, the
gods had bestowed the gift of perpetual old age. Of the
year 1880 Beerbohm observes: "To give an accurate and
exhaustive account of that period would need a far less
brilliant pen than mine." Although when at school, he
says in "Diminuendo," he read Pater in bed by the light
of a dark lantern, he was disappointed, upon coming to
Oxford, by Pater's military demeanor and bright dogskin
gloves. The cult of the moment was too arduous in any
case; for to be at the focus of all experience, as Pater
advised, one would have to be the Prince of Wales. "I
belong," sighed Beerbohm, announcing its end, "to the
Beardsley period."

Yeats, who also belonged, was the friend of Wilde,
Symons, and all the Rhymers. His poetry and more especially his prose of the nineties reveal the cult of Morris
and Rossetti. Like Swinburne before him, Yeats based his
æsthetics largely upon Blake's and conformed to the laws,
not of society, but of the imagination. Looking back in his
introduction to *The Oxford Book of Modern Verse* (1936)
at the poets of his group, Yeats saw Pater behind their
abandonment of "moral earnestness" and their attempt to
"purify poetry of all that is not poetry." The style of "Rosa
Alchemica," a story Yeats published in the *Savoy,* shows
this influence, and so does the increasing richness of his
expository prose.

Communication was of small concern to an enemy of
the people. Yeats's father, an artist without commercial

[1] *Collected Poems* (1902); *Days and Nights* (1889); *Silhouettes*
(1892); *Images of Good and Evil* (1899). Symons wrote two essays
and a book on Pater.

talents, had taught his son to despise getting ahead and to hold in contempt those who had got ahead. That contempt embraced the middle-class world. Yeats addressed his writings to men outside this world, to poets, peasants, and aristocrats, who would know by instinct and tradition what he meant. In his essay "What is Popular Poetry?" (1901) he glances with disdain at those who, conforming to the requirements of the middle class, have written abstract, didactic verse. "The triviality of emotion, the poverty of ideas, the imperfect sense of Beauty" of Longfellow, for example, or Mrs. Hemans or even Burns, show their remoteness from the great tradition.

When Yeats set out to reform Ireland and liberate her, he found himself in a quandary. The situation demanded didactic, patriotic poetry and propaganda in prose; the Irish middle class cried for this poetry and this prose. But, refusing to compromise with his ideal, he set about the work of reform with a difficult poetry of music and suggestion and the prose of Walter Pater. He would enchant them with beauty. His defeat was inevitable, and, on the whole, good for his poetry, which got from it the loftiness it lacked.

The other master of English in our time, James Joyce, was no less indebted to the æstheticism of the nineties, but he hid it like a Jesuit. Refusing to accept the "tyranny of the mediocre," young Stephen of *Stephen Hero* (1944) calls himself an "outlaw" and makes a philosophy of self-expression. The æsthetic theory that he expounds here and in *A Portrait of the Artist* (1916), though based upon sentences from Aquinas, has no place in it for religious, moral, or social purpose. Art, says Stephen, is the "human disposition of sensible or intelligible matter for an esthetic end," and beauty, which resides in the most pleasing relations of part to part, has three qualities: "wholeness, harmony, radiance." Good art is static, above desire or loathing; bad is kinetic, either pornographic or didactic. "That," says Lynch, "has the true scholastic stink." The president of the Jesuit college with whom Stephen debates this theory in *Stephen Hero* is even more penetrating. To use Aquinas in order to justify art for art's sake, he moderately observes, is paradoxical.

It took a Jesuit to see what Jesuitical Joyce had done. Reared during the nineties by Yeats and the Jesuits, Joyce had combined his two traditions. He admired the Paterite prose of Yeats so much that he committed the stories to memory and imitated their rhythms in his own essay on Mangan. Echoes of Yeats's poetry fill Joyce's prose. The verses of *Chamber Music* (1907) strain memories of Ben Jonson through the tradition of Dowson and Yeats, and that, perhaps, is why Arthur Symons found them good. "The good," says Stephen, echoing the nineties, "is the beautiful." But Joyce was to pursue unsocial beauty into obscurities beyond the lights of the English nineties. The prose that he developed for these further excursions was not in the tradition of Pater or Yeats but in that of Flaubert and the symbolists, and, like Flaubert's, Joyce's prose does its work with precision.

The critical habit of the æsthetes was generally impressionistic. For this Pater was also partly responsible: the æsthetic critic, he says in the preface to *The Renaissance,* looks for pleasurable sensations, each unique, in the fairer forms of art. His aim is to know his "impression" as it really is. What the book or picture is hardly matters. What, Pater asks, is it "to *me?*" After determining the unique impression, the critic may support his feeling by analysis or find its causes in history. In his criticism of La Gioconda, Pater does not tell us about the picture but about his feeling about it.

In "The Critic as Artist," a dialogue in *Intentions,* Wilde repeats Pater's ideas with some exaggeration. The æsthetic critic, he says, does not analyze or tell the history of an object, but on the basis of his impression, exploiting his personality, creates a new work of art, often better than the object. Only a poet, he continues, can be a critic. In practice, however, he criticized by epigram.

George Moore, who called Pater the "president of the high court of criticism," says in *Impressions and Opinions* (1891): "I understand criticism more as the story of the critic's soul than as an exact science." Of Rimbaud he says: "My object is . . . to convey a sensation of this strange boy." Moore's criticism of literature in this book and in his *Confessions* is impressionistic; but in *Modern Painting* (1893), on a subject of which he had some technical knowledge, he is often analytic and controversial.

Under Pater's personal direction, Symons most closely approximated the method of the master. "On Criticism" in *Dramatis Personæ* (1923) and the essay on Pater in *Studies in Prose and Verse* (1904) praise Pater for making criticism a fine art. Fixing the peculiar quality of each work, determining its effect upon his soul, extracting the essence of beautiful moments, noting nuances, the critic, says Symons, appreciates the good and ignores the bad. Good critics, like the Goncourts, aim to "give sensation, to flash the impression of the moment." From the eighties to recent times Pater's method commonly appealed to those who, revolting against the external world, whether of science or society, wanted a congenial refuge.

The criticism of Virginia Woolf is the climax of this romantic tradition. Her *Common Reader* (1925) and its sequel, showing the familiar prejudice against analysis, history, and scholarship, reflect her anti-intellectual position and the delicacy of her feelings. An essay on Hazlitt gives her principles. This critic, she says, "builds up with the freest use of imagery and colour the brilliant ghost that the book has left glimmering in his mind. The poem is re-created in glowing phrases. . . . He singles out the peculiar quality of his author." In the essay on Christina Rossetti, Virginia Woolf restates the critic's aim: "to expose the mind bare to the poem and transcribe in all its haste and imperfection whatever may be the result of the impact." Haste and imperfection, however, are no part of her work. She was as meticulous as Pater, whom she echoed, and the most benign and generous of critics.

Recent critics of impressionism have been less generous. In *Principles of Literary Criticism* (1924) I. A. Richards attacks it as inexact, and art for art's sake as mistaken. Rebelling against the moralists, the æsthetes, thinking the æsthetic experience different in kind from other experi-

ences, fell into worse error. For the experience of art,
says Richards, differs from other experiences only in
higher organization; and form, despite Whistler, Clive Bell,
and Roger Fry, cannot be separated from substance. Although crude, moralists are nearer than æsthetes to the
truth. Moral, utilitarian, pragmatic, Richards proposes in
place of impressionism a method based upon pseudo-
science. The critic, unconcerned with moving the reader,
must determine meaning by semantic analysis, and value
by behavioristic psychology.[2]

T. S. Eliot also rebelled against the school of Pater
and Symons. In the essays on criticism in *The Sacred
Wood* (1920) and in *The Use of Poetry and the Use of
Criticism* (1933) he says that criticism must be objective,
impersonal, cold, making use of comparison and analysis
to support the sensibility. To the impressionists, criticism
was a kind of poetry, but poetry misdirected; for although
criticism enters poetry, poetry must not enter criticism.
The unpoetical critic, Aristotle, Dryden, or Gourmont, displaying universal intelligence, avoids the condition of Symons. Eliot's criticism, as one might suppose, is dogmatic
and austere; and its tone, as he confesses, is one of "pontif-
ical solemnity." Its happiest effects are those of tone, taste,
and poetry. The value lies in those poetic penetrations (of
intellects at the tips of senses or of Marvell's identity with
Laforgue) which have served to misguide a generation
through the past.

Although condemned as "emotive," impressionism or
the sensitive reader's response to a book, which after all
is what concerns other readers next to their own response,
is as valuable as analysis or dogma, and perhaps their
basis. Impressionism differs in manner and tone from the
methods of Richards and Eliot, but it also fixes fine shades
and the quintessence of things.

"To fix the last fine shade, the quintessence of
things," says Arthur Symons in "The Decadent Movement
in Literature" (1893), is the "ideal of the Decadence."

[2] In *Coleridge on Imagination* (1934), condemning Pater as meaningless, Richards renews his plea for scientific criticism. Clive Bell:
Art (1914). Roger Fry: *Vision and Design* (1920).

Decadent, an epithet applied by Philistine malice to impressionists and æsthetes, was received by them as a badge of distinction. Symons, Wilde, and, in France, the generation of Laforgue were called and called themselves decadent. The word, however, does not imply value, but rather a difference in character due to time. A decadent work may be good or bad, better or worse than nondecadent works; but it differs in nature from those of an earlier period as Camembert differs from Gruyère. Both are good; but Camembert has a past.

A literary tradition, having exhausted its normal possibilities, invites three courses. The poet may imitate the perfect expression of his predecessors, in which case he is dead. He may start a new tradition, but this is permitted to few and only with the help, apparently, of social change. Or, keeping within the limits of the old tradition, he may make it extraordinary. This poet is decadent.

Pope and Swift perfectly expressed the Augustan tradition, Erasmus Darwin and Gibbon its decadence. Darwin is inferior in value to Pope, but it cannot be said that Gibbon is remarkably inferior to Swift. With the help of the French Revolution, Wordsworth started a new tradition, which expressed itself in the work of his contemporaries and the early Victorians. After such perfection nothing was left for Wilde and his contemporaries but imitation, the course of William Watson, or extraordinary variation, the course of all artists with life in them. "Strangeness added to beauty," which Pater, defining his quality, called the quality of romanticism, better defines its decadence.

The decadents of the nineties differ from their successors in being aware of their condition and proud of it. Symons was an ostentatious decadent. In "The Decadent Movement in Literature" he finds the younger generation enjoying the *"maladie de fin de siècle,"* that "new and beautiful and interesting disease." Artificial, morbid, without simplicity or sanity, he and his companions, refining upon refinement, seek the exceptional and the remote. As might be expected, the verses that Symons composed before and after this manifesto are decadent, especially his hothouse verses on the hothouse.

Oscar's garden must have supplied it. A carnation, like a primrose, is Wordsworthian; but a green carnation, though of the family, is abnormal. Although a lily is romantic, a gilded lily is decadent.[3] As Wilde observes in "The Critic as Artist":

> The subject-matter at the disposal of creation becomes every day more limited in extent and variety. Providence and Mr. Walter Besant have exhausted the obvious. .... The old roads and dusty highways have been traversed too often. Their charm has been worn away . . . and they have lost that element of novelty or surprise which is so essential for romance.

Under these circumstances, he continues, the artist must seek out fine moods, exquisite moments, curious new sensations. No better definition of decadence has been framed. Nor has decadence been more obviously illustrated, as Symons said, than by *Dorian Gray*, "The Sphinx," or *Salomé*. Cyril in "The Decay of Lying" belongs to the Tired Hedonists' Club, whose members, adoring Domitian, wear faded roses. But "the very flower of decadence," said Wilde, is Pater's *Renaissance*, which should have provoked the last trump. The decorative elegance of Beardsley, the exquisite refinement of Dowson, and the depravity of John Gray are no less extraordinary than Oscar's garden. But these are products of the declining century, and since the disgrace of Wilde, decadence, displaying itself in private, has become obscure.

II

Of the difficult writers in our time, some are exiles from middle-class society, others followers of these exiles.

---

[3] In *The Green Carnation* (1894), Robert Hichens burlesqued the enormities of Wilde. In *Degeneration* (translated 1895), Max Nordau mistook decadence for disease. However foolish his conclusions, his analysis is almost as sound as that of Mario Praz, whose *Romantic Agony* (1933) traces the decadence to its romantic roots.

The French symbolists and their followers have been the most influential of the exiles and the most obscure. Though Baudelaire was an exile, he never had recourse to that obscurity which later on became the response of those in his position. The French classical tradition of clarity and craftsmanship remained too strong for him to break, and he translated his hallucinations into the clear, impeccable, and final terms of his tradition. Whatever his implications, he drew his images from familiar reality and maintained coherence on the manifest level where he might outrage the reader without confusion. "I have cultivated my hysteria," he remarked; but he cultivated it in the manner of a formal gardener.

Before glancing at his informal successors it might be well to consider the case of another early exile who went further toward predestined obscurity. Gerard Manley Hopkins, a spiritual exile from the heretics of his time, was a literary exile from them and from the Jesuits to whom he had fled. Isolation and faithfulness to his own nature produced those maddening ellipses, those distortions of common usage, those syntactical innovations which even today keep his poetry from common readers. The knowledge that he had no audience but Robert Bridges exempted him from the obligation to temper his honesty. "I do not write for the public," he said, and added: "No doubt my poetry errs on the side of singularity," but "indeed I was not over-desirous that the meaning of all should be quite clear." He confessed he was dismayed that Bridges found him unintelligible; but it was his aim, said Hopkins, to express, not to communicate:

> If it is possible to express a subtle and recondite thought on a subtle and recondite subject in a subtle and recondite way and with great felicity and perfection, in the end, something must be sacrificed, with so trying a task, in the process, and this may be the being at once, nay perhaps even the being without explanation at all, intelligible.[4]

[4] Quotations are from *The Letters of Gerard Manley Hopkins to Robert Bridges* (1935).

They disorder these things better in France. Exile, which permitted Hopkins to cultivate his honesty, drove the followers of Baudelaire to extremes of privacy that make Hopkins seem almost social. Since Hopkins remained unpublished until 1918, it was permitted the French to teach future exiles a becoming obscurity.

Rimbaud was a better teacher than Scotus. This genius of fifteen emerged from a middle-class home, looked at the world, and found it "full of grocers." Following Baudelaire, he proceeded first to shock and confound them, and then, leaving grocers to their grocery, he tried to penetrate the unknown. The defeat of this endeavor caused him to abandon poetry and to become, like his grocer, a man of substance. That gun-running in Abyssinia which has been considered his exile from society was not an exile, however, but rather, like the top hat he purchased in London, a symbolic, bitter, and self-mortifying acceptance of things as they are. The exile of Rimbaud was his life in France while still a poet. "One is an exile," he exclaimed, "in one's own country."

Exile brought privacy and obscurity with it. He did not write for grocers, but for himself. He made no attempt to make his poems comprehensible or, indeed, to publish them. Turning what Verlaine called the "face of an exiled angel" inside out, he embarked upon an exploration of his unconscious. Logic and the categories of reason were discarded. He suppressed the interference of his conscious mind by drugs, fatigue, and depravity, and penetrated beyond his deranged senses to the domain of dream and madness where few could follow him. In *Illuminations,* that great, strange, and very private book, he made words express vision and, using them as a means of discovery rather than of expression, compelled them to do what they cannot do. "I noted the inexpressible," he said. Had Dr. Johnson been around, that sociable man might have observed of Rimbaud as he once observed of some obscure eighteenth-century predecessor: "Sir, if Mr. X has experienced the unutterable, Mr. X should not attempt to utter it."

Observing the manners of Rimbaud, Mallarmé, and

the other exiles, Jean Moréas in 1886 decided to assert
their patterns as principles, to make obscurity, if not an
end, an estimable means, and to declare the poet's independence of the common reader. Once established, the
pattern would serve as a guide for younger exiles; and
even for those who were as yet indifferent to exile it would
be a badge of unfashionable fashion. Moréas made it clear
that the symbolist poem, avoiding description, statement,
logic, and references to matters external to itself, was a
complex structure of overtones, indirections, and private
images.

The labyrinth of obscurity had been established, and
poets great and small, exiled and fashionable, honest and
knavish, followed its conventions as the only normal
course for men so abnormal as they. By the time of the
surrealists Rimbaud was not the only guide to the country
he explored, for by this time Freud and Jung had come to
his assistance. Reason and common sense, the hope of
classicist and bourgeois alike, had ceased to please. The
increasing disorder of society had turned the eyes of artists
within and above themselves. The new physics, displacing
old dogmas of matter and continuity, now permitted truths
of equal validity to get along together, and, seeming to
affirm the unimportance of cause and effect, reinvited the
metaphysical and the irrational.

The symbolist tradition from Baudelaire to surrealism
produced much of the greatest poetry of our time. It is a
pity that this poetry should remain unintelligible to the
society that unintentionally produced it. The decay of
logical structure, its replacement by free association and
the unconscious, the conception by poets of the poem as
a self-contained organism with internal but without clear
external references, the natural desire to baffle the vulgar,
the emphasis upon expression rather than communication
—all these, while improving poetry, have placed it beyond
the common understanding. The separation of poet from
audience, which gave poetry its present character, must be
deplored even by its readers as socially unhealthy. But the
blame for this separation falls more upon society than
upon the poet; for society exiled the poet before he exiled

himself. And popular education, confirming exile, continues to prepare the reader for Tennyson.

In England the French symbolist tradition did not
produce significant obscurities until around 1910. For the
æsthetes of the nineties the strangeness of Baudelaire was
enough. They knew of Mallarmé and Rimbaud, but their
obscurity was too advanced perhaps to suit the purposes
of more backward exiles. With the appearance of T. S.
Eliot, however, French obscurity found British tongue.

Eliot was an exile in a society composed of Sweeney,
Bleistein, Krumpacker, Klipstein, and of Burbank and
Prufrock at its best. "I have never," Eliot once said in an
address to Americans, "I have never met Sweeney on a
footing of social equality." Nevertheless, Eliot left home;
and it was not to Sweeney but to Laforgue that he turned
for suitable incoherence, free association, and the idea of
poetry as a drama of suggestive images and overtones. To
this he and Pound added the allusiveness of disappointed
professors. Although Elliot's difficulty comes largely from
his careful suppression of intellect, for a long time it was
customary to call him an intellectual poet. His pedantry,
his ceaseless praise of the marriage of feeling and intellect,
and his denial of emotion obscured the fact that he is a
very emotional poet.

Eliot has used his rational prose to explain the irra-
tionality of his verse. His essays, better as manifesto than
criticism, compose the best rationalization of obscurity.
The seasoned reader, he says, does not bother to understand poetry. He just enjoys it. He himself, confesses Eliot,
enjoyed the French long before he could understand them.
They had omitted transitions, statements, logical framework, and other things of low intensity. They were complex; for the complexity of our civilization, playing on a
refined sensibility, trying to be true to thought and feeling
at once, must produce complexity. Moreover, poetry is as
unintellectual as a secretion. The meaning or prose sense
of a poem is superfluous, and if there at all, is there to
keep the mind of the reader diverted while the poem does
its work. The work of the poem is not communication.
Standing alone between poet and reader, the poem cor-

responds to the feeling of the poet and may excite a feeling in the reader, but the poet may feel pink, the reader blue. These essays are of social significance; for through them Eliot has tempered the loneliness of recent poets, who, thanks to him, enjoy a considerable audience. For this audience, which seems compelled to attend poetic plays of the most baffling kind, Eliot is a kind of Dr. Johnson.

Joyce's exile was darker than Eliot's and more genuine. In *The Day of the Rabblement* (1901), a two-page pamphlet directed against the Irish Literary Theatre for coming to terms with the public, Joyce says: "No man can be a lover of the true or the good unless he abhors the multitude; and the artist, though he may employ the crowd, is very careful to isolate himself." Employing the crowd, Joyce maintained his isolation, increased it by physical exile, and created characters to illustrate the exile of their creator. Stephen Dedalus, whose name implies the artist martyred by society, deliberately severed his connections with mother, father, church, and country. "I will not serve that in which I no longer believe," he says, "whether it call itself my home, my fatherland or my church: and I will try to express myself in some mode of life or art as freely as I can and as wholly as I can, using for my defence the only arms I allow myself to use, silence, exile and cunning." Mr. Bloom and H. C. Earwicker are outlanders and symbolic exiles. And by its title and implications the play *Exiles* reveals Joyce's preoccupation with his state.[5] Although he felt that art can exist today only in isolation from society, Joyce suffered from a sense of guilt over his own exile. Stephen's hunt for a father, his brooding over his mother, and his concern with country and church show Joyce's longing to recover what he had renounced.

The early works seem simple enough. But as Joyce's exile deepened he became more and more deeply involved with himself. His mind, lost in the labyrinth of its own being, turned in upon itself, and to express what it found

---

[5] Cf. Thomas Mann's "Tonio Kröger," Conrad's *Victory*, and the works of Kafka for exemplary exiles.

there, turned naturally to the French tradition. In *Finnegans Wake* Joyce surpassed Rimbaud in creating a self-
contained private universe into which he might retire to
deepen his exile and his sense of guilt. Exile and guilt are
among the recurring themes of *Finnegans Wake*. Both are
expressed in the fragmentary and distorted allusions to
St. Augustine's phrase *"securus iudicat orbis terrarum"*:
"The calm judgment of the world is that those men cannot
be good who in any part of the world cut themselves off
from the rest of the world."

Since Joyce never expected to find the "ideal reader
with an ideal insomnia" who could read his book, it is not
clear why he bothered to publish it unless even the exiled
ego requires this social support. But the few imperfect
readers he has secured are as grateful to him for this inconsistency as the commoner reader is indifferent. True to
the policy of silence, exile, and cunning, Joyce issued no
explanations. But his fellow exiles in Paris, Stuart Gilbert,
Eugene Jolas, and Elliot Paul, published a manifesto (*transition*, June 1929) that, since it seems not to refer to their
work, may refer to his. Proclaiming the end of grammar
and communication, the autonomy of the imagination in
search of a fabulous world, the litany and hallucination
of the word, and the triumph of Rimbaud, they stated
what the tradition of exile implied: "the plain reader be
damned."

Lamenting the separation of artist and audience, poets
of the early thirties in *New Signatures* (1932) promised
clearer poetry when the audience for poetry was greater.
The generation of Auden was clearer than the generation
of Eliot, but not clear enough to be commonly read. Dylan
Thomas's excellent poems are as obscure as *Finnegans
Wake*.

Complaining about such darkness, readers call for
meaning. Reviewers for the larger periodicals, celebrating
popular fiction or middlebrow essay, make short work of
poets whom most periodicals refuse to print. Through
editors and the laws of commerce the middle class pun-
ishes its exiles by denying them a hearing. Hence "little
magazines" where, unpopular and strange, exiles may dis-

play their isolation.[6] These magazines, contemporaries of the *Daily Mail,* are almost peculiar to our times. Rossetti's *Germ* and the innumerable magazines of the French symbolists started the current tradition. The first little magazine of importance in England was the *Yellow Book* (April 1894–April 1897). Published by John Lane, who published Wilde, edited by Henry Harland and Aubrey Beardsley, this quarterly was intended to organize the decadence.[7] Prose and poetry by Moore, James, Beerbohm, Symons, pictures by Beardsley and Nettleship, proclaimed art for art's sake and offended the public with their wickedness, realism, or beauty. But John Lane, astutely tempering the effect, also printed "Reticence in Literature," by Arthur Waugh, Evelyn's father, who expressed the moral position of the Philistines. The fourth issue, January 1895, is the last good one; for in April, Wilde was tried and the celebration of beauty became dangerous. To save himself Lane purged the *Yellow Book*. Subsequent issues are dull except for a story by young Enoch Arnold Bennett and another by H. G. Wells.

With Beardsley and Leonard Smithers, a publisher more daring than Lane, Arthur Symons started the *Savoy* to succeed and surpass the *Yellow Book*. In this periodical, which survived public displeasure for eight issues (January to December 1896), Symons published æsthetes, naturalists, and intellectuals, and wrote the last issue himself. Outraged by Beardsley's drawings and his prose, booksellers refused to sell the abominable magazine.

The *Egoist* (1914–19), founded as a feminist periodical, turned under the influence of Ezra Pound to the advancement of imagism and French literature. Dora Marsden and Harriet Weaver, who was to become Joyce's patron, were editors, Richard Aldington and T. S. Eliot assistant editors. This radical magazine published the prose of Wyndham Lewis, eccentric poetry in free verse, Joyce's *Portrait of the Artist,* and parts of *Ulysses*. More splendid than this were Eliot's *Criterion* (1922–39) and Cyril Connolly's *Horizon* (1940–49).

[6] Frederick Hoffman, Charles Allen, and Carolyn Ulrich: *The Little Magazine, a History and a Bibliography* (1946).

[7] J. Lewis May: *John Lane and the Nineties* (1936).

Of the editors, aside from Eliot, Cyril Connolly, critic and novelist, is the most remarkable. In the guise of Palinurus, the submerged pilot, Connolly devotes *The Unquiet Grave* (1945) to *maximes* and *pensées* that fix a mental climate, not his alone but his world's. These exquisite mutterings of anxiety, petulance, and guilt are nothing like the sounds from *The Condemned Playground* (1945), a miscellany of reviews, essays, and wicked parodies that prove him the exile's spokesman. In "Writers and Society," which distinguishes between entertainer and artist, he laments the artist, free alone in middle-class society, but barely tolerated where free and condemned by indifference or hostility to his solitude.[8]

While poets admired or loathed one another in their magazines, while Eliot, defining poetry as poetry, justified it as independent organism, while other critics said a poem does not say but is, I. A. Richards and William Empson provided a method for bringing poet and reader together again. If poetry is communication, says Richards in *Principles of Literary Criticism* (1924), it follows that reader and critic must determine the meaning of a poem. Since the ambiguity of words is profound and emotive words are easily confused with references, the reader must be aware of the doubleness of talk and of the semantic scale along which words slide from meaning to meaning.[9] The reader of a poem must know that meaning is not sense alone, but also feeling, tone, intention. When, at Cambridge, Richards confronted his students with poems, the results as analyzed in *Practical Criticism* (1929) were deplorable. Missing one meaning or more, these readers showed they could not read. Richards blames the state of society for their inability; for taste, he says, has declined, democracy has lowered the level of culture, traditions have died. As his first cure he proposes semantics. The possibilities of the new science are explored in *Coleridge on Imagination* (1934), where, sliding the words of Coleridge along the

[8] Cf. *Enemies of Promise* (1939), criticism and autobiography. *Ideas and Places* (1953), editorials and articles from *Horizon*.

[9] Cf. *Mencius on the Mind* (1932), *The Philosophy of Rhetoric* (1936), and his earlier, more difficult study (with C. K. Ogden), *The Meaning of Meaning* (1923).

scale, Richards shows that idealistic Coleridge meant what materialistic Richards means. Basic English, his second cure, improves communication by destroying poetry; but poetry, he says in *Science and Poetry* (1926), is pseudostatement.

In these books Richards continually speaks of recent poetry and its critics, attacking those who complain that poetry is unintelligible, those who think the whole meaning of a poem is its prose sense, and those emancipated men who claim that prose sense has no place in poetry. From such ignorance of fourfold meaning he defends Hopkins, Auden, Empson, and Eliot, whose allusiveness and ambiguity are products of the time, whose sense is subordinated to feeling and tone. Some modern poetry, he admits, is truly private, failing in communication; but failure in that is commonly the fault of reader not of poet.

Elaborating ideas from Richards and Robert Graves in *Seven Types of Ambiguity* (1931), William Empson makes of them an instrument for penetrating obscurities. Since words of poetry are ambiguous and ambiguity is multiplied by context, the proper approach is analytic. His method, which amounts to careful reading or *explication de textes,* is excellent when applied by a reader of Empson's acuteness to metaphysical poetry of the seventeenth century and to difficult poetry of our time.[1] Having adapted criticism to exiled poetry and having inflamed the New Critics of America, Empson proceeded to what he calls the pastoral. *Some Versions of Pastoral* (1938) contains first-rate analyses of Marvell's "Garden" and other obscure documents in verse and prose. *The Structure of Complex Words* (1951), narrowing a field at the border of semantics and criticism, tests single words for overtones. Not only Richards but the logical positivists as well seem behind this enterprise.

[1] Empson confesses a debt to the analysis of a Shakespearian sonnet by Robert Graves in *A Survey of Modernist Poetry* (1928). Empson's method was also anticipated by Graves in *Poetic Unreason* (1925). René Wellek: *A History of Modern Criticism, 1750–1950* (1955—). Stanley Edgar Hyman: *The Armed Vision* (1948). David Daiches: *Critical Approaches to Literature* (1956).

CHAPTER TWO: *Left*

*T*HE terms Left and Right, always ambiguous and now confounded by events, have almost lost their meaning; but they will still do as labels for what used to be two tendencies. Leftist critics of the middle class were less radical on the whole than moderate. From the eighties, however, writers occupying positions somewhat to the left of center expressed in novel, tract, play, or poem their impatience with convention or economy. The works of Bernard Shaw and of the Auden generation excellently illustrate this literature in all its varieties.

I

Around 1880 Shaw showed his contempt of bourgeois morality by becoming an anarchist. But after reading a French translation of *Das Kapital,* he became a socialist, at first a member of the Social Democratic Federation, a Marxist society, then in 1884 a member of the Fabian Society. Finding his spiritual home among the "gas and water socialists," he managed to combine more effectively than William Morris the traditions of socialism and art.[1]

[1] For social background see Helen Lynd: *England in the Eighteen-eighties* (1945); Esme Wingfield-Stratford: *The Victorian Sunset* (1932), *The Victorian Aftermath* (1934); Edward Pease: *The History of the Fabian Society* (1916); Sidney Webb: *Socialism in England* (1889).

Archibald Henderson: *Bernard Shaw, Playboy and Prophet* (1932);

From 1879 he had occupied his leisure with the composition of five edifying novels, unpublishable except in socialist magazines. Of these novels *An Unsocial Socialist,* written in 1883, is best. Trefusis, the wealthy hero, turning against his caste, expresses his contempt of Philistine society, its economic foundations, its virtues, and its sentiments. Leaving his lovely wife because love interferes with duty, he retires to a young ladies' seminary, where he works for his living disguised as a lawn-mower. In this capacity he ceaselessly repeats the ideas of Marx to all who will listen. This eloquent egoist, enemy of capitalists, clergymen, physicians, and wives, set the pattern for the Shavian hero. Although the novel abounds in outrageous paradoxes and, except for the interminable orations of its hero, is lively enough and gay, the characters are less convincing than what they represent. The rational and the preposterous deserved, and later got, a better vehicle. But William Morris read the novel, liked the ideas, and became Shaw's friend.

The hero of *The Irrational Knot* is rational to the point of inhumanity. This novel, written in 1880 before Shaw's conversion, deals with the effect of caste upon marriage. Edward Conolly, the Irish-American engineer, is far from respectable; for he has neither an unearned income nor a public-school education. The creature dares marry a lady despite the apoplectic disapproval of her father. Unable to endure the rational and the infra dig, she sensibly elopes with one of her own class, an Eton man, who abandons her with illegitimate child. The deserted engineer, applauding her superiority to convention, offers in vain to take her back. In the 1905 preface to this shocking, second-rate novel, Shaw finds his fault to have been ignorance of money, the moral basis of that cultured class which will murder or steal "in the name of law and

---

Hesketh Pearson: *G.B.S., a Full Length Portrait* (1942); Eric Bentley: *Bernard Shaw* (1947); Edmund Fuller: *Bernard Shaw* (1950); Louis Kronenberger, editor: *George Bernard Shaw, a Critical Survey* (1953); A. H. Nethercot: *Men and Supermen* (1954).

Shaw: *A Manifesto* (1884), *Fabian Essays in Socialism* (1889), *William Morris as I Knew Him* (1936), *Anarchism versus State Socialism* (1889).

order." But his own original morality, he says, makes this novel one "of the first order." Such morality is almost the only value of his other early novels.[2]

Knowledge of money at last forced upon Shaw the desirability of making some. He saw his chance in the "new journalism," the attempt to adapt journalism to the needs of an expanding, newly literate public. The headline, the interview, and other seductions made their appearance during the eighties. To please the unaccustomed eye, journalists adopted a colloquial style, filled at its best with wit and color, and descending at its worst, as Shaw confesses in *Dramatic Opinions,* to the split infinitive. The brilliant styles of Wilde, Henley, Chesterton, and Shaw were formed in this cynical school. Writing in his direct, easy manner for many journals, Shaw discovered in himself a commercial shrewdness far from socialistic, and he enjoyed a calculated success. The music criticism in which by praising Wagner he puzzled the Philistine is filled with harmless irreverence and common sense.[3]

As Shaw continued to please, astonish, and displease, he discovered in the "new drama" of Ibsen another vehicle for his talents. Shaw had ignored the English theater of the eighties, which specialized in melodramas, sentimental farces, and adaptations of the well-made play of Scribe, Sardou, and Dumas the younger. None of these had intellectual or æsthetic interest, none was realistic in dialogue, character, or action, and none gave any sign of the social and domestic problems attending the advance of the middle class. The artificial excitement of melodrama stopped short of sex and other natural endeavors. Plots of well-made plays were so well made that, as John Mason Brown has observed, if a character was to get tuberculosis in the last act, in the first he must have had at least catarrh.

Changing all that, Ibsen adapted the stage to modern conditions. Like Lillo and Heywood before him, he wrote

[2] *Immaturity,* written in 1879; *Love among the Artists,* written in 1881; *Cashel Byron's Profession* (1886).

[3] *Music in London, 1890–94* (1932); *London Music in 1888–1889* (1937).

bourgeois and domestic tragedy, in which, surpassing his early predecessors, he revealed by conflict of character and idea the depths of human nature and of society. His frankness in exposing domestic and social troubles and all the horrors of the suburb lifted the protective convention by which they had been concealed. In *A Doll's House* (1879) he presented the nature of middle-class marriage, in *Ghosts* (1881) he exposed respectable hypocrisy, and in *An Enemy of the People* (1882) he showed a humanitarian at war with middle-class interests. These and other problem plays were followed by the enigmatic *Hedda Gabler* (1890), a character study that elevated the stage to the level of the novel. Technique was as revolutionary as substance. Ibsen established the convention of the stage as a four-walled room, in which, while the audience peered through an imaginary wall, the characters spoke and acted as if the imaginary wall were real and the room their own. Soliloquies disappeared with asides. Plots, depending now upon character and situation, became unmechanical. Symbols of duck and tower presented a reality beyond the limits of such realism. And from these northern austerities arose what Yeats considered an odor of spilled poetry. Edmund Gosse was the first Englishman to discover Ibsen. His propaganda and that of William Archer made Ibsen known in England during the eighties, and their translations made him available to readers. With this preparation *A Doll's House* was produced in London, to the displeasure of the middle class, in 1899.

A Doll's House contains little that Shaw had not said in *The Irrational Knot*. It was for this reason that he remained unexcited when during the middle eighties he, Eleanor Marx, and other Fabians took part in a private performance of the play. Later, however, converted by his friend William Archer, Shaw realized that Ibsen's value for him was a form for the ideas he shared with the master.

Dazzled with the possibilities of the theater, Shaw became an Ibsenite. In July 1890 he lectured the Fabians on the new drama of ideas, and, expanding this lecture, published in 1891 *The Quintessence of Ibsenism*. By this

time Florence Farr had appeared in *Rosmersholm* and
J. T. Grein had produced *Ghosts* at the Independent Theatre, founded in 1891 on the model of Antoine's Théâtre
Libre. Shaw took occasion in his tract to defend these productions against Clement Shorter and the other Philistine
critics who found Ibsen long, nasty, and brutish. Far from
being an enemy of virtue, says Shaw, Ibsen is the first moralist of Europe, the enemy of conventional virtue. His
plays show that middle-class ideals of marriage, family,
and love disguise a shocking reality, especially the ideal
of the womanly woman, Ibsen's doll and her husband's
slave. Although his interest in Ibsen seems no more than
moral, social, and domestic, Shaw must have seen beyond
the didactic moralist to the artist and technician; for what
he learned from Ibsen was not morality, of which he had
enough, but how to write a play. In the light of the plays
he wrote this tract appears less tract than manifesto.

Widowers' Houses, his first play and the first of the
"new" or "higher" dramas, was written for Grein and produced by him in 1892 at the Independent Theatre. At each
of the two performances socialists applauded what others
hissed. Both were right; for the play is a socialist attack
on landlords of slum property, who, while oppressing the
poor, profess philanthropic ideals and maintain respectable
demeanors. The plot involves municipal fraud and the defeat of an idealist by landlord and womanly woman. Although the idea is important and the technique up to date,
the dialogue is too clever for orthodox Ibsenism and the
play too poor.

Shaw's next two plays could not be produced, the first
because no producer would produce it, the second because
the official censor, true to his class, found it immoral. *The
Philanderer,* written in 1893, produced at last in 1907,
deals with the womanly woman and the "new woman,"
with marriage as slavery to a middle-class ideal, and with
the vogue, displeasing to Shaw, that Ibsen was enjoying
among the unworthy. The characters, members of an Ibsen club, talk about woman's freedom to smoke, use roller
skates, or leave the home; yet all but two of them are imperfect Ibsenites, Philistines in disguise. Charteris, "an

Ibsenist philosopher," is the real thing. He despises marriage, ideals, and respectability, and he trifles with virtue. It is his fate to be pursued by womanly women, whose disguise as Ibsenites he easily penetrates. But Sylvia, who smokes, dresses like a man, and derides marriage, is a comfort. In this fantastic play Shaw discovered his destined mixture of frivolity and Ibsenism, of the real and the unreal. *Mrs. Warren's Profession,* written the same year, is more of the same and somewhat better. Against the clergymen, capitalists, and men of leisure who form the detestable background stand Vivie Warren, a new woman, and her mother, who manages a chain of brothels for Sir George. Vivie, a formidable creature, has been to Girton College. She smokes, of course, dresses sensibly, and is devoid of attractiveness. This new woman, reared in ignorance of her mother's profession, is attracted, when she discovers it, by its unsentimental character, but on second thought rejects it as respectable and capitalistic. She also rejects her suitor and his unearned income, and leaves her home to earn her living. When Ibsen's Nora slammed that Norwegian door, the noise went farther than could have been predicted. Vivie Warren is an Ibsen girl.

Mrs. Warren's Profession, whose virtues are its dialogue and idea, not its realism or character, was timely. It reflects the feminist movement, which since the time of John Stuart Mill had proposed a distinction between women and property, and now, abetted by Ibsen, rocked the pillars of society. Fabians were feminists. Shaw's friend Annie Besant had left her husband. Everywhere new women ascended bicycles and were off to college or to work. Shaw, reflecting upon these things, was but one of many, of whom Grant Allen was easily the most notorious. In *The Woman Who Did* (1895), a novel, Allen tells of Herminia, another Girton girl, whose rejection of marriage surprises her conventional suitor. "Surely, surely," he exclaims, "you won't carry your ideas of freedom to such an extreme, such a dangerous conclusion!" [4]

[4] For later developments of feminism see H. G. Wells: *Ann Veronica* (1909); Virginia Woolf: *A Room of One's Own* (1929), *Three Guineas* (1938). To illustrate a feminist point, Orlando of *Orlando* (1928), changing sex, remains the same.

Finding no stage for these "unpleasant" plays, Shaw finally published them in 1898, providing them with preface and elaborate stage directions in order to help the reader of novels to visualize the action and understand its meaning. The thwarted dramatist had learned, however, that attacks upon middle-class society were unprofitable unless tempered to the capacity of the middle class. The "pleasant" plays that followed represent a prudent compromise between his ideals and his needs.

The best of these, *Candida*, written in 1894, is an Ibsenite problem play, still too shocking for immediate production. It concerns the intrusion into a middle-class home of a poet who asks the woman of the house to choose between her husband and himself. Marchbanks, the poet, is a fluttering, ambiguous creature, calculated to annoy the manly man. Morell, the clerical husband, instead of kicking Shaw's idea of a poet downstairs, abides his wife's decision. Clear-eyed Candida decides to remain at home on the ground that her husband, more childish than Marchbanks, needs her more. These decisions provide the dated shocks. Morell's decision, rising above the rights of property, admits the independence of his wife, and her decision reflects an unconventional superiority to duty. For the first time Shaw's characters and their psychology are almost human, and for the first time he approximated Ibsen.

In 1895 Shaw became drama-critic for the *Saturday Review*. The selections from this column printed in *Dramatic Opinions and Essays* (1906) are among his most readable writings. As Wagner served as criterion in Shaw's music criticism, so Ibsen served in this. Shaw condemned pre-Ibsenite and pseudo-Ibsenite drama. Shakespeare wrote well before the time of Ibsen. Blaming the bard for intellectual and moral sterility, Shaw called attention to himself. This campaign against Shakespeare, which annoyed the respectable, was designed to advance the cause of Ibsen and, by breaking the grip upon the stage of established actors who found in Shakespeare their best vehicle, to clear the way for new drama with new actors and new conventions. Shaw all but destroyed the well-made play, his chief rivals, and Mrs. Pat Campbell, who acted in their plays. His cruel brilliance was made bearable by the extravagance of the new journalism and by the extremity of his judgments. Having established his reputation and the new drama, Shaw yielded his chair in 1898 to Beerbohm, the "incomparable Max," whose urbane columns were reprinted in *Around Theatres* (1924).

The London Stage Society, founded in 1899 to produce Shaw and Ibsen, staged *Candida* in 1900 and *Mrs. Warren's Profession* in 1902. When Granville-Barker began to produce Shaw and other new dramatists at the Court Theatre in 1904, Shaw found in the noncommercial theater the commercial success of his dreams. His socialism naturally declined, his religious inclination increased, and the plays he wrote for the next few years, when of social significance, concern marriage and caste, softened for middle-class consumption by farce and sometimes comedy. His prefaces of this period often concern the virtue of money, an idea of his own corroborated by Samuel Butler. This idea was shocking only because it was so implicit in the middle-class mind that few had mentioned it.

Getting Married (1908) is announced as an attack upon those who regard an attack upon marriage as an attack upon property. The daring preface on sex and society suggests easy, cheap divorce and economic independence for wives. But the inaction of the play that follows takes place in a kitchen where all sit around and talk about the preface upon which the play depends. Shaw had discovered the secret of sedentary farce as had Ibsen that of static tragedy. The clever lines and fantastic characters make good theater, and the harmless conclusion, avoiding the issues dangerously approached, is less illustrative of the new drama than of a new prudence. The setting of *Misalliance* (1910), another farce, is the house of a rich manufacturer of underwear. But the social meaning, if any, is diffused by conversations among new women, superwomen, and miseducated men, whose words and characters are innocuously grotesque.

Fanny of *Fanny's First Play* (1911) is a Fabian and a suffragette. The critics of her indecorous play within a

play think Shaw wrote it because of the tedious speeches
and the author's "physiological incapacity for passion."
They are not so far wrong, however, as he thought. For
years he had called himself better than Shakespeare. But
Shaw's inhumanity, whether physiological or psychological in origin, his prosaic mind, his growing dependence
upon preface and round-table discussion, and his reluc-
tance to dramatize his ideas made Shaw Shakespeare's opposite. One night Yeats dreamed of Shaw as a "smiling
sewing machine." The portrait is excellent. But Shaw had
all the virtues of his defects. His passionless intellect gave
intellectual vigor to a stage that wanted it. His strange
characters and their lines proved capital vehicles for actors. And his plays, good theater even at their least dramatic, combine at their best some merits of Ibsen, Wycherley, and Bunyan. This original confusion, working by its
assumptions and its tone, amused and taught its audience.
And Shaw wickedly announced to enemies of didactic art
that "art should never be anything else."

He described *Pygmalion* (1914) as "intensely and deliberately didactic." That is one of his jokes, as the play,
confounding his critics, was one of his surprises. Whatever didactic element it contains is so well dramatized
that, remaining unstated, it insinuates itself through art.
The creation of the artificial duchess suggests that accent,
the artificial mark and instrument of caste, is the only difference except wealth between the classes. The inhumanity of Higgins, based upon subtle observation, is thoroughly human. These subtleties, however, do not injure
social point.

In 1911 Shaw abandoned the conservative Fabians.
But the war or the boredom of prosperity turned him
again to social and political problems and to the composition of longer manifestoes, talkier plays. *The Intelligent
Woman's Guide to Socialism and Capitalism* (1928) presents his post-Fabian position. Like the Fabians he abhors
Marx, class war, class dictatorship, and revolutionary violence. But he condemns trade unions and democracy, preferring dictatorships. After their fashion, he says, all men
must be forcibly fed, clothed, lodged, taught, employed,

and, if reluctant, "executed in a kindly manner." *Every-body's Political What's What* (1944) need not detain the intelligent woman. Somewhat rambling in structure but brisk in style, this product of what he calls his "second childhood" recommends equal income for all except Shaw and the selection of rulers by competitive examination. These repeated ideas emerge with difficulty from long attacks on vaccination, Cæsarian operations, tonsillectomy, disinfection, Pavlov, and orthodox religion which make it plain that the ancient journalist, as a wit remarked, had outlived the time for which he was born too soon.

Before we glance at the political plays of Shaw's senility, *Heartbreak House* (1921) demands notice. In this house and its occupants Shaw symbolized "cultured, leisured Europe before the war" as Chekhov, his model, had before him. The tragedy of England, says Shaw in the excellent preface to this excellent play, is the refusal of the best part of the ruling class to rule, the separation of culture from power, and the resulting government by business men seeking private gain. In the first two acts of the play Shaw introduces a group of eccentrics, who gradually harden into types: the practical businessman, the burglar, the colonial official, the horsy woman, the futile socialist, and the enjoyer of unearned income who has read Shaw, understands all things, and does nothing about them. Through these two acts these morally emancipated, cultured, foolish, or reactionary people move about the parlor of superior light comedy; and the spectator thinks this their element until the last act, when what seemed domestic comedy, expanding now on the terrace, becomes far larger than the limits of the original parlor and much more sinister. In the last act, lest his moral miss its point, the anxious author made the play a conversation piece. But even this return to habitual explicitness is not without drama. Hardly has Hector Hushabye condemned his class as useless, dangerous, and—for leaving government to business men—responsible for what is coming, when a bomber drops a bomb on them, as one of them observes, to keep the home fires burning. This play, tracing the collapse of civilization to the irresponsibility of the civilized,

the "blunders of boobies," and "the cupidity of capitalists," could not be produced while hostilities continued.

The depression sent Shaw back to the social and political play. *The Apple Cart* (1929) is trivial. But the preface neatly restates Shaw's objections to irresponsible plu-
tocracy. *Too True to Be Good* (1932) concerns the misery
of riches. What seems at first a Shavian paradox seems
next the work of a tractarian for Sunday schools, and finally seems a more or less serious treatment of labor and
leisure and their distribution. In the play the wealthy
heroine, having eloped with a clerical burglar to enjoy
the leisure of theft, asks, in her boredom and spiritual starvation, freedom for what? As the curtain descends she
finds a purpose of a sort, and the burglar preaches as if
words were still effectual. The characters are authentically
Shavian; the play, a farce, is bright, witty, and full of the
old extravagance; but, wanting unity of theme and action,
it remains as ineffectual as the burglar's words. As the curtain falls on the first act, Shaw observes: "The play is now
virtually over; but the characters will discuss it at great
length for two acts more." The reference of "it" is unclear,
for the characters proceed to discuss not only freedom but
Freud, the quantum theory, the ending of certainties, relations of parents and children, disease and medicine, cocktails, cuddling, and the younger generation. Shaw's trouble was not so much his disregard of Aristotelian unity as
his attempt to compress the chaos of the thirties into a
form suitable for the neater problems of the nineties. The
preface of *On the Rocks* (1933) commends the liquidation
of incorrigibles for the public good, as practiced by Stalin
and Pontius Pilate. But Shaw's approval of this end is con-
tingent upon the means since he dislikes cruelty, he says,
"even cruelty to other people." The play that is appended
to this preface proposes a ready and easy way to establish
a new commonwealth. Painless liquidation is also the
theme of *The Simpleton of the Unexpected Isles* (1935),
a fantasy. The angels who perform the social task of Ogpu
attend to stockbrokers, medical men, and other parasites.
An attempt by capitalistic police to arrest an angel in
Leicester Square fails to arrest the Last Judgment. *The*

Millionairess (1935) establishes the need of controlling those whose talent is money-making, and, in the person of Epifania, presents a plutocrat whose unscrupulousness and indifference to social good are exemplary. The English bishop of *Geneva* (1938) is such another. Embodying the prejudices of the middle class, he faints when confronted with a commissar and, upon resuscitation, dies. In these ultimate farces Shaw speaks almost as kindly of Stalin as of Mussolini.

Shaw had outlasted the new drama. When it began, however, he was but one, though easily the first, of many. During the eighties Arthur Wing Pinero wrote well-made sentimental comedies in the manner of the French or dramas remotely in the manner of T. W. Robertson, author of *Caste*. Brought face to face with reality by Ibsen, Pinero rapidly reformed. *The Second Mrs. Tanqueray* (1893) is his first good play and the first good play of the new drama. The problem is that of a woman with a past, who, upon her marriage to a respectable widower, is compelled to endure social ostracism, her husband's effort to shield his daughter from contamination, and his daughter's coldness. When her cold stepdaughter is about to marry an old lover of Mrs. Tanqueray's, Mrs. Tanqueray solves her problem by suicide. This pathetic play, which misses tragedy, takes its well-made plot from France but its natural dialogue and action from Ibsen. *The Notorious Mrs. Ebbsmith* (1895) presents a new woman, hostile, of course, to marriage. The attempt of this sensible, dowdy, socialist agitator to brave opinion and live in sin with Lucas Cleeve is defeated by his conventionality and the worldliness of the Duke (played by George Arliss), who thinks women toys. An attractive dress symbolizes the victory of convention, and the rescue of the Bible from the stove the defeat of emancipation.

To Shaw, reviewing for the *Saturday Review,* this Ibsenite play was pseudo-Ibsenite, and, since it showed the defeat of the new woman by Philistine society, almost immoral. There may have been something to these charges, for Pinero's plays found ready acceptance in the commercial theater. Unable to find even a little theater for most of his, Shaw could find no merit in his fortunate rival.

The hand of the established craftsman, too apparent in the tooled perfection of Pinero's plays, and an emphasis greater upon character than upon problem, though not unlike that of *Hedda Gabler,* displeased didactic Shaw. It was clear to others, however, that Pinero had more power than Shaw to create human beings and display their discomforts in middle-class society. But Pinero proved unable to develop, and, like Ibsen and Dumas *fils,* his masters, he wanted wit.[5]

Henry Arthur Jones, whom Shaw admired, evolved into a social playwright by way of melodrama. *The Silver King* (1882), a melodrama as splendid in its kind as *Sweeney Todd, the Demon Barber of Fleet Street,* was financially the most successful play of the eighties. It is still of interest not only for its soliloquies, asides, sentiment, and violence but for the villain's justification of middle-class villainy by Darwin's survival of the fittest. Although melodramatic, *The Middleman* (1889) concerns social problems, the exploitation, for instance, of worker by capitalist and the hypocrisy of the respectable; for under Robertson's influence Jones was turning to the realities around him. In 1884 Jones adapted Ibsen's *Doll's House* for popular consumption, giving it a happy ending and *Breaking a Butterfly* for title; but he admitted later that he had been unaware of Ibsen's value. Realizing this value in the nineties, he studied Ibsen to some purpose, but never to such purpose as Pinero or Shaw.

The Case of Rebellious Susan (1894) is the first of the comedies under which Jones concealed the aim of the social critic. Like Nora, Susan walks out of the middle-class home, but here the resemblance ceases. Susan matches her husband's infidelity by her own, but, advised

[5] Of Pinero's later plays, three are conspicuous: *Iris* (1901), *The Thunderbolt* (1908), and *Mid-Channel* (1909). Granville-Barker, who became the chief producer of new dramatists, wrote competent plays according to their patterns: *The Voysey Inheritance* (1905), *Waste* (1907), and *The Madras House* (1910). Cf. St. John Hankin: *The Return of the Prodigal* (1905), *The Cassilis Engagement* (1907); St. John Ervine: *Jane Clegg* (1913), *John Ferguson* (1915). The best short survey of the new drama is in Allardyce Nicoll: *British Drama* (1925).

by cynical Sir Richard Kato, preserves appearances. This cynical conformity carries Jones's criticism of Mrs. Grundy, to whom he addressed, with the published play, an epistle. *Michael and His Lost Angel* (1896), his favorite, though primarily a study of character, bears in its treatment of the cleric and his fallen woman a social burden. After the financial failure of this strange, dark play, one of the most powerful of the nineties, Jones returned to the social comedy at which he excelled. *The Liars* (1897) and *The Hypocrites* (1906) deal, as their titles suggest, with the "organized hypocrisy" forced upon the governing class by its moral code. The first of these is among the most smoothly contrived of well-made plays; the second with its squires, vicars, and ladies is a gallery of detestable middle-class portraits, relieved by that of the curate, an honest, unsuccessful man. *Mrs. Dane's Defence* (1900) is Jones's closest approach to Ibsen, but the problem is too unreal to support the elaborate apparatus of detection with which society surrounds it. Although the cruelty of respectable people has never been more faithfully presented, the play loses its force in melodrama and sentimentality.

Jones shared the views of Shaw and Ibsen, but in the person of the *raisonneur,* borrowed from Dumas *fils,* upheld the hypocrisy each play attacked. This worldliness strangely invited the critical applause of Shaw, who seems to have been able to pass beneath surfaces to the didactic intention they conceal. It is likely, moreover, that Pinero's enemy saw less of a rival in Jones.

In 1900 James Joyce's essay "Ibsen's New Drama" appeared in the *Fortnightly Review.* Joyce, who had learned Danish to read the master, praised him not for action or character but for the perception of naked truth. Admiration of Ibsen's static quality and his "lofty impersonal power" seems to have assisted Joyce in achieving these qualities in *Ulysses,* but before this he had written *Exiles,* published in 1918, an Ibsenite triangle involving that change in family relationship which became Joyce's constant theme. Although it is one of the best of the Ibsen tradition, this play, overshadowed by Joyce's greater works, is prized mostly for what light it sheds on his mind and his development as an artist.

From among these good, small, higher dramatists one emerged higher than they and more thoroughly representative of their kind. In the hierarchy they compose, John Galsworthy[6] stands below Shaw alone and somewhat to his right. Legal Galsworthy began with *The Silver Box*, discovered and produced in 1906 by Granville-Barker. This play involves the difference between the justice accorded by the middle class to its own members and that to workers and the unemployed. Through his austerities of plot and dialogue Galsworthy presents a problem not for solution but for contemplation. He seems dispassionate, but as the children cry without and as the innocent are rejected or led away, his sentiments project a slight mist from the wings. There are no villains around, nor heroes, but only commonplace men, little victims of social pressures larger than their comprehension, which make them irresponsible and pitiable. Galsworthy is concerned less with his people than with the ponderous forces of middle-class society.

This admirably constructed play, in which nothing is irrelevant or weak, was followed by another better and no less severe. *Strife* (1909) presents the problem of worker, union, and boss. The unauthorized strike of tinplate workers proves as wasteful as it is inevitable. Only the death of a woman is accomplished and the breaking of two emergent men, stronger than most of Galsworthy's characters: Roberts, the symbolic worker, and Anthony, the capitalist. *Justice* (1910) concerns the injustice of the criminal code. More complicated than the usual Galsworthy play, which achieves its end by monolithic simplicity, this one appears scattered. In *The Fugitive* (1913) sentiment triumphs. Fleeing the middle-class home, the heroine receives the weight of the social displeasure poised over Nora's door. Bourgeois marriage is bad; prostitution, to which she is driven by her nurtured incapacity, worse.

[6] H. V. Marrot: *The Life and Letters of John Galsworthy* (1936).

These two comparative failures were atoned for by *The Skin Game* (1920), which reveals the hidden conflict within the middle class between landlord and capitalist, and by *Loyalties* (1922), among the finest studies of caste. Into a country house, swarming with products of the public school, comes De Levis, a Jew, an outsider, and a cad, of course, but suffered for his riches. Ignorant of the code, he breaks it. Loyalties, torn between truth and playing the game, generally incline toward the latter, except the loyalty of the lawyer, which, transcending caste, inclines toward law. This is a good play, differing from some of Shaw's in dramatizing the problem. In *Old English* (1924), Galsworthy's last important play, sentiment emerges from the wings to moisten an ancient capitalist, who nevertheless remained an adequate vehicle for George Arliss.

By the time of *Old English* the social-problem play, except for vestigial Shaw's, was all but extinct. His preface to *Heartbreak House* tells of the war's effect. Never financially profitable, the new drama was driven from even the littlest theater during the war by rising rents, which, permitting nothing less entertaining than whimsy or musical comedy, made the stage respectable again. For a time the serious drama found refuge in the suburbs, then in the provinces, but pursued by rents, against which it had once exclaimed, it gradually tired or, what was worse, moved on to Dublin or New York. After the war the situation proved little better. The war created new problems, but these problems were unsuitable for Ibsen's parlor. Three walls and a fictive fourth, admirably designed for domestic problems and for limited intrusions by labor, finance, or caste, were insufficiently elastic for problems now international or all but universal in their dimensions. What the theater needed was a new stage, one adapted, for example, to the production of Hardy's *Dynasts,* a stage, as Allardyce Nicoll has suggested, something like a three-ring circus. In the absence of this improvement, the theater, always dependent upon its stage, lost touch with current reality, which was now and again attended to by the movies.

Maugham, Coward, Milne, and others, however, continued
to fill what once was Ibsen's stage with charming plays.[7]

II

Once thought red, writers of Auden's generation were
little more than pink. After the excitement was over, certain things besides this color emerged: some of the poems
of Auden and MacDiarmid, Caudwell's criticism, the novels and essays of Orwell, and Spender's autobiography.
But poets clamoring for blood in the early thirties had
historical sanction.

The depression, the failure of the general strike of
1926, and the greater failure of the Labour government of
1929–31 had destroyed hope of social democracy. Hence,
after years of obscure bickering with Labour, the Communist Party enjoyed a boom. As antidote to dying capitalism this party offered a classless society, production not for
profit but for use, and the right to work. After the violence
of the inevitable revolution, society would submit to the
dictatorship of the proletariat until society and proletariat
were one. In this classless condition human nature, expanding, could realize its possibilities, and culture, no
longer confined to a leisure class or menaced by profit,
would be universal. Consisting of a few intellectuals and
workers, the party was as exclusive and enigmatic as the
Society of Jesus. But it welcomed the aid of those middle-
class men who, realizing the necessity of necessity, walked
leftward and within their bourgeois limitations were proletarian in tendency. Writers of this kind (and few were of
any other) were known as fellow travelers.

John Strachey, Etonian and ex-Labourite, was the
party's first important apologist. In *The Coming Struggle
for Power* (1933) he proves by Marx and Lenin that
capitalism is destroying itself through monopoly and im-

---

[7] J. B. Priestley: *Dangerous Corner* (1932), *Laburnum Grove*
(1933), *They Came to a City* (1942); James Bridie: *A Sleeping Clergyman* (1933), *The Last Trump* (1938), *The King of Nowhere* (1938),
The Golden Legend of Shults (1939), *What Say They?* (1940).

perialism, that Shaw and Wells are thoroughly bourgeois, and that communism, which he describes with sober lucidity, is the only hope for Britain. His literary criticism was moderate. *Literature and Dialectical Materialism* (1934), though partly devoted to exposing the "fascist unconscious" in D. H. Lawrence and others, maintains that literature is literature. We do not pretend, says Strachey, that a poet is good because he is a Marxist or bad because he is not, nor are we too hard on fellow travelers. Such moderation was peculiar.

According to many writers for *Left Review,* a critical journal that flourished from 1934 to 1938 under the editorship of Edgell Rickword, art is propaganda. This orthodox opinion, which replaces æsthetic value with political expediency, was held by Anthony Blunt, for example, and Edward Upward. The latter's essay in *The Mind in Chains* (1937), a leftist symposium edited by C. Day Lewis, proclaims that no book at the present time can be good "unless it is written from a Marxist or near Marxist viewpoint." Applying this standard, Upward finds Joyce and Proust to be without value; for talent without dialectical materialism is helpless before reality. Other essays of this volume urge artists to embrace the proletariat and be free.

In *Illusion and Reality* (1937) Christopher Caudwell, the ablest and most philosophical of Marxist critics, rejects this notion of art as propaganda. Art, he says, is the product of society and performs a social function; its purpose is to adapt responses to economic co-operation by adjusting conflicts of individual, society, and nature. This theory, which combines the anthropologists with I. A. Richards and Marx, permits a criticism at once orthodox and reasonable. Although Caudwell finds Shakespeare bourgeois, he does not find him bad. The trouble with recent poetry, he says, is the isolation of poet from society; but this isolation, as illusory as the bourgeois idea of freedom, merely reflects the individualism of the poet's class.[8]

[8] In *Studies in a Dying Culture* (1938) Caudwell (Christopher Sprigg) detects the bourgeois illusion of freedom in Shaw, Wells, and Lawrence. Cf. Alick West: *Crisis and Criticism* (1937); Philip Henderson: *The Poet and Society* (1939).

While critics theorized, poets were adjusting their responses to the proletariat and to bloody revolution. Of these poets Hugh MacDiarmid was first and, by proletarian standards, best. His "First Hymn to Lenin" is good by any standard. Written in Scots dialect, this muscular prayer, which uses the language of daily speech, heightened by feeling and given finality, captures something of the grandeur of Yeats. MacDiarmid's other poems show that his proletarian façade conceals the bourgeois technician who knows and profits by the work of Rilke, Joyce, and Eliot. Exercises in erudite verbalism and lovely ambiguous lyrics like "O wha's been here afore me, lass," are commoner than Marxist poems. Although Burns's successor writes too much indifferent verse, he is memorable for having made poetry out of the "Cheka's necessary murders." [9] "Above all, my poetry is Marxist," he says in *Lucky Poet* (1943), his autobiography and manifesto. *"Vive l'anarchie!"* A working man, a Scottish nationalist, and apparently a party member for a while, he gives the back of his hand to the bourgeois leftists of England.

Following MacDiarmid's lead came younger poets— Auden, Day Lewis, Spender, and their chums—constituting the main literary current of the early thirties. All were products of public school and university, but all had ostensibly abandoned their class for a hypothetical proletariat. Some of them became or appear to have become members of the Communist Party for a time, but, whether members or not, all were fellow travelers. According to Caudwell, this group consisted of bourgeois anarchists, destructive of their own class but incapable of joining its successor. Socialists in economics, these "romantic revolutionaries" remained individualists in art. The party welcomed their aid while rebuking their limitations. Events have proved the accuracy of Caudwell's analysis.

This group announced itself in two anthologies, *New Signatures* (1932) and *New Country* (1933), both edited by Michael Roberts, who saw the end of isolated, erudite

---

[9] MacDiarmid (Christopher Grieve): *First Hymn to Lenin* (1931), *Second Hymn to Lenin* (1933), *Selected Poems* (1944).

poetry and the achievement by his contributors of new proletarian attitudes toward life. Both are represented by William Plomer's "Epitaph for a Contemporary" who was shot by the proletariat for remaining a gentleman. But on the whole the volumes are less revolutionary than their prefaces announce them to be and far less exciting. Auden, Day Lewis, and Spender were the most hopeful signs. These anthologies were succeeded by *New Writing* (1936–39), a semiannual of poetry and prose, in which the original group was augmented by John Cornford, whose poems in the fourth volume seemed to John Lehmann, the editor, the only successful poems produced on "hard-thinking Marxist lines" by an English writer—and perhaps they are.

The best poet of the Auden generation is Auden. His *Poems* (1930) reveal new social awareness by colloquial diction, conversational rhythms, and suitable images of deserted factories, frontiers, invalid chairs, glaciers, and schoolboy games. Ideas for improvement, resembling those of D. H. Lawrence and Homer Lane (a kind of Mary Baker Eddy), generally stop short of Marx, who had little use for the individual change of heart that Auden prescribed. "Doom is dark" and "Venus Will Now Say a Few Words" celebrate the Marxist and Darwinian necessity that drives young men to exile from a dying culture. Yet "no ruffian badge" of party membership or "bombs of conspiracy" spoiled an energetic preoccupation with death. In *The Dance of Death* (1933), Auden's most Marxist poem, music-hall techniques lead to the entrance of Karl Marx, muttering about liquidation as he brings the curtain down. Even this burlesque of their convictions was gratefully received by waiting multitudes. Auden's later poems, those of *Look, Stranger!* (1936) for example, illustrate nothing but his occasional lyric power and his protean variety. Of the three poetic plays he wrote with Christopher Isherwood on the relapse of the present world into fascism, imperialism, and war, *The Ascent of F6,* produced in 1937, is the most remarkable. It seems significant that the theme of this political allegory is the plight of the intellectual, torn between the pulls of left and right, disloyal to both and therefore to himself.[1]

Of these fashionable poets Stephen Spender is next best and somewhat more orthodox. Toward the end of *Poems* (1933) are several revolutionary lyrics, threatening death to exploiters, pitying the unemployed, and, in their imagery of aerodromes and railways, looking to a Wellsian future. Advising "young comrades" to forsake their fathers' houses, Spender points to dawns "exploding like a shell" and to new roots seeking water. These poems, mostly in free verse, show lyric intelligence and Spender's admiration of Whitman and Lawrence. Aside from "Pylons," "The Funeral" is worthiest of notice and most original. Here Russian workers carry to a grave (while red flags wave) a dead worker, "one cog in a golden and singing hive." Revolutionary enthusiasm may excuse the presence of cogs in the hive and explain the general looseness of these poems, which were, however, a welcome change from Eliot. But *Vienna* (1934) is imitation Eliot and imitation Auden. Technically derivative as it is, this poem is the first celebration of a revolutionary theme by one of the group. Spender's waste land is Vienna, where, in January 1934, rebellious socialists and workers were destroyed by capitalists. Although his essays on literature and communism seem Marxist enough to an outsider, Spender's defense of the artist's individuality and his right to choose theme and treatment displeased Caudwell.[2] Other severer critics began to call Spender the Rupert Brooke of the depression, but it would have been better to call him the Shelley.

Less like something by Shelley, however, than like something by Rousseau, Spender's autobiography, *World Within World* (1951) is not only his important work, but also the tallest memorial to the Auden period. In this

[1] Auden: *Collected Poetry* (1945). Auden and Isherwood: *The Dog Beneath the Skin* (1935), *On the Frontier* (1938), *Journey to a War* (1939). Isherwood: *Lions and Shadows* (1938) concerns the Auden group. Richard Hoggart: *Auden* (1951). John Lehmann: *The Whispering Gallery* (1955), autobiography.

[2] *The Destructive Element* (1935), *Forward from Liberalism* (1937), *Trial of a Judge* (1938), *Collected Poems* (1955).

sincere disclosure of himself, his friends, and his loves, Spender tells not only how he met Auden and Isherwood, but how he enjoyed an unearned income, finally met a working man, wrote for the *Daily Worker,* joined the Communist Party, and on a visit to Spain fired a borrowed rifle in the right direction. What chiefly moved him was "a thirst for moral knowledge," of which his experiences afforded plenty.

In *A Hope for Poetry* (1934), a group manifesto and an explanation of technical ancestry, C. Day Lewis praises Auden and Spender in return for their praise, as if taking in one another's washing could make it red. *Revolution in Writing* (1935) is Day Lewis's defense of poetry and of the individual's rights against bourgeois society and demanding Marxists. Rejecting propaganda, he calls, while trying to be true to Marx, for liberal æsthetics. The position of Day Lewis and the other fellow travelers was a difficult one. Bourgeois by nature, proletarian by sympathy, they found themselves neither here nor there. Some of Day Lewis's verses are revolutionary in theme, but more concern internal conflict. "I look to the left, comrades," he exclaimed, looking to the right.[3]

The menace of fascism did more than the unaided Communist Party could to provide a credible cause. In the later thirties when the People's Front, under party control, embraced all leftist groups but Labour, leftist literature became anti-fascist literature. Franco's Spain provided from 1936 to 1938 the emotional center. Finding at last a clear position, poets abandoned pacifism, visited Spain, wrote poems about it, or enlisted in the International Brigade. Tom Wintringham, small poet and political commissar in the brigade, fell wounded. Christopher Caudwell died manning his machine gun; John Cornford, Julian Bell, and Ralph Fox died manning theirs. To celebrate these heroes and symbolic Spain, Spender edited *Poems for Spain* (1939), to which he, Wintringham, Corn-

---

[3] *Transitional Poem* (1929), *From Feathers to Iron* (1931), *Noah and the Waters* (1936). Louis MacNeice: *Poems* (1935), *Plant and Phantom* (1941), *Modern Poetry* (1938). MacNeice and Auden: *Letters from Iceland* (1937). E. A. Osborne, editor: *In Letters of Red* (1938).

ford, Auden, and others contributed. Spender's verses, descriptive and pathetic, lack revolutionary conviction. Auden's "Spain," reprinted here, is a rhetorical triumph and plainly the best poem of that war. By "poets exploding like bombs" Auden ambiguously intends his more desperate comrades and by "the flat ephemeral pamphlet and the boring meeting" the life of the party.

Spain may have been what English poets needed, but it was not enough to inspire the proletarian novel, which, defeated by orthodoxy, continued to languish. Ralph Bates, who worked and fought in Spain, devoted one of the best of these, *The Olive Field* (1936), to Spanish workers and landlords and the insurrection of 1934. His individuals (according to Marx) are less alive than the group and its relation to the symbolic trees. Although not proletarian, the fantasies of Rex Warner and the Berlin and Vienna novels of Christopher Isherwood are anti-fascist.[4] The only real proletarian novel of the period is *Living* (1929) by Henry Green, capitalist.

Loyalist politics and Stalin's pact with Hitler in 1939 finally diverted fellow travelers. A sudden shift of party line, which made of England's war against fascism an imperialistic adventure, enabled poets to see the value of what they had surrendered for something thought better. They saw the party plain, no longer as guide to the world's proletariat, but as the instrument of Russian policy.[5]

The relapse of George Orwell (Eric Blair) was spectacular. This Etonian, whose knowledge of workers and bums was intimate, as he tells us in *Down and Out in Paris and London* (1933), was moved by hatred of fascism to join the Republican militia in Barcelona. After fighting by the side of workers and anarchists and having been gravely wounded, he found himself and his fellows

---

[4] Isherwood: *Prater Violet* (1945). Arthur Calder-Marshall: *Pie in the Sky* (1937). John Sommerfield: *May Day* (1936).

[5] The disillusionment of Strachey, Laski, and Victor Gollancz of the Left Book Club is recorded in their *Betrayal of the Left* (1941). Herbert Read, who had once called himself a communist, proclaimed himself an anarchist in *Poetry and Anarchism* (1938) and other tracts. His position, not unlike that of the other poets, is more precisely defined.

condemned as Trotskyites by the Stalinists of the International Brigade. The story of this ordeal and of his escape across the French border, one jump ahead of the commissars, is told in *Homage to Catalonia* (1951), the most moving book to come out of England's Spain. The betrayal of his ideals also accounts for his attack in *Inside the Whale* (1940) on fellow travelers, whose innocence blinds them to the intellectual dishonesty of Communism. Intellectual honesty and straightforwardness of style distinguish his *Critical Essays* (1946), *Shooting an Elephant* (1950), and *Such, Such Were the Joys* (1952); and disillusionment accounts for the bitterness of his political satires. *Animal Farm* (1945), one of the most brilliant since Swift's, is directed against Stalin and his commissars. As the pigs betray the barnyard revolution, they change its slogans. All animals are equal, to be sure, but some "are more equal than others." *1984* (1949) reveals the totalitarian nightmare to which both left and right have been tending and which, it seems likely, they must produce. Under the eye of Big Brother, war is peace, freedom is slavery, and ignorance is strength. While the Ministry of Love attends to liberals in the cellars, another bureau attends to history upstairs so that "oligarchical collectivism" may continue to enjoy power for power's sake.[6]

Backsliding in *The New Realism* (1939), where he defends the artist's integrity, Spender reveals his complete relapse into liberalism in the verses of *Ruins and Visions* (1942). A liberal of his generation may be defined as one who was once a Communist. Having replaced necessity by choice, he makes the right one with sensations of commitment. Having discarded politics, he makes literature morality and morality a kind of politics. Liberal Auden and Isherwood departed for capitalistic America, Isherwood to become a yogi and Auden a Christian. But while Louis MacNeice, whose interests were less political than those of his friends, was composing his "Epitaph for Liberal Poets," illiberal MacDiarmid was founding a quarterly to main-

---

[6] John Atkins: *George Orwell* (1954). Lawrence Brander: *George Orwell* (1954). Orwell: *Keep the Aspidistra Flying* (1936), *The Road to Wigan Pier* (1937). Cf. William Golding: *Lord of the Flies* (1955).

tain the heat of dialectical materialism. Sean O'Casey, who had once been secretary to James Connolly's militant workers in Ireland, presented in 1940 *The Star Turns Red*, the ideal Marxist melodrama. *Oak Leaves and Lavender* (1946), which remains unproduced, finds promise of life in the Red Army. With these loyal Celts to his left and the Labour Party to his right, moderate Laski surveyed the empty field.

CHAPTER THREE: *Right*

*T*HIS chapter deals less with reactionary philosophies than with their effects, direct, peripheral, and indirect. Nationalism, imperialism, fascism, and neoclassicism produced propaganda, of course, and with it much of greater excellence.

I

"Imperialism," said Lenin—and it is foolish to quarrel with him—"is the monopoly stage of capitalism." Faced at last with the failure of *laissez faire,* capitalists turned to monopoly, state control imposed from above, and the geographical extension of monopoly. Colonies gave them the markets and materials they needed and the chance to export their capital. In the late nineteenth century, trusts and the great powers representing them extended monopolies to empty places. Rival monopolies, established by small wars, led to greater wars, which threatened to destroy what they were designed to protect.

British imperialism of this time seems the attempt of the middle class to prevent its decline. This attempt, inspired by growing German and American competition, was supported by doctrines of racial supremacy, formulated by Houston Chamberlain and others, by a theory of state supremacy, expounded by Bernard Bosanquet, and by Dar-

win's ideas of fitness. The *Daily Mail* was founded in
1896. Here and elsewhere journalists and poets made empire glamorous enough to serve as a substitute for religion.
Fear and hate, the principal sentiments, accompanied
thoughts of righteousness. The Liberal Party, representing
an earlier stage of capitalism, declined and fell, to be succeeded in 1895 by the Tory government of Lord Salisbury,
of which Joseph Chamberlain was the significant member.
Under him British imperialism attained its perfection.
Rudyard Kipling was its simple-minded singer.[1]

It would be simplest to dismiss his verse as doggerel;
but the verses Kipling wrote, from *Departmental Ditties*
(1886) to those which interrupted his last collections of
prose, are often more than that. Some are ballads suitable
for baritones in parlors, some are hymns suitable for Anglicans at worship, and some, like "If—," are suitable for
framing on walls. A master of thumping, splendid rhythms,
of the language of daily speech, and of rhyming abstractions, he generally wrote what Yeats called popular poetry,
verse that pleases a class commonly indifferent to literature. The sensitivity is limited, the response to reality is
crude, the whole escapes becoming poetry because it is
conscious and contrived. But in this kind, a kind in which
Longfellow excelled, Kipling's verse is good. Good journalism, metrical talent, and simple morality never produced anything more haunting than "Mandalay" or "Gen-
tlemen-Rankers" or "Gunga Din." Sometimes Kipling rose
above this kind to poetry: "Recessional," a triumph of
tone, "Cities and Thrones and Powers," and a translation
from Horace. In "The Way through the Woods" he approached the Georgians.

A poet with such gifts was fitted to become the laureate of Joseph Chamberlain's designs. Although Kipling rejected Tory honors, and thought himself independent, he
was among the last of public poets. While others, express-

[1] See Élie Halévy: *A History of the English People, 1895–1905*
(1926). Rudyard Kipling: *Something of Myself* (1937). Edward Shanks:
Rudyard Kipling (1940). Hilton Brown: *Rudyard Kipling* (1946). Edmund Wilson: *The Wound and the Bow* (1941). George Orwell:
Critical Essays (1946). C. E. Carrington: *The Life of Rudyard Kipling*
(1955).

ing themselves alone, exiled themselves from the middle class, Kipling, sharing its sentiments, expressed it. That he was unconscious of doing this made his conscious verses better and assured their sale.

His idea of empire may be deduced from "Recessional," "The White Man's Burden," and "Loot." It was the duty of the chosen race to bring order to "lesser breeds without the Law." These unfortunates, all right when servile, consisted of Irishmen, Indians, Russians, Burmese, and Americans. The Law, the middle-class Englishman's idea of what was what, was enforced by a thin red line, keeping the borders against unarmed outsiders. The ascetics who administered the Law were gentlemen trained for the purpose by playing games at public schools. No profit or reward softened their Indian discomforts save their sense of work well done. They were aided by common men, soldiers of the line, fine fellows, respectful of their betters. Kipling was so far from knowing what his sahibs were about that he despised business men and members of Parliament. Unaware that imperialism was capitalism and that democracy was their necessary condition, the confused, angry man allied himself with feudal aristocracy, which, though dead, was their disguise. He consorted when he could with Cecil Rhodes and the Viceroy.

But Kipling had started as a common journalist. His earliest stories, unlike the verse of his imperial days, are filled with sympathy for all the swarming humanity about him. *Plain Tales from the Hills* (1888) presents the follies and wisdom of Anglo-Indian society at Simla, especially those of "wonderful" Mrs. Hauksbee. At the other end of the social scale are a native girl who loses the hands that embraced a sahib, and three soldiers, Mulvaney and his companions. The prose, swift and sure, and the impeccable craft suggest long study of Maupassant and Stevenson. Slight characters are supported by local-colored places. Exploiting India as artist, not as sahib, he pleased by his sharp, exotic flavor.

Having tired of India, Kipling tried to become an American, but, defeated by Vermont, became an imperial Englishman instead and spent his time abusing Americans.

Even in his hate he was fortunate, for the middle class of
England, fearing American machines, found his hate their
own and paid him well for it. Expanding from Vermont
to include the non-English world, his hate provided protective shells into which he could withdraw to shield his
wounded sensitivity and limit it. Upon the reality that he
had warmly welcomed he began to impose middle-class
patterns. These emotional and moral limitations and the
growing technical proficiency that made his stories a little
slick made him the symbol as well as the prophet of his
class.

The success of the American stories is their British
tone. "An Error in the Fourth Dimension" shows an irresponsible American capitalist breaking the British code
and, rejected by responsible British capitalists, fleeing to
the "unkempt" banks of the Hudson. "An Habitation Enforced," no less condescending, shows good rich Americans in England. Having learned that in England only
Englishmen may speak, these boobies are grateful when
spoken to. The squire's lady accepts them, they attend the
established church, and are happy ever after. Kipling, who
simplified all, had succeeded in simplifying Henry James.
"The Captive," a story of the Boer War, presents Laugh-
ton O. Zigler, an Ohio capitalist, who, unfaithful to the
breed, has been "fighting for niggers, as the North did."
He sees his error, becomes an acceptable subject, and in
"The Edge of the Evening" breaks the law with impunity
as a sahib may.

Stories of triumphant empire accompany these. In
"The Devil and the Deep Sea" English pearl-poachers
poach pearls in waters of one of the "lesser law-breaking
Powers." The moral is that England protects her pirates
and that Englishmen can repair machinery. An English
gunboat in "Judson and the Empire" subdues a Brazilian
democratic revolution that threatens to interrupt the exploitation of Brazil by the General Development Company. Such stories are too numerous to list, but it is impossible altogether to ignore those which attack democracy
in favor of government by sahibs. In "A Walking Dele-
gate," conservative, perhaps Republican, horses on a Ver-

mont farm trample a social-democratic yellow horse who advises revolt against oppression. "With the Night Mail" and "As Easy as A.B.C," Wellsian dreams of mechanical Utopia, reveal a time when government by self-appointed experts has succeeded the "rule of the mob." With intolerable machines these specialists come from London to subdue a democratic rebellion in Illinois. Other stories praise machines, which by their order, co-operation, and discipline symbolized the Empire. As Romance brought up the 9.15, the simplest reader could feel its splendid inhumanity.

Mechanical perfection of plot and efficiency of prose, however admirable, were not enough to make Kipling a novelist; for a novelist must have greater understanding of people than Kipling's self-imposed limitations generally allowed. *The Light that Failed* (1890) failed; and *Captains Courageous* (1897), however salty, is flawed by the sudden reformation of the hero. But in *Kim* (1901) Kipling triumphed. This great nostalgic novel, recapturing his earlier delight in the multitudes of India, presents with sympathetic tolerance not only sahibs but men of lesser breed, the excellent Lama, the horse-trader, and the lady of the litter. The Grand Trunk Road, embodying the essential theme, presents the color, confusion, and humanity of India. What Kipling called his "Daemon," that part of his nature which was uncommercial, must have had a hand in *Kim*.

In *Stalky and Co.* (1899) Kipling made his semi-public school more public by introducing the practical jokes, vengeances, and small cruelties that were his obsession. *The Jungle Book* (1894) is loved by every child, but even here that didactic nature inherited from many Methodists made his jungle an allegory of empire. The Bander-logs, democratic outsiders, are destroyed by the Law of the Jungle. If, like a child, one can ignore their imperial function, Kaa and the other animals are fine people. "How the Rhinoceros Got His Skin," and the other metamorphoses of the *Just So Stories* (1902), are among Kipling's best. *Puck of Pook's Hill* (1906), inferior to these, celebrates imperial virtues in the Roman defense of the wall, but is generally concerned with the glories of little England and "all her thousand years."

It was the Boer War that made a Little Englander and an introvert of imperial Kipling. Disillusioned by the hollowness disclosed, he never fully recovered. "Recessional" had warned against boastfulness and pride, and "The Lesson," written at the end of the war, is filled with the apprehensions that plagued old, suffering Kipling, a master of prose who had kept himself from other greatness.

W. E. Henley, small poet, critic, and editor, patron of Kipling, Shaw, and Wells, was a lesser poet than Kipling but of the same breed. He admired piracy, served Stevenson as the model for John Silver, and preached the cult of virility. His early *Poems* (1888), some of them composed in primitive free verse, deal for the most part with his experiences in hospital where he lost a leg. "Invictus" with its courageous platitudes belongs with "If—" among poems of middle-class philosophy. During the Boer War, Henley wrote jingoistic verses, popular, obvious, and hysterical. These imperial sentiments had been expressed somewhat better in 1890 in his "Song of the Sword," a celebration in free verse of military violence and survival of the fittest. With Kipling he shared the dream of unending progress through empire and machine. This dream is the subject of "A Song of Speed," his last poem. In mechanical free verse he tells how Alfred Harmsworth, proprietor of the *Daily Mail*, took him for a ride in a 1901 Mercédès. As he handled her pipes and her cylinders Henley succumbed to religious awe.[2] There were other poets of that kidney—Henry Newbolt, for instance, an even more nautical Kipling, and, later, Rupert Brooke, whose patriotic sonnets, agreeable to patriots, are of less importance than his poems of fish and dust.

The parents of W. H. Hudson were North Americans, he was Argentinian, but, disregarding these accidents, he remained an Englishman. Fascinated by the British ranchers of the pampas, he regarded himself as one of them, though he differed from his neighbors in being in-

[2] Jerome Buckley: *William Ernest Henley* (1946).

terested more in the birds and flowers than in the other natural resources of the pampas. In *The Purple Land that England Lost* (1885) the British hero regrets that England did not seize Uruguay in 1807 when it had the chance. England would have introduced system and cleanliness into a lawless dirty land. But faced there with nature's noblemen, he reconsidered the point, confessing a British readiness to regard people of other nationalities with a certain amount of contempt. "With us, perhaps, the feeling is stronger than with others, or else expressed with less reserve." [3]

As Hudson occupies a thin red circle, somewhat more remote from the center than Kipling's, Charles M. Doughty and T. E. Lawrence occupy circles still more remote but in the same system. More or less unintentionally these two great men assisted imperial designs upon Arabia. England needed control of Arabia, as of Egypt and the Sudan, in order to protect the flow of wealth from India. In 1875 England acquired the necessary shares in the Suez Canal. It was not accidental that Doughty's exploration of Arabia commenced in 1876. Unconscious of his function, however, he resembled those explorers and missionaries who commonly preceded the flag. *Travels in Arabia Deserta* (1888), the great sprawling story of his adventures, is no less peculiar for its matter than for its style, which fits the matter like a blanket. Crabbed, cantankerous, and archaic, formidable in diction, original in syntax, this wonderful style, repelling all but the hardiest reader, succeed in exposing the author and itself. Emergent Doughty is of the rough-hewn tribe of Hardy, Hopkins, and the author of *Beowulf*. T. E. Lawrence's *Seven Pillars of Wisdom* (1926) is equally singular.[4] Starting as archæologist in Mesopotamia, and as spy disguised as archæologist in the region of Sinai, Lawrence became in 1916 the organizer of the Arab revolt against the Turks.

---

[3] Hudson's autobiography, *Far Away and Long Ago* (1918), is one of his best works. Morley Roberts: *W. H. Hudson* (1924).

[4] *Revolt in the Desert* (1927) is an abridgment of *The Seven Pillars*. *The Mint* (1955). B. H. Liddell Hart: *Colonel Lawrence* (1934). Flora Armitage: *The Desert and the Stars* (1955). Richard Aldington: *Lawrence of Arabia* (1955).

He was a British agent, but his independence and whimsicality and the original character of his strategy and tactics incurred official displeasure while ensuring his success. Far from being a conscious imperialist, he promised the Arabs freedom from "colonial schemes of exploitation," allayed their natural fears of England, and did what he could to foil the French. But the promises upon which he relied did not survive Versailles and its mandates. French Syria and British Iraq took the place of an Arab state. Troubled by thoughts of England's dishonor and his own, Lawrence retired monastically to the air force, where, as private, he found comfort in speed and in the friendship of Winston Churchill. Lawrence's book, recounting his Arabian exploits, tells of exploding trains and of politicians and camels. Written in the most familiar of grand manners, pungent and clear, this book approaches the epic as Lawrence the heroic.

Concerning thin red circles: some, epicycles on the system, were occupied by other writers. The commercial exploitation of inferiors had opened up new territories for literary exploitation, producing many novels and stories that without being imperialistic are colonial. Of these, those of Joseph Conrad are important.

Conrad spoke of himself as "a Polish nobleman, cased in British tar," and his political conservatism is what one might expect. During his nautical career he was gunrunner for a royalist faction. In a letter of 1886 he condemned socialism as a doctrine born in Continental slums and socialists as unscrupulous rascals. The socialists, anarchists, and nihilists of *The Secret Agent* (1907) and *Under Western Eyes* (1911) are vain and foolish, though presented with exemplary detachment. Ever puncturing the illusions of his friend Cunninghame Graham, socialist and adventurer, Conrad was cynical, yet enamored of British law.

Although Conrad favored the extension of British law to less fortunate countries, he was not an imperialist. He sometimes sneered at Kipling, even at his "Recessional," found Henley "a horrible bourgeois," disapproved of the Boer War and the Spanish-American War, which inspired

"The White Man's Burden." But while ironic or indignant about the pretensions of American, Belgian, Dutch, French, and German imperialism and convinced that taking the earth away from defenseless people is "not a pretty thing," he saw little but good in British imperialism. In "Heart of Darkness" Marlow finds the red patches on the map of Africa good "because one knows that some real work is done in there." Although most imperialism is "robbery with violence," British imperialism is redeemed by efficiency, "idea," and conscience. In his colonial stories Conrad generally avoided British colonies, preferring instead those of the Belgians and the Dutch.

Taking empire as his frame and traders as his people, Conrad pondered what man and nature do to man within this frame. *Almayer's Folly* (1895), his first novel, is a story of Dutch and English traders, half-castes, and natives in Borneo. The incursion of Dutch empire is part of the plot, but the emphasis falls upon the minds of Almayer, his native wife, and his daughter. Dealing with some of the same people in similar contact, *An Outcast of the Islands* (1896) makes tragedy of misalliances that Kipling would have treated within the categories of caste. Trade, empire, and the indignation of natives form the background for a slow-motion adventure story in which introverts, clogged with their dream, move about like sleep-walkers. Pages of brooding or analysis separate the question from its answer and the gesture from its object. Even the semicolons are a little sleepy. British progress in the Malay States and German competition frame "The End of the Tether" (1902), much livelier and more readable, a story of conflict between love and duty. These heavy studies of the soul in trouble are involved in their exotic places; but no ideas emerge, for Conrad had little use for them. They are implicit, however, in his two accounts of the Belgian Congo, which, though further studies of human suffering, are almost attacks upon colonial policy. "An Outpost of Progress" (1898) is an ironic picture of ineffectuals in a Congo trading post. After reading an article on "Our Colonial Expansion," these bringers of light feel for a time an almost British sense of mission, and question the exchange of ivory and slaves. "Heart of Darkness" (1902), Conrad's most powerful and enigmatic story, is another nightmare. The discovery by Marlow of the nature of things and of himself and Kurtz's dying exclamation are themes for which the forest provides intrusive darkness, but on the edge of that darkness the "imbecile rapacity" of the Belgians is exposed to British contempt.

In Patusan, Lord Jim's enterprise shows British imperialism at its best, but in the composite South American republic of *Nostromo* (1904) Mr. Gould's silver shows it to less advantage. Mr. Gould and other British capitalists, who control silver mine and railroad, control that country's politics, backing a reactionary dictator in the interests of order. Mr. Gould's integrity is British, but his American backer, a capitalist without ideals, is unredeemed. Emerging from political chaos, the mine absorbs the country, exploited natives resent it, and Mr. Gould loses his soul. Nostromo, that vain, simple man, loses his life for silver, which has become symbolic. Only Mrs. Gould and Decoud, the detached cynic, remain above materialism. Yet this great novel, with its sleepy power, remains, like all of Conrad's art, essentially ambiguous.[5]

Darkest Africa provided W. Somerset Maugham with the scene for *The Explorer* (1907), a novel in which an Etonian explores, subdues wicked slave-traders, establishes a virtuous British trading company, and enables England to claim a territory larger than herself. Maugham matured; and the short stories he wrote in the 1920's, though imperial in setting, are far from imperialistic in aim. His places are Samoa, Malaya, and Borneo, his people sahibs; but his themes are the effect upon them of lonely places and colored people. Mixed marriage, caste, infidelity, and tropical anxieties are presented with the detachment, lucidity, and form of Maupassant. "Rain" and "The Letter" are the most famous and the most cynical.

[5] G. Jean-Aubry: *Joseph Conrad, Life and Letters* (1927). Conrad: *Tales of Unrest* (1898). H. M. Tomlinson (a follower): *Gallions Reach* (1927), *The Sea and the Jungle* (1912). Cf. Joyce Cary: *Mister Johnson* (1939). Susanne Howe Nobbe: *Novels of Empire* (1949).

As Maugham says of himself, he is "competent" and "readable." His most readable stories are those of *Ashenden or the British Agent* (1928), where want of substance permitted triumph of style. No writer of our time commands an easier elegance or shows to better advantage the effect of the eighteenth century. *The Moon and Sixpence* (1919) is colonial in part; but this embellishment of the life of Gauguin is important for presenting the artistic morality of the nineties with the kind of wisdom that ensures popularity. Maugham is among the most excellent of commercial artists. But more than that, he is remarkable among Englishmen of his generation and class for treating outsiders, even colonials, without arrogance.[6]

The skeptical twenties, looking wickedly at things, looked wickedly at empire. Maugham's stories have the detachment and cynicism of that happy time. But E. M. Forster's *Passage to India* (1924), having irony, is even more typical. Here Forster, a Little Englander in other novels, displays sahibs and natives, the first maintaining white supremacy with the emotions of Southern colonels, the second, insulted and injured, nursing hysteria upon despair. He impartially exposes the injustice of officials, the shoddiness of educated natives, and, in the diminishing coda, the Anglo-Indian dilemma.

The responsible thirties, Christian or socialist, sometimes failed to include empire among their responsibilities. Azania of Evelyn Waugh's *Black Mischief* (1932) is Abyssinia, which civilized powers long to civilize. Sharing this longing, Seth, the Emperor, introduces boots, contraceptives, and other signs of progress and culture. His subjects eat them. European fools or knaves increase the turbulence, which brings a Franco-British mandate. At once horrible and funny, Waugh's satire, not unlike Voltaire's, is impartial. If native disorder is hopeless, British order is suburban or stupid. If Basil Seal eats his mistress at a

---

[6] The short stories are collected in *Altogether* (1934) (in the United States entitled *East and West*). *The Gentlemen in the Parlour* (1930), *The Narrow Corner* (1932). *The Summing Up* (1938), autobiography. Cf. Graham Greene: *The Quiet American* (1955).

cannibal banquet, it is no worse than might occur under more civil auspices.[7]

II

Reaction invites equal and opposite or sometimes greater reaction. British imperialism produced Irish nationalism, and with it a literature better at its best than that of contemporary England. The westward course of empire was not extraordinary. Civilized by British garrison, police, landlords, and business men, the population of Ireland declined from eight million in 1841 to four million in 1911. Some starved while landlords exported food, some emigrated, and some survived. The remnant became impatient, destroying Englishmen in alleys now and then or in Phoenix Park, and even the Anglo-Irish complained a little and celebrated Ireland in poetry or in prose. Ornaments of the renaissance were Yeats and Joyce, the one Anglo-Irish, the other Irish. A third was Anglo-Irish Synge.[8]

This quickening, in which oppression, the compactness of Dublin, and genius conspired, began in the eighties. When it began, Parnell was giving hope of independence by parliamentary action. His Land League was helping peasants against landlords, to the displeasure of George Moore, landlord, who expressed it in *Parnell and His Island* (1887). The failure of Gladstone's Home Rule bill in 1886, the death of Parnell in 1891, and the return of Tories to power brought promise of more coercion and for most an end to hope of constitutional remedies. Parnell's fall and death split Irish patriots into factions. Fenians of the Irish Republican Brotherhood constructed bombs and Maud Gonne carried them about or planted them

---

[7] Winifred Holtby: *Mandoa, Mandoa!* (1933). Waugh: *Scoop* (1938). George Orwell: *Burmese Days* (1934). Aubrey Menen: *Dead Man in the Silver Market* (1953).
[8] Dorothy Macardle: *The Irish Republic* (1937). Ernest Boyd: *Ireland's Literary Renaissance* (1922). Arland Ussher: *Three Great Irishmen* (1953). Estella Taylor: *The Modern Irish Writers* (1954).

in likely places.[9] Sublimating poets, disgusted by the betrayal of Parnell, turned from politics and found happiness in a heroic past which, by enlarging the soul, might ensure a future.

Standish O'Grady's *History of Ireland* appeared in 1878 and 1880. Before this, Sir Samuel Ferguson had made poems of Ireland's heroic past, but it was O'Grady who fathered the renaissance by disclosing in his imaginative, unorthodox history the glories of Finn MacCool and Cuchulain. Here was the matter that James Clarence Mangan, no scholar, had wanted to make his patriotic verse better. After O'Grady came George Sigerson, translating Gaelic poems, and Douglas Hyde, founder of the Gaelic League, who restored the forgotten language and by his *Love Songs of Connacht* (1893) and other translations provided an English style, Irish in rhythm, extravagance, and idiom, for Lady Gregory and Synge. Folklorists went about interrupting peasants. T. W. Rolleston and John Todhunter, inspired by these labors, commenced as Irish poets; and Katherine Tynan turned her small Catholic instrument to pagan song. Anthologies announcing these and other poets confirmed the revival.[1]

When Yeats commenced as poet in 1885, he had used the techniques of Spenser and the English romantics for Arcadian and Hindu themes, but now, instructed by O'Grady and the folklorists, he began to write ballads about priest and peasant and songs about the little people. From the legendary cycles he took Cuchulain, Fergus, and the Land of Youth. Distorting his materials to fit his problems, he used Fergus as his symbol and became obsessed with Cuchulain's fights with son and wave. The most ambitious of these legendary poems is "The Wanderings of Oisin" (1889), in which by inventing much and by covering the severe original with ornament he made it nineteenth-century rococo. Adjectives like "pearl-pale" and "glimmering" try to anticipate effects and to create a twilight atmosphere, which, a product of the English romantic

[9] Maud Gonne MacBride: *A Servant of the Queen* (1938).
[1] *Poems and Ballads of Young Ireland* (1888), *A Treasury of Irish Poetry in the English Tongue* (1900).

movement, is no more Celtic than a London fog. In this
diffuse, dreamy narrative Yeats debated facing reality or
escaping it.

Yeats collected folk tales from the peasants or from
the collections of earlier folklorists. When Lady Gregory
became his patron, they visited her tenants and published
the result of their inquiries in 1920 as *Visions and Beliefs
in the West of Ireland.* For her excellent versions of the
two epic cycles, written in peasant-flavored prose, he provided enthusiastic introductions. Her prose taught him
much and he rewrote his own collections in it. Surveying
the work of Irish folklorist and poet, he observed that
there is no fine literature without nationality, and, pro-
nouncing England dead, claimed a place near Davis, Mangan, Ferguson.[2]

Yeats did not thoroughly approve, however, of the
abstract and sometimes jingoistic verses of Thomas Davis
and his school; nor did he thoroughly approve of the Irish
Republican Brotherhood, of which for a time he was a
member. His adoration of Maud Gonne was tempered by
dismay at her conspiracies and her eloquence. Like his
friend John O'Leary, the old Fenian, Yeats followed a
more pacific ideal. He proposed to liberate the Irish by
symbolic poetry and poetic drama, by the examples of
Cuchulain and Oisin, by swooning diction and suitable
rhythms. For a while Yeats remained true to this ideal,
but his patriotism, never free from thoughts of Lady
Gregory and Maud Gonne, was complicated by prudence
and love.

The Irish Literary Theatre provided further complica-
tion. Founded in 1899 by Yeats, George Moore, and Edward Martyn, its financial backer, this uncommercial theater endured for three bad seasons. Their venture was

[2] Yeats: *Collected Poems* (1950), *Letters to the New Island* (1934),
edited by Horace Reynolds. Joseph Hone: W. B. Yeats (1943). A.
Norman Jeffares: W. B. Yeats (1949). Graham Hough: *The Last
Romantics* (1949). T. R. Henn: *The Lonely Tower* (1950). Allan
Wade: *A Bibliography of the Writings of W. B. Yeats* (1951). Thomas
Parkinson: W. B. Yeats, *Self-Critic* (1951). Richard Ellmann: *The
Identity of Yeats* (1954). Augusta Gregory: *Cuchulain of Muirthemne*
(1902), *Gods and Fighting Men* (1904).

doomed from the start by disagreement about ends, Moore and Martyn wanting Ibsen, and Yeats poetry and legend. His *Land of Heart's Desire,* a mild poetic play on fairies, had been produced in London by Florence Farr in 1894. *The Countess Cathleen,* far greater, was the first choice of the Literary Theatre for the season of 1899. At the first performance the lovely lines and sleepy atmosphere failed to prevent a riot (described by Joyce in *A Portrait of the Artist*) of Catholics injured by theological irregularity. Undiscouraged, Yeats continued to think he could elevate that audience by the power of poetry and by the nobility of an aristocrat selling her immortal soul for potatoes. Martyn's *Heather Field,* produced the following night, was quietly received. This well-constructed play about the defeat of a landlord by wife, weeds, and madness reflects Martyn's admiration for *The Master Builder* and *The Wild Duck.* Pulled in two directions, the theater collapsed, but it had shown the possibility of a national drama and had introduced Yeats to Lady Gregory. Under their management an Irish theater, avoiding Ibsen, was to become bucolic, urban, and great.

This theater, later known as the Abbey or the National Theatre Society, was established by Frank and William Fay in 1901 for native actors acting native matters, heroic or peasant, especially the latter. They replaced Anglo-Saxon attitudes with those of Irishmen and the idiom of London with that of the Western World. Distinguished actors—the Fays, Sara Allgood, Dudley Digges, and others—attracted distinguished dramatists, whose plays are among the best of our time. A. E. composed for them his twilit *Deirdre,* a prose play in three acts, remarkable for an invocation of Mananaun MacLir. This tentative play was produced in 1902 with Yeats's *Cathleen Ni Houlihan,* written for and acted by Maud Gonne. The success of these plays assured a native drama.[3]

[3] A. E. Malone: *The Irish Theatre* (1929). Una Ellis-Fermor: *The Irish Dramatic Movement* (1939). W. G. Fay and Catherine Carswell: *The Fays of the Abbey Theatre* (1935). Peter Kavanagh: *The Story of the Abbey Theatre* (1950). George Moore: *Hail and Farewell.* Denis Gwynn: *Edward Martyn and the Irish Revival* (1930).

Pursuing his ideal, Yeats had seen possibilities in this company. *Cathleen Ni Houlihan,* first of many folk dramas it produced, was his only popular play. In the symbolic figure of the Poor Old Woman who had "the walk of a queen" he embodied Ireland's wrongs and her desire to rid the house of strangers. By verse no longer lyric but dramatic he centered Irish feelings and pleased his girl. Bred to a harder thing than triumph, he and Lady Gregory quickly assumed control of the theater and perfected its policies. In *Samhain,* its publication, he dissociated the company from Martyn's middle-class drawing-room, announced a return to the people, and promised a poetical drama "which tries to keep at a distance from daily life." For ten years plays and controversies constituted his daily life.[4]

The Pot of Broth, a slight prose comedy, was produced in 1902. Written in collaboration with Lady Gregory, and in her peasant idiom, the play is more hers than his. More typical of Yeats, *The King's Threshold,* played in 1903, expresses by the poet's hunger strike his fight for recognition by a world hostile to poetry. This theme from the Finn cycle served to suggest Yeats's own position and his desire. *On Baile's Strand* (1904), another one-act poetic play, reveals again his obsession with Cuchulain and elevates a familiar theme by majestical verse. The austerities of Yeats's *Deirdre* (1906) renew this favorite. Condensation, the chorus of musicians, and the subtlety of his heroine combine to make this version greater than A. E.'s if less than Synge's. Of the many plays Yeats wrote for the Abbey, these are representative and best. He had dreamed of a theater for verse plays remote from nature and society, but defeated by society, which, clamoring for pedestrian comedy, displayed indifference to his beautiful verse and to the symbols he substituted for characters, Yeats retired to his parlor, where with plays for dancers he pleased fit audience though few. In the Japanese Noh play, commended by Ezra Pound, Yeats had found at last

[4] Yeats: *Plays in Prose and Verse* (1922), *Plays and Controversies* (1923), *Collected Plays* (1952). *Autobiography* (1938).

a congenial form.[5] *The Only Jealousy of Emer* (1919) and *Purgatory* (1939) are the best of his plays in this kind and among the best of poetic plays. Maybe, as some say, Yeats was not a great dramatist but a great poet, and it is true that starting with the desire to hear his verses spoken he wrote fine poems, like *The Shadowy Waters*, disguised as plays; but he gradually adapted himself to the theater, learned its craft, and achieved dramatic poetry. One of its values was to give his lyric poetry hardness and power; but to the theater the poet's value was also practical. In the capacity of director he served as Synge's bulldog.

Having found J. M. Synge trying to be Arthur Symons in Paris, Yeats persuaded the mistaken man to try the Aran Islands.[6] There he learned the rhythms and idioms that became his instrument and he learned there about the people in whose passions he found what was hidden in himself. On his return to Dublin, in love with life and art, he wrote those plays that assured his place as one of the two principal dramatists in English in his time.

The Shadow of the Glen, a one-act comedy produced in 1903, is an old wives' tale of husband pretending death to test his wife's fidelity. He is old, the place is lonesome and she is bored. What might have been problem play or cynical farce rises to the plane of myth. Synge turned in 1904 to high tragedy. *Riders to the Sea* reveals in the death of Maurya's sons the death of all men and the sorrow of women. The sea is fate's agent and its symbol, the keening a chorus. Nothing greater, starker, or less restrained had appeared on the contemporary stage, and nothing, though the medium is prose, so poetic. *The Well of the Saints* (1905) is strange, bitter comedy, no less universal. The conflict of dream and reality, Yeats's theme, is also Synge's. Martin and Mary Doul, blind beggars, think each other beautiful. A Saint, coming with his can of holy water, restores their sight. Examining the world,

[5] "Certain Noble Plays of Japan" and other essays in *Essays* (1924).

[6] Synge: *The Aran Islands* (1907). Maurice Bourgeois: *John Millington Synge and the Irish Theatre* (1931). Daniel Corkery: *Synge and Anglo-Irish Literature* (1931), a plea for intolerant nationalism.

they do not like the look of it. She finds him a horror, he her a hag. Blind again, they refuse another cure. *The Tinker's Wedding,* published in 1908 but never played at the Abbey for fear of Irishmen, is a Chaucerian fabliau of covetous priest and blasphemous peasants.

The Playboy of the Western World (1907), Synge's greatest comedy, work of a poet and a craftsman, triumphs by abundant, laughing speech and by what Yeats called "astringent joy and hardness." A delight to read, the play is a greater delight to see and hear. But the extravagant characters, their confusion of the heroic with the eloquent, their freedom from common things, displeased. Patriots hissed, and puritans, purer than elsewhere, booed. Their riots lasted all that week. Yeats, Synge's champion, offending nation, defended art.

It was the word "shifts" that bothered some who did not understand the shifts of Synge. For these Wicklow and the Aran Islands had provided patterns to be improved by imagination. For the speech Hyde and Lady Gregory had provided patterns; but such speech as Synge's had not been heard. Such people as his had not been seen. Patriots, however, wanted in place of the stage Irishman of tradition, not Synge's invention, but an impeccable dummy, suitably speaking. Maud Gonne resigned in anger from the National Theatre Society.

Deirdre of the Sorrows, left unfinished, was posthumously produced in 1910. Done in Synge's language, this three-act tragedy makes folk tale of legend, and heroic peasants of heroes. His Deirdre, more conscious than most of his characters, knows lovers age, and this knowledge makes her welcome doom. His other characters, uncircumscribed by logic, are generally careless of reasons for what they do. They are fabulous, acting less than existing, and existing through their speech.

Lady Augusta Gregory, who patronized Synge at Coole along with Yeats, Hyde, and others, was greater as patron, manager, and translator than as playwright. But not the least of her services to the Anglo-Irish renaissance are the one-act comedies she wrote to provide the Abbey with relief from the intolerable greatness of Synge. These comedies, written in her peasant idiom and dependent upon the mugging of her players, display a landlord's tolerance for the humors of tenants and for the complications of their simplicity. Her achievement is *The Gaol Gate* (1906), a one-act piece approaching tragedy and the gruesome humor of Synge.[7]

Lennox Robinson, who followed Synge among the Abbey's directors, wrote several fine plays of which *The Whiteheaded Boy* (1916), a comedy, is the most important. Unlike many good plays, this one is good reading not only for its dialogue but for the stage directions in Irish idiom and the author's asides, which, destroying his characters' characters, are as queer as Irish humor itself. An earlier play, *The Cross-Roads* (1909), in which nationalistic aspiration is defeated by a return to the land, shows that harrowing combination of darkness and austerity which distinguished the Cork realists, those gloomy men who had learned from Ibsen and Turgenyev ways of dissecting suffering peasants.[8]

Under Robinson's management the Abbey produced the best plays since Synge's, those of Sean O'Casey, Dubliner. His characters are Dubliners the bleakness and violence of whose lives, though proper to a slum, reflect the tradition of Zola. *The Shadow of a Gunman* (1923) concerns poets, gunmen, and the Black and Tans. Comic at first, the tone changes and the tension rises until the appalling climax. Nationalism, ceasing to be ideal and implicit, openly occupies the turbulent center. *Juno and the Paycock* (1924), one of O'Casey's best plays, creates against the background of civil war the character of Captain Jack Boyle, the paycock. Made for the use of Barry Fitzgerald, the paycock displays himself while his wife scolds, his daughter loses her virtue, and his son, crippled

[7] Gregory: *Our Irish Theatre* (1913), *Lady Gregory's Journals* (1946), *Seven Short Plays* (1908). Padraic Colum: *The Fiddler's House* (1907), *Thomas Muskerry* (1910). T. C. Murray: *Maurice Harte* (1912).

[8] Robinson: *The Clancy Name* (1908), *Plays* (1928), *More Plays* (1935), *Curtain Up* (1942), autobiography. *The Irish Theatre* (1939), edited by Robinson. *Ireland's Abbey Theatre* (1951).

by a bomb, is carried away by Irregulars. The screaming violence of the climax yields in memory, however, to the humors of Boyle, who is less comic relief than comic triumph set off by surrounding tragedy. *The Plough and the Stars* (1926) is an excellent loosely constructed tragedy, not unlike the histories of Shakespeare in design and, not unlike them, better seen than read. Without outstanding characters, the play deals with the tenants of a single house, communist, republican, Orangeman, together with consumptives, wives, and whores. Their individual tragedies during Easter Week stand for Ireland's troubles, but the play, far from propaganda, is a dramatist's job. Not that delight in language by which O'Casey resembles Synge, but that similar delight in people which moved O'Casey to create imperfect patriots caused the audience to riot, though soothed once more from the stage by Yeats, O'Casey's discoverer. Whether the reception of *The Plough and the Stars* or the Abbey's prudent rejection of his next play was the immediate cause of his departure for London, where some of his subsequent plays were produced, is debatable. The rejected play, *The Silver Tassie* (1929), starting realistically enough in a Dublin kitchen, becomes symbolic fantasy and war's indictment. The scenes at the front or in the hospital, where people bound about and break into bad verse at the drop of a hat, are less effective, though sufficiently nightmarish, than the domestic scenes at which O'Casey excelled. But distracted by Eugene O'Neill and the Continental expressionists, O'Casey turned his back on realism and slum. *Within the Gates* (1934) is a symbolic play of a London park in which a kind of rhythm takes the place of plot and significant creatures appear, reappear, and mysteriously declaim. The point, unclear as in many symbolic plays, appears to be the disorder of the world. As the gramophone announces the fall of London Bridge, as the man in plusfours pursues his girl, as the chorus of down-and-outs goes down and out, the park appears another waste land, depression-born and portentous. Attempting too much, the play achieves too little. Two of O'Casey's later plays celebrate Russia and its "holy city," but *Purple Dust* (1940),

Red Roses for Me (1942), and *Cock-a-Doodle Dandy* (1949), also unproduced, are nonpolitical fantasies.[9]

Increasingly neither here nor there, O'Casey dissipated that realistic gift which had helped save the Abbey, weakened by the troubles and almost destroyed by the curfew. The financial backing of Miss A. E. F. Horniman, an Englishwoman, had been withdrawn, the audience declined, and unpaid actors left the scene. But a subsidy from the Free State, new actors, such as Barry Fitzgerald, and the appearance of new dramatists restored the Abbey's fortunes.[1] Most notable of the newcomers were Denis Johnston and Paul Vincent Carroll.

Rejected at first by Lady Gregory, Johnston got his start at the Gate Theatre, where in 1929 Michael Mac-Liammoir and Hilton Edwards, the managers, produced *The Old Lady Says 'No'!* Commonly supposed to allude to Lady Gregory, but actually alluding to the Poor Old Woman, or Ireland herself, this brilliant nightmare shows Robert Emmet wandering in search of his love through the streets and homes of modern Dublin, meeting flappers, Trinity students, animate statues, and bohemians. As the discouraged patriot wanders, talking in tags from Pearse and Parnell, the fluid scenery shifts and those he meets talk in tags from Swift, Thomas Moore, Yeats, O'Casey, and Joyce. These memories and the conflict of ideal and real constitute a commentary upon Ireland past and present and upon the sentimental tradition of the Poor Old Woman. Most of what occurs on the stage occurs in the hero's head, whence, after the expressionistic manners of Strindberg and Joyce, it is projected and given substance. *The Moon in the Yellow River,* produced at the Abbey in 1931, is almost equally sardonic. This grotesque, witty play of the Shannon River project and the conflict be-

[9] Autobiographies: *I Knock at the Door* (1939), *Pictures in the Hallway* (1942), *Drums under the Windows* (1946), *Inishfallen, Fare Thee Well* (1949), *Rose and Crown* (1952), *Sunset and Evening Star* (1954). *Collected Plays* (1949–51). *The Story of the Irish Citizen Army* (1919). *The Flying Wasp* (1937), reply to critics.
[1] See Curtis Canfield: *Plays of Changing Ireland* (1936). Lord Dunsany's fantasies are somewhat apart from the movement: *The Glittering Gate* (1909), *A Night at an Inn* (1916).

tween Republic and Free State, between Ireland and her idealists, is the kind of play Shaw might have written. That zeal for experiment which is Johnston's distinction and the Gate's was never more admirably illustrated than by *A Bride for the Unicorn,* written for the revolving stage and produced without it at the Gate in 1933. Not expressionistic by the author's own assurance, this queer play, mythical at least, pursues ideas of love, time, and death. Nothing could be less Irish and nothing a clearer anticipation of Auden and Isherwood.

As the intolerance of Eire increased so did the critical spirit, commoner among exiles than among those successful at home. The plays of Paul Vincent Carroll, as severe as Johnston's, are anticlerical and hostile to insularity. *Shadow and Substance,* produced at the Abbey in 1937, owes much of its excellence to Canon Skeritt, an actor's delight, whose austere conception of Catholicism quarrels with the vulgarity and emotionalism of his curates. His priggishness and inhumanity, expressed in some of the finest lines of the modern drama, yield to the simpleminded saintliness of Brigid, his servant. This play could be produced in Eire because criticism is subordinated to character. But the bitterness of *The White Steed* (1939) proved more suitable for New York. In this play Carroll's usual conflict between schoolmaster and cleric serves as a center for a secular rebellion against a book-burning priest whose "clerical fascism" threatens the state.

To understand these Irish dramatists and the poets, the course of politics or something of it must be known. During the early years of the Abbey three political factions quarreled with England and each other, John Redmond's Parliamentary party, Arthur Griffith's Sinn Fein, and James Connolly's organized workers. Griffith's plan to destroy the English by nonrecognition, which attracted Edward Martyn and Maud Gonne, seemed bourgeois to Connolly, who desired class war. Padraic Pearse and Thomas MacDonagh, poets and critics, and Constance Markiewicz, daughter of Lord Gore-Booth, favored all radicals. The Boy Scouts, for example, received from Constance Markiewicz heroic tales and directions for using bombs. In August and September 1913 the strike of Connolly's workers was punished by a general lock-out and consequent famine. Defeated, Connolly and Larkin organized the Irish Citizen Army to rival and finally to aid the I.R.B. Volunteers, who drilled incessantly and conspired. Constance Markiewicz and Sean O'Casey, conspirators, drilled with the Citizens; Pearse, de Valera, Joseph Plunkett, and Roger Casement with the Volunteers. Despairing of pacific remedy and encouraged by England's preoccupation with Germany, Padraic Pearse proclaimed the Irish Republic on Easter Monday 1916 and led both armies into action. Constance Markiewicz led her battalion, the Boy Scouts charged the magazine in vain, and near the Post Office the O'Rahilly fell. The British, victorious by artillery, executed sixteen leaders, Pearse, MacBride, Connolly, MacDonagh, Plunkett, and Casement among them, and imprisoned Constance Markiewicz. The surviving Boy Scouts were ignored.

Griffith's Sinn Fein was dead, but taking its name, republicans maintained under the I.R.B. a campaign of peaceful, then violent resistance. In 1918 Constance Markiewicz, at large, was imprisoned again. Discouraged Englishmen, borrowing from Germans the policy of frightfulness, invented the Black and Tans, and by 1921 besides ambush and murder there was open war. The treaty ending this war split the Irish into two factions, those who tolerated British Home Rule and those of the I.R.B. and the I.R.A., who wanted independence. In 1922 these factions engaged in civil war, out of which, exhausted and dismembered, de Valera's nation slowly emerged.

These matters appear not only in the plays of O'Casey and Carroll but in the political poems of Yeats. Standing somewhat above action like old O'Leary, Yeats used events to enlarge imagination and elevate it. During the lock-out of September 1913, while A. E. wrote passionate letters to the press in defense of Connolly's workers, Yeats wrote "September 1913," a lofty poem attacking employers who, "born to pray and save," were faithless to "romantic Ireland." Rooted hostility to the middle class gave

Yeats a clear position on Connolly's side, but the Easter
rising found him on the fence. Curiously, it is to this ambiguous position that "Easter, 1916" owes its force. The
great bare poem is less concerned with the rising than
with the conflicts it produced in the poet, compelled by
love of country to praise those whom he despised or
despised and loved. His allusions are to Constance Markiewicz, Pearse, MacDonagh, and MacBride. Pearse and
MacDonagh were bad poets, and MacBride, that "vain-
glorious lout," had married Maud Gonne. By surprise
and disharmony of sense and tone Yeats makes them fools
and heroes at once. In the last part, asking if their excess
was vain, he approaches the position of Lady Gregory.
Too close to landlords to be undivided, the poet was none
the less aroused, and in "Sixteen Dead Men" and "The
Rose Tree," poems on the executions, excitement conquers
division. As for Constance Markiewicz, the poet's feelings
were mixed. Yeats had known her in Sligo when, young,
she rode to hounds from Lissadell, her father's house. That
this aristocratic deportment, this elegance and grace, should
have yielded to politics seemed a pity to be lamented in
song. "On a Political Prisoner" records her transformation
into something "bitter and abstract." "In Memory of Eva
Gore-Booth and Con Markiewicz" is her elegy and her
sister's. Taught by Maud Gonne to dread what makes
women windy, unlovable, and plain, Yeats used perfection
of rhythm and tone to condemn not only politics but time
itself. The ending, obscure because compressed, grandly
proposes the destruction of time by fire and escape to that
Georgian gazebo, fireproof and timeless, beyond all common folly. This fine poem shows Yeats a reluctant republican if a republican at all.[2] "Nineteen Hundred and Nineteen" and "Meditations in Time of Civil War," poems
occasioned by the troubles, reveal Yeats a sorrowing spectator of violence, called from his tower by Irregulars or

---

[2] "Coole Park, 1929" expresses fear that agrarian policy threatened
great houses. The fear was justified. The government, instead of making
a national monument of Coole, razed the house and established a
sawmill in the Seven Woods.

hiding the sight of them by philosophy. In these poems there is little to choose between the mother-murdering Black and Tans and the "leveling" Irish.

Surpassing most of the earlier poems in excellence, these poems differ in kind. The rhythms, no longer relaxing, are firm, the surfaces hard, the words general; and the phrasing is sometimes colloquial. That mixture of "passion and precision" which Yeats had noticed in great houses was his. These poems, "cold and passionate as the dawn," though no less personal than the earlier poems, seem by their austerity impersonal and dramatic. The themes are new. Instead of dream and legend these poems handle life. Half are occasional, some are bitter epigrams upon the Abbey's audience or the middle class, and some, as we have seen, are political. These poems approach the classical state of charged emotion, of surface impassibility, and, within tight limits, of perfection.

This finality has many causes. To replace the pre-Raphaelites Yeats had turned to cleaner models—Landor, Ben Jonson, Donne, and classical Blake. Maud Gonne's marriage had discouraged Yeats, practice in dramatic verse had given him impersonality, and the bitterness of conflict with the Abbey's pit had made his softness hard. Defeated in his hope of a theater remote from life, he had retired to a "place of stone" whence, facing the world, he could defy it. Defeat and defiance are suitably expressed in "To a Friend Whose Work Has Come to Nothing," "Lines Written in Dejection," and "The Fisherman." Their tone, born in part of drama and defeat, owes as much to aristocracy. At Coole, Lady Gregory had shown him spaciousness. When he went with her to Italy, he discovered Ferrara and Urbino, and on his return, in the pages of Symonds's *Renaissance,* the culture of their courts. With patrons like the good dukes, whom Lady Gregory distantly approximated, a poet could be free from mob and middle class. Later at the court of Sweden, walking backward down the stairs after receiving the Nobel prize from a royal hand, Yeats felt his convictions fortified. For him the ideal society, banishing the middle class, consisted of noble patrons and their retainers, poets and peasants, each happy

in their degree.[3] Understandable and foolish alike, this
ideal, a product of the middle class, gave theme, form,
and tone to many of his finest poems, among them "To
a Wealthy Man Who Promised a Second Subscription
. . ." and "Sailing to Byzantium." In the latter poem Byzantium, replacing as symbol the Land of Youth, gave
Yeats as the mechanical bird of the Emperor Theophilus
freedom from time and nature and the opportunity to sing
of both to lords and ladies there. Expressing world and
self by their opposites, Yeats had found adjustment and
a kind of ease.

To secure or perhaps to rationalize this success, Yeats
had invented the doctrine of the mask. Torn between the
pulls of abstraction and lushness, dream and reality, circumstance and self, trying to be true to one or another, he
had made poems that seemed to him too full of feeling
or too empty. Intellectual and emotional by turns, he
needed a device to make him both at once and to unite
reality with dream. His mask, the necessary device, is his
attempt to be his opposite. However hopeless this attempt
may seem, it had practical value. Placing his conflicts
upon a stage, the mask dramatized them, enabling him to
regard them coldly with an artist's eye. Art is not self-
expression, he announced, but what is most unlike it. This
useful fiction, persuading romantic Yeats that he was
classical, enabled him to be impersonal and personal at
once, dramatic and lyric, and to write better than he could.
In a romantic time when direct expression of the self is
easy and often fatal to perfection, the classical ideal of
impersonality, as Eliot was also to decide, is an instrument
for romantic success. His mask upon him, Yeats wrote
the noble poems of his middle and later periods, and by
being untrue to self became most true to it. Many of his
earlier poems, now sentimental in his eyes, passed through
the mask and emerged in grandeur. Archaic, particular,
and descriptive diction has been replaced by general terms

---

[3] Yeats gave more space to Lady Dorothy Wellesley in the *Oxford
Book of Modern Verse* than he gave to Eliot. See *Letters on Poetry
from W. B. Yeats to Dorothy Wellesley* (1940). *The Letters of W.
B. Yeats* (1954), edited by Allan Wade.

of Latin origin, yet their colorless restraint is charged with a new intensity and greater humanity. By his classical tone Yeats increased the energy of romantic feeling, and by their discord created a kind of conceit. The first poem of his second period is "Adam's Curse" (1902).

His "humanistic" position is shown again in the preface to *Fighting the Waves*, a poetic play for maskers, produced by the Abbey and published in *Wheels and Butterflies* (1934), where Cuchulain's fight, like Irving Babbitt's, represents hostility alike to science and to flux. Some years earlier, after considering Catholicism, Yeats had bade Von Hügel, the theologian, good-by, but this passing interest is significant. In tradition Yeats was seeking an antidote to Cosgrave's or de Valera's Eire and the world itself. For a time he thought he had found what he wanted in General Eoin O'Duffy, who led his blue-shirted Irish Brigade in Franco's cause, but after writing "Three Marching Songs" for Irish fascists, Yeats repented and revised.[4]

In old age Yeats returned to the romantic Ireland of his youth. The *Last Poems* (1940), mostly of politics and love, attack Eire for failing to live up to his ideal, condemn Cromwell, and praise Ireland's heroes. These nostalgic, lusty poems, different from anything Yeats had written, owe form and spirit to translations from the Gaelic by F. R. Higgins and Frank O'Connor.[5] In the heartiness of Higgins and in Egan O'Rahilly's laments for vanished aristocracy, translated by O'Connor, Yeats found himself expressed. He assisted O'Connor with these poems before going home to imitate and improve them. That Yeats should have been attracted by O'Rahilly's aristocratic yearning needs no explanation, but that he should have been attracted by the lustiness of other eighteenth-

[4] Their first state, with his political commentary, may be found in *The King of the Great Clock Tower* (1934), their second in *Last Poems* (1940). Cf. *On the Boiler* (1939).

[5] Higgins: *The Gap of Brightness* (1940). O'Connor: *The Fountain of Magic* (1939). See Daniel Corkery: *The Hidden Ireland* (1925), on eighteenth-century Gaelic poetry. Yeats's growing interest in the eighteenth century is shown in *Words upon the Window Pane* (1930), *Essays* (1937).

century Gaels would be astonishing in one so old were it
not known that he had submitted to an operation for restoring youth. It is to this perhaps that we owe the songs
of the chambermaid and that which begins "Come swish
around, my pretty punk."

Of other Irish poets, those who wrote before 1920
may be classed with the Georgians. In *New Songs* (1904)
A. E. presented the work of several young poets, among
them Seumas O'Sullivan, Padraic Colum, Susan Mitchell,
Eva Gore-Booth, and Ella Young. Colum's *Wild Earth*
(1909) is the poetic equivalent of his earthy plays. Seumas
O'Sullivan, inspired by A. E. and the softer Yeats, lost
himself in Celtic twilight. James Stephens, also A. E.'s
disciple but odder than these, combined the fantastic and
sometimes the divine with urban and pastoral reality. Some
poems of *Insurrections* (1909) and *Songs from the Clay*
(1915) achieve the quality of his better novels. But words
like "thrill," "rapture," and "robed in flame" indicate the
conservatism with which he and A. E.'s other poets sang
the rustic, the urban, or the imaginative. From the ordinary productions of the group one brilliant book emerges,
Susan Mitchell's *Aids to the Immortality of Certain Persons in Ireland* (1908). Her witty preface and wittier
verses parody or caricature George Moore, the principal
victim, Yeats, Martyn, and all the politicians. "Ode to the
British Empire," a parody of "Recessional," is the final
word on the subject.[6]

The novels of James Stephens are better on the whole
than his poems. His best work, uniting as works of Irishmen are supposed to do the fantastic and the real, is *The
Crock of Gold* (1912), and of this the best part is the first
chapter, on philosophers and wives. Stephens's humor, his
gift of simple statement, and his unfortunate love of phil-
osophizing about men and women are again displayed in
The Demi-Gods (1914), the story of Patsy MacCann, the

[6] Oliver St. John Gogarty (Joyce's Mulligan): "Begone, Sweet
Ghost," *Selected Poems* (1933), *As I Was Going down Sackville
Street* (1937), *It Isn't This Time of Year at All!* (1954). Later poets:
Denis Devlin: *Intercessions* (1938), *Lough Derg* (1945); Patrick Kav-
anagh: *A Soul for Sale* (1947).

guardian angels, and Brien O'Brien. But *The Charwoman's Daughter* (1912), a story of the Dublin slums inspired by Barrie perhaps, is sweet and sentimental.[7]

Liam O'Flaherty's slum is closer to Zola's, and its creatures, by Dostoyevsky's aid, are more appropriate than Stephens's Mary Makebelieve. A political melodrama of extreme violence, *The Informer* (1925) deals with communistic opposition to the middle-class Free State during the twenties. *The Martyr* (1933) is a melodrama of 1922. These crude novels and his others owe their power to O'Flaherty's experiences with Connolly's workers in 1913, with the British army during the war, and with the Irish communists in the troubles. After *I Went to Russia* (1931) his political position was neither left nor right, but betwixt and between.

Two Cork realists, Frank O'Connor and Sean O'Faolain, are the most considerable of Eire's remaining writers. Frank O'Connor, known for poetic translations from the Gaelic, is better known for short stories which, like most in our time, follow Maupassant's pattern or Chekhov's mood, generally the latter. In *Guests of the Nation* (1931) brief episodes from the English troubles or the civil war, suggesting more than they say, reveal character and establish tone. *Bones of Contention* (1936) employs bare lucid prose, and *Crab Apple Jelly* (1944), somewhat tarter, the rhythms and syntax of Cork, for local ironies. Schoolteachers, peasants, priests, shopkeepers, lady doctors, and small officials compose a cross-section of Cork and its county. The implications of discouragement and decay that fill these stories become explicit in *Dutch Interior* (1940), a novel built of short stories, each complete and incomplete. Apparently incoherent at first, the episodes, cohering at last, become symphonic. The title implies the kind of reality through which obscure people move in the rain (for it is always raining), hiding their hopelessness under buffoonery or wit. It cannot be supposed that the resemblance between Joyce's Dubliners and O'Connor's Corkers is al-

---

[7] Stephens: *Irish Fairy Tales* (1920), *Deirdre* (1923), *In the Land of Youth* (1924).

together casual. In his later stories, "The Holy Door," for
example, and "Uprooted," O'Connor emerges as a master
of comedy.[8]

Decay, irrelevant violence, and the lovable dampness
of Cork fill the stories of Sean O'Faolain, whose work, relatively free from plot, resembles that of O'Connor and the
Russians. The decline of big houses, the fanaticism of the
I.R.A. and Black and Tan, the tragedies of people trapped
in the pitiful struggle, are themes of *Midsummer Night
Madness* (1932). Nowhere has the spirit of place been
caught more happily than in this excellent book. His best
novel, *A Nest of Simple Folk* (1933), an epic of rebellion's
birth from provincial decay, follows the misfortunes of a
dull man through Fenianism to the rising of 1916. More
than patriotic, this novel is a gallery of living creatures
with windows through which Cork, its vicinity, and its
times appear with solidity and brilliance.[9]

O'Faolain's quarrel with Eire, whose soil and people
he loves, is shown in *She Had to Do Something,* a bitter
comedy hissed at the Abbey in 1937. This slight Chekhov-
ian play concerns the efforts of a puritanical canon to suppress a ballet, immoral because inadequately clothed. The
angry audience of the Abbey is rebuked by O'Faolain in
the preface to the printed text. More bitter than the play
itself, this document is his declaration of war against the
mob, sterilized by patriotic and religious fervor, which, imposing vulgarity upon the artist, demands not national but
nationalistic literature, not life but piety. Harried by mob
and middle class, against whom Yeats had fought in vain,
and silenced by censorship, the remaining artists of Eire,
says O'Faolain, are strangers at home. The nation that
hooted Synge and exiled Joyce was less inimical to art than
this bourgeois theocracy.

That O'Faolain exaggerates a little is proved by Dub-

[8] Frank O'Connor (Michael O'Donovan): *The Common Chord*
(1947), *Traveller's Samples* (1951), *The Stories of Frank O'Connor*
(1952), *More Stories* (1954). Cf. James Plunkett: *The Trusting and
the Maimed* (1955), stories of Dublin. Bryan MacMahon: *The Red
Petticoat* (1955).
[9] *Bird Alone* (1936), *Come Back to Erin* (1940), novels.

lin's Bloomsday celebration in 1954, the fiftieth anniversary of that great day. Led by Myles Na gCopaleen of the *Irish Times,* about fifty Dubliners started out in the morning from Sandycove tower to follow the course of Stephen and Bloom through their city. The success of this endeavor was prevented only by the number of pubs in the way of it. Although the works of Mickey Spillane are banned in Ireland, those of Joyce are displayed in bookshops. Reporting the centenary of University College, the *Irish Independent* placed Joyce's name above that of Padraic Pearse among eminent graduates; and many priests nowadays, instead of burning *Ulysses,* explicate it.

Stealing the Stone of Scone was the Scottish equivalent for the Easter rising in Ireland. The central figure of Scottish nationalism is Hugh MacDiarmid, who is not only a communist, but also an "anglophobe" and a patriot. In *Lucky Poet* (1943), his manifesto, he uses English in order to be understood, but for his poems he prefers Lallans or "synthetic" Scots, a selection of words from all local dialects for literary purposes. His lyrics, those of *Penny Wheep* (1926), for example, and his long poem, *A Drunk Man Looks at the Thistle* (1926), owe much of their success and obscurity to this medium. MacDiarmid has been followed by Lewis Grassic Gibbon in prose and by William Soutar, Sydney Goodsir Smith, and many others in verse. Smith's *So Late Into the Night* (1952) contains some of the finest and simplest lyrics of our time, "Exile," for example, and "Defeat O the Hert." Not all Scots, however, approve of this nationalistic enterprise or of Lallans. Edwin Muir prefers the United Kingdom and the Queen's English.[1]

[1] MacDiarmid: *Sangschaw* (1925), *To Circumjack Cencrastus* (1930), *In Memoriam James Joyce* (1955). David Daiches: "Hugh MacDiarmid," *Poetry,* LXXII (July 1948). Sydney Goodsir Smith: *Selected Poems* (1947). William Soutar: *Collected Poems* (1948). Lewis Grassic Gibbon (J. L. Mitchell): *A Scots Quair* (1932–34). Geoffrey Wagner: "The Scottish Renaissance," *Adelphi,* XXX (fourth quarter 1953).

For Welsh nationalism see Keidrych Rhys: *Modern Welsh Poetry* (1944) and the magazine *Wales.*

III

Meanwhile some English writers became more reactionary than the imperialists. Among older writers Shaw, and among younger Lawrence, Hulme, Wyndham Lewis, and Eliot represent this retreat in all its kinds. No longer imperialist, it turned toward fascism, classicism, or religion. From right as well as left, artists, seeking order, kicked at the decaying body of liberalism.

That Shaw's socialism was skin deep in spots was shown in the late nineties by his passion for Nietzsche's superman, more congenial to his somewhat sadistic temper than the undifferentiated man of Sidney Webb.[2] The appearance of amoral supermen in *Cæsar and Cleopatra* (1907), *Man and Superman* (1905), and *Major Barbara* (1905), his growing distaste for democracy, and his later admiration of dictators indicate the shape of his thought.[3] Perhaps its most curious expression is *On the Rocks* (1933), to all appearances a fascist play with a socialist preface. It is true, of course, that fascism is sometimes difficult to distinguish from socialism; but if socialism at all, the socialism of *On the Rocks* is national socialism. Liquidation, discussed in the preface, increasingly appealed to Shaw. Sometimes, as here, he condemned Hitler's abuse of this instrument. Sometimes he damned the Jews or praised the Russians. But this ambiguous evidence is less difficult than it seems. The great eclectic was neither socialist nor fascist but Shavian, and his varieties of doctrine were good business.

Bucolic theocracy was D. H. Lawrence's remedy for confusion. Seeing money and machines as enemies of soul,

[2] Although Shaw's preference for effeminate or supermanly heroes and for supermanly heroines may be explained by his desire to be outrageous, it fits the pattern of sadism traced through nineteenth-century literature by Mario Praz in *The Romantic Agony* (1933).

[3] The superman is also celebrated in *The Devil's Disciple* (1899) and *The Doctor's Dilemma* (1906). *Geneva* (1938) ambiguously presents Hitler, Mussolini, and Franco. See Shaw: *Bernard Shaw & Fascism* (1927).

Lawrence prophesied doom to money-changers and mechanics. He did not take his stand with the workers from whom he had sprung, however, or with the aristocrats with whom, like Yeats, he snobbishly consorted, but somewhat apart from them. To destroy democratic liberalism he proposed dictatorship by a hero, descended on one side from Nietzsche and Wagner and on the other from Mme Blavatsky and the noble savage. Under this great pious man natural aristocrats would replace the middle-class world with another, better and more natural. Lawrence's novels and stories describe the emergence of this savior, and two novels describe his political career. Bidding good-by to socialists and Jewish financiers, Somers of *Kangaroo* (1923) finds suitable refuge in the semifascistic cult of Kangaroo, whose plan, however, turns out to be too tentative and imperfect for devotion. But Don Ramon of *The Plumed Serpent* (1926) is the ideal dictator. Convinced that Mexicans are oppressed by socialists, Catholics, and international financiers, this great man founds a fascist organization, primitive and religious in character, and by a coup imposes theocracy upon Mexico. Destroying machines or thinking with the blood, Mexicans find their peace in his will and, when unoccupied by love, dance beneath the vital sun. This partial anticipation of Hitler's Germany owes its resemblance to similar causes. It might be supposed that, had he lived, Lawrence would have become a Nazi; but although he liked the German youth movement, he was too much of an individual to follow the leader. What Lawrence wanted was to become dictator himself. He had a few followers. By some of the British fascists of the thirties *The Plumed Serpent* was taken as text and Don Ramon as pattern. But this enormous novel is so seductive with its hypnotic rhythms, its barbaric splendor, its characters on the border of trance, that these thoughtless men can hardly be blamed.

Similar reaction in politics accompanied the rise of classicism. This chaste development, so exotic in our age as to seem more romantic than our other excesses, generally comes from France. But Robert Bridges, the earliest of contemporary classicists, no less indifferent to France than to politics, expressed his traditionalism by tone, rhythm, and diction. Experiments with these and a comfortable income produced poems of almost incredible emptiness. Yeats admired their grandeur and Hopkins their technique.[4]

A distaste for romantic extravagance and for the abundant but somewhat vulgar language of Shakespeare, whose impropriety revolted Bridges, caused that fastidious man to adopt the general diction of the eighteenth century. In his lyrics the Thames is "silver," the verdure of its banks "declines" while zephyrs cool the "sweltering pasturage" and "fleecy clouds disport." Forgetting Wordsworth, the idle reader awaits the reappearance of the finny tribe and, with Dr. Johnson, dismisses the streaks of the tulip. Lest such neoclassicism seem worthless, the reader, recalling the severities of Lionel Johnson or of the later Yeats, should remember that general diction, which turns the bird-infested, individual tree into something regular like an artichoke, has virtues for evil times, as Grant Wood, in another medium, discovered. The "Ode to Spring," as classical as lawns, is representative. And for examples of more experimental prosody "Wintry Delights," in classical hexameters, and "A Passer-by," that splendid poem in sprung rhythm, will serve.

In phonetic spelling and loose Alexandrines *The Testament of Beauty* (1929) expresses the philosophy behind experiment and decorum. It was Platonism that allowed Bridges, ascending from beauty to beauty, to ignore evil as irrelevant. The happy philosopher turned aside from war and poverty and walked alone with the Muse in her garden. Lest this reaction to our times seem extraordinary, the reader should remember that Eliot's Tiresias turned his back upon the waste land and went fishing off the edge of it. Given a waste land, some will contemplate tin cans and rusty springs, others lawns or, like Chirico, corridors.

[4] Bridges: *Poetical Works* (1914), *Milton's Prosody* (1921), *Collected Essays* (1927–36). Albert Guérard: *Robert Bridges, a Study of Traditionalism in Poetry* (1942). Cf. the splendid, empty poems, existing by surface tension, of Sacheverell Sitwell: *Collected Poems* (1936). *All Summer in a Day*, an *Autobiographical Fantasia* (1926). *Canons of Giant Art* (1933).

Although as up to date as *The Waste Land, The Testament of Beauty* is less exciting and, like most didactic verse since Pope, lacks his virtue. But not even Eliot has given a more suitable expression to the humanism of the middle class.

In France classicism, also a memory of past grandeur, was a tool in the service of religion or politics, and a cry against Rousseau, Bergson, and the symbolists. French classicists were of several varieties, each professing love for Racine. There was Charles Maurras, editor of the *Action française,* who progressed from literature to politics, first royalist, then fascist. As fascist he was sentenced by angry Frenchmen in 1945 to life imprisonment. Jacques Maritain progressed from secular literature to Thomas Aquinas, under whose austere auspices he gave Christians again the illusion of being rational. Julien Benda, immune to politics and religion, upheld the claims of pure reason and the Latin tradition against Bergson and his followers. These intolerant men, whose existence would be enough to establish the romantic character of our age, were matched in America by Irving Babbitt and Paul Elmer More, who, trying to dam romantic flux by taste, culture, and traditional wisdom, announced balance as cure for the unbalanced. In England the principal classicists, disciples of these, were T. E. Hulme, Wyndham Lewis, and T. S. Eliot.[5]

T. E. Hulme, the most thoughtful, was their leader. Alone of classicists a follower of Bergson, he atoned for an inconsistency no Frenchman could allow by approximating the neo-Thomist position. In "Humanism and the Religious Attitude" he condemns the relative values of recent times and praises the absolute values of the Middle Ages. Absolute or religious values are based upon the acceptance of original sin, relative or humanist values upon its rejection. Art based upon humanist values, the art of Zola, for example, or Shelley, is realistic, subjective, and

<hr />

[5] For classicism: P. M. Jones: *Tradition and Barbarism, a Survey of Anti-Romanticism in France* (1934). Benda: *Belphégor* (1918). Michael Roberts: *T. E. Hulme* (1938). T. E. Hulme: *Further Speculations,* edited by Sam Hynes (1955).

unlimited. Art based upon religious values, the art of
Byzantium or Chartres, is unnatural and limited. In "Romanticism and Classicism," the other important essay of
Speculations (1924), Hulme enters the humanist field,
previously condemned, and divides it into two parts, good
and bad. Classical art, crowding man's limits, is good; romantic, overflowing them, bad. He foresees the end of
romanticism and a period of dry hard verse, descriptive
in character, adorned by fancy, lit by common day. The
new classicism will not be a return to Alexander Pope, but,
different as a result of the emotional metaphysics we have
had to endure, will be original though spare. These manifestoes, representing what his disciples heard, may owe
their inconsistencies to developing thought.

Shortly before Hulme was killed in the war, his classical disciples began to repeat or to illustrate his teaching.
Vorticism, in part a hoax, was its most violent application.
To *Blast, Review of the Great English Vortex,* an outrageous magazine, two issues of which appeared, one in
1914, the other in 1915, Wyndham Lewis and Ezra Pound
together with Gaudier-Brzeska and Eliot contributed manifestoes, pictures, or poems. Demanding classicism, Lewis,
the editor, praised castor oil, machines, and hairdressers
as violations of nature. In painting and sculpture vorticism
was the cubistic abstraction Hulme recommended. In poetry
it was a more violent kind of imagism. Hulme's invention,
imagism had grown too soft and ladylike. Vorticism was
the attempt of his followers to rescue it from Amy Lowell
and recapture his ideal of dry, hard, classical verse. Pound
and Eliot were the vorticist poets. Abandoning petals, turning to satire, Pound composed verses, still imagistic, but
harsher now and dry. His models were the classical epigram and the chiseled verses of Gautier. "The Bath Tub"
and "Mœurs Contemporains," epigrams, were followed by
the Mauberley poems, Pound's best. His companion simultaneously composed the Sweeney poems, his happiest.
These elegant quatrains mix Gautier with the symbolists
according to Hulme's prescription.

Hulme's disciples were extravagant: Pound became a
fascist and Eliot a royalist, but even among these right-

thinking men Wyndham Lewis seems extravagant. Starting as cubist painter, but soon defeated by public indifference, he turned to propaganda and satire in the attempt to defend art and destroy stupidity with "laughter like bombs." *The Art of Being Ruled* (1926), his manifesto, is a declaration of war against Bergson. Against flux and time Lewis upholds the static, the spatial, the intellectual. Classing himself in all but theology (an important exception) with the neo-Thomists, he takes his stand with Benda and with Hulme. Art, he says, is menaced by the democratic mob and by a conspiracy among capitalists trying, by debasing taste, to assure their gains. To this end these wicked men encourage the cults of childishness, feminism, savagery, and anti-intellectualism, all traceable to Bergson's flux, and all inimical to proper art. In a series of angry books, of which *Time and Western Man* (1927) is first and most notable, the "enemy," as he called himself, attacked each of these cults and their literary adherents. He attacked Joyce for his fluid relativity, Lawrence for his primitivism, the surrealists for their unconsciousness. African music, sun-bathing, and feminine sensibility, he said, further ensure the doom of white, adult, Western civilization.[6]

Lewis found relief from propaganda in satire. In *Tarr* (1918) and *The Wild Body* (1928), Rabelaisian experiments in the gigantic and the grotesque, he laughed at man, that mechanical animal, particularly at man in his bohemian character. *The Apes of God* (1932) is his most considerable satire. This attack upon Bloomsbury bohemians, especially the three Sitwells, whose cult of "childishness" affronted him, is a fictional version of his tracts, its merit gusto, its defect diffuseness. In this long novel the hero behind the scenes is Pierpoint, a kind of fascist, who directs the half-wits toward Lewis's ends.

[6] *Paleface* (1929), *The Diabolical Principal* (1931), *The Doom of Youth* (1932), *Men Without Art* (1934). *One-Way Song* (1933), verse. *The Enemy* (1927), a magazine. *Blasting and Bombardiering* (1937), *Rude Assignment* (1950), autobiographies. *The Human Age* (1955), a continuation of *Childermass*. Terence Armstrong: *Apes, Japes, and Hitlerism* (1932). Cecil Melville: *The Truth about the New Party* (1931). Hugh Kenner: *Wyndham Lewis* (1954). Geoffrey Wagner is the principal authority.

As early as 1926 Lewis had seen Italian fascism as a cure for romantic disorder. His increasing distaste for capitalism and communism led him to Hitler, in whose praise he wrote a book called *Hitler* (1931). Here Lewis sees that man defending the Aryan West against Jews, blacks, Bergsonists, and other exotics. Interested in what is under his nose, Hitler is classical.

Lewis's retirement to Canada during Hitler's war is the subject of *Self Condemned* (1954), a discursive novel that proves its hero no fascist but an honest man driven to exile by hatred of evil and love of art. Barbarous Canada, to which he is unable to adjust himself, defeats that hero, who, like the hotel where he stays, becomes a burned-out, frozen shell. Although satirical portraits prove Lewis's continued mastery of the "absurd," the hero, who is regarded with pity, should be the object of this satire. Increasingly Tory, Lewis devotes the satiric sketches of *Rotting Hill* (1951) to the decay of his own country under a socialist government and *The Revenge for Love* (1952), a loosely constructed novel, to the shams, pinks, and pseudo-artists of London. It may be that none of these three books is successful, but Lewis has kept a painter's eye for the grotesque and the bogus; and he has emerged from the precincts of fascism as the authentic voice of the postwar middle class.

Roy Campbell, the South African poet, was another, lesser Lewis, and his disciple. Having produced gorgeous dithyrambs and pseudo-classical satires upon Bloomsbury bohemians, especially Lesbians, he wrote *Broken Record* (1934), an autobiography, to explain his position. Like Lewis an enemy of Jews, communists, and softies, he sees fascism, Italian and German, as the only hope for the Western tradition. He salutes Maurras and Léon Daudet as masters, attacks Hugh MacDiarmid, and expresses devotion to bull-throwing, shark-catching, and pugilism. This furious convert to Catholicism made Franco's cause his own. In *Mithraic Emblems* (1936), singing the Spanish civil war, he sees fascists as "Christs in uniform." In *Flowering Rifle* (1939), a long satiric poem in suitable couplets, he celebrates Franco's victory, applauds Chamberlain's umbrella, and condemns those misguided Englishmen who had sided in humanitarian and liberal zeal with Jew against Christian, black against white. The final scene discloses the Blessed Virgin smiling upon her triumphant fascists.[7]

Similar in tendency, T. S. Eliot differs from Campbell and Lewis as his lucidity differs from their violence. To counteract romantic confusion, Eliot, demanding impersonality, assumed at first the position of the secular traditionalist. In "Tradition and the Individual Talent" and "The Function of Criticism," essays written in 1917 and 1923, he professes allegiance to something outside himself, at this period the great tradition of European letters. During the twenties his sensibility, requiring stimulation, turned to politics. In the *Criterion*, which he was devoting to the advancement of classicism, he expressed contempt of democracy and a guarded affection for fascism. Indecorous Mussolini, like the Church of Rome, seemed too foreign to the ideals of the public school. It was a pity, said Eliot, surveying the British fascists, that these almost wholly admirable men should go to Italy for name and symbol. How much better and more British to go to Charles Maurras and the *Action française*.[8] Inflamed by Maurras, whom he published and lauded, Eliot, once unitarian, found classicism a trinity. In *For Lancelot Andrewes* (1928) he proclaimed himself "classicist in literature, royalist in politics, and Anglo-Catholic in religion." These congenial posi-

[7] *The Flaming Terrapin* (1924), *Adamastor* (1930), *The Georgiad* (1931), *Wyndham Lewis* (1932), *Flowering Reeds* (1933), *Talking Bronco* (1946). Campbell translated the poems of St. John of the Cross (1951).

Evelyn Waugh, another convert, expressed admiration of Italian fascism in *Waugh in Abyssinia* (1936). In *Authors Take Sides* (c. 1937), a questionnaire on the Spanish war, Waugh took his stand with Franco, and, if a choice had to be made, with fascism. Pound and Eliot professed neutrality.

[8] See Eliot's editorials and a dialogue in the *Criterion* (January 1925, February 1928, and *passim*). Eliot printed an article by Maurras (January 1928) and praised his politics (March and December 1928). Eliot's assistant editor, Herbert Read, however, called himself "anarchist, romanticist, and agnostic," and Dylan Thomas, announcing his independence, called himself a Welshman, a drunkard, and a heterosexual.

tions, which, providing an emotional center, invited song, seem plainer than they are.

Paul Elmer More wanted to know why his friend, so austere and classical in his prose, should be so romantic in his poetry. To this Eliot replied that his prose reflects his ideals, his poetry the reality around him; and since this reality is romantic, his poetry can be no more than classical "in tendency." His classical prose reflects admiration of Benda, Maurras, Maritain, and above these, of Hulme. The two essays on Irving Babbitt and humanism, where Eliot rebukes his first master for secularity, restate ideas of Hulme. Eliot is after heretics again in *After Strange Gods* (1934), which, by references to racial homogeneity and "free-thinking Jews," falls into a familiar pattern. Since even in British politics the king is no longer or hardly ever an issue, Eliot's position as royalist must reflect that of Maurras, serve as the objective correlative of Midwestern aspiration, or else mean nothing but Tory. Tory standards alone seem to account for his approval of Kipling and his disapproval of Milton.

With Eliot's lecture on Milton in 1947, however, it became plain that his disapproval was less of Milton's politics than of his technique. Enamored of conversational rhythm and diction, and directing a revolution to those ends, Eliot had condemned a rhetoric distant from his own. Now that the revolution is successful, he said in 1947, we can safely go back to Milton to learn structure and the use of detachable simile. The second part of *Four Quartets* offers evidence of this return and the reference to Milton in the fourth is charitable.[9] Agreeing with this development, the later plays announce an end to the dissociation of sensibility that once made Eliot seem a theocrat on the one hand and a poet on the other.

[9] "A Note on the Verse of John Milton," *Essays and Studies by Members of the English Association*, XXI (1936). *Milton* (1947). *A Choice of Kipling's Verse* (1943). *Selected Essays* (1932).

CHAPTER FOUR: *Disenchantment*

*D*ISENCHANTMENT and its effects, the cynical, the disgusting, and the grotesque, though products of the first World War, existed before it as products of science and bourgeois self-contemplation. With these effects came others, the comic, the ironic, and the fantastic, the last of which appears an attempt of the disenchanted to recover enchantment. Attitudes of disenchantment, found at their happiest in the work of young Huxley and young Waugh, occur so abundantly that, like politics and religion, they discover the times.

"Come, my lad, and drink some beer," cries Dr. Johnson in one of his satiric ballads. But Shakespeare on golden lads and girls anticipates a commoner theme of A. E. Housman's *Shropshire Lad* (1896). In these poems, as every adolescent knows, gloomy, ironic Housman was preoccupied with lads dying, going off to nameless wars and getting shot or staying at home and getting hanged, especially the latter. To understand this obsession, we must remark his singular experience. Having decided at Oxford to be the greatest Latinist, he failed in his examination and went down with no degree. This failure, a center of his emotional life, may help to explain the cruelty of his prefaces and his obsession with the lads. The hanging lad is not theme but symbol. As he hangs, youth and promise are frustrated and Housman flunks again. This obsession, after sinking into his unconscious, where it became

more general than particular, emerged with dreamlike
intensity. For this reason the poems of youthful frustration are poems.

His emotions remained the baffled undergraduate's.
Because he never developed, his poetry, never developing,
appeals to adolescents, whom it expresses; but, beyond
these, it appeals to some who find his symbols the expression of our world. Within his limits and because of them
he wrote some of the best "public" poems of our time,
finer, on the whole, than Kipling's.

"Terence, this is stupid stuff" is among them because
it expresses not the hidden self but what Yeats called the
anti-self. Addressing Terence, the supposed author of
these poems, Housman laughs at his sentimentality. Such
wit, although it appears along with cruelty in the prefaces,
is absent from most of the other poems. If he had not
held with some earlier romantics that wit is inimical to
poetry, he might have expressed the whole instead of part
of what he was.

The Name and Nature of Poetry (1933) defines not
poetry, of course, but Housman's romantic principles.
Poetry, he maintains with the surrealists, is close to madness. To approximate this condition, or at least to quiet
his intellect, he drank his beer and let the poetry come.
It came like a secretion. But he was accustomed to improve the result. The first half of "Terence, this is stupid
stuff" came by secretion, the second by conscious art. And
for "coloured counties" he tried and rejected many adjectives before the right one came.

The result is excellently simple, though complicated at
times by unintentional ambiguity; but many of the poems
are less simple than obvious. The famous poem of cherry
trees is exemplary. Dismayed by blossoms, Housman feels
that time is passing, he must age. "Now" at the end of the
first line expresses this reaction, and occupying the remain-
der of the stanza, a suggestive image supports this ominous
word. A Japanese poet would have stopped here. But Housman dilutes what is already thin, first by mathematics,
then by stating what has been implied. Less final than it
seemed at first, the examined poem becomes diffuse and

tentative. Its merit is saying what the average man feels but cannot say as he would say it if he could.[1]

With Housman and Hardy, E. M. Forster belongs among the prewar ironists. Although he has the gifts of intelligence and humanity, resembling James at times and at others Lawrence, he somehow avoids their greatness in all but his final novels. His aim, the exposure of his class, is more impressive than his early achievement, the apparatus of exposure more elaborate than the results require. The trouble, perhaps, is that, unlike the exiles, he remained a resident critic, too near his kind and too far from others to see them properly. "It is impossible," he says, "to see modern life steadily and see it whole," but facing both ways, he tried. Refusing clear-cut issues and easy solutions, he approached comedy or tragedy.

Howards End (1910) and *A Passage to India* (1924) are the most impressive statements of his themes. At first glance *Howards End* appears another *Man of Property,* but upon consideration it appears far more complex and of greater value. Mr. Wilcox, like Soames, epitomizes the Philistinism and repacity of the ruling class. The Schlegels, representing the culture and intelligence of that class, are almost outsiders. Leonard Bast, an instrument for revealing Wilcoxes and Schlegels, is not only an outsider, but a bounder who aspires to a culture belonging to his betters. Mysterious Mrs. Wilcox, a symbol like her house, represents the fine ignorance of the county, the unspeakable result of tradition, leisure, and Little England. These exemplary creatures are not so clear-cut as Galsworthy's. Wilcox may be a man of property who regards even that symbolic house as his, but he is the steady backbone of the nation, and her creator. Bast, his opposite, is not only pathetic but absurd. Seeing around and through his people, Forster sees them as they are, as mixed and dubious as gryphons. Although dull and, through most of the book, dead. Mrs. Wilcox alone emerges with full honors. Wilcox,

[1] *Last Poems* (1922), *More Poems* (1936), *Collected Poems* (1940). See prefaces to editions of Manilius (1903) and Juvenal (1905). Laurence Housman: *My Brother, A. E. Housman* (1937). A. S. F. Gow: *A. E. Housman* (1936). Grant Richards: *A. E. Housman* (1941). Housman Supplement to the *Bromsgrovian*, October 1936.

compounded of bad and good, is real because Forster, wearing the same tie, knows him, but Bast, from whom he is separated by chasms of class and culture, remains unreal. The unreality of Bast, the principal instrument, is the defect of the novel. *A Passage to India,* in part a parallel exposure of the ruling class, is more effectual because Forster was more familiar with his instruments of exposure, the Indians, than with the lower caste at home.

The Longest Journey (1907), less successful than these but no less fascinating, concerns the nature of reality and of Cambridge. Reality is a cow and Cambridge is intellect, imagination, and humanism. Stephen Wonham, the child of nature, more or less conforms to the one, Ansell, the Jewish intellectual, to the other. But Rickie, untrue to nature and to Cambridge alike, weds conventional Agnes, who does not exist. Her effect upon him and her defeat by Ansell and Wonham, outsiders, agents and, despite their imperfections, ideals, constitute the plot. During its progress pompous Mr. Pembroke and his public school, mother of prigs, bullies, and imperialists, are destroyed, but all else, seen by the double eye of Cambridge, is mixed.

In *A Room with a View* (1908) the Emersons, outsiders of low degree, occupy the place of Wonham and Ansell. Life, Passion, and Beauty, quarreling with middle-class emptiness, win a doubtful victory. Made a snob by his public school, Cecil is shown up. But Lucy, rising above the conventions of her class, elopes with young Emerson. Nothing, however, could be more painful than their Florentine honeymoon, for Passion and Beauty, remaining ideas in Forster's head, fail to emerge upon the scene. But if the Emersons are failures and if the ideas for which they stand remain unconvincing, the hotel full of clerics and old maids is a success.

Forster, who had one complicated thing to say, tried to say it again and again. *Where Angels Fear to Tread* (1905), the first, is the most nearly perfect among his early novels and the most Jamesian. The suburban Herritons, sending ambassadors to Italy, are Forster's most disgusting Philistines. And Carella, the Italian who receives them, is as convincing as the Indians of *A Passage to India*. Like Lawrence's gamekeepers, Carella has the vitality vainly attributed to Emerson or Wonham. With his useful child, Carella reveals Harriet and her mother, improves Miss Abbott, and makes Philip aware of his powerlessness. Despite the ambiguity of Carella and the ironic inconclusiveness of the ending, the impact of the book is final. Even its melodrama serves the effect.

To make his defectives come alive and show themselves, Forster contrives for each of his novels a series of climaxes and melodramatic surprises. Although most of these do what they should, some are only odd, and some, after their violent introduction, are diminished by understatement or with a kind of public-school diffidence, deliberately avoided. His plots, somewhat old-fashioned and contrived, are excellently contrived for his purpose. His archaic intrusions, after the fashion of Fielding or Thackeray, compose an explicit chorus for what were better implicit. Urbanity of manner, irony, and occasional restraint expose more than Forster's subject. So exposed, the emotional defects of Philip or of Rickie and the wise incapacity of Mrs. Wilcox or Mrs. Moore seem withering comments by the author upon himself. Instead, however, of the silvery laughter that might accompany these comic practices, comes the smile of lucid pessimism.[2] This humor became that of the Cambridge-Bloomsbury school that called him master.[3]

To understand the postwar disillusionment of literate civilians, the disillusionment of literate belligerents must be remembered. Most of them were killed, but some—poets, novelists, and essayists—survived to unfold a tale of bungling, confusion, and horror that increased despair at home.

[2] Forster: *Abinger Harvest* (1936), *Two Cheers for Democracy* (1951), *The Hill of Devi* (1953). Lionel Trilling: *E. M. Forster* (1943). Virginia Woolf: "The Novels of E. M. Forster," *The Death of the Moth* (1942). Rose Macaulay: *The Writings of E. M. Forster* (1938).
[3] Virginia Woolf: *The Voyage Out* (1915) and Rose Macaulay: *Potterism* (1920) are imitation Forster. Cf. Macaulay's *Told by an Idiot* (1923): postwar disenchantment.

Disenchantment (1922) by C. E. Montague, *Her
Privates We* (1930) by Frederick Manning, and *In Paren-
thesis* (1937) by David Jones are typical reactions to the
first war. Reactions to the second, though less bitter on the
whole, are bitter enough. Alexander Baron's *From the
City, From the Plough* (1948) is moving and desperate;
and Evelyn Waugh's *Officers and Gentlemen* (1955) is an
ironic disclosure of official incompetence and of its victim,
a Catholic gentleman.[4]

Georgian poets also provided equivalents to Barbusse
and Remarque. The Sherston autobiographies of Siegfried
Sassoon are the best in their kind.[5] Conspicuously gallant
but maturing, entrenched Sherston gradually becomes
aware of war's futility, of official bungling and civilian
greed. His story is Sassoon's minus poetry and intellect,
which are attended to in another autobiography, *The
Weald of Youth* (1942) and its sequel.[6] In *Good-bye to
All That* (1929) Robert Graves, a fellow officer in the
Royal Welch Fusiliers, repeats Sherston's progress. Honest
and more pedestrian, Graves notes horrors of public school
and war. He also suffered from neurasthenia, and, re-
nouncing his caste after the war, also became a socialist.

Georgian by nature, Graves and Sassoon were encouraged by Edward Marsh, who published them in his
anthology. *Fairies and Fusiliers* (1917), the war poems of
Robert Graves, now seem of less value than the childhood
reminiscences, the dreams, and the mythical excursions of
his later volumes.[7] Sassoon's war poetry, printed in *The
Old Huntsman* (1917) and in *Counter-Attack* (1918), is
more impressive. Converted from a conventional preoccupation with nature and music by the impact of Masefield,

[4] C. E. Montague: *Disenchantment* (1922), an essay on the
war. R. H. Mottram: *The Spanish Farm* (1924–27). Evelyn Waugh:
Men at Arms (1952). John Wyllie: *The Goodly Seed* (1953). Stuart
Hood: *The Circle of the Minotaur* (1950). Henry Green: *Caught*
(1943), *Back* (1946). Denis Johnston: *Nine Rivers from Jordan*
(1954). Alistair MacLean: *H.M.S. Ulysses* (1955).
[5] *Memoirs of a Fox-Hunting Man* (1928), *Memoirs of an In-
fantry Officer* (1930), *Sherston's Progress* (1936).
[6] *The Old Century* (1938), *Siegfried's Journey* (1946). *Selected
Poems* (1925).
[7] *Collected Poems* (1955).

Sassoon used Masefield's colloquial diction and conversational rhythms for bitter ironic accounts of what he saw in France, "sodden buttocks" protruding from the "sucking mud" and other wastes of youth and courage. Aside from Owen's these poems are the best attempts at rendering an experience too enormous for poetry.

While at Dr. W. H. R. Rivers's hospital for the shell-shocked, Wilfred Owen met Sassoon, read his poetry, and was inspired. The poetry Owen wrote upon his return to the front is notable for its profound humanity and its technique. Discarding Georgian conventions, he used dissonance, assonance, and alliteration. He paired "world" with "walled," "shelling" with "shilling," and "fleers" with "feet." These discords, setting the teeth on edge, are what his horrors needed. But the poetry, as Owen said, "is in the pity." He was killed one week before the armistice.[8] Pity and dissonance alike commended him, long after, to the devotion of Auden and Day Lewis, but Yeats, making his anthology, refused to admit that unhappy warrior.

The reactions of Edmund Blunden, Robert Nichols, and W. W. Gibson conformed to the Georgian tradition, less pastoral now than disillusioned.[9] To his fellow poets, the noble sentiments of Rupert Brooke, dead too soon, now seemed archaic. Even the imagists, discarding petals, shared Georgian bitterness.

Making a hokku of flowers one night in his trench, Richard Aldington was interrupted by a rat. For a time he had devoted his images and the decorous freedom of his verse to flowers, then to impressions, more sensuous than thoughtful, of immediate reality. The later verses of *Images of War* (1919) express disgust. In *Death of a Hero* (1929), one of the best war novels, he bitterly describes

[8] *Poems* (1920), with introduction by Sassoon.

[9] Edmund Blunden: *Undertones of War* (1928), *Poems* (1930). Robert Nichols: *Ardours and Endurances* (1917). W. W. Gibson: *Collected Poems* (1926). Isaac Rosenberg: *Collected Works* (1937).

Poets of the second World War: Sidney Keyes: *Collected Poems* (1945). Alun Lewis: *Raider's Dawn* (1942). Alan Rook: *Soldiers, This Solitude* (1942). T. R. Hodgson: *This Life, This Death* (1943). Roy Fuller: *A Lost Season* (1944). Alex Comfort: *A Wreath for the Living* (1942).

the war again and the despicable civilians who help make war what it is. Betrayed by these and depressed by former friends, the "hero" invites his death. The savagery of Aldington, which owes much to war, more to the success of friends, is at its most agreeable in the satires of *Soft Answers* (1932).[1]

Herbert Read is a better poet than Aldington or Graves. Commencing as disciple of Aldington, H. D., and Hulme, Read wrote poems in their manner. Tidy visual images in free verse convey impressions of accidental beauties and, increasingly, of battle and its mess. Some of his war poems are narratives, some dramatic monologues, some lyrics; but even the last are more objective and serene than most, as *In Retreat* (1925), his brief history of a discouraging episode, is more detached than its longer parallels. Retaining in France something of the artist's aloofness, he used discouragement and atrocity less for personal complaint than as "focus for feeling . . . otherwise diffuse." After the war, following the development of Eliot and Pound, his imagistic colleagues, he wrote satiric quatrains, but his later work is closer than theirs to their flowery originals. Their happiest pupil, he sometimes approaches their effects.[2]

The sensibility of T. S. Eliot, who took Aldington's place on the staff of the *Egoist* when that angry man went off to war, was stirred, if not by war, by war's aftermath. The cynical quatrains of Sweeney, Bleistein, and the hippopotamus, written at the end of the war, and the images and people of *The Waste Land* express his reaction. No poet of our time has captured the mood of that decade so well or more thoroughly embalmed its bounders and parasites.

The "terrible gaiety" of Edith Sitwell and her luscious artifice parallel Eliot's austerities, conveying the same despair in fancier words. *Gold Coast Customs* (1929) is her *Waste Land,* footnotes and all. Emerging from her nursery in this, she confronted what she once transformed. *Street*

[1] *Poems* (1934). *All Men Are Enemies* (1933), *Rejected Guest* (1939).
[2] *Poems, 1914–34* (1934).

Songs (1942), different in manner from her frivolities, contains "Lullaby," one of the best and most terrible reactions to the second war. The war poems of her brother Sir Osbert Sitwell, who served at the front, concern the iniquities of civilians. These angry poems, in free verse or meter, which lament youth's slaughter for the profiteer, are less interesting than the satiric quatrains with which he expressed the peace. Since 1940 he has devoted himself to composing a memoir.[3]

Sacheverell Sitwell, belongs here for his discovery of the baroque, which, like Owen's dissonance or Donne's conceit, became a vehicle for the ambivalent and the polite. By interruptions of solidity, sublime irrelevancies, frivolous pomposities, the baroque diverted, while it expressed, the age. What had been the expression of magnificence and authority became the most florid expression of disenchantment. *Southern Baroque Art* (1924) and his other elegant studies, though anticipated by Germans, defined a cult already ensplendored by Edith Sitwell and Aldous Huxley. From these it broadened down to men of fashion and, after an interval, to critics and scholars.

Sweeney's mood was recaptured in the postwar novel of Aldous Huxley and Evelyn Waugh, for whom a form had been established by Norman Douglas. *South Wind* (1917), urbane and skeptical, is a symposium, plotless or all but plotless, in which opinions of eccentrics are interrupted by outrageous circumstance and innocents transformed by the spirit of place or the oddness of people. Pagan Mr. Keith, Miss Wilberforce, who undresses herself in public, and innumerable others, pious, gaga, or indecorous, became types and their eloquence a pattern for later novelists.[4] Less immoderate than its successors, *South*

[3] *Collected Satires and Poems* (1931). Novels: *Before the Bombardment* (1926), *The Man Who Lost Himself* (1929). Stories: *Triple Fugue* (1924), *Dumb-Animal* (1930). Memoirs: *Left Hand, Right Hand* (1944), *The Scarlet Tree* (1946), *Great Morning* (1947), *Laughter in the Next Room* (1948), *Noble Essences* (1950).

[4] In the Douglas tradition: Cyril Connolly: *The Rock Pool* (1936); Aubrey Menen: *The Prevalence of Witches* (1947), *The Duke of Gallodoro* (1952).

Wind is mellow, golden, prewar; and far less dismayed, it supports against immoderation and repression a classical ideal. With its bland preposterous lives of the saints, its catalogue of fountains, its "luminous asides and fruitful digressions," this panorama of Capri is as individual as *Tristram Shandy* and almost as fine. The exotic pedantry that Douglas shares with Sterne appears again in *Old Calabria* (1915), a travel book distinguished by lives of flying saints, and in the learned apparatus of *Some Limericks* (1928). Douglas, who wrote more novels than one, is a man of one novel.[5]

Huxley, a man of more than one but of none better, had a capacity for continual disillusionment. Nineteenth-century science and the war had made all meaningless. A solitary undergraduate in an Oxford depopulated by war, he became increasingly cynical and civilized. For a time he enjoyed his disillusionments and the feeling of irresponsibility that accompanied them, and it was long before he tried to restore a meaning. He made fun of those earnest mystics and vegetarians who were trying. But his pleasure was a kind of pain. Delighting like Swift in self-torment, he took his stand in the heart of a waste land where he forced himself to contemplate the disgusting and the inane.

Friendly with Sitwells, Huxley wrote strange poems, at once luscious, elegant, and desperate. Of these the philosopher's songs of *Leda* (1920) are typical. An idiot's merry-go-round became his image, and in the neighboring menagerie the "gorgeous buttocks of the ape" put him in mind of "sunsets exquisitely dying." These learned grotesques were followed by short stories of similar character, some owing shape to Katherine Mansfield, all their mood to war and peace, and all, as a character remarks, "the ingenious products of a very cultured and elaborate brain." Those of *Mortal Coils* (1922) are typical. As Mr. Hutton of "The Gioconda Smile" kisses his mistress he thinks of fabulous sea cucumbers in the aquarium at Naples. Sidney Dolphin, the decadent poet of "Permutations among the Nightingales," a one-act play anticipating Coward, sees life

[5] *Siren Land* (1911). *Looking Back* (1933), autobiography.

as a bad joke and love itself as meaningless. On these façades the curves are broken, the ornament is florid.[6]

Huxley's baroque novels are even better and more desolating. *Crome Yellow* (1921), a country-house symposium, made in the fashions of Douglas and Peacock, consists of digressions from nothing. Mr. Scogan, the commentator, fixes the point. "We all know," he says, "that there's no ultimate point." A gallery of fools and eccentrics proceeds to illustrate it, and innocent Denis is continually deflated. The Elizabethan privy proves that Huxley had read Sir John Harington, and the story of the dwarf that the period of Wilde and Beardsley was not wholly extinct. These grotesques compose Mr. Scogan's ideal for the novel: something fantastic, witty, erudite, and rich. Huxley was never more successful.

But *Antic Hay* (1923) is of almost equal value and shapelier, for the concentric meaningless circles and the arabesques surround a fixed, if empty center. While Coleman, a diabolist of the nineties, rapes, he lectures his girls upon the tediousness and pointlessness of debauchery. Shearwater's science is as futile as Gumbril's pneumatic trousers or Lypiatt's painting. Only Mozart and Christopher Wren emerge from the circles of Huxley's hell, which is symbolized by the night club and the taxi of Mrs. Viveash, the promiscuous and miserable. As she sees the twitching lights of Piccadilly, she has for a moment the illusion of being cheerful, but tomorrow, she knows, will be as awful as today.

Those Barren Leaves (1925) is less nearly perfect. Of the cynics, fools, and knaves at Mrs. Aldwinkle's house party, Chelifer, the masochistic editor of the *Rabbit Fanciers' Gazette,* is the most amusing and the most desperate. But he and Cardan are less triumphant than Calamy, a mystic, for meaning was beginning to intrude upon a meaningless world. This mixture served to introduce *Point Counter Point* (1928), Huxley's most ambitious novel, in which the usual gallery of caricatures, now fixed and recurrent, is matched by hopeful specimens. Burlap in his

[6] Stories: *Little Mexican* (1924, in America entitled *Young Archimedes*), *Two or Three Graces* (1926), *Brief Candles* (1930).

tub belongs to the familiar world, but Rampion to another better. Philip Quarles, in betwixt and between, is a critical self-portrait. Far from being a natural novelist, Philip concludes, he does by intellect and fancy what others do by instinct. And the form of this novel, written by one of its own characters, helps to prove his contention. Based upon Gide's *Faux-Monnayeurs* and Bach's *Suite No. 2 in B Minor,* it illustrates elaborate heartlessness. This defect was soon to be remedied.

But even among Huxley's works of mystical vegetarianism traces remain of his talent for the disgusting and the bizarre. In *After Many a Summer* there are still baboons and antiquaries and the Marquis de Sade. The diary of the Fifth Earl is as good as the digression on plumbing in *Crome Yellow,* his fate as exquisite as Gumbril's beaver. But baboons and antiquaries are all but lost among the sermons of Mr. Propter. Although comparatively free from preaching, *Time Must Have a Stop* (1944) is tedious. From the wealth of meaning, however, Uncle Eustace's infantile lips protrude to suck a clear perfecto. That cigar, a relic of civilization, is, of course, a *Romeo y Julieta.*

In *Ape and Essence* (1948), a satiric scenario of the world after an atomic war, Huxley reveals our apelike indifference to essentials. This novel lacks the power of *1984* or even of *Brave New World,* but something of the old mixture of brilliance, learning, and disgust is recaptured in *The Genius and the Goddess* (1955), a monologue on man's condition, especially that of an infantile atomic physicist. The wisdom seems worldly again, but cynicism has yielded to understanding.

While Huxley, the offended idealist, suffered from night clubs, Michael Arlen, once popular, took them as ideals. The manner of *The Green Hat* (1924) is warm, pink, and confidential. As Mayfair dotes on cocktails, he invokes the mews, and all the nymphomaniacs and drunks assume for him a kind of glamour. Arlen saw postwar society, but, misunderstanding its meaning, made the desperate meretricious, the horrid shoddy.

Ronald Firbank made them bizarre. Replacing the shoddy by the elegant and the baroque by the rococo, he fulfilled the promise of Aubrey Beardsley, whose *Under the Hill* seems to have served as model. Rose-lipped orchids with lilac beards crowd Firbank's hothouse; his private orchestra renders deliquescent waltzes from *Der Rosenkavalier;* and the ambiguous undulations of a *fête galante* suggest depravities more delicate and enormities more refined than earlier dandies had dreamed of. But, far from being revolting, such artifice is redeemed by gaiety and humor. The "frou-frou," as Firbank observes, is "gay-gay." Ghosts of plot haunt his novels, and his prose, however precious, is not only glittering but functional. All conspires to create a vision of what is most unlike the postwar world. Firbank's creation may seem what Mallarmé called an *"aboli bibelot d'inanité sonore,"* but this complicated emptiness is a form for presenting an inverted reality.

The Artificial Princess (1934), an arabesque on the theme of Salomé, is what Wilde might have approached had he been a little more decadent. Like him and Beardsley, Firbank was a Catholic; and in his novels humors of relics, holy water, confessors, flagellation, and choirboys abound. *The Flower Beneath the Foot* (1923) is a kind of saint's life, somewhat more off-centered than even Graham Greene could devise. *Concerning the Eccentricities of Cardinal Pirelli* (1926) discloses a prelate whose cheeks are stained by a choirboy's lipstick. Having baptized a blue-eyed puppy at the font, the cardinal, who looks like a geranium, pursues his choirboy through the dark basilica until, beneath a fresco of the eleven thousand virgins "or as many as there was room for," he expires in those ecclesiastical pursuits.[7]

Evelyn Waugh, another Catholic, differs from Firbank in being somewhat less bizarre, from Huxley in being funnier and more savage, and from Arlen in almost everything. "All Mayfair," Waugh observes in one of his novels,

---

[7] *Valmouth* (1919), *Prancing Nigger* (1925). For Firbank see Cyril Connolly: *Enemies of Promise* (1939); Sir Osbert Sitwell: introduction to *Five Novels by Ronald Firbank* (1949); Ernest Jones: introduction to *Three Novels* (1950).

"seemed to throb with the heart of Mr. Arlen." But it only seemed. Waugh's heartless Mayfair is also a "world that had lost its reason." Its occupants, who display with bright energy their indifference to value, their freedom from scruple, combine and recombine in situations so appalling that the weeping reader laughs aloud.

Decline and Fall (1928), the first of his excellent novels, is speedy, deplorable, and very funny. The central character, like all of Waugh's victims, takes what comes to him without reflection. This passivity increases the horror of what surrounds him: Oxford, the private school, Mayfair, and white-slavery. As symbol of this world Margot Beste-Chetwynde's chromium-yellow house lamentably obtrudes, its drawing-room embellished with octopuses, its conservatory with India-rubber fungi, and for its floor green glass. The people are outlines or shadows, their speech laconic, but standing without the support of the author's comment they have a kind of vitality. Their victim, who learns at last to cultivate his garden, returns to his theology. *Vile Bodies* (1930) is brisker and more sickmaking as Miss Runcible, Miles Malpractice, or other Bright Young People would say. Mrs. Beste-Chetwynde, now Lady Metroland, gives parties, Mrs. Melrose Ape conducts her choir of synthetic angels, Father Rothchild, the omniscient Jesuit, intrigues, and society columnists report or invent these things for the *Daily Excess*. After the symbolic motor race, Adam, a simpleton like Waugh's other victims, finds himself in the war his world has invited.

Waugh took the title for *A Handful of Dust* (1934), his best novel, from Conrad's *Youth* by way of Eliot's *Waste Land*. The allusion should have been to "Heart of Darkness"; for the waste land's heart, shown here, was never darker. With quiet power this novel proceeds through gruesome comedy to tragedy. Pity and fear attend the fall of Tony Last, whose innocence and responsibility are out of fashion. His inevitable fate as idiot's reader is the more tragic for being absurd.

Put Out More Flags (1942) is somewhat less successful than its predecessors. But Waugh regained his power with *Brideshead Revisited* (1945), a sober review of the twenties and thirties from the vantage point of the second war. The first part, concerning Oxford in the twenties, contains Waugh's most entertaining and most three-dimensional eccentrics: Sebastian with his Teddy bear, and Blanche, who paints his toenails red. The second part, far more serious than the first, concerns Sebastian's family, the ruin of Sebastian by his mother, and the conflict in their hearts between religion and the world. This subtle study of imperfect Catholics and of Catholicism triumphant is Waugh's most open treatment of his faith.[8] Like Huxley, Waugh found in religion a refuge from the world and a point of view from which to regard it; but unlike Huxley he remained an artist, leaving sermons to the clergy. His public religion, improving his art, gave to his moralities intensity and that monkish loathing by which he pleases.

Returning to pure satire in *The Loved One* (1948), Waugh presents the Englishman's idea of America, with its beautiful boneheads, its beautified stiffs, its earnest morticians, and elaborate graveyards. Wicked, hilarious, and gruesome, this satire on a barbarous people displays a hero, who, unlike most Englishmen confronted with Hollywood, emerges from passivity with British fortitude and enterprise. But the hero of *Scott-King's Modern Europe* (1947), a vision of Yugoslavia maybe, remains a victim while human values yield to totalitarian indifference. It is a pity that this satire, which begins and ends so well, lacks a middle. *Tactical Exercise* (1954), a collection of desolating stories, presents lunacy, ruin, and the welfare state in England from a Tory's point of view. Waugh's two novels of the second war have enough eccentrics and boobies to embody the old disgust.

Venusberg (1932) by Anthony Powell, a mellower Waugh, discloses the absurdities of a totalitarian world; and *Agents and Patients* (1936) is another victim's re-

---

[8] Waugh was converted in 1930. *Edmund Campion* (1935). *Helena* (1950), a saint's life, one of Waugh's best books. Christopher Hollis: *Evelyn Waugh* (1954).

sponse to what we are faced with.[9] *Lucky Jim* (1954) by Kingsley Amis is a somewhat less brilliant picture than Waugh's of academic incompetence. But *Nothing* (1950) and *Doting* (1952) by Henry Green, though similar in tone to some of these satires, are comedies of growing older. As symmetrical as *Cosi fan tutte, Nothing* figures the follies of two generations.

From comical satire to sardonic comedy is a small step and Ivy Compton-Burnett took it. Her novels of gentry in country houses at the close of the Victorian period reveal a world of self-centered hypocrisy and cruelty—a world without love. No retribution follows, no moral indignation attends, her aloof exposure of the disparity between pretension and things as they are. This comic area was that of Jane Austen, but whereas she was rational and humane, Ivy Compton-Burnett, facing a more terrible world, is clinical.

Her surgery is crowded with patients of limited variety. There are tyrannical fathers, matriarchs, suffering children, butlers, governesses, tutors, and an assortment of parasites, cooks, and maids. Few of these emerge as created beings, but all are brilliantly and ceaselessly articulate. Undifferentiated speech, almost disembodied and autonomous, may be unnatural and, in the absence of description and characterization, artificial; but, bringing the hidden to light, it reveals nature. Even servants and children converse with an adult lucidity, a freedom from inhibition, and a dispassionate logic which, however heartless, reveal the heart and its obscure motives. Her speakers say what people might say if they had words for thoughts they do not have. Never has discourse performed less discursively or in the service of so much beyond its common

[9] Powell: *Afternoon Men* (1931), *From a View to a Death* (1933), *What's Become of Waring?* (1939). V. S. Pritchett: *Mr. Beluncle* (1951). William Plomer: *Museum Pieces* (1952). John Wain: *Hurry on Down* (1953 in America, *Born in Captivity*). Kingsley Amis: *That Uncertain Feeling* (1955). In *The Picnic at Sakkara* (1955) P. H. Newby unites virtues of Waugh, Menen, and Forster. More general and more desolating than these, *Cards of Identity* (1955) by Nigel Dennis is a satiric vision of man's identity or his lack of it.

capacity. But concentration, making demands upon the reader, fatigues him, and if his attention wanders for a moment, he is lost. Though less demanding, the plots, which employ all the resources of melodrama, are as artificial as the dialogue, but no less functional in the business of exposure. As Ivy Compton-Burnett wrote the same book again and again, to have read one is to have read all; but *Manservant and Maidservant* (1947, in America *Bullivant and the Lambs*), at once typical and outstanding, may be singled out for praise.[1]

Lytton Strachey is to biography what Waugh and Huxley are to the novel. Civilized, a member of the Cambridge-Bloomsbury set, he too found in satire and irony fitting expressions of the postwar world. During the war he had been a conscientious objector, and, when asked by the inquisitors what he would do if he found a German ravishing his sister, replied that he would try to get between them. Such reasonable ambiguity became his instrument.

The improvement of biography in our time is largely Strachey's affair. In the nineteenth century, biography had been scholarly or panegyrical, the one careless of art, the other of truth. Proposing to make biography once more a truthful art, he succeeded in making it an art. His merits and his defects come from his point of view, his manner, and his tone. These belong to his adorable eighteenth century and to France, on which he wrote his first book, *Landmarks of French Literature* (1912), one of the most sympathetic studies in English of the classical spirit. He adored that mildness of surface which hides a catlike malice; he adored the elegant, the urbane, and the aloof. He liked to use his ironies on what he disliked. The war having sharpened his instrument, he used it not upon the world around him but upon Victoria's world, which, with some reason, he held responsible for our condition.

The preface to *Eminent Victorians* (1918) states his

[1] *Men and Wives* (1931), *Daughters and Sons* (1937), *Elders and Betters* (1944), *Two Worlds and Their Ways* (1949), *The Present and the Past* (1953), *Mother and Son* (1955). Pamela Johnson: *I. Compton-Burnett* (1951). Robert Liddell: *The Novels of I. Compton-Burnett* (1955). Cf. Thomas Hinde: *Mr. Nicholas* (1952).

purpose and defines the "new" biography. Lamenting
those two fat volumes with which Victorians were accustomed to celebrate their dead, he proposes fact, not com-
pliment; brevity and selection, not copious dullness. He
will expose. In the essays that follow he exposes four Victorians who had been stuffed and whitewashed by their
contemporaries. But the treatment of Cardinal Manning
as an unprincipled politician seems unfair. This impression
is not altogether unwarranted. Reference to Edmund Purcell's two-volume biography, Strachey's principal source,
proves his facts correct but reveals his malice. In its interests his facts are selected, juxtaposed, or emphasized. The
quotations are deadly, the sequences incongruous and anti-
climactic. The result is swift, irreverent, readable; but truth
is partial or colored. Dr. Arnold, an "earnest enthusiast"
who is blamed for the public school, is destroyed by the
same method; but General Gordon and Florence Nightingale, humanized a little, are improved.

In *Queen Victoria* (1921), perhaps the best biography
of our time, this method has been refined. What had been
crude at times or obvious is now easy and impeccable.
Everything follows from the method. Victoria, absurd,
middle-class, noble, admirable, becomes convincing and
many-sided, and the portraits of the men to whom she was
so susceptible are at once brilliant and lifelike. For suave
malice nothing in English exceeds the portrait of Albert.

But this well-balanced book was followed by *Elizabeth and Essex* (1928), which lacks Strachey's particular
merits. Irony has been succeeded by romantic enthusiasm,
knowledge by ignorance. Strachey, at his best at what he
detested, loved Elizabethans; and his many essays on the
seventeenth and eighteenth centuries, though not without
penetration, might have been composed by another.

Strachey had reason, in his essays on "Six English
Historians," to commend the styles of Gibbon and Hume
and to dismiss Macaulay's as "one of the most remarkable
products of the industrial revolution." The classical virtues
of clarity, elegance, and wit, so often wanting in the nineteenth century, were more than Strachey's instrument.

They were his refuge from the times and, like Yeats's mask, the means to keep his own disorder down.[2]

Before Strachey, Edmund Gosse in *Father and Son* (1907), a study at once kindly and detached of his father, anticipated many of the effects of the new biography. After Strachey, biographers abounded, moved by him, but all, save for their common preoccupation with the nineteenth century, dissimilar. Philip Guedalla, the most important of these, wrote *Palmerston* (1926) and *The Duke* (1931). Guedalla's intention as expressed in the preface to the first of these is Strachey's. But more scholarly than Strachey, Guedalla consulted documents, discovered facts, and left none except the unmentionable unmentioned. Where Strachey used a scalpel, Guedalla used a flashing shovel, each stroke so brilliant the effect is dull. Conclusions and character alike are left implicit in the heap. Recreating the Whig aristocracy in *The Young Melbourne* (1939), David Cecil is swift, elegant, and urbane, but not inaccurate. This civilized book, the finest of Strachey's tradition, is the outstanding biography of its decade.

Noel Coward, no less postwar in attitude than these biographers and novelists, found his vehicle in the comedies of Wilde and Maugham, which it is necessary for their sake and his to review. The comedy of manners, as historians know the type, often departs from the tradition of Congreve toward sentiment, fantasy, or purpose. Whether true to type or not, its element is wit. Before the war wit was demanded by the decadence of society and after the war by the war.

Between 1892 and 1895 Wilde wrote four comedies, increasingly good, in which he cleverly combined the virtues of Congreve, Pinero, Ibsen, and W. S. Gilbert, who had restored the tradition of comedy. Unrealistic, these plays create a bright imaginary aristocracy who talk like

[2] *Books and Characters* (1922), *Portraits in Miniature* (1931), *Characters and Commentaries* (1933), *Pope* (1925). Guy Boas: *Lytton Strachey* (1935). Max Beerbohm: *Lytton Strachey* (1943). Harold Nicolson: *The Development of English Biography* (1928). Mark Longaker: *Contemporary Biography* (1934). Nicolson's preface to *Tennyson* (1922) states the aims of the new biography. His best book: *Some People* (1927), is autobiographical.

Wilde himself in epigram and paradox. Since Burke's peer-
age, as Wilde's Lord Illingworth remarks, is the best example of English fiction, Wilde, like James, was compelled
to invent what he could not discover. His middle-class
fantasy pleased the middle class and flattered those members of the aristocracy who were still around. Giving his
plays something of the appearance of Ibsen's gratified the
advanced as the cordial reviews of Shaw attest. But that,
while maintaining appearances, he avoided real problems
and appeased the conservatives whom he excited is shown
by his commercial success.

In his first three plays, dull virtue, confronted with
glittering vice, is more or less victorious. In each there are
a proper lady, a dandy, who carries the burden of antino-
mian wit, and several dowagers, sometimes witty too. As
the ill-made play proceeds, with soliloquies and asides and
creakings at the joints, a curious conflict develops between
sentiment and wit, morality of theme and amorality of
epigram. *Lady Windermere's Fan* (1892) and *A Woman
of No Importance* (1893) are less comic on the whole
than sentimental. Approaching pure comedy in *An Ideal
Husband* (1895), which deals with political and financial
unscrupulousness, Wilde achieved it in *The Importance of
Being Earnest* (1895), where wit, for once at home with
theme, shines in a moral vacuum.

Having learned his craft from Wilde and Jones, and
disillusioned by science, Somerset Maugham commenced
writing plays in 1903, his object, like Wilde's, money.
Lady Frederick (1907) is Wilde minus sentiment, and
Jones minus problem. Like most of Maugham's plays, it
was a commercial success. Maugham defines the commercial play as one that people will go to see. Seeking delight,
they want good construction, interesting theme, amusing
characters and dialogue or, in two words, good theater.
Since plays depend upon the many-leveled audience, most
of which is indifferent to ideas, plays should avoid them.[3]
This cynicism reappears in the entertainments he contrived for many-leveled London.

[3] In *The Summing Up* (1938) and in the prefaces to his *Plays*
(1932), Maugham discusses his principles and plays.

Of these witty plays *The Circle* (1921) is among the best. Here aristocrats in a country house keep reality at several removes, but enough of a problem is suggested and cleverly avoided to keep an audience in stitches and to please the cynical. That history repeats itself is at once familiar, hopeless, and amusing. If the purpose of the theater is not to inform or complain, this is the perfect play. *Our Betters* (1923), as savage as Wycherley, discloses wartime Mayfair, peopled with irresponsible aristocrats and rich Americans, mostly the latter, who have lost one code and failed to find another. These intruders almost transform Maugham's worldly tolerance into moral indignation. But this feeling, one feels, is what he felt his audience would feel. Equilibrium is restored with *The Constant Wife* (1926), which, taking its theme of woman's financial and sexual independence from the problem play, demoralizes it. Comic indifference had become an expression on the popular level of the postwar mind.

Having studied Maugham and the tempo of New York, Noel Coward gave the disenchanted the bitter sweetness they desired, uniting for them the worlds of Huxley and Arlen. Coward knew the theater and how to write a play. His craftsman's cunning made farces like *Hay Fever* (1925), thin when read, effective on the stage.

At once smart and moving, *The Vortex* (1924), though subsidized by Michael Arlen, presents a world as dark as Huxley's, symbolized, like his, by circling dancers. The vortex is postwar beastliness, in which mother and son revolve with the other flotsam of Mayfair. The critics and the censor, less up to date than the audience, wanted to know why Coward chose unpleasant subjects and decadent types, why his characters drink cocktails, take drugs and lovers, or circle to the gramophone. In "The Author's Reply to his Critics" (*Three Plays,* 1925), Coward maintains that, far from trying to be shocking, he tries to express his view of reality and will continue to do so in the teeth of the middle class. Unlike cynics who regard the stage as a commercial opportunity, he regards it as the place of reality and art. Preserving these, he intends to provide an "evening's entertainment." He did that, and his plays helped retard the decay he laments in audience and stage.

Coward's well-made entertainments fall into two kinds, the ironic and the sentimental. Those of the first kind, called "brittle" by critics, are spare and swift, with splendid surfaces, their themes the moral anarchy of the times. *Easy Virtue* (1926) is an old-fashioned problem play on the conflict between a woman with a past and bourgeois respectability. But, faster in every sense than her predecessors, she is less victim than conqueror, and the open door at the end implies sophistication beyond Pinero's capacity. *Fallen Angels* (1925), slight, amusing, and symmetrical, concerns Mayfair wives and husbands and a Frenchman. No point is made, but the ambiguous ending seems to condone what moralists deplore. In *Private Lives* (1930), another symmetrical farce, Coward selects from the people of Waugh and Huxley two couples, who, intricately recombining, cut across conventions. Their lines are clever but not too clever, their conduct hilarious, and nothing, apparently, matters. This amusing play was followed by a better, *Design for Living* (1933), on a similar theme. What Ernest calls a "disgusting three-sided erotic hotch-potch" is illustrated by two men and one woman who love each other very much. At his words, as the curtain falls, the three laugh and laugh, but it is unclear at what—at him, at life, or at themselves?

Such pleasing ambiguities amused and reassured the audience, which understood, as many critics failed to do, that Coward's meaning was not to be confused with his surfaces. Beneath them beat a conventional heart, moral, sentimental, and serious, located, moreover, in the proper place. That the audience was correct is shown by his plays of the other kind. *Bitter Sweet* (1929), his favorite, spurns the jazzing world for what he calls "seminostalgic sentiment." *Cavalcade* (1931), a pageant of enormously clever construction, of magnificent theater, expressed for wet-eyed Britons the pathos of empire and the ruling caste. It is not enough to say that such plays are what Coward's dramatic intelligence told him his audience wanted. They are also what he wanted. The curious thing about them is the importance, surely symbolical, of the cocktail. *Blithe Spirit* (1941) begins with dry Martinis, but this excellent farce of the husband and his shades, symbolical of nothing, is an entertainment.[4]

The poetic comedies of T. S. Eliot may owe something to Coward; certainly those of Christopher Fry owe something to Eliot, if only the idea of using verse. Whereas Eliot employs an inconspicuous rhythm not far from that of common speech, Fry's robustious, ranting speech is as uncommon as possible and his verse is commonly blank. At times Fry seems not unlike Alexander Pope's victim "whose Fustian's so sublimely bad,/It is not Poetry, but Prose run mad." But in *The Lady's Not for Burning* (1949), Fry's successful play, the fustian is the instrument of comedy. What seems at first "a lot of amphigourious stultiloquential fiddle-faddle," as one of his ranters puts it, becomes functional at last. No one since Rabelais and Nashe has found more fun in fustian or more in fiddle-faddle.[5]

Before the first World War and after it other writers presented their world in comic novels or stories, some of which are sardonic, some sentimental, all more or less fantastic. A normal medium for Englishmen in our time, fantasy has enabled them to escape what they faced. With its aid it became possible to contemplate middle-class reality without the pain of Huxley or of Waugh, for reality, when passed through this medium, became agreeable. But the adoption of this protective enchantment argues a kind of disenchantment.[6]

[4] *Play Parade* (1933), *To-night at 8:30* (1936), *Second Play Parade* (1939). *Present Indicative* (1937), autobiography.

A. A. Milne, best remembered for "The King's Breakfast" and excellent children's stories about Winnie-the-Pooh, which compare in value with Kenneth Grahame's *Wind in the Willows* (1908), shared the postwar stage with Coward but not the postwar attitude: *Mr. Pim Passes By* (1920), pleasant comedy; *The Dover Road* (1922), fantasy.

[5] *A Phoenix too Frequent* (1946), *Venus Observed* (1950). *The Dark is Light Enough* (1954), lacking fustian, is dull.

[6] Fantasies: T. F. Powys: *Mr. Tasker's Gods* (1925), *Mr. Weston's Good Wine* (1927); A. E. Coppard: *Adam & Eve & Pinch Me* (1921); David Garnett: *Lady into Fox* (1922), *A Man in the Zoo* (1924); Sylvia Townsend Warner: *Lolly Willowes* (1926); John Collier: *His Monkey Wife* (1930); Archibald Marshall: *Simple People* (1928);

The precocious disenchantment that tempered Max Beerbohm's essays and fantasies of the Beardsley period reached dandier levels in *Zuleika Dobson* (1911), one of the best novels of our time. At once heroic and comic, this tender malicious story of Oxford takes the form of Greek tragedy with all the machinery of fate, the messengers and owls. The characters are caricatures in Beerbohm's manner. The Duke is the middle-class Englishman's ideal, Oover his most kindly idea of the intruding American, and Noaks his idea of the intruding proletarian. These portraits, which imply the class that made them, are matched by those of frigid Zuleika and the careless dons, who would be intolerable in another atmosphere. Fantasy is preserved not only by the preposterous plot, the perspiring Emperors, and the affair of the studs but by a style dandiacal, concerned with its own perfection, lucid, yet precious as Beardsley's, light, yet ensplendored with turns of classical rhetoric.[7]

However malicious, the comic fantasies of Beerbohm are sunny and urbane. Those of Saki (H. H. Munro) are savage. The callousness of his short stories, *The Chronicles of Clovis* (1911), for example, or *Beasts and Super-Beasts* (1914), is that of a sadistic child. His effect depends in part upon regarding the affairs of the adult world with the cold-blooded eyes of such a child and in part upon brevity and casual speed. Appalling practical jokes, infantile revenge, and meaningless horrors compose a world (not unlike that of Kipling) peopled by children, carnivorous animals, and the ruling caste. After the child has been devoured by the hyena, the fox-huntress moves on to take her tea. Ascetic multitudes devour Filboid Studge while applauding Cousin Teresa and the big borzoi. It is hardly a surprise when the bishop is reported to be liquidating Jews with the assistance of Boy Scouts. Though these cruel stories present a vision of the world before the first World War, in which Saki died, they anticipate the

---

Bruce Marshall: *Father Malachy's Miracle* (1933); T. H. White: *The Sword in the Stone* (1939); Eric Knight: *Sam Small Flies Again* (1943). J. R. R. Tolkien: *The Lord of the Rings* (1954–55).
[7] *A Christmas Garland* (1912), parodies.

world before the second, and from our point of view are less fantastic than they seemed.[8]

The world between two wars was oyster for Bertie Wooster and Jeeves, his man. By humorous exaggeration with the effect of fantasy, P. G. Wodehouse made unearned incomes bearable even by those who do not have them. It is unclear, however, whether he intended satire of the idle or their defense. As Wilde had made his idlers wits, Wodehouse made his fools, whereas most are neither. But as one or the other they are harmless, to all appearances, and tolerable. Whatever the intention, therefore, the effect was less satiric than protective, and the vogue of Wodehouse, assured by his hilarity, was reassured. When his young men in spats tool off to country houses to become involved with uncles and horsy ladies, from whom Jeeves, alone intelligent, will rescue them, their dilemmas are at once unlike and like what's what. For these pure and amiable distortions of Mayfair and the counties, no more extreme in one direction than those of Waugh in another, Wodehouse invented an idiom parallel to that of polite society, but inimitable and far from tiresome.

Depending less upon word and situation, the humor of Angela Thirkell is inconspicuous. Her theme, like that of Wodehouse, is the gentry, not of Mayfair, however, but of the county, and the county, of course, is Trollope's Barsetshire. Her purpose, whether conscious or not, is their defense. As Wodehouse made them foolish, she made them charming, and the result, in a world they try to ignore, is pleasantly fantastic. Her self-contained province as displayed in *The Brandons* (1939) or *Northbridge Rectory* (1942) abounds with squires, their ladies, their vicars, and their servants. Some, like Mrs. Brandon, are helpless, and some, like Sir Edmund, are bluff, but all, as they enjoy their property, conceal hearts of gold. Their rounded characters, their placid idleness, and their diversions afford matter for comedy of manners. But into this lovely place

[8] *The Short Stories of Saki* (1930). *The Novels and Plays of Saki* (1933). *The Unbearable Bassington* (1912). Ada Leverson's novels, e.g. *The Limit* (1911), are comedies of the Edwardian period in the urbanest manner of Wilde.

the war intruded, and the later novels concern the impeccable reactions of these people.

The people of Barrie—or most of them—have hearts of gold, but while we are smiling about it we are asked to weep. His humorous fantasies are often sentimental, as every woman knows, but Barrie is neither as bad as he has been considered nor as good. His early work in imitation of the sentimental Kailyard school is best represented by *A Window in Thrums* (1889), sketches of village folk. A shrewd ear for speech and a shrewder eye for familiar detail of scene or character welcome all signs of goodness or of tears. It was against such sweetness that George Douglas directed *The House with the Green Shutters* (1901), a dour, nightmarish melodrama of the village Scot.

Although some of his craftsmanlike commercial plays[9] are free from sentiment and whimsy, such freedom was not Barrie's merit. Both are present in *Peter Pan*, his best work, whether as play or novel. In this fantasy of the boy who refused to grow up, as in *Margaret Ogilvy* (1896), Barrie expressed what was nearest his heart. Instead of covering reality, the sentimental, the whimsical, and the fantastic became keys to what reality he could know.

The moonlit fantasies of Walter de la Mare, like those of Machen, which they resemble, are responses to the world of science and the middle class. Uncanny and antiquarian, these stories draw atmosphere from the prose of the seventeenth century, which de la Mare loves and often approximates. In *The Return* (1910), a novel of morbid psychology, the hero, loitering at twilight in a churchyard, finds himself possessed by the tenant of a convenient grave. The displeasure of his suburban wife and his discovery of her nature and his own, providing an accompaniment of grisly humor, indict the world. Of the stories collected in *The Connoisseur* (1926), some are nightmares, others fantasies. Relying like Maeterlinck upon

---

[9] *Quality Street* (1902), *The Admirable Crichton* (1902), *What Every Woman Knows* (1908), *The Twelve-Pound Look* (1910), *A Kiss for Cinderella* (1916), *Dear Brutus* (1917).

tenuous indirections, de la Mare approaches demons in
"All Hallows" and nameless horrors in "Mr. Kempe." His
best novel, *Memoirs of a Midget* (1921), is beautiful and
strange, though somewhat Victorian in gait. His poppet's
account of her relations with the normal world displays it
as gigantic and incomprehensible. This vision, several fine
characters, and the feat of penetrating, without loss of
credibility, the mind of one so small are virtues of this fantastic romance.

The poems of de la Mare are similar in character to
the stories, but more exquisite. His scenes are church-
yards, forests, and ruined towers. His flora, from old her-
bals, is bindweed and dittany; his fauna the moth and
vole; his people travelers, innocents, and revenants. Much
possessed by death, he approximates the "metaphysical
shudder" of Donne, and, renewing the Gothic, recaptures
effects of Beddoes and Hölderlin. Freed by these antecedents from Georgian rhetoric, he is seemingly archaic,
actually timeless. The title poem of *The Listeners* (1912),
his best collection, is a conspiracy of suggestions. His happiest lines,

> *Through what wild centuries*
> *Roves back the rose,*

are not unlike the perfections of the seventeenth century.
In this and his other volumes the flora, the fauna, and all
the symbols of his private world maintain their enchantment, the incantation of sound and rhythm prolong the
dream, and the simplest means add beauty to strangeness.[1]

Those metaphysicals of the seventeenth century, together with Eliot's Sweeney and Pound's Mauberley, provide suitable precedent for William Empson's witty, ambiguous poems, which seem to have been composed as
puzzles for explicators.[2] In his train came the "University
Wits" with clever verse of the dry, hard sort that T. E.

[1] *The Riddle* (1923), *Ding Dong Bell* (1924), *Collected Poems*
(1941), *The Burning-Glass* (1945). Forrest Reid: *Walter de la Mare*
(1929).
[2] *Poems* (1935), *The Gathering Storm* (1940). *Collected Poems*
(1949).

Hulme esteemed. Kingsley Amis, A. Alvarez, Thom Gunn, and John Wain are of this academic company; and there is also Donald Davie, who, from his exile in Dublin, led those who refused to mourn the death of Dylan Thomas. It almost seems, as Bonamy Dobrée observes, that this verse by dons is written for dons to read.[3]

The light verse of John Betjeman, agreeably preserving in aspic the manner of late Victorian Oxford, is tender and witty. He writes not only of picnics, punts, belfries, and all the apparatus of academic sentiment, but also of suburbs, tea shops, the aspidistra, dissenting chapels, and all that holds the peculiar sensation of England. Although what Auden calls Betjeman's "topophilia" is often directed by the satiric eye, his verse chiefly appeals by nostalgia to mourners of a fading culture.[4]

[3] University Wits: for a good selection of their verse see *Springtime, an Anthology of Young Poets and Writers*, edited by G. S. Fraser and Iain Fletcher (1953). Donald Davie: *Articulate Energy* (1955), on poetic syntax.

[4] *Continual Dew* (1937), *Old Lights for New Chancels* (1940), *New Bats in Old Belfries* (1945), *A Few Late Chrysanthemums* (1955), *Slick but not Streamlined* (1947), a selection of verse and prose edited by W. H. Auden.

CHAPTER FIVE: *The Troughs of Zolaism*

*E*NLARGED by Zola and Flaubert, some English novelists tried to see life steadily and, if possible, whole. This effort is called realism or, in one of its forms, naturalism. Other English writers, more or less indifferent to the realistic French, were enlarged by science or by philosophies based upon it. For writers of both kinds the new reality was as knowable as a slot machine and not unlike it in character.

French realism itself was based upon science or deductions from it, partly upon the work of Darwin and of Claude Bernard, who applied the laws of matter to the study of creatures, and before these upon the Positivism of Auguste Comte, who in the first half of the century applied what he knew of physical science to the study of man in society. Matter and mechanics were triumphant. From their applications to man it was but a short step to literature. Taine took it, extending in the fifties and sixties the ideas of Comte and the scientists to the practice and criticism of literature. His *Histoire de la littérature anglaise* (1864) proved that literature, rigorously determined, illustrates the laws of cause and effect. For the instruction of novelists Taine held that psychology is physiology, that virtue and vice, like vitriol and sugar, are products of material causes. Justifying writers in the contemplation of any subject, however revolting, he became the philosopher of realism.

That Balzac, its first practitioner, had Comte in mind during the latter part of his vast inquest upon society is shown by the preface (1842) to *La Comédie humaine,* where he justifies himself as a student of "social species." Delighted, Taine saw Balzac's work as a collection of scientific documents on human nature. Balzac was not a scientist, though he presented actual life on every level. By his example, however, he pointed the way for subsequent realists, who with the aid of Positivism and science went further along it but not always so well. The development of realism by Balzac's followers is best represented by three great novels: *Madame Bovary* (1857), *Germinie Lacerteux* (1865), and *L'Assommoir* (1877). These novels were read and, to the limit of social or individual capacity, imitated by most French and English realists of the eighties, the nineties, and the new century.[1]

Although Flaubert denied that he was a realist and displayed through his life a taste for the exotic and the remote, he devoted *Madame Bovary,* his first novel, to a commonplace woman of the middle class whose like might be found in twenty villages. To Flaubert, Madame Bovary seemed less an individual than a type; for the novelist, working like a scientist, he sometimes held, should deal in "probable generalities." The authentic details, carefully observed and selected, that compose the life, character, and environment of his heroine are presented with divine aloofness and impersonality. This attitude, so moving in its effect, was one of Flaubert's contributions to the novel. Another was his care for art. Maupassant, Flaubert's disciple, makes this plain in his preface (1885) to *Bouvard et Pécuchet* and in the preface to his own *Pierre et Jean* (1888). Painfully searching for the precise word, the one noun, adjective, verb, the one rhythm that would distinguish a particular janitor or horse from others, Flaubert immortalized his observations of common things and their uncommonness. *Bovary,* so composed by the greatest artist among realists, became the Bible of realists, turning some to thoughts of art, others to thoughts of life.

[1] For French realism see P. Martino: *Le Naturalisme français* (1923).

Germinie Lacerteux, a servant, is a woman of lower degree than novelists had been accustomed to handling; and during the course of the novel she becomes still lower. The stages of her degradation, presented without reticence, proceed from illicit love to drunkenness, lying, theft, sexual debauch, tuberculosis, and rupture of the bowels. This infamous decline follows logically from her passionate, generous nature and from her environment. The brothers Goncourt, her creators, regard her with sympathetic detachment as the victim of circumstances. Social historians and, to some extent, Positivists, they applied historical method to modern horror. Recording what they found, they produced a "documentary novel," which to most early reviewers seemed *"littérature putride."*

But when Émile Zola reviewed *Germinie Lacerteux* in 1865, he admired the "excessive and feverish," yet somehow scientific character of the documentation. In 1868 he visited the brothers Goncourt to express his adoration and that same year he published *Thérèse Raquin,* his first "scientific novel." This novel owes its character not only to the Goncourts but to Taine, whose materialism Zola exaggerated. Almost immediately Zola conceived a plan, as large as Balzac's but more systematic, of studying the history of a family through five generations. The two branches of this family would evolve under the influence of heredity and environment through all the strata of society. Having read a book on heredity, Zola provided the original Rougon-Macquarts with suitable distempers. During the twenty volumes of their "natural history" these unfortunates, who became merchants, peasants, priests, laborers, or prostitutes according to their surroundings, display, according to their inheritance, the symptoms of hysteria, imbecility, scrofula, ataxia, and alcoholism.

Le Roman expérimental (1880) is the clearest expression of Zola's plan. This manifesto is based upon *L'Introduction à la médecine expérimentale* (1865) by Claude Bernard, who applied the methods of physical science to medicine, previously considered an art. Substituting the word "novelist" for "doctor," Zola paraphrased Bernard. The novelist, says Zola, must be a scientist, indifferent to moral convention and art, using hypothesis, examination of evidence, and verification of hypothesis. The laws of nature that his experiments confirm are, of course, heredity, environment, and the physiological nature of the sentiments. The conduct of fictional characters is determined by these laws. "A like determinism," said Zola, "will govern the stones of the roadway and the brain of man."

But Zola's science was pseudo-science, and his faith in it was premature. Carried away by his enthusiasm, he was unaware that the laboratory method requires a laboratory. As he pursued the laws of heredity and environment, he forgot that a family so tainted as his could not have survived three generations, still less five; and he forgot that a dog born in a stable is not necessarily a horse. But his faith in what he took for science stimulated his imagination and his zeal for fact. His novels are less experimental than documentary.

In *L'Assommoir,* the most nearly perfect illustration of Zola's method, Gervaise Macquart, like Germinie Lacerteux, is the victim of temperament and environment. Her marriage to Coupeau, at first a sober worker in zinc, is happy until, having fallen from a roof, he learns the charm of idleness and drink. She borrows money of a tender boltmaker, starts a laundry, supports her degenerating husband. But her generosity and his excess bring them to ruin. They starve in a dismal room. Their daughter Nana, to whose career Zola devoted another volume, goes bad. Coupeau expires of delirium tremens, Gervaise of starvation.

Already familiar with the slums of Paris, Zola visited them again, notebook in hand. He studied public washhouses, bolt-factories, home industries, flower-factories, dance halls, tenements, and the outer boulevards. He recorded the smells, sights, and sounds of laundries and saloons. He observed marriage feasts, birthday feasts, confirmations, fights among women, and wife-beating. He consulted police reports, read books on alcoholism. From a mass of notes and observations he constructed, not a plot in the usual sense, but a logical chain of causes and effects. He described environment and typical conduct in detail;

for environment, the chief element in the book, produces the characters, and however tedious at times his descriptions, none is irrelevant. Forgetting, now and again, his scientific pretensions, Zola abandoned dispassionateness for gusto and, not infrequently, elevated objects, like the steam engine of the wash-house, the coal mine of *Germinal*, or the apartment house of *Pot-Bouille*, into symbol.

Au Bonheur des Dames (1883) concerns a great Parisian department store. In this environment clerks illustrate Darwin's struggle for existence, and the store itself, which puts its less efficient rivals out of business, illustrates the survival of the fittest. Here, as in *L'Assommoir* the documentation is relevant; but in many of his novels, carried away by a natural desire to use his notes, Zola forgot that description should be used where needed, not where not. As some of his novels are over-documented, some are inadequately documented, especially those that deal with the life of the upper classes, the clergy, or farmers, where neither ignorance nor imagination could supply the background. At times a tendency to melodrama injured his scientific demeanor.

Zola called his novels naturalistic. By naturalism, a term for critics to quarrel over, he meant scientific or, better, Positivistic realism, which he hoped by this name to distinguish from the artistic realism of Flaubert. Naturalism is an exaggeration, with the aid of Comte, Taine, and the scientists, of the methods of Balzac and Flaubert. Although *Germinie Lacerteux* is as naturalistic as *L'Assommoir*, it is customary to reserve the label for Zola's novels and the work of his followers, the early novels of Huysmans, for example, and the stories of Maupassant. The naturalistic novel usually differs from the realistic in the kind of reality it includes. Realists contented themselves with average reality, but naturalists, carried away by their scientific or humanitarian ardor, delighted in revealing what decorum had hitherto concealed. Their novels are filled with brutality, ugliness, and degradation. A novel about the slums that contains wife-beating, drunkenness, and sexual promiscuity is usually naturalistic. But this test is not infallible. Some novels with these ingredients are sentimental melodramas; others, like *Au Bonheur des Dames,* which lack these ingredients, are thoroughly naturalistic. It might be best, avoiding these difficulties, to call the realistic novel realistic.

French critics are accustomed to consider realism antithetical to romanticism, but their definitions are traditional and a little academic. There is every reason to consider realism as romantic as transcendentalism. In their search for a wider reality romantics not only soared above the old limits but descended below them. Back to nature, a romantic cry, means not only back to flowers but back to life as it is. The slums and their inhabitants were as attractive to these later romantics as flowers to their predecessors. The war between idealists and realists, in which Zola was a champion, was a war between romantic factions.

The last of these romantic realists to influence the English was Maupassant, whose first short story, *"Boule de Suif,"* appeared in 1880 with the blessing of Zola. Though Maupassant belonged to the group of Médan, his realism is closer to Flaubert's than to Zola's. From Flaubert he learned the art of exact and lucid prose, the attitude of ironic detachment, the habit of minute observation, and hatred for the middle class. For his three hundred stories of Norman or Parisian life he had no need to study documents, for he wrote of what he knew. Maupassant differs from his master chiefly in his increasing pity for mankind. *Une Vie* (1883), his first novel, is the story of an innocent provincial woman, who, though disillusioned by husband, mother, and son, says at the end: "Life is never as good or as bad as one thinks." *Pierre et Jean* (1888) is an "objective" novel, in which actions and speech take the place of psychological analysis. The black pessimism and the physical horror of man that complicated Maupassant's sympathy are implicit in his impersonal art.

Meanwhile, when Victorian novelists confronted reality, they generally kept within limits set by middle-class decorum. When they examined brutality, bastards, and slums, they softened the focus by sentiment or by moral conclusions. Personal intruders, they had little use for the aloofness of scientist or artist. They imposed artificial plots upon observed reality or turned it into melodrama. These distortions were necessary; for their novels, issued in three volumes, were dependent upon the great circulating libraries and these upon public opinion. George Moore changed all that.

When Moore went to Paris in the latter seventies, he discovered naturalism. In *Confessions of a Young Man* (1888) he tells of reading *L'Assommoir,* which he considered abominable, and, later, the propaganda of Zola. This converted him. Awed and excited by the "new art based upon science," which embraced all of life, avoiding puerility of plot and of imagination, he sought out Alexis, of Zola's school, and the Goncourts. He read Flaubert, Huysmans, Balzac, and resolved to become the first English naturalist. On his return to London in 1880 he wrote *A Modern Lover* (1883).[2] This novel, which anticipated Maupassant's *Bel-Ami,* concerns an artist who makes unscrupulous use of women to pursue his ends. The reviewers who found traces of Zola in this book were too acute.

Moore's first naturalistic novel, the first in English and still one of the best, is *A Mummer's Wife* (1885). The epigraph from Victor Duruy is significant: " 'Change the surroundings in which man lives, and, in two or three generations, you will have changed his physical constitution, his habits of life, and a goodly number of his ideas.' " Taking a respectable woman of the lower middle class, the wife of a nonconformist, asthmatic shopkeeper in a pottery town, Moore causes her to elope with an actor. Her temperament, her romantic reading, and her dismal environment, of course, lead her to this step. She is gradually coarsened, takes to drink, has an illegitimate child, and finally marries the actor, who is not a bad sort. She beats him. Finding this very tiresome, he is compelled at

[2] Rewritten as *Lewis Seymour and Some Women* (1917). Joseph Hone: *The Life of George Moore* (1936). William C. Frierson: *L'Influence du naturalisme français sur les romanciers anglais de 1885 à 1900* (1925). M. L. Cazamian: *Le Roman et les idées en Angleterre,* Vol. I, *L'Influence de la science* (1923).

last to leave her. She drinks until her liver rots, and, nursed by a madwoman, she dies. For this relentless sequence of cause and effect Moore took his notebook to the pottery district, traveled with actors, and mastered the symptoms and progress of alcoholism. Like Zola he provided detailed descriptions of the motivating environment: asthma, the shop, the potteries, the theater. His attitude is sympathetic but aloof. He refuses to moralize, to soften or distort. The novel is massive, the action appears inevitable, and the portrait of Kate is convincing. Her character is drawn in part from Madame Bovary's and her career in part from *L'Assommoir,* but she is independently alive.

Reviewers found the book "repulsive" or, at best, "a powerful study of the commonplace." Tennyson, reflecting opinion as a laureate should, appears to have alluded to Moore in "Locksley Hall Sixty Years After" (1886):

> *Feed the budding rose of boyhood with the drainage of your sewer;*
> *Send the drain into the fountain, lest the stream should issue pure.*
> *Set the maiden fancies wallowing in the troughs of Zolaism,—*
> *Forward, forward, ay, and backward, downward too into the abysm!*

Mudie's circulating library was of the same opinion. In *Literature at Nurse, or Circulating Morals* (1885) Moore attacked Mudie for restricting, in accordance with middle-class morality and commercial prudence, the freedom of the artist. To circumvent the libraries, Moore had persuaded Vizetelly, his publisher, to issue novels in a single volume. By this device Moore and his publisher liberated the novel, for many readers, interested in science and hence in scientific fiction, proved to be more tolerant than librarians or critics.

Vizetelly, who had published translations of Flaubert, now undertook translations of Zola. Moore provided the enthusiastic preface for *Piping-Hot* (1885), a translation of *Pot-Bouille.* These translations, though somewhat expurgated, proved intolerable. The National Vigilance Association, charging Vizetelly with obscenity, brought him to official notice. The publisher was tried and fined in 1888, and, after renewed offenses, imprisoned for three months in 1889 despite a petition signed by Hardy, Moore, Havelock Ellis, and Gosse. But Vizetelly prospered during the nineties. And when Zola visited England in 1893 he received almost universal homage.

Moore, who was largely responsible for this development of middle-class taste, met Zola on this occasion. But he had been corresponding with the master since 1881 and, as recorded in "A Visit to Médan," had visited him. Moore's letters to Zola and his continual propaganda show a disciple's devotion.

A Drama in Muslin (1886) presents the Irish upper class and the marriage market of the Dublin season. However elegant the theme, this documentary study of silks and ballrooms, as Moore informed Zola, is fundamentally naturalistic. But there are significant intrusions from René Ghil, Jane Austen, and Balzac; and Moore's new concern for style shows other influences. For Moore was turning from Zola at this time under the influence of Pater, Huysmans, and the symbolists. Confessing in *Confessions* his inability to recapture his old ecstasy over naturalism, Moore saw Zola as crude and wanting art. In *Impressions and Opinions* (1891), praising Balzac and Turgenyev, Moore condemned Zola as too objective to be realistic and, in later essays, as too unspiritual.

But before Moore had got quite clear of the "shallows and mudbanks of naturalism," he wrote *Esther Waters* (1894), his last novel in the manner of the French realists and one of his best. This excellent story of a servant girl and her illegitimate child conforms to naturalism in theme, documentation, and detachment. Moore was full of his subject. In his *Confessions* he speaks of a servant girl whom Dickens would have sentimentalized or laughed at. But Moore, with French eyes, "studied the horrible servant as one might an insect under a microscope. 'What an admirable book she would make. . . .'" Like the Goncourts, however, Moore tempered detachment with sympathy; and although declaring it his intention merely to "exhibit life," he was as pleased as Zola with the moral effect. Smith's circulating library banned the book. It enjoyed great success.

With "Mildred Lawson" of *Celibates* (1895) Moore bade a farewell to the school of Balzac. *Evelyn Innes* (1898) and *Sister Teresa* (1901), second-class novels of love, music, and religious experience, distantly resemble the later novels of Huysmans. For the details Moore consulted friends familiar with music and nunneries.

George Gissing was an imperfect realist. A self-centered man, he was at his best in semi-autobiographical fiction like *New Grub Street* (1891) and *The Private Papers of Henry Ryecroft* (1903) where, enamored of his subject and full of pity for it, he could display his sentiment or his mellowness. Although in *Workers in the Dawn* (1880) he wrote about the slums, where poverty once compelled him to live, he described their victims with a fastidiousness that confirms his later confession of hatred for them. Even hatred failed to give him detachment. He is always personal, intrusive, emerging for exclamations and asides, pointing morals and social deductions. His style is crude, his observation limited, his occasional humor or irony ponderous. No writer could be further from Flaubert. Yet Gissing was aware of Flaubert and Balzac, whom he mentions in his study of Dickens (1898), and he was to some extent affected by the French realists. His achievement in novels of the lower classes was to confound Zola with Dickens.

The Unclassed (1884), described by Gissing as pure narrative without moral, deals as he says "in a romantic spirit with the gloomier facts of life." His heroine, investigating a slum, finds bad smells and a dead baby in the garbage. Among less gloomy facts are unhappy marriages, poverty, and prostitution. Ida, the heroine, is a prostitute. Driven to this profession by economic necessity, she does well at it until her "nobility of character" moves her to become respectable. She finds a job in a laundry, inherits riches from her reappearing grandfather, and spends her virtuous days in rebuilding Grandfather's slum or taking poor children on picnics. The intricate, sentimental plot with which Gissing distorted probability saved him and his readers from the dangers of his subject. Waymark, the hero, who marries Ida, is a realistic novelist like Gissing. His job of rent-collecting in Grandfather's slum gives him the materials for his art. He plans a novel, he says,

> such as no one has yet ventured to write, at all events in England. . . . The novel of every-day life is getting worn out. We must dig deeper, get to untouched social strata. Dickens felt this, but he had not the courage to face his subjects; his monthly numbers had to lie on the family tea-table. Not *virginibus puerisque* will be my book, I assure you, but for men and women who like to look beneath the surface, and who understand that only as artistic material has human life any significance.

Elsewhere Waymark modifies this position of artistic detachment by announcing that art should be "the mouthpiece of misery." When his novel appears, reviewers class it with "the unsavoury productions of the so-called naturalist school." If Waymark's novel resembles *The Unclassed*, and the implication is that it does, these reviewers are ignorant of Zola. But it is probable that *The Unclassed* is the closest approximation of Zola that English convention, always too strong for rebellious Gissing, allowed him to make. Intending Zola, he produced Victorian melodrama.

The Nether World (1889) is no less dismal. From Zola come the long descriptions of the environment that determines the viciousness and brutality of Gissing's London slum. But upon this Zolaesque material Gissing once more imposed an artificial, melodramatic plot, filled with improbable coincidences, vitriol, nicks of time, and missing wills. And Jane Snowdon, the heroine, whose purity is unsullied by her slum, is a sentimental invention. The trouble is that Gissing's characters, intellectually conceived, are unfelt; and all his "hapless spawn of diseased humanity" remains a little inhuman.

It would have been better for Gissing had he resembled Harold Biffen, the realist in *New Grub Street* who wrote a novel called *Mr. Bailey, Grocer,* "unutterably tedious" but true to life. This fictional fiction has no drama, no art, but only cold serious reporting. Biffen says:

> What I really aim at is an absolute realism in the sphere of the ignobly decent. The field, as I understand it, is a new one; I don't know any writer who has treated ordinary vulgar life with fidelity and seriousness. Zola writes deliberate tragedies; his vilest figures become heroic from the place they will fill in a strongly imagined drama. I want to deal with the essentially unheroic, with the day-to-day life of that vast majority of people who are at the mercy of paltry circumstance. Dickens understood the possibility of such work, but his tendency to melodrama on the one hand, and his humour on the other, prevented him from thinking of it.

But Gissing, who also understood this possibility, resembled his own unfortunate Reardon, and it was left for others to follow Biffen's plan. Among them were short-story writers and novelists of the nineties and of the new century who found form and attitude in Maupassant and Flaubert, theme sometimes in Zola.[3]

For these realists reality consisted of what earlier Victorians had endeavored to avoid. Unlike Zola, these morally detached or semidetached observers had no scientific pretensions; but the reality they observed was also limited by scientific materialism to environment and to predictable responses. Nothing mysterious, nothing above or below the conscious, the mechanical, or the social could

---

[3] Hubert Crackanthorpe: *Wreckage* (1893). Arthur Morrison: *Tales of Mean Streets* (1894), *A Child of the Jago* (1896). Rudyard Kipling: "The Record of Badalia Herodsfoot," *Many Inventions* (1893). Somerset Maugham: *Liza of Lambeth* (1897). (In *The Summing Up* (1938) Maugham explains his adherence to the doctrine of determinism, telling how he was affected by Darwin, Maupassant, the Goncourts, and Morrison.) Richard Whiteing: *No. 5 John Street* (1899). Frank Swinnerton: *Nocturne* (1917). James Hanley: *The Furys* (1935). Richard Llewellyn: *None but the Lonely Heart* (1943).

intrude. Within this area, as limited in its way as that of their decent predecessors, the realists found their reality in prostitutes, wife-beaters, and servants (preferably with illegitimate children) or in the tedious affairs of the lower middle class. These French subjects were more or less adapted to English taste by humor or by judicious reticence.

In spite of Moore's success, the English public was not altogether at home with the new realism. Enough readers were converted to assure a moderate success for moderate realism, which the excesses of Wilde and the æsthetes had made appear comparatively innocuous. But Philistines remained true to their ideals. Arnold Bennett, while making the new realism commercially profitable, felt to the end the need for compromise; and the banning of *Ulysses,* which defined middle-class capacity, justified his prudence. It was enough for realists to contemplate the dregs without stirring them up.

Arnold Bennett belongs with Moore among superior products of France. During the nineties Bennett read the French realists, learned of cause and effect from Taine and Herbert Spencer, and with Moore and James came to share Flaubert's idea of the novel, not as so much material, but as art, selective, impersonal, final. He made elaborate technical studies of form and development; and he counted verbs. Of English realists Moore, whose *Mummer's Wife* Bennett read three times, seemed most admirable. Like Moore and Zola, Bennett recorded what he observed in notebooks and in the *Journals* he kept after the fashion of the Goncourts. Priding himself, like Moore, upon knowledge of women, whom he observed with and without his notebook, Bennett arrived at the point of being astonished at nothing. By his own devices this provincial man had freed himself from the puritanism of his youth to arrive at a moral disinterestedness unusual among Englishmen. He freed himself, that is, to a point; for like his heroes he remained in part the creation of his lower middle-class commercial and religious environment. He was all the French can do to a Wesleyan Methodist.

A Man from the North (1898), Bennett's semiauto-
biographical first novel, concerns a young clerk from
Bursley, who, coming to London with literary ambitions,
is frustrated and doomed to the suburbs by heredity and
circumstance. This "natural history" reflects Bennett's admiration of Zola, Gissing, and especially Huysmans, whose
A vau-l'eau is the closest parallel. This was Bennett's ap-
prentice work in amused detachment. He did better in
Anna of the Five Towns (1902), a serious study of a commonplace woman in the pottery district, a satire on Methodism and parental tyranny, and a firm re-creation of
environment. The extensive, often ironic, descriptions
of the potteries, of the revival meeting at the chapel, and
of Anna's kitchen are less irrelevant than they seem; for
they serve to account for their creatures. With this admirably restrained story of dullness and frustration Bennett found his subject and his manner. *Leonora,* which
followed this in 1903, is of less value. The excellent portrait of a woman of forty is injured by an improbable plot
and left unsupported by the surrounding caricatures. Bennett was attempting to combine realistic psychology with
something that would appeal to popular taste. He wanted
a yacht.

This natural desire led Bennett about this time to the
composition of what he called commercial fiction, novels
designed by their worthlessness to please the reader and
make their author rich. The best of these sensational novels
is *The Grand Babylon Hotel* (1902). Though this "fantasia
on modern themes" reflects Bennett's own provincial devotion to urban splendor, it is otherwise unserious. It concerns dark doings at the Savoy: trapdoors, secret passages,
abductions on yachts, a disappearing corpse, poisoned
wines, gilded adventurers, rouged girls, international
crooks.

Along with these thrillers Bennett produced several
humorous novels of merit, *A Great Man* (1904), for example, and *Buried Alive* (1908). Alice Challice in *Buried
Alive* is one of Bennett's best portraits; and the triumph
of his craft is nowhere more evident than in Priam Farll's

emotion at his own funeral. *A Great Man* is a hilarious account of the popular writer and of his publishers, critics, and readers.

That the same man at the same time could have written *The Old Wives' Tale* (1908) increases the wonder of Bennett's capacity. This novel, one of the best of our time, is one of the best in the French tradition. As he tells us in the preface, he found his theme in a Parisian restaurant where he observed an eccentric lady, once young. His novel would concern women and time. Instead of eccentric he made his heroine commonplace, as the realistic tradition required. Maupassant's *Une Vie,* he said, was his model. But one woman was too easy for a student of women and insufficiently illustrative of heredity and environment; so he provided his heroine with a sister of different temperament. Placing them, like an experimental novelist, in the environment of a drapery shop in Bursley, he removed one to another environment, reunited them after a while, and observed that however different their lives and tempers, time had brought both to a common end. With what he called "an infinite number of infinitesimal changes" he revealed his provincial women in the grip of heredity, environment, and time. Of these, time, which levels all, is chief. To convince the reader of its passage he resorted to many technical devices—concentration, monotony, selection here, detail there, and, more dramatic than these, generations of dogs and deaths of husbands. The book is an epic of dull lives and of all life, the more moving and tragic because aloof in manner, restrained in style, and filled with what Bennett himself called a "lofty nobility." Lafourcade cannot be blamed for finding this romantic novel a monument of classical art.

Bennett's sources were observation and notebook and, for the melodramatic and somewhat inferior scenes in Paris, newspapers of the time. From Maupassant came Constance's relationship with her son. But a principal model seems to have been Moore's *Mummer's Wife,* and it was probably this book that showed Bennett the literary possibilities of the Five Towns. As Moore's heroine is lured away from her draper's shop in the pottery town

by a traveling actor, so Bennett's Sophia from hers by a
traveling salesman. These travelers are but devices to
effect a change of environment. Their similarity means
perhaps that Moore and Bennett alike were in the naturalistic tradition.

Bennett's virtues, his patient building of external reality, his mastery of the illusion of time, his understanding
of character, simple or complex, in relation to environment
and time, reappear in *Clayhanger* (1910), which belongs
with *The Old Wives' Tale* among masterpieces of realism.
Edwin's life in solidly constructed Bursley, his development as an individual, and his frustrated love for Hilda
are presented in humdrum scenes selected from a period of
thirty years, crystallized now and then by small symbolic
climaxes designed to flash the meaning: the Sunday-school
centenary, for instance, and the death of Darius. The clinical details of Cheyne-Stokes breathing, the steam printing
shop, the streets and squares and kilns are re-created in the
spirit of naturalism; but the psychology of Edwin and
Hilda, who rise mysteriously above their surroundings to
heights of complexity, is indebted to Stendhal and Dostoyevsky. *Riceyman Steps* (1923), the story of a book-
selling miser and his appropriate death, is a triumph of
realism, dull and inevitable.

Bennett's last important book, *Imperial Palace* (1930),
unites his interest in detailed environment, his knowledge
of women, and his love of luxury. The plot and the characters of the capitalist and his daughter are contrived in
Bennett's best commercial manner. But the hotel represents the climax of naturalistic documentation. Notebook
in hand, Bennett had explored a luxury hotel, its laundry,
kitchens, stores, its housekeeping, catering, and accounting
departments. The portrait of this elegant machine is the
single point of the novel and its success. Equally romantic
but more frivolous, *The Grand Babylon Hotel* was a first
study for this portrait. For years Bennett had been fascinated with hotels, department stores, and steamships, which
assumed in his eyes the importance of symbols, representing not only the repressed provincial's dream but the world
in little. The resemblance between this microcosmic novel

and Zola's *Au Bonheur des Dames,* his study of a department store, is far from accidental.[4]

By the time of Bennett's greatest novels, objections to realism by reputable critics were less commonly moral than æsthetic or metaphysical. In *Notes on Novelists* (1914), Henry James complained on æsthetic grounds of Bennett's excessive and irrelevant materials. If reality is an orange, said James, in reading Bennett we are immersed, to be sure, in its juice, but to what end? This objection to Bennett's naturalism by the disciple of Flaubert repeats Flaubert's objection to Zola. But it is odd that James should have rebuked for want of art one who was no less preoccupied with art than he or Moore and no less a part of the French tradition. When Virginia Woolf attacked Bennett, together with Wells and Galsworthy, in *Mr. Bennett and Mrs. Brown* (1924), her complaint was that Bennett's reality is unreal. His materialism, his elaborate concern with surroundings, fails, she said, to convey life itself. Amid so much well-constructed solidity and such craft, character and soul as well are lost. This metaphysical objection to realists' reality marks a change in the nature of reality to something perhaps no more real. But for the generation of Mrs. Woolf, though he was certainly as much a realist as she, Bennett was out of fashion.

While disciples of Zola or Flaubert were reaffirming the possibilities of their reality, other English writers, more or less immune to France, were learning similar realities from science. Thomas Hardy is the most eminent of these. Early in his development he read Darwin, Spencer, and Colenso, lost his faith in revealed religion, and, seeking no substitute for it, faced the universe like an Englishman. Natural selection and mechanical determinism had taken the place of special creation and design. Man was cog or victim of a machine. The governing forces, laws of Newton's physics and of Darwin's biology, determining and themselves determined, seemed casual at best or at worst

[4] *Hilda Lessways* (1911) and *These Twain* (1915) complete the Clayhanger trilogy. *The Pretty Lady* (1918). *The Journals of Arnold Bennett* (1932–3). Georges Lafourcade: *Arnold Bennett* (1939). Reginald Pound: *Arnold Bennett* (1953).

malign. This deplorable universe was also Zola's. But
Hardy differed from Zola in being sad about it instead of
happy. Where Zola saw cause and effect, Hardy, seeing
them as they seem, saw chance and made it plain by arbitrary plot. Reading Greek tragedy, he read chance for fate.
References in *Tess of the D'Urbervilles* to Huxley and
Æschylus fix the frame he imposed upon observed reality.
The Return of the Native (1878), an evocation of the
blasted heath, is the first novel in which the hero is articulate about his condition; but *Two on a Tower* (1882), revealing the disparity between human affairs and the
indifference of the stars is even more disturbing. The
pattern of melodrama that Hardy inherited from Wilkie
Collins became a fitting vehicle for the disclosure of accident and design.

Of Hardy's novels in our time, *The Mayor of Casterbridge* (1886) and *The Woodlanders* (1887), like some
of the earlier novels, are tragedies of Darwin's man in
Newton's universe and Mrs. Grundy's parlor. *Tess of the
D'Urbervilles* (1891) and *Jude the Obscure* (1895), as
dramatic in form, are closer to Zola's reality. What is true
of these, however, is more or less true of all. Their power
comes from the feeling with which Hardy contemplated
human significance and insignificance, their irony from
the disparity he found between chance and will, their density from love of native soil, a love the more intense (as
Darwin fought inside him with Wordsworth and Lord
Nelson) for his awareness of nature's cruelty or indifference.

Tess is another servant with illegitimate child. Like
Germinie and Esther Waters, she is the blameless victim
of nature and of social convention, which wears in middle-
class England the aspect of a natural force. Chance in the
ordinary sense is there. Tess's letter goes under instead of
over the rug. But chance is less important than usual in
Hardy. Here for the most part chance in the sense of determinism operates like Darwin's selection through heredity and environment. Tess does what she has to do because
half D'Urberville, half peasant; and Angel, torn between
theological emancipation and moral convention, acts ac-

cording to his half-lights. Tess is sex, Angel, in his degree, intellect. Under "cruel Nature's law" they converge in a social environment ill adapted to their natures or desires. The background is half the book, for it is the environment out of which the victims grow and in which they move. A fellow sufferer, nature is also there to reflect and intensify mood. When happy, Tess milks idyllic cows at the dairy farm; when sad, digs turnips on the blasted heath.

Continual intrusions of the author to announce the pity of it, to blame the First Cause, or to make a terminal flourish grow tiresome at last. The style is heavy; and it is easy to see why Moore, amorous of the impersonal art of France, found Hardy intolerable. Too amorous of France, however, Moore could not see native virtue or tragedy in homely dress.

The genteel protests to which Hardy, protesting truth, responded in the preface to *Tess* were nothing to those occasioned by *Jude*. The book was banned by the circulating libraries, defended by Havelock Ellis, and publicly burned by a clergyman. Even the last of these actions is understandable; for, attacking caste, Hardy presented the clergy of Oxford as agents of respectability alone. And at his hands the sacrament of marriage appeared to be endangered. Having read Ibsen, and thinking of the Parnell case and his own affairs, Hardy arranged the four people of *Jude* in displeasing marital or extra-marital combinations. Of Jude, victim not only of society but of Darwin's universe as well, Hardy says: "Nature's logic was too horrid for him to care for." Jude's ideals are defeated by the blind forces of nature, by sex, for example, which compels the scholar to embrace a woman little better than a beast. He knows the folly of free will; but even Hardy's littlest victims are not regardless of their doom. Little Father Time has Hardy's view of things before he is old enough to take it. Among other victims Sue is the most disturbing, as complex and unpredictable as someone from Dostoyevsky. With these unnatural creatures and the natural laws, Hardy was attempting Greek tragedy with Darwin in place of the Eumenides. He failed. The pattern was too capriciously imposed; and evil is unrelieved by good. Wanting catharsis, the gloomy reader is forced to conclude that, however violent, this is a morbid book.

Hardy was even more explicit about determinism in the cantankerous lyrics he wrote. In "Hap," for example, and "In Vision I Roamed" he deplores "that Universe taciturn and drear," and in "The Ivy-Wife" and "In a Wood," the struggle for existence among vegetables. These dismal little philosophies, whose virtues are irony and crabbedness, fail as poems. Perhaps, as T. S. Eliot observed in the *Criterion,* Hardy is a minor poet; and it is certain, as Yeats observed in his anthology, that Hardy "lacked technical accomplishment." Yet "The Last Signal" is a poem as good as something by Hopkins, and "The Ruined Maid," with its grim humor, is best of its kind. Hardy was a poet, but not enough of a poet to distinguish between good poems and bad or to invent an appropriate form for his individual feeling. As Victorian form takes one line and Hardy's matter another, agreeing and disagreeing, the effect is contrapuntal. From this his failures and his triumphs. But form and mood happily conspire in *The Dynasts* (1903–8).

This grandiose mixture of epic and drama, of blank verse and lyric chorus, is modeled upon Shelley's *Prometheus Unbound.* Since there are nineteen acts and one hundred and thirty scenes, many of which are cosmic, the play is ill adapted to the stage and even worse to the closet, for which it was written. For years Hardy had been fascinated with the Napoleonic Wars, partly because an ancestor had received Lord Nelson's last exclamation. But *The Dynasts* surveys the wars from the point of view of Darwin and Newton. Fancying free will, Napoleon is determined; and even Englishmen are puppets of Schopenhauer's Immanent Will. The pointlessness of mechanical determinism is expressed by a machinery of celestial observers, Spirits of the Years and Choruses of Pities. As the First Cause blindly works Its clocklike laws or like a vast fermenting-vat brews evolution, the Spirits sing:

> *Of Its doings if It knew,*
> *What It does It would not do!*

The conflict between Pities and Years, the one a projection of human sentiment, the other of Flaubertian indifference, reveals the theme of the play, the conflict between will and chance. However philosophical their demeanor, these spirits are there to tighten structure, effect transitions, and, like a Greek chorus, provide the obvious comment and some relief. Although philosophical, the play is less philosophy than vision. As T. S. Eliot tolerantly observed, Hardy apprehended his matter as a poet should. But Chesterton, confronted with Hardy's exploitation of the nineteenth-century universe, an exploitation as great as Zola's, heard only the "mutterings of the village atheist." [5]

Although Catholic, Joseph Conrad shared Hardy's view of nature and of man. In a letter of 1897 to Cunninghame Graham, that eupeptic idealist, Conrad explained the nature of the universe. It is a machine, he says, that evolved itself

> out of a chaos of scraps of iron and behold!—it knits.
> I am horrified at the horrible work and stand appalled.
> I feel it ought to embroider,—but it goes on knitting.
> . . . The infamous thing has made itself: made itself
> without thought, without conscience, without fore-
> sight . . . without heart. It is tragic accident,—and
> it has happened. You can't interfere with it. . . . It
> knits us in and it knits us out. It has knitted time,
> space, pain, death, corruption, despair, and all the
> illusions,—and nothing matters.[6]

Like Hardy, Conrad considered man's consciousness his tragedy. Like Hardy, he had a gloomy temper.

[5] David Cecil: Hardy the Novelist (1946). William Rutland: Thomas Hardy (1938). Florence E. Hardy: The Early Life of Thomas Hardy (1928), The Later Years of Thomas Hardy (1930). H. C. Webster: On a Darkling Plain (1947); Albert Guérard: Thomas Hardy (1949). Evelyn Hardy: Thomas Hardy (1954). Cakes and Ale (1930), one of Maugham's best novels, is generally supposed to be an irreverent portrait of Hardy, but Maugham denied the likeness.

[6] From: Joseph Conrad, Life and Letters, by G. Jean-Aubry, copyright 1926, 1927 by Doubleday & Co., Inc. John Gordan: Joseph Conrad (1940). M. C. Bradbrook: Joseph Conrad (1941). Albert Guérard: Joseph Conrad (1947). Paul Wiley: Conrad's Measure of Man (1954).

By storms and calms and jungles Conrad presented the indifference or malevolence of nature, against whose alien might man's life is struggle. The sea of *The Nigger of the Narcissus* (1897) is the "terrible sea," and the jungle of "Heart of Darkness" holds the "horror" of Kurtz's final lucidity. Marlow, obsessed with the machinery of chance, speaks in Lord Jim (1900) of the "working of the implacable destiny of which we are the victims—and the tools."

But Conrad differed from Hardy in the belief that nature, claiming victims, may create heroes. Testing men, she may increase their moral stature, discovering courage, honor, and integrity. In *Typhoon* (1903), Captain MacWhirr confronts his tempest like a teapot. Refusing to change his charted course, attending to the neatness and order of his hold, he emerges with his engineers and the builders of his ship as a symbol of human integrity. In *The Shadow Line* (1917), the young captain confronts his calm. Bringing ship and crew through their ordeal and gaining moral maturity, he becomes no less symbolic.

Nature, which made Conrad the moralist of emergent occasions, explains the invention of Marlow, his moral detective. This cynical sentimentalist, obsessed with man's integrity, is compelled to spend his time assuring himself of its existence. Lord Jim was his first case. Faced with two accidents, Jim succumbed to one, unsettling Marlow, and, cheering him, conquered the other by death. This equivocal victory foreshadows that of Heyst in *Victory* (1915). Trying to defend himself by insularity from man and nature, Heyst falls victim to accident, in the person of Mr. Jones, to his own nature, and the nature of man. His elegant refusal to fight is atoned for, however, by the gesture of death, somehow an assertion of defiance and contempt. The defeat of Lingard in *The Rescue* (1920), Conrad's most complicated morality, amounts to success because of that hero's scruples. Torn between loyalty to his rajah and to the woman he adores, frustrated by circumstance, Lingard has done what man can do.

Yet, however central, morality is an illusion; and illusion is the "destructive element" in which, according to

Stein of *Lord Jim,* we must immerse. At once necessary and deadly to heroic minds, illusion remains our noblest answer to natural law. Stein's discourse appears to be a key to Conrad's attitudes and themes. Plainly *Lord Jim* is the story of an illusion lost, pursued, and recovered; and *Victory,* no less plainly about the destructive element, ironically celebrates a dream of apartness and ancestral elegance in conflict with intrusive, modern fact. The irony that reveals these glorious defeats reveals Conrad's divided mind.

Like most of those concerned with circumstance, Conrad owed something to the French realists. From Flaubert and Maupassant, whom he admired with moral reservations, Conrad took method, attitude, and some notions of style. He admired their disinterested art, and, using morality as matter alone, he refrained like them from preaching it. He admired their ideas of diction, and, hunting precise words, he endeavored to make the reader see, hear, smell, and taste experience. But never satisfied with the precise word, Conrad used many precise words, succumbed to the vice of word-painting, and blanketed his stories with description that, far less evocative than drama, defeated its end. Few can read the first chapter of *The Rescue,* where for page after page Conrad describes the sea, the ship and its sails, and then the sky. At last someone comes on deck to light a cigar.

This ponderous motion, however, helps create a vision of life no less than the dullness of these heroes. Lord Jim is far from bright; Lingard is dumb, and Nostromo simple. Incapable of thought, these moralists brood, and Conrad, wisely disdaining analysis, broods over their brooding. Nothing comes quite clear. Motions and punctilios emerge from wading-glue. But this effect, the portrait of his world, is Conrad's triumph.[7]

Science, which made Hardy regard and distort reality, made H. G. Wells regard, discuss, and try to change it. Wells was excited by Huxley's lectures on biology at the

[7] For Conrad's aim as an artist see the preface to *The Nigger of the Narcissus. Notes on Life and Letters* (1921) contains an essay on Maupassant; and two stories in *Tales of Unrest* (1898) seem imitations of Maupassant. In his letters, however, Conrad is hostile to the external realists.

Normal School of Science. Duller lecturers on physics, geology, and astronomy bored him. But his mind was formed by these studies, and his knowledge, though superficial, was greater than that of other literary men. While Kipling optimistically sang of piston and connecting rod and saw in the evolution of caveman to imperialist a promise of larger imperialists, and while Henley in his "Song of Speed" complacently fondled the pipes and cylinders of the horseless carriage, Wells, better informed, saw danger in complacency and optimism. Science had shown him that nature is cruel or at best indifferent, that the position of man, dwarfed in the perspectives of astronomy and evolution, is precarious, that more science and more wisdom are required. He devoted his scientific fantasies to grave warnings. *The Time Machine* (1895), ostensibly a frivolous romance of the fourth dimension, shows that evolution may produce degenerates, that the future is likely to belong to giant crabs, and that, according to the second law of thermodynamics, sun and earth must die. The horrors of *The Island of Dr. Moreau* (1896) blasphemously reveal the cruelty of the Creator, the animal nature of the highest creatures, and their liability, despite moral ideals, to relapse. *The War of the Worlds* (1898), another assault upon complacency, demonstrates the insignificance of man and the dangers of intellectual development. Wells was not a scientist but a critic of science and, unlike Jules Verne, with whom he was often confused, a moral philosopher. In his romances the fantastic occupies the commonplace. *The Invisible Man* (1897), despite a preposterous premise, concerns actualities of London and Kent, and the manner, pedestrian and easy, suits things as they are.

Wells had little use for Frenchmen. When he turned to the realistic novel, he used Dickens and Gissing as models. But Gissing, at whose death-bed Wells presided, lacked science and in Wells's eyes was little better than a humanist. It was science that gave Wells his air of examining as in a laboratory the human specimens before him. Science had nothing to do, however, with the gusto that complicated his view of the trials and errors of little men in bad environments. From *Love and Mr. Lewisham*

(1900) and *Kipps* (1905) down to *The History of Mr. Polly* (1910), many of Wells's characters are caricatures; but the exaggerations are of observed reality. *Tono-Bungay* (1909), "a cross section of the British social organism," is at once typical and transitional. The servants' basement, the bakery, the chemist's shop, and all the other sets are substantially presented. Nicodemus Frapp and Ponderevo are Dickensian grotesques. But while Ponderevo puffs his worthless potion, George, the potential savior of society through science, experiments with flying machines and talks. As he talks, what began as novel threatens to become essay. Managing this transition without awkwardness by the autobiographical method, which enables George to present or to interpret as he pleases, Wells happily balanced his interests and his talents.

In *The New Machiavelli* (1911) and in the later novels, ideas of reality increasingly take the place of reality; imagination and concreteness are replaced by abstract monologues. But science, more abstract than concrete, was also behind this development. Dreams of the New Republic and of natural aristocrats are scientific dreams of order, clarity, and foresight, of all that is opposite to muddle. No longer used to examine muddle, science is used to show the way out of it. Wells cheerfully admitted that he had become less interested in character and circumstance than in ideas about them. And as for the art of the novel, dear to most realists, he rejected it with violence. He quarreled with Henry James, Bennett, and Conrad over Flaubert's empty ideals, and called himself a journalist. "A Digression about Novels" in *Experiment in Autobiography* (1934) reaffirms his denial of realism and art. And in his preface to Swinnerton's *Nocturne* Wells claimed, forgetting his earlier works, that he had never "presented" life.[8]

Wells, Bennett, and Galsworthy, grouped by long custom, have little in common save, as Virginia Woolf insisted, a common materialism. John Galsworthy, though in a sense a realist like the others, had little to do with

---

[8] During his Fabian period Wells wrote *This Misery of Boots* (1907) and other tracts. *A Modern Utopia* (1905) is a cross between a novel and a treatise. Geoffrey West: *H. G. Wells* (1930).

science and, though a follower of Flaubert and Turgenyev at a suitable distance, little to do with France. But science and realism were at large in the atmosphere, and *The Forsyte Saga* is a monument to cause and effect, heredity and environment.[9] Even sports like young Jolyon, who have attained the power of self-analysis, have the sense of property. Although this sense is probably the product of middle-class environment, young Jolyon, when speaking of it or defining a Forsyte, implies an evil heritage. The metaphors of the preface imply a scientific purpose, as if Galsworthy thought of himself as pickling a species for some museum.

The Man of Property (1906), the first of the novels that compose the *Saga,* is best. The trouble is that Irene and her Bosinney, symbols of beauty, never come to life, whereas Soames, whom Galsworthy understood, is enormous and vital. As the *Saga* proceeds through a series of family dinners and conferences, of rather obvious symbols of house, hat, mutton, or picture, the matter disintegrates into the unconvincing affairs of Fleur, Jon, and Mont, creatures of the fast twenties, whom Galsworthy could not know and could not wish to know. What started as excellent satire upon a class that he could anatomize if not transcend is lost in tenderness or, as D. H. Lawrence savagely remarked, in "fake."

Heredity and environment and the effort to escape them are also the theme of the novel of adolescence. This form, which had flourished throughout the nineteenth century, producing *Wilhelm Meister, David Copperfield,* and *Richard Feverel,* received new life toward the end of the century from the science of biology and later from psychology.[1] In novel after novel sensitive lads are apprenticed to life, formed by its forces, rebelling against them, sometimes failing, sometimes emerging in victory. Their

[9] Sagas, combining Galsworthy's pattern with Zola's: G. B. Stern: *The Rakonitz Chronicles* (1932); Louis Golding: *Five Silver Daughters* (1934); Storm Jameson: *The Triumph of Time* (1932); Henry Handel Richardson: *The Fortunes of Richard Mahony* (1930).

[1] Justin O'Brien: *The Novel of Adolescence in France* (1937). Susanne Howe (Nobbe): *Wilhelm Meister and His English Kinsmen* (1930).

trials and errors, like those of rats in a maze, are painfully displayed. And all the horrors of adolescence, the theater of biology and spirit, are examined. The popularity of this form may be traced in part to the philosophy of determinism and in part to the growing revolt against it. The danger, since these novels are commonly autobiographical, is sentimentality. From 1903 onwards almost every first novel by a serious novelist was a novel of adolescence. So usual was the practice that Aldous Huxley in *Crome Yellow,* his first, congratulated himself too soon on having avoided the dangerous tradition. But it produced some of the best novels of the early twentieth century.

The Way of All Flesh (1903), which started the vogue, is not one of these. Samuel Butler wrote this book between 1872 and 1884 to express hatred for his father, admiration for himself, and his dearest prejudices. He could not publish it at once for fear of being disinherited, and since he was his father's parasite, this fear was not irrational. Mainly autobiographical, the book concerns Ernest's apprenticeship to life, his revolt against his father, and its success. His ancestry is traced in an essay on heredity, which in its ebb and flow, says Butler, tends to skip a generation. This happy circumstance keeps Ernest from resembling his father. Ernest's own children, however, inherit his acquired maturity; for, hating Darwin, Butler followed Lamarck. As for environment, Ernest's education through trial and error in religion, money, caste, and marriage occupies the rest of the book. He learns that money is all that matters, that inherited money is the only conceivable kind, that "tangible material prosperity in this world is the safest test of virtue," that "nice people" or those, like Towneley, of superior caste alone are nice, and that there is an impassable gulf between the classes. This Philistine position at which Ernest arrives after all his trials was Butler's own. In his maturity Ernest does what Butler did, thinks what Butler thought, but, happier than he, is able to avenge himself upon his father by inheriting money from another. The trials that precede this victory are painful. He loses money in the stock market, mistakes a nice girl for a whore and lands in jail, marries a bibulous

servant girl because he thought he had to. Cambridge,
which had failed to teach him about the stock market,
nice girls, and whores, was to blame. From this sentimental story one caricature emerges, that of Theobald
Pontifex, the father, who is good because hatred gave
Butler detachment. Hypocrite, bully, Victorian clergyman,
this Philistine is less Philistine than his son and far more
lovable.

Addressing the reader, depending upon statement instead of drama or symbol, Butler evaded art. The isolated
man, driven in upon himself, could not separate himself
from Ernest. But the book is not without incidental merit.
The style is straightforward. Scenes, especially Theobald's
courtship, are excellent, and the epigrams are clever.

The Way of All Flesh was a tremendous success.
Time, which explains much, explains this. The age, prepared by Ibsen and Shaw, was ready for another attack
upon the Victorian family. Converted to Butler, Shaw, a
master of publicity, converted others. At the annual dinners in Butler's honor, at which Shaw, for his own purposes, presided, his assurance that Butler was "advanced"
kept diners from perceiving his middle-class conservatism
and enabled them to confuse personal revenge with criticism. The publication of the *Note-Books* (1912), which
Butler indexed for posterity, and of Jones's carefully
whitewashed biography (1919) expanded the cult. While
intellectuals were finding their affinity in Butler's ideas,
romantic authors found in his happy form the vehicle they
had looked for. Novels of adolescence, each with hateful
father or, sometimes, uncle, abounded. Some are better
than *The Way of All Flesh,* but none was of more importance.

In *Clayhanger* (1910), Bennett, who liked Butler, followed his pattern. The quarrel with the father, the struggle
of the sensitive boy to escape the environment which had
partly formed him, the experiments in life are there. Bennett's troubles with his own father gave pattern point. But
Bennett made Darius Clayhanger, the father, a credible
human being; and Edwin, the son, though in part the
author's portrait, is an independent creature. The venge-

ance vowed against his father for thwarting his æsthetic and amorous desires turns to pity. And his struggle with environment is unsuccessful. For Butler's fantasy of wish-fulfillment Bennett substituted reality.[2]

The novels of adolescence that have appeared in England since 1920 depart from Butler's tradition, which departed for America and flowered again in Thomas Wolfe's *Look Homeward, Angel*. *Blindness* (1926), Henry Green's first novel, follows the development of a blinded boy through the stages of caterpillar, chrysalis, and butterfly. The last, supplemented by images of rose and bird, seems to imply adjustment and the realization of creative power. Blindness itself, maybe suggesting inner light, is the center of symbolic insinuations that promise Green's later triumphs. Dylan Thomas's *Portrait of the Artist as a Young Dog* (1940), consisting of brilliantly original stories of the poet's youth, is a quieter evocation of the strange world of his poetry. Exceeding other novels of this sort in frankness and many in value are *Maiden Voyage* (1943) and *In Youth Is Pleasure* (1945) by Denton Welch. But the best books in this tradition are *Of Human Bondage* (1915) by Somerset Maugham and James Joyce's *Portrait of the Artist as a Young Man* (1916).

Philip, the victim of Maugham's clinic, has an uncle in place of the father. Uncle, of course, is a Victorian clergyman, a hypocrite, and a Philistine. Thwarted by uncle, oppressed by nature, Philip endeavors to assert his individuality, only to accept at last the lot of a country doctor. His character and his career are determined by his club foot, his sexual instinct, and circumstance. "He acted as though he were a machine, driven by the two

[2] Novels of adolescence: Henry Handel Richardson: *Maurice Guest* (1908); J. D. Beresford: *The Early History of Jacob Stahl* (1911–15); Compton Mackenzie: *Sinister Street* (1913–14). In 1910 Gilbert Cannan translated Rolland's *Jean-Christophe*, one of the best French examples of the type. Forrest Reid: *Peter Waring* (1937); L. A. G. Strong: *The Garden* (1931); Stephen Spender: *The Backward Son* (1940); Anthony Powell: *A Question of Upbringing* (1951), *Buyer's Market* (1952), *The Acceptance World* (1955); Alexander Baron (Bernstein): *With Hope, Farewell* (1952); Jack Common: *The Ampersand* (1954). Cf. Lawrence's *Sons and Lovers* and May Sinclair's *Mary Olivier*.

forces of his environment and his personality." He sees at
last that all men are "helpless instruments of blind
chance." This Hardyesque determinism presides over his
trials of accountancy, of art in Paris, of medicine, of spec-
ulation in the stock market, of entanglements with women.
His affair with Mildred, the waitress, is almost too painful.
Like obscure Jude, he is compelled to love his "vulgar
slut" despite all reason and his loathing and to return to
her again and again. This mechanical experience, however,
helps him to understand the meaning of life. He sees that,
like the figure of Cronshaw's carpet, it has no meaning.
This knowledge, which he has sought for years, brings acceptance at last and a kind of happiness. If his philoso-
phizing sounds like a sophomore's, it must be remembered
that he is young and that Maugham, as he showed again
in *The Razor's Edge*, is fascinated by adolescent philosophy. Maugham's style is plain but not, as in the Ashenden
stories, felicitous. His detachment, ironic to the point of
indifference, is scientific. He differs from Butler, his chief
model, not only in this but in adherence to the arts of
Maupassant. These auspices and his craft produced one of
the more depressing masterpieces of English realism.

A Portrait of the Artist, the story of Stephen Dedalus,
concerns his formation by the Jesuits, whom he disliked,
and by his country, his experiments with sin and repentance, his conflict with father and mother. For the sake of
artistic integrity he determines to detach himself from
environment, and though he remains essentially attached,
he succeeds to the point of using what he is. The pattern
of his struggle and development is the pattern of this kind
of fiction. That Joyce had Butler in mind is shown by
Simon Dedalus, the father, whom literary convention made
Stephen despise. Joyce liked his father, an agreeable man,
capable of saying when shown Brancusi's abstraction of
his son as a bedspring: "Well, Jim hasn't changed much."
Joyce followed the pattern, but the pattern directed genius.
The *Portrait* is by far the greatest English novel of adolescence. Its early version, *Stephen Hero*, first printed in
1944, enables us to admire the selection, emphasis, and
style, the attached detachment, of Joyce's artistic maturity.

It was this maturity that prevented the dangers of sentiment. Like all novelists of adolescence, Joyce was writing
about himself and his conflict with the hostile world, but
he regarded himself as another. The essential words of his
title, as he himself observed, are *as a Young Man*. In
presenting him Joyce approximated Stephen's ideal of the
artist, who, "like the God of the creation, remains within
or behind or beyond or above his handiwork, invisible,
refined out of existence, indifferent, paring his fingernails."

Ulysses (1922), which continues the story of Stephen,
brings to their British climax the French traditions of realism and art. The bright, solid reconstruction of Dublin and
the scenes of degradation may owe something, if not
much, to Zola. The impersonality, form, and firmness of
the whole are in the tradition of Flaubert, to whose tradition we must also ascribe the style, the fixing of the unique
impression by the precise noun, adjective, verb, and
rhythm. Though this great novel is less scientific than symbolist and humane, the penultimate chapter, the return of
Odysseus to Ithaca, is the logical development of the
scientific method in literature—and its parody. Proceeding
by scientific or catechismal question and answer, this chapter reduces all things to matter, space, and motion, presents man in the world of mechanical physics, and provides a cross-section of the scientific mind, Bloom's mind
in contrast to Stephen's.[3]

The fiction of cause and effect (naturalism and, to
some extent, the story of adolescence) declined because
the universe it celebrated died. Pure mathematics took the
place of mechanism and biology, determinism with all its
causes and effects gave way to atomic free will and statisti-

[3] Biographies: Herbert Gorman (1939), Richard Ellmann (forthcoming). Critical introductions: Harry Levin (1941), W. Y. Tindall
(1950), W. P. Jones (1955), Hugh Kenner (1956); John Slocum
and Herbert Cahoon: *A Bibliography of James Joyce* (1953). Stanislaus
Joyce and Ellsworth Mason, editors: *The Early Joyce: the Book Reviews, 1902–1903* (1955). Marvin Magalaner and Richard Kain: *Discovering Joyce* (1956). For details of biography see: Leon Edel: *James
Joyce, the Last Journey* (1947); J. F. Byrne: *Silent Years* (1953);
Oliver Gogarty: *It Isn't This Time of Year at All!* (1954); W. R.
Rodgers, editor: *Portrait of James Joyce* (1950), transcription of a
B.B.C. program.

cal probability. No longer a machine, the universe became
a thought, matter a wave, and wave a fiction. Time complicated space, which unimaginably curves. In short, the
universe of the engineer-physicist, where Darwin's creatures grew, gave place, if there is place, to the universe
of the mathematical physicist and he alone can think it;
for he alone can multiply the time-space continuum by
the square root of minus one, which does not exist. This
unthinkable universe is the creation of Max Planck, whose
quantum theory (1900), all but destroying cause and
effect, made nature discontinuous, and of Einstein, who
in 1905 welded space with time, energy with mass and
velocity. "E," he said, equals "mc^2." Since, as Jeans observes, this universe is mysterious, news of it took time to
descend from laboratory and thinking-room to literary
circle. Even Wells, though he spoke of four dimensions in
the nineties and in an essay cast doubt upon predictability,
waited until the 1920's to say more. It was in this decade
that philosophical mathematicians, possessed of limpid
style and poetic imagination, spread the news. As far as
literary people were concerned the new physics was an
invention of the twenties. *The Mysterious Universe* (1930)
by Sir James Jeans is the clearest of these books. Proceeding by concrete analogy, his admirable prose leads almost
to the understanding of what words cannot express.[4]

The effect of these books, though in some cases no
doubt indirect, was pervasive. They confirmed the old romantic distaste for mechanism and matter, supplying the
war waged by Lawrence, Woolf, and Aldous Huxley on
both. To these romantics Hardy's universe seemed antiquated, Zola's objective reality unreal. And the new
physics, unlike the old, could not deny the religious possibilities of which they dreamed; for if electrons have free
will, and matter is thought, there may be a place in the
crumpled continuum for angels or a god. The new physics
encouraged the subjective novelists, already encouraged by
psychoanalysis. Although the stream of consciousness was

[4] A. N. Whitehead: *Science and the Modern World* (1925).
Bertrand Russell: *The A B C of Atoms* (1923). Arthur Eddington:
The Nature of the Physical World (1928).

designed before the discontinuous continuum, and consciousness is thought by Jeans to 'lie outside it, the stream of consciousness is as discontinuous as the stream of quanta. Although the illogical conduct of heroines and heroes in these novels and those of Lawrence owes much to Dostoyevsky and Freud, their attractiveness may have been increased by the conduct of matter. The new physics, hastening the rejection of Taine's historical criticism in favor of the analysis of separate virtues, immune to cause and effect, affected criticism. This is not to say that William Empson read Jeans and immediately applied him; but he had created a climate where critics too must live. Physical discontinuity as well as psychological free association may lie behind the incoherence of poetry, in which casual meetings and departures parallel the behavior of electrons. If it is the business of literature to arrange or to reflect reality, there is nothing odd about the appearance of a discontinuous literature in the age of physical discontinuity. Since Niels Bohr, who invented the atom, prefers this hypothesis to that because this is more "elegant" than that, it may be that science and æsthetics, despite old quarrels, are of a kind; and it may be that Roger Fry and Einstein, enjoying sofas in the same chamber of paradise, are served by the same brisk cherub.

Without better evidence than parallels and the former laws of cause and effect provide, all this, of course, is tentative. But some important works unmistakably illustrate the new physics. *The Waves* (1931) by Virginia Woolf is a symbolical demonstration of Jeans's statement that all is waves. Having little use for such symbolism, Shaw made his talkers talk about the new physics. Although he attacked it in *St. Joan* (1923) as evidence of modern credulity, he was delighted with the death of determinism, which he had religiously defied. In *Too True to Be Good* (1931) The Elder, an old-fashioned materialist, laments the end of Newton's universe. The capricious electron obeys no law, he complains, and "the calculable world has become incalculable." In *Finnegans Wake* (1939) Joyce presents the universe of relativity, and, in spite of Jeans, of cyclical regeneration. The private universe Joyce created is finite, discontinuous, and curved. That he had the new physics in mind is proved by his references to the quantum theory, the "abnihilisation of the etym," and the expanding universe, and by such phrases as "Eins within a space" and "whorled without aimed." As Hardy's *Dynasts* is the greatest exploitation of the old universe, so *Finnegans Wake* of the new.

CHAPTER SIX: *The Hunt for a Father*

F R O M Blake's time to Lawrence's, men of feeling lamented a world in which physics, displacing metaphysics, limited reality to matter. The world of their desire extended from matter to spirit. In that world a chain of being, connecting all things by correspondences, linked microcosm or man himself with macrocosm. That was the world of the astrologers, who, since celestial and human bodies were analogous, could predict man's future by the stars and earn a decent living. It was the world of the alchemists, who, by increasing the spiritual contents of baser metals, could turn them into gold. And it was the world of those who could speak with assurance about choirs of angels, music of the spheres, and siren song. Although it would not work, it was a good world and a hopeful one in which all things, whether souls or metals, could be promoted a little or refined.

This happy order, made to fit man's emotions and his need for unity, was so tightly constructed that doubt cast upon one part imperiled the whole. Copernicus and Galileo cast such doubts. The new philosophy, said Donne, as his world fell about his ears, puts all in doubt. Indifferent to poets and their anguish, followers of Bacon and Newton gave a kind of unpoetic stability to the eighteenth century by omitting metaphysics from the universe of their design. Safe in the horizontal world of physics, few regretted the vertical. Poets became exact and descriptive, scanning lines without presuming God to scan.[1]

But this universe, which denied so much, was too limited and artificial to last. Long before it died in its turn men of feeling had rebelled against it. The transcendental revolt that began in the eighteenth century, impairing its stability, has continued to our time. Even after the universe of Darwin and Newton yielded to the newer physics, which replaced determinism early in the twentieth century, the spiritual revolt against materialism persisted because news of the new disorder was slow to get around among poets who had not taken calculus. Where it did get around, the physics of discontinuity, permitting various kinds of truth on different levels, encouraged spiritual exercise.

Some turned to Rome, some, for whom science had made Western orthodoxy untenable, found comfort in Hinduism or Theosophy, others in amateur religions like vitalism. Seeking the reunion of matter and spirit, these transcendentalists sought personal integration. The reunion of matter and spirit symbolized union of self and world and, beyond this, of the unconscious with the conscious. Religions offered ends and means. If these religions had been kept out of polite literature, they would not concern us, but they have had an enormous effect, at times producing sermons, at others poetry.

Samuel Butler, the first of these romantic men in our time, was destined for holy orders. After going down from Cambridge in 1858, he became a lay worker in the slums. But he was unsettled by a difficulty: the good little boys in his care had not been baptized, the bad ones had. This, together with inconsistencies he detected in the Gospels, led him to refuse ordination. His disappointed father sent young Butler to New Zealand, where instead of becoming a pastor he became a shepherd.

To increase his disillusionment he read Strauss and the other "higher critics" who were examining the Scrip-

---

[1] E. M. W. Tillyard: *The Elizabethan World Picture* (1943). R. G. Collingwood: *The Idea of Nature* (1945). Marjorie Nicolson: *The Breaking of the Circle* (1950).

tures with scientific zeal, and in 1861 he read Darwin. In "Darwin on Origin of Species" (1862), the first of three articles Butler contributed to New Zealand newspapers, he announced his acceptance of the new doctrine, chance variation and all. He was answered, to his delight, by a bishop. In hope of another, he devoted "Darwin among the Machines" (1863) and "Lucubratio Ebria" (1865) to playful applications of Darwinism. Machines, he said, developing by the same mechanical laws that control animal and man, may supplant us; and since "a fertile union between two steam engines" is unlikely, man, a slave to machines, will serve to reproduce them. In the second of these articles Butler saw machines as limbs and those who possessed most limbs as fittest. No bishop disputed this capitalistic sentiment.[2]

These articles provided Butler on his return to England with the main ideas of *Erewhon* (1872), a Utopia in reverse. Seeing the danger of being supplanted by machines, the Erewhonians had abolished them. This book with its excellent introductory narrative, its direct style, its effective satire against church, university, and criminal code, is imperfect only because Butler, unable to decide where he stood, could not maintain a tone. He is sometimes serious, sometimes ironic, always too copious. The ironic accounts of Chowbok's baptism and of the Musical Banks reflect the author's recent emancipation from sham. Higgs, the hero, is at once the author's spokesman and his victim. The section on machines, the best in the book, is serious; for Butler, in the odd position of accepting Darwin's mechanical system while rejecting machines, seems to have seen something of the danger to man in his growing dependence upon them. The efficient prose is the triumph of

[2] Henry Festing Jones: *Samuel Butler* (1919). Malcolm Muggeridge: *The Earnest Atheist* (1936). Butler: *A First Year in the Canterbury Settlement* (1914) contains the New Zealand tracts.

Mrs. Humphrey Ward's *Robert Elsmere* (1888), the most popular and the most earnest novel of the eighties, takes its theme from the higher criticism. Clerical Elsmere reads Germans, gets doubts, succumbs. Albert Schweitzer: *The Quest of the Historical Jesus* (1948), a survey of the higher criticism.

all the ideas of utility that scientists, Puritans, and men of business had carefully fostered from the time of Bacon. In all but his fear of machinery Butler proves himself in this book to be the child of science and his class.

Fair Haven (1873), his chief contribution to the higher criticism, exposes the inconsistencies of the four Gospels and the myth of the Resurrection. Pious reviewers, unaccustomed to irony, mistook it for earnestness and Butler's mock defense of faith for its defense; and even Darwin, to whom Butler sent a copy in the hope of impious applause, was not amused. Darwin and the pious reviewers were more discerning than Butler, who, distracted with admiration of his wickedness, failed to see that his book, in which irony quarrels with sentiment and skepticism with vague aspiration, is more earnest than wicked. For irony a point of view is requisite. Of his models, Swift had faith, Gibbon skepticism. But Butler, betwixt and between, reflects the confusions of his age.

In *Erewhon Revisited* (1901), a sequel to *Fair Haven* and *Erewhon*, Butler shows the development of a religious myth. The ascent of Higgs in a balloon had been interpreted with some reason by the unmechanical Erewhonians as the Ascension and exploited by the clergy. Attempting wickedness again, Butler succeeded in being more tiresome and much more sentimental.

Butler was less ironic shepherd than lost sheep. But Darwin, who had made return to the Church of England impossible, offered no solace for the yearner. Butler began to resent Darwin for destroying what he could not replace. Moreover, at tea one day with Darwin, misinterpreting Darwin's British demeanor as the sign of coldness and contempt, Butler found himself hating the scientist. Driven by his need and his dislike, he proceeded to invent a substitute for the religion Darwin had destroyed, something that would satisfy mind and feeling at once and baffle Darwin.

The idea of evolution still appealed to Butler, but evolution by chance variation offended his need of spiritual design. He made a private religion by removing Darwin from evolution and substituting Lamarck, whose giraffe owed his neck not to chance but to desire. The religious tracts that Butler proceeded to write attack the mechanical, mindless universe of Darwin and, replacing luck by cunning, reintroduce mind and purpose into nature.[3] "Faith and hope," said Butler, beckon the world of chance and blindness to his dream. Ignorant of science, he attributed equal ignorance to Darwin and Huxley, whose foolish theory of protoplasm Butler demolished. That later men corrected Darwin does not make faith or hope a better instrument of correction. He wisely ignored the pugnacious amateur, who, failing to correct him, liked him less.

This one-sided quarrel had no common terms. Darwin, according to his tradition, inhabited the world of physics. Butler, in revolt against this tradition, demanded metaphysics. Darwin was concerned with immediate causes, Butler with final causes. Darwin asked how, Butler why. Less one-sided than Darwin, Butler was trying to combine physics with metaphysics again. But their unfortunate separation needed stronger glue than his.

The religion of Samuel Butler may be called vitalism. This neo-Lamarckian faith celebrates the progress of the life force, which penetrates matter and, improving it by desire, design, and purpose, makes spottier bodies or longer necks. In his later years Butler called his hopeful faith Broad Church, a name as good as another for evolution without Darwin and Christianity without Christ. This religion is expounded in *Erewhon Revisited;* and it is to this religion that Ernest turns after his trials and errors.

Having attended to Darwinism, Butler turned to other heresies and shams. In free-verse poems he disconcerted the entrenched rhymesters, in tracts the entrenched and indifferent scholars.[4] In *Narcissus* (1888), a Handelian

---

[3] *Life and Habit* (1878), *Evolution Old and New* (1879), *Unconscious Memory* (1880), *Luck or Cunning* (1887).

[4] *The Authoress of the Odyssey* (1897), *Shakespeare's Sonnets Reconsidered* (1899). Of the poems (printed in *The Note-Books*) the best, and Butler's most successful work, is "A Psalm of Montreal" (1878).

cantata, he confounded the entrenched musicians. These confusions of heresy illustrate that final success of Protestantism in which every man his own church assails from within its walls the heresy without. His transcendentalism, as divided as his age, carried him above all matter but money and above all categories but those of caste. In his last years, not quite alone in his belief, he found a convert in Bernard Shaw.

In the preface to *Man and Superman* (1905) Shaw declares himself a preacher with a popular method, and his conscience the "genuine pulpit article." When he said that, he smiled; for what he said, however odd it sounds, is true enough. Although as Protestant as Butler and more of a puritan, Shaw as a boy had little religion to lose, soon lost what he had, and spent much of his subsequent career seeking a suitable substitute for what he should have had. He had had no formal creed, but he had the religious impulse, which, like Freud's sex, when repressed in one place, reappears in another. In a more favorable time Shaw might have been Bunyan, whom he admired above most other men; but in the nineteenth century he was compelled to become a playwright. It is not altogether correct to say that his plays are sermons; for, confusing the two, he produced something with the beauties of both kinds and few of their defects.

Every age has its idiom. That of the nineteenth century was not religious. At first Shaw expressed his religious ideas under the guise of socialism, as during the seventeenth century, when the idiom was religious, lay preachers expressed their social ideas under the guise of religion. However satisfactory socialism was to his intellect, it left his emotions unappeased. In 1896 Nietzsche, newly translated into English, presented in the idea of the unsocialistic superman an object for Shaw's groping devotion. The name rather than the idea was new to Shaw, for supermen, equally beyond good and evil, had served him as heroes of his novels and plays for many years. Provided now with a name and a more splendid destiny, Shaw's hero acquired from Wagner's Siegfried an even more heroic deportment and took his place alongside Bunyan's Christian in a private pantheon.[5]

Dick Dudgeon, the hero of *The Devil's Disciple* (1899), a Nietzschean superman, is compared not only to Siegfried but to Shelley's Prometheus. A puritan by inclination, he is forced by the nature of society to abandon organized religion, now the property of the middle class, and take the Devil's side or romantic private religion. This excellent allegory, which reflects Shaw's own nature and development, rejects materialistic society as well as philosophical materialism.

Taken with old unsuccessful Butler, whom he met in 1897, Shaw permitted him to lecture on Nausicaa before the Fabians, six of whom attended. Not content with this, Shaw persuaded a publisher to accept *Erewhon Revisited*, and after Butler's death, in 1902, he secured too late by ceaseless propaganda the fame that Butler had always wanted. This propaganda began with the preface to *Major Barbara* (1905), in which Shaw credits Butler with the discovery of "mystical vitalism." It was this that Shaw took from Butler to add to his private religion. The superman of Nietzsche and Wagner was to be produced by Butler's Lamarckian life force, struggling through matter with the aid of desire and purpose. This up-to-date religion involved, like Butler's, the excommunication of science. By its happy union of physics with metaphysics it satisfied emotions and intellect as well.

The attack upon the science of medicine in *The Doctor's Dilemma* (1906) follows from Shaw's religious position, which was fully expounded in *Man and Superman*. This work, says Shaw in his preface, is a Bible for the "modern religion of evolution." The heroine of the play, directed by the life force, seeks a father for the superman and, despite his protests, finds one. The interlude, which interrupts this pursuit, is a round-table discussion, hilarious

[5] "Nietzsche in English," *Dramatic Opinions; The Perfect Wagnerite* (1898); preface to *The Devil's Disciple* (1899). Eric Bentley: *A Century of Hero-Worship* (1944), *Bernard Shaw* (1947).

The preface to *Androcles and the Lion* (1913) is Shaw's principal attempt at the higher criticism.

and tedious by turns, of Shaw's religion by the characters
of Mozart's *Don Giovanni*. At the end of the play itself
Tanner's enormous speeches, which, apparently directed at
our minds alone, have become increasingly tiresome, are
suddenly elevated by Ann's curtain line to comic triumph.
Never, we discover, has discourse functioned less discursively or in the service of greater insight. What seemed
a sermon emerges, transfigured, as brilliant drama.

In *Back to Methuselah, a Metabiological Pentateuch*
(1924) "the most advanced man" of his time, having
come across Bergson ten years late, added creative evolution to his vitalistic synthesis. The preface to this play, one
of the best commentaries upon the battle between science
and aspiration, is an attack upon the "materialistic nihilism" of the nineteenth century, under which the soul
starved. As antidote to Darwin and food for the soul, the
"vitalist philosopher," as he calls himself, offers Butler's
Lamarckian evolution once again under its new name,
and, he says, he awaits disciples.

Saint Joan (1923), Shaw's most popular play, also
concerns the life force. But instead of making his creatures
sit around talking about it, Shaw discussed it himself in the
preface and dramatized it in the play. He approved of
Joan, for although her imagination made use of an old-
fashioned religious iconography to express the life force,
she was a superwoman whose religion is nearer the truth
than the gospel of St. Louis Pasteur or the other saints
created by modern credulity. Taking her from the Papists
and saving her from materialists, Shaw makes her a saint
of his own faith. But almost alone among human beings
she appealed to him less as a representative of something
else than as a person. For this reason he could create a
living woman with a life independent of his intellect. Yet
much of her strength comes from the significance he alone
detected and artistically used.

Subsequent years saw the cooling of Shaw's religious
fervor. Increasingly political in character, as the times demanded, his prefaces and plays continue to mention his
diet and his faith. But he became so lukewarm about them
that in the preface to *On the Rocks* (1933) he refers to

his creed of creative evolution as a "provisional hypothesis," a "useful illusion," differing from older creeds in this and, unlike them, continually adapted to the times. For the coming state he tolerantly advises creeds for different capacities. In the preface to *The Six of Calais* (1934), removing another of his prophetical robes, he says:

> Now a playwright's direct business is simply to provide the theatre with a play. When I write one with the additional attraction of providing the twentieth century with an up-to-date religion or the like, that luxury is thrown in gratuitously; and the play, simply as a play, is not necessarily either the better or the worse for it.

The playwright with a private religion, since he constitutes his church, must be priest as well as artist, and though it may be his business to write plays, it is his plain duty to preach. According to the doctrine of art for art's sake or the æsthetic theory of Stephen Dedalus, the art of such an artist, being didactic, cannot be good. If the artist is good enough, however, whatever his intention, his work is likely to be art. Shaw, like Bunyan, was usually good enough.

The religious impulse, which turns literature to tract, has no power to injure tract. For this reason the works of Samuel Butler escaped all injury. And the only effect of this impulse upon Shaw was to make those abstract interminable dialogues longer and more abstract. Intellectual by nature, and more at home in essay or debate than play, Shaw wrote prefaces that sometimes dwarf their plays. And many of the plays, avoiding character, action, and symbol, ape their prefaces in explicitness. Shaw, said Shavian Beerbohm, would be a good dramatist if he wrote plays. Under these circumstances religion could but add at times to the intellectual load a transcendental straw.

Not always plays in the usual sense, Shaw's plays brought new intellectual vigor to the theater and with it brilliance, grotesqueness, gaiety, a few substantial characters, and Shaw's bright inhuman smile. These virtues, creating a kind of drama, give life to the roundest tables. Shaw is not unlike the man who told Dr. Johnson that although he had tried to be a philosopher, cheerfulness would break through.

The religion of H. G. Wells is no less symptomatic of our disorder. Half schoolmaster, half visionary, he arrived in his later years at a religion of humanity, secular and benevolent, not unlike that of Comte. The high priests of this unmetaphysical faith, which he offered as a substitute for old theology, were scientists, its prophet Wells.

The Open Conspiracy (1928), the key to Wells's later work, is the bible of this religion. "This is, I declare," says Wells, "the truth and the way of salvation." Though once deficient in a religious sense and a rebel against religion before he had any, he now feels that what is wrong with the world is the want of religion. The old religions are of no use to order chaos. Only a new one will do; and the best of new religions is the world state. It is his hope that religious men, reading his books to one another, will advance his plan. Far from being a union of physics and metaphysics, this modern religion is the elevation of physics by faith and hope to a plane where it may move men's hearts.

Wells regarded his later works, both expository and fictional, as tracts for this religion. The purpose of his outlines and guides is clear. And in "A Digression about Novels" he explains the purpose and character of his later novels. The objection that he fails to write the old kind of novel is irrelevant, he says; for, driven by his hope, he is writing a new kind of novel based on Plato's dialogues and the Book of Job. *The World of William Clissold* (1926), that monstrous monologue on all things, serves to illustrate what social purpose inflamed by piety can do to fiction.

Butler, Shaw, and Wells revived religion and adjusted it to the world about them. More transcendental than these, Yeats, Lawrence, and Huxley, turning back the clock, recovered a former piety. They saved self and world not by reuniting physics with metaphysics, but by fleeing

to a time when they were united. This happy time is represented by the Oriental or the occult, by Hinduism, alchemy, or the wisdom of Mme Blavatsky.

"I am very religious," says Yeats in his *Autobiography*,
"and deprived by Huxley and Tyndall, whom I detested,
of the simple-minded religion of my childhood, I . . .
made a new religion, almost an infallible church, of poetic
tradition." His scriptures were the spiritual, the old, and
the imaginative, his prophets adepts or poets. The arts, he
says in an essay, "are about to take upon their shoulders
the burdens that have fallen from the shoulders of priests."
At first a refuge from the middle class, this poetic church
excited his imagination and provided for a time the illusion of unity.

The works of Shelley and Blake were among Yeats's
sacred books, and to them he soon added those of the
Theosophists. Theosophy, founded by Mme Blavatsky in
1875, is a synthetic religion that, embracing the Oriental
and the occult, is good for those who are weary of Huxley
and Tyndall. A. P. Sinnett was Blavatsky's apostle to the
British, and Colonel H. S. Olcott her apostle to the Americans. In 1885 Yeats read Sinnett's *Esoteric Buddhism*
(1883), an account of reincarnation. Excited, he showed
the book to A. E. and Charles Johnston; and together
they founded in Dublin a Hermetic Society, which Sinnett
chartered in 1886 as the Dublin Lodge of the Theosophical
Society. At their meetings these vegetarians discussed
Blavatsky's *Isis Unveiled* (1877) and, when it appeared in
1888, her *Secret Doctrine*. On Blavatsky's arrival in London in 1887, Yeats visited her and was permitted to smell
spectral incense, hear spectral bells. Following her advice,
he placed the ashes of a rose in the receiver of an air-
pump, reduced the pressure, placed the apparatus in the
moonlight, and watched all night for the ghost of the rose.

When, in 1885, Yeats also became a poet, his poems,
of course, reflected his spiritual interests and the nature
of society. The heroine of the closet drama *Mosada*
(1886), summoning phantoms by her art, exclaims: "I'm
eastern-hearted once again." Such fancies, whether Eastern
or Western, offered the poet refuge from men of science,

"merchants grey," and from time, change, and confusion.

Yeats improved his wisdom in the late 1880's by joining in London the Order of the Golden Dawn, a Rosicrucian, cabbalistic, and alchemical cult under the direction of MacGregor Mathers. References to the cabbala and to famous alchemists like Lully, Flamel, and Paracelsus began to appear in Yeats's poetry and his prose. Pledged to read all occult literature he could come by, Yeats seems to have been faithful to his vow.

MacGregor Mathers enjoyed familiar relations with two societies in France, the Martinists, under Papus, a follower of Eliphas Lévi, and the Kabalistic Order of the Rosy Cross, under Stanislas de Guaita, the "magus," who offered magic and alchemy as antidotes to materialism. And to French poets rebelling against the bourgeoisie, he offered that "unity of being" which was the desire of the nineteenth century. Through the doctrine of Hermes, "as above, so below," the seekers of his time might discover that harmony of matter and spirit for which they looked. Seeking these things, Yeats visited the Martinists in Paris during the nineties and on one occasion at least saw great Guaita at his home. Excursions to these awful places, where mysteries were celebrated under the image of the Sabbatic Goat and alchemists sought the formula for Hermetic gold, gave Yeats the pleasing sense of being magus as well as poet. In 1896 Yeats drew upon Guaita to furnish his Rosicrucian story "Rosa Alchemica." Michael Robartes, the hero, is a magus, using alchemy for spiritual exercise. But it is Yeats's poems that bear in theme and image the weight of this wisdom.

In "Fergus and the Druid," King Fergus abandons the real world of politics to become an Irish magus and poet. Immediately he is oppressed by unspeakable knowledge. Politics was bad; magic and metempsychosis are worse. The occult, Yeats felt, was what a poet needed in order to free himself from matter; but at the same time he knew that a poet's place is the real world, not the world of dream. Oisin, who flees time, change, and the implacable laws of nature for the Land of Youth in *The Wanderings of Oisin,* is unhappy there; for evil is needed for happiness as well as good. "To Ireland in the Coming Times" expresses fear that the occult may separate the poet from his nation, and hope that, though haunted by elemental spirits and the "red-rose-bordered hem," he may yet be one with Davis, Mangan, Ferguson.

"Who Goes with Fergus?" the most enigmatic and the best of the early poems, can be understood only in the context of these poems and this situation. Fergus is a poet or magus who, like Yeats, has abandoned reality, not politics this time, but love; for Yeats was suffering his first disappointment with Maud Gonne. Fergus has regressed, like Oisin, to the Land of Youth, that "woven" or integrated place where love can bother him no more. An invitation to leave this world with Fergus and be as happy as children in the womb, this poem celebrates a passing mood. Such retreats, whether to infancy, the Lake Isle of Innisfree, or the occult, brought Yeats a bitterness that drove him to confront and flee again his love, his nation, and his world.

These poems, representing in rhythm, tone, and diction all that was opposite to his world, seemed sentimental to older Yeats. The occult, which had helped give them this character, now seemed no less unsatisfactory. Far from giving Yeats the integration he desired, the occult had replaced the chaos of the world by a more shadowy chaos. For relief he confronted Ireland, and the world of the middle class that he had fled was now his arena. His poems became harder, colder, more precise. But Yeats's old interests were dormant, not dead.

"The Phases of the Moon" (1919), a didactic poem, announced an occult system of his own, fully expounded in the prose of *A Vision* (1925). At first he ascribed this system to the researches of Michael Robartes, but after some further attempts at mystification he confessed in *A Packet for Ezra Pound* (1929) that certain benevolent demons had dictated the whole business to Mrs. Yeats, a medium. Their revelation, which presents the nature of man, his history, and the progress of the soul under the symbolism of the moon and its twenty-eight phases, seems, however, to be the poet's work. Rewriting it in 1937, Yeats made it even more complicated and less readable. But that a poet of the Celtic twilight could command that intricate geometry improves the effect by wonder.

For this system, inspired partly by Blake's, Yeats seems to have combined astrology, Plato's great year, the Hindu symbol of light and dark fortnights, and the Buddhist wheel of destiny with Sinnett's metempsychosis. On the whole the system may be regarded as a simplification of astrology. The moon is taken, like the stars, as a sign of that union of microcosm and macrocosm which enables one to account for present, past, and future. Yeats used astrological and alchemical symbols on his diagram of the wheel. The moon and wheel, like the earlier rose, appear to signify unity and generation.

This system made Yeats at home in the world. Reconciling spirit and matter, self and world, it gave him the framework our age desires and with it unity and myth. Yeats's poems now, like Dante's, could depend for image and reference upon something external to themselves. By explaining confusion as part of a great order, Yeats could confront and use what he abhorred, and almost alone could be man of the world and poet too.

Yeats's system had further values. Ridding him of abstractions that had plagued him for years, it left him free to write the poems it inspired. And sending him for corroboration and support to the records of the past, it gave him a liberal education, such acquaintance with the European tradition from Homer to Jung that he could fill his poems with common images and references to familiar knowledge. Through his private system he became a public poet.

To be sure, some of the later poems, such as "The Double Vision of Michael Robartes," which refers to the first and fifteenth phases of the moon, are unintelligible without reference to *A Vision*, which Yeats published to help readers through poems like this. And though "Byzantium" has every appearance of unity and though such images as the dome are readily intelligible, the poem remains enigmatic in parts even with the help of *A Vision*. Such privacy is uncommon.

That apocalyptic poem "The Second Coming," presenting the disintegration to be expected at the end of a cycle, presents a vision of our time. In a nightmare from Blavatsky's Anima Mundi or Lévi's Astral Light, Yeats sees how the Sphinx, a symbol of the previous cycle, was vexed at the rocking cradle of Christ, and he wonders what symbolic beast will represent the approaching cycle. Despite the elaborate implications, the images are plain to the common understanding. Even more public in character, "Two Songs from a Play" requires no reference to *A Vision,* for Yeats presented his idea in images that have been familiar for two thousand years. His virgin is the Virgin and his wheel is Plato's year.

Public and private at once, "Sailing to Byzantium," like all great works of art, says what cannot be said another way. Sense cannot be separated from sensation nor sensation from rhythm, feeling, and tone. But while the whole remains inexplicable, the parts may be explained and their functions determined. "The mackerel-crowded seas" summarizes the world's condition, struggle, limited survival, and time. Part of its power comes from the unconscious symbolism, part from inevitable statement, and part from contrast with neighboring abstractions, "those dying generations" and the trite, mysterious trinity of "fish, flesh, or fowl." The single word "commend" is by position and tone the central magic of the stanza. Caught in that noble rhythm, the dissonance of time yields in the last couplet to anticipations of timelessness. But even here the tone is complex, and one becomes aware that compulsory timelessness is but an old man's substitute for time. The idea of this voyage, having come from Yeats's unconscious, had smoldered so long in his consciousness, forming many poems, that now, glowing, it emerged final, easy, and triumphant.

Noting that his later poetry had gained in assurance and power, Yeats ascribed the improvement to his wheel. But one may wonder with Katharine Tynan how far a man of his intelligence believed what he professed. "Some will ask," says Yeats in *A Packet for Ezra Pound,* "if I believe all that this book contains and I will not know how to answer." This important question, however, had been answered earlier in other essays. Of his occult studies in Paris he had said: "My critical mind . . . mocked, and yet I was delighted." Not intellect but imagination needed the excitement, myth, and unity that our age could not provide. He intelligently invented what he wanted. The pragmatic occultist, never as transcendental as he seemed, was first of all a poet.

Reproving the folly of Yeats, Lawrence, and Wells, I. A. Richards in *Science and Poetry* (1926), the neatest of his books, observes that science, which deals with references, is right, religion, which deals with emotive terms, wrong. To satisfy our emotions without the danger of believing what is wrong, Richards suggests that poetry, which also consists of emotive terms and pseudo-statements, may take the place of religion. Annoyed by this pragmatic attitude toward belief, T. S. Eliot accused Richards of confusing poetry with religion. He might have been accused more reasonably of confusing Yeats's religion with religion; for he failed to see that Yeats's substitute for religion was as pragmatic as his own.

But in his last years Yeats returned to Hinduism. Poems in *The King of the Great Clock Tower* (1934) celebrate this return and his friendship with a learned yogi named Shri Purohit Swami, whom he met in 1931. His introductions to the swami's works assert that Hinduism, seen at last without Blavatsky's aid, satisfies mind and feeling and gives unity to the chaos of occult experience. In his new enthusiasm he wrote an essay on the "Mandookya Upanishad" for Eliot's *Criterion,* and with the swami's help translated *The Ten Principal Upanishads* (1937). Yeats, though old and ill, undertook these labors to provide young poets with a more public myth than his *Vision,* to which he referred less and less. And the excellent poetry of these final years is secular.

Unlike Yeats, George Russell (A. E.) was a mystic. He also became a member of the Dublin Lodge, where he read the Upanishads, the yoga aphorisms, and the works of Mme Blavatsky. His paintings and poems[6] are the product of mystical raptures with which critical intelligence was not permitted to interfere.

The Candle of Vision (1918) is A. E.'s spiritual autobiography. Given to trances and visions from early youth, he says, he spent half his time in Anima Mundi, whence he returned to paint pictures of what he saw there or write poems about it. In Song and Its Fountains (1932) he tells how easy it is for a mystic to write verse. Going into a trance, he receives the poem from spirits and sets it down with automatic hand. On waking, the poet reads with surprise and gratitude the finished poem. These early Theosophical visions are diffuse and misty, typical in diction, feeling, and tone of the softer romanticism. Later his visions lost their intensity, and he was compelled to write his own verses.

The practical side of A. E. is represented by his work for Sir Horace Plunkett's Agricultural Society. Going about on a bicycle, A. E. persuaded farmers by talk of fairies to establish co-operative dairies. Of his many books on politics and economics, The National Being (1916), advocating rural communism and Anima Mundi, is representative. Essentially a prophet, though the most agreeable of men, he made economics and art serve piety. Even young Joyce attended A. E.'s Sunday evenings.

Arthur Machen, another Celt, was preoccupied like Huysmans and Yeats with black magic and its horror. To Machen, too, nature seemed a veil embroidered with signs of a reality unveiled at peril, but useful for counteracting science and Maupassant. Enormities are evoked in The Great God Pan (1894), in which Helen Vaughan, an initiate, sends men mad with knowledge. The Three Impostors (1895) discloses the doings of an occult society off Oxford Street in Babylonian London, their Sabbatic rites, and their vengeance upon a faithless member. These stories, which gain their effects through indirection, are chiefly remarkable for their exquisite style. Like "Rosa Alchemica," they unite the worlds of Pater and Huysmans,

[6] Homeward: Songs by the Way (1894); The Earth Breath (1897); Collected Poems (1913); The Living Torch (1937) essays.

and like it are less indicative of worship than of refuge in spiritual horror from the greater horrors of the world.

In contempt of the world that had destroyed the Primitive Methodism of his youth, D. H. Lawrence also found relief from matter and reason in Theosophy. Between 1912 and 1915 he read the works of Mme Blavatsky. Mixing this spiritual literature with anthropology, he made a private religion, which he preached in his novels and essays. Lawrence was an enthusiast and, unlike Yeats, was prophet before poet or novelist. Prophetical purpose sometimes gives his novels of the unconscious a didactic and allegorical character foreign to their substance and makes what should be lyrical a little grim.

In *The Secret Doctrine,* Mme Blavatsky had described Atlantis as a spiritual Utopia from which, after the Flood, swimmers had carried fragments of the truth to shores where today they may be found in the doctrines and symbols of Hindus, American Indians, and Etruscans. Theosophy is an attempt to reassemble this secret doctrine from its fragments and to return in spirit to a better past. That Lawrence shared this endeavor is evident from the preface to *Fantasia of the Unconscious* (1922). And his best novel, *The Plumed Serpent* (1926), recovers the truth of Atlantis from its Aztec vestiges. Here Lawrence, seduced perhaps by the splendor of Mexico, assimilated what he preached and subdued it to purposes of art.[7]

Sometimes, as Lawrence says, a "demon" shook a poem out of him. From Hardyesque descriptions of nature, rhymed but irregular in metre, he progressed to songs of his mother, his body, and his religion. "Virgin Youth," which celebrates his genitals, anticipates the religious preoccupation of his maturity. But the characteristic early poems are those in which he loves his mother, "Piano," for instance, that fine Proustian memory restored by the "great black piano appassionato." These poems have the energy of something overcharged and suddenly released.

[7] For more about Lawrence's occultism see W. Y. Tindall: *D. H. Lawrence and Susan His Cow* (1939). *The Letters of D. H. Lawrence* (1932), edited by Aldous Huxley. Willian Tiverton: *D. H. Lawrence and Human Existence* (1951).

Burningly personal, evading censor and objective correlative alike, they leave him almost naked. When symbols interrupt directness, they are Freud's, used unconsciously at first, then consciously, but—of the most public sort—they complete exposure.

After Lawrence discarded rhyme, an uncongenial impediment, and adopted the rhythms of Whitman, he was even better able to follow the contours of passion. His best poems, those of *Birds, Beasts and Flowers* (1923), express him entirely. Conversational, tender, fierce, and incandescent, they draw morals from figs and other natural things, and prove the poet a Georgian who, having read wonderful books, has left the suburb for a distant pulpit. There like a medieval friar he uses the *exemplum* to compose his bestiary. But whereas Hopkins and the friars used nature to celebrate God, Lawrence, by turns chatty and apocalyptic, uses nature to celebrate nature. His poems of peach, goat, and snake, models of didactic art, are among the first religious poems of our time. Besides satiric trifles, *Last Poems* (1932) contains a few vital lyrics on gentian, for example, and whale. But, death upon him, Lawrence was declining into abstraction. "The Ship of Death," though symbols of apple and ship remain unreconciled, is a good poem, stricter than the others and final by circumstance.[8]

The crusade against science that Lawrence preached by allegory and symbol seems less absurd today than it used to seem. And Aldous Huxley's contention that science has gone far enough is proved by atomic fission and the irresponsibility of scientist, capitalist, and politician. About to be decomposed, we can return with understanding to these prophets. Surely, what we need is one religion or another, preferably both.

Aldous Huxley, Lawrence's disciple, was an apparent cynic when he met the prophet in 1915. War and science had destroyed all meaning; and to express his disgust with the world, Huxley was writing desperate verses and planning elegant novels. Lawrence invited Huxley to join him

[8] *Collected Poems* (1928); *Pansies* (1929); *Nettles* (1930). Horace Gregory: *Pilgrim of the Apocalypse* (1933).

in a Utopia he was going to establish in Florida. Touched
by sincerity and passion, Huxley accepted; but, circumstances preventing Utopia at that time, cynicism resumed.
In *Antic Hay* (1923) Huxley made fun of Lawrence's
chakras. But longing for unity and truth expressed itself
in *Those Barren Leaves* (1925), whose hero retires from
fools and cynics to meditate; and when Huxley met Lawrence again in 1926, both were ready and Huxley succumbed. Rampion, a spiritual man among knaves in *Point
Counter Point* (1928), is Huxley's interpretation of Lawrence. Huxley remained a disciple until Lawrence's death
and, after it, piously edited his letters. The savage from
New Mexico who dies a martyr to H. G. Wells in *Brave
New World* (1932) is Huxley's second portrait of Lawrence. In the absence of Lawrence's attractive presence,
Huxley's fervor cooled, and after going to Mexico to check
up on Lawrence's Indians, as Huxley confesses in *Beyond
the Mexique Bay* (1934), he was disenchanted. But Lawrence, softening Huxley's intellect, had left the former
cynic ready for Gerald Heard.

No less attractive than Lawrence, Heard had the ad-
vantages of respectability and omniscience. For years he
had delivered over the B.B.C. his famous lectures on all
things, and he had written books on the same subject. Anthropology, psychoanalysis, and intuition prove, he says
in *The Social Substance of Religion* (1931), that man's
disunity and that of the world may be cured by religion.
Huxley fell under the influence of the new prophet in
1934 or 1935. After writing tracts for the Peace Pledge
Union, which promoted "the redeeming power of Love"
as a refuge against bombs, Huxley and Heard prudently
left for America. As they traveled, they composed almost
identical tracts, Heard *The Third Morality* and Huxley
Ends and Means, both published in 1937. The mechanical
philosophies of Newton, Darwin, and Freud, they say,
have made life meaningless by ignoring the spirit. Man
needs a new religion to embrace all levels of reality. Samuel Butler and Lamarck have shown the possibility of
spiritual evolution. The wise men of the East have revealed
the power of a vegetable diet and, through yoga and

Buddhistic contemplation, the proper training of the mind-body unit. Heard and Huxley propose, therefore, the improvement of man by spiritual and physical exercises, a diet of vegetables, and systematic meditation.

In *Eyeless in Gaza* (1936) Huxley had told of his conversion to Heard and his system. Anthony Beavis, the hero of this religious novel, meets Mr. Miller, who advises yoga, vegetables, and enemas as cure for skepticism. Immediately convinced, Beavis practices, eats, and takes these things. Meditation and mystical ecstasies improve his sermons for Mr. Miller's Peace Pledge Union. This is the story of Huxley and Heard up to their departure for America.

Finding little to their purpose in the East, they departed for the congenial West, where in Hollywood Heard wrote *Pain, Sex and Time* (1939), a further exposition of his religion, and Huxley *After Many a Summer Dies the Swan* (1939), a fictional twin to Heard's tract. In this novel Mr. Propter presides in California over a little cult of meditators. This neo-Brahmin, like Heard, spends his time transcending personality and time when he is not preaching to the materialists who surround him. He has a greenhouse for the vegetables. *Time Must Have a Stop* (1944), more allusive on the whole, leaves particular treatment of Huxley's religion to the notebook at the end. But Uncle Eustace's limbo is a warning to materialists; Rontini is a reminiscence of Lawrence; and the desperate hero, of course, is converted.[9]

Huxley is less to blame for this perhaps temporary decline than our times, which, making writer prophet and writing tract, invite correction or escape. Some of his later novels illustrate that indifference to art which he proclaims in *Time Must Have a Stop*. Although it is foolish to blame for æsthetic failure one who has abandoned the plane of æsthetics for a higher one, the pity is that good cynics are as uncommon in English literature as preachers are common.

[9] Cf. *Grey Eminence* (1941); *The Devils of Loudun* (1952); *The Perennial Philosophy* (1945); *Science, Liberty and Peace* (1946). See David Daiches: *The Novel and the Modern World* (1939).

Around 1940 Huxley came under the influence of Swami Prabhavananda of the Ramakrishna Mission, who, in his miniature Taj Mahal in Hollywood, expounds the Hindu scriptures on Tuesdays and Thursdays. So instructed, Huxley wrote for *Vedanta and the West,* the magazine of the Vedanta Society, and in 1942 contributed a foreword to Swami Nikhilananda's *Gospel of Sri Ramakrishna.* Living in the desert with no neighbors but his cows, Huxley assumed yoga postures, breathed deeply, and meditated.

For a time the altar boy, if that is the name for him, of Huxley's Hollywood temple was Christopher Isherwood, late novelist and collaborator with Auden in left-wing plays. Having more or less abandoned the world, Isherwood assisted Swami Prabhavananda at services, helped him edit *Vedanta and the West,* and prepared himself with austerities for the priesthood.[1] The example of Isherwood appears to have inspired Somerset Maugham's *Razor's Edge* (1944), a novel about a worldly boy who, converted to Hinduism, leaves his inheritance for the holy life. Similar in theme to Huxley's later novels, this novel differs in other respects. Seeing his material with a novelist's eye, Maugham is content with the wonder of human nature.

Less need be said of those who in despair of modern or exotic remedies found what they required in a Western church, usually that of Rome or Canterbury, since the appeal of Geneva has visibly declined. The effect of conversion upon Catholics and Anglo-Catholics has been great, but not, on the whole, injurious. Because their churches maintain a salaried clergy, the convert may allude to what is commonly known or celebrate it, leaving the preaching to the proper authorities. Under different auspices, Huxley and Eliot left time for eternity. The result of one departure is tract and of the other poetry.

Although a preacher of a sort in his sermons, Gerard

[1] *Vedanta for the Western World* (1946), edited by Isherwood. In 1944 Isherwood and the swami translated the *Bhagavad-Gita.* *The World in the Evening* (1954), a novel on varieties of love, commends charity and the Quakers.

Manley Hopkins was a poet in his poems. He is not only the greatest religious poet of England in our time, but one of the greatest poets. He was not a mystic like Huxley, A. E., or Lawrence, but a poet who used his art for the greater glory of God.[2]

While at Balliol in the 1860's, Hopkins was attracted by the higher criticism of Jowett and Strauss, and his sensuous nature was stimulated by the teaching of Pater. But the Oxford Movement and the defection of Newman, proving more congenial to his temper, made him aware of the void left by skepticism and sent him, in the endeavor to fill it, to former certainty.

With the extravagance of the convert he became a Jesuit. The Society of Jesus promised an austerity that seemed opposite to his own sensuousness and to the doctrine of Pater. Ordained in 1877, Hopkins remained faithful to his vows—indeed, somewhat overscrupulous—and as happy as his neurotic constitution permitted. After he had preached in the seventeenth-century manner a sermon upon the church as a cow, whom we must milk and feed and whose moo we must follow, his colleagues came to regard him as one who would be better employed perhaps as a schoolteacher. In this capacity he spent his later years at that university in Dublin which Newman founded and Joyce was to make illustrious.

Hopkins tried to repress his eccentricity, his sensuousness, and his dangerous delight in nature. He burned his verses. But the possibility of compromise appeared in Loyola's permission to employ sensuous beauty for God's sake. Far from impairing his poems, as several critics have held, his vocation improved their quality, gave them character and exciting matter, and disciplined their romantic confusion. Since he became a great poet, his vocation did not prevent him from becoming one. It is idle to suppose

[2] The Note-Books and Papers of Gerard Manley Hopkins (1937). G. F. Lahey, S.J., Gerard Manley Hopkins (1930). Eleanor Ruggles: Gerard Manley Hopkins (1944). John Pick: Gerard Manley Hopkins, Priest and Poet (1942). Martin D'Arcy, S.J., "Gerard Manley Hopkins," Great Catholics (1941), edited by Claude Williamson. W. A. M. Peters: Gerard Manley Hopkins (1948), on inscape. Norman Weyand, editor: Immortal Diamond (1949).

that under other circumstances he might have been greater.

His poems, written between 1876 and 1889, were published in 1918. Their editor, Robert Bridges, has been blamed for delaying so long, but he was wise to wait until the times, prepared by other excesses, could receive poems so peculiar for rhythm, diction, metaphor, and syntax.

Sprung rhythm, in which Hopkins composed, is the rhythm of *Piers Plowman,* but he developed it from the choruses of Milton's *Samson Agonistes.* With syncopated accents and effects of counterpoint, sprung rhythm looks formidable, but it raises few problems of scansion; for as Hopkins observes, it is the "natural rhythm of speech," and though elaborately composed is easily read.[3] Like Whitman's verse, sprung rhythm is a major development in prosody, an attempt to complete the romantic revolution, which, correcting words, had let rhythm alone. But Hopkins was conservative in rhyme. Retaining it at the cost of awkwardness and—in the "Eurydice"—of bathos, he prized it as an extra value.

His diction, though he had no German, Anglo-Saxon, or Middle English until late in life, seems Germanic. He knew Welsh prosody, however, and his alliteration, his kennings, his internal rhymes and dissonances, as "blood-gush blade-gash" or "lush-kept plush-capped," exaggerate Welsh usage. Such oddities, at once sensuous and uncouth, kept him at several removes from Tennyson.

That "naked encounter of sensuality and asceticism" which offended the nineteenth-century reverence of Robert Bridges excellently describes the metaphors of Hopkins, who, combining Pater and piety, made discordant concords of heaven and earth. Unlike the dry metaphysical conceit, these sensuous emblems present the spirit so palpably and flamboyantly that they approach the grotesque. But the sensualization of spirit, as in the images of barn, stallion, and deliquescent sloe, is redeemed by ecstasy. All material things, however common or mean, sanctified by the Incarnation, comprised a store of poetic con-

---

[3] For Hopkins's explanation of sprung rhythm see "Author's Preface" to *Poems* (1930), edited by Robert Bridges, with a commentary by Charles Williams, or to *Poems* (1948), edited by W. H. Gardner.

traries, agreeing and disagreeing with spirit in pleasing tension. Hopkins differed from the other Jesuits of his time (who, while admitting the rule of *"tantum quantum,"* inclined to severity) in having recaptured the baroque spirit that inflamed Crashaw and his Jesuits, leaving as it swept through Europe a trail of florid churches with voluptuous altars.

Prizing singularity and encouraged by Duns Scotus, its philosopher, Hopkins called the essence and the underlying design of a thing its "inscape." His endeavor to be true to his inscape and his theme's, making him singular and, he feared, repulsive at first reading, demanded those distortions of syntax, the ellipses, the grammatical improvisations, that make his poetry difficult. In this interest and for intensity he condensed as he distorted. So made and charged with the profound experiences of his faith, his poems seem not recollections in tranquillity but experience in progress. Songs of becoming, not of being, they are opposite in kind to the perfections of Yeats.

"The Wreck of the Deutschland," Hopkins's first great poem, improves upon acquaintance. Dealing with the problem of evil, this ode unwinds in three congruent strands, the first of Hopkins and God, the second of the wreck, the third of nuns and God; and the point is discovered in the broken exclamations of the twenty-eighth stanza.[4] Following this tumultuous success, Hopkins wrote those sonnets of nature that comprise his most agreeable achievement. "God's Grandeur," a marvelous unity of rhythm, sound, and meaning, proceeds from the conceit of the Leyden jar to the traditional image of the Holy Ghost, redeemed from commonness by a magical "Ah!" "The Windhover," a more incredible sweep of pace, harmony, and image, puzzles by its ambiguities. Is the falcon a bird, the critics ask, or the poet or Jesus Christ? He is, of course, all three at once, but in the last three lines is dominantly Christ addressing Hopkins, priest. The theme

---

[4] See the explications by John Pick and by W. H. Gardner: *Gerard Manley Hopkins* (1948–49). The Kenyon Critics: *Gerard Manley Hopkins* (1946). Among recent poets who have studied Hopkins with profit are Auden, Day Lewis, Barker, Thomas, and W. R. Rodgers.

is the apparent conflict between two kinds of beauty, that of vocation and that of life. Elaborating another "conceit" in "The Blessed Virgin Compared to the Air We Breathe," Hopkins proves himself Donne's rival.

Poems of men, Purcell, Duns Scotus, Felix Randal, follow with tenderness and future perfect imperatives; and these in turn are followed by the self-questioning poems of the eighties, "Spelt from Sibyl's Leaves," tortured and grim, and the other sonnets of the "terrible" period, of which "Carrion Comfort," "I wake and feel the fell of dark," and "No worst" are best, their theme his own unworthiness and, as a reader of William James should know, of normal religious experience. But even these cries of anguish reveal the passionate grammarian. The wonder is not that Hopkins, confined by self-imposed punctilios of syntax and prosody, wrote poems so good, but that he wrote poems at all. Their excellence is a tribute to his constant burning faith, for only by this fire could that syntax and that prosody prevail.

Almost to a man, the Paterites of the nineties, having pursued hedonism to its limit, turned for relief to the Church of Rome as Huysmans had done before them. In an essay on Huysmans, Arthur Symons said that Catholicism is the religion of the decadence "for its venerable age, valuable in such matters as the age of an old wine, its vague excitation of the senses, its mystical picturesqueness." Dorian Gray in his search for odd sensation delighted not only in flowers and rugs, but in the ritual of the church. Oscar Wilde, going further, became a convert. So did Lionel Johnson, Ernest Dowson, Henry Harland, John Gray, Aubrey Beardsley, and Frederick Rolfe or, as he preferred, Baron Corvo, author of *Hadrian the Seventh* (1904). The literary results, except for the religious poetry of Johnson and Dowson and the eccentric novels of Rolfe, were meager.[5]

[5] A. J. A. Symons: *The Quest for Corvo* (1934). *The Last Letters of Aubrey Beardsley* (1904), edited by John Gray. The richly metaphorical poems of Francis Thompson (e.g., *Sister Songs*, 1895) recapture the baroque lusciousness of Crashaw and Marvell and the drier wit of Donne. "The Hound of Heaven" (1893), more austere, triumphs by the scenery of dream, but that it is overelaborate can be seen by

While the Catholicism of G. K. Chesterton was more medieval in character than that of Hopkins or Rolfe and more jovial, it served a similar purpose. The scientific materialism and the decadence of the nineties left him dissatisfied. Groping for something better, he was attracted, as he tells in his *Autobiography* (1936), to Theosophy. He met Yeats, considered Blavatsky and the Celtic twilight, but preferred the London fog. The only trouble with Yeats's *Land of Heart's Desire,* he said, is that "the heart does not desire it." In 1905 he devoted *Heretics* to Shaw, Wells, and others whose solutions were eccentric. The optimistic pantheism that attracted him at this time underlies that fine, fantastic novel *The Man Who Was Thursday* (1908). Policemen and anarchists and the insane light in which they move indicate the personal nightmare of nihilism, materialism, and æstheticism from which he was beginning to emerge; and Sunday is his provisional god. That same year, however, he wrote *Orthodoxy*.

The appeal of order and tradition had led Chesterton to the company of eminent Anglicans and then to Father John O'Connor (Father Brown), who told him about sin. Chesterton became a Catholic at last in 1922 and devoted his journalistic brilliance, his paradox, wit, and outrageous simplicity to tracts in verse and prose.

Graham Greene, who shares with Evelyn Waugh the highest eminence among more recent converts to Catholicism, devotes his compassionate and moving novels to imperfect or seemingly imperfect Catholics. *The Heart of the Matter* (1948), centering upon impious communion, is a drama of two kinds of love—and God knows which wins. *The End of the Affair* (1951), also involving conflict between loves, is an off-centered saint's life. Revealing holiness in unlikely places, Greene plays Roman tradition against the peripheral and the secular to promote charity.

Eliot expressed despair in his early poems and, in the poem on the hippopotamus, irreverence as well. Elegantly allusive, he piled fragments of culture about the ruins. That culture was not enough becomes evident in "Geron-

---

comparison with George Herbert's "Collar." Cf. "The Shepherdess" and the other sweet, delicate verses of Alice Meynell.

tion," a desperate monologue on the need and unlikelihood of salvation. *The Waste Land* (1922) objectifies the spiritual desert in which he felt half alive, a cross between Dante's Hell and London. The second part of this excellent poem proves the desert moral. Hindu and Buddhist overtones, dark references to ruined chapels, the Grail, and the Resurrection of Christ, which accompany the regenerating rain, point the way to salvation. Images from Dante's Purgatory and Limbo, together with cactus and stuffed shirts, define "The Hollow Men." But these spiritual allusions are so oblique that I. A. Richards may be pardoned for thinking Eliot happily represented freedom from all belief. To correct this error and to make his conversion plain, Eliot announced in 1928 his adherence to the more pompous faction of the Church of England.[6]

It is difficult to detect the piety that must underlie *The Idea of a Christian Society* (1939), which offers a kind of theocracy as the only substitute for liberalism, democracy, and godlessness. He excludes America and the Dominions from comprehension in his state because the mixture of people in those places makes them irredeemable. Not all Englishmen, however, are worthy, for not all have attended the better public schools. In England the lower orders, incapable of religion, will be kept within the Anglican frame by the "Community of Christians." Although in *Notes Towards the Definition of Culture* (1948) Eliot is somewhat less illiberal, he still finds culture dependent on the religion of a "governing élite."

Essays Ancient and Modern (1936) announces that the poet has no objection to being called a bigot. Although one may be inclined to separate his bigotry from his poems or, dismissing it, praise them, the two are inseparable and the poems are bigotry's excuse. In bigotry—and for one of his temper nothing less would do—Eliot found the integration a poet needs. The "still point" of the turning

[6] Eliot's spiritual career is presented as a saint's life by Richard Aldington in "Stepping Heavenward," *Soft Answers* (1932). Eliot did not become a Roman Catholic because, as he says in the *Criterion* (October 1927), Anglicanism is essentially Tory and Catholicism in our time is essentially American and democratic.

Quartets, a symbol of God, is also the symbol of this integration. As Yeats's queer system provoked poems, so, after long silence, did Eliot's. In *Ash Wednesday* (1930), liturgical incantation and the clear allegorical images he took from Dante objectify a penitential mood and his desire to desire faith. In *Four Quartets* (1943), less purgatorial than heavenly, bare, incantatory statements of time and eternity reveal a feeling that almost redeems Mr. Eliot's Sunday morning service.[7]

It is true that *The Rock* (1934), a pageant composed for an ecclesiastical occasion, is heavy. But *Murder in the Cathedral* (1935), also written for an ecclesiastical occasion, is a successful play of great emotional power. This play and the even more successful plays that followed it are his most public poems.

In his essays lamenting the separation of poetry and drama Eliot had asked how our craving for poetic drama could be satisfied. Not, he replied, by imitating the Elizabethans, but by creating a form. Since drama must be popular, he suggested the development of some popular technique, that of the music hall, for instance, or of the Mass. For *Sweeney Agonistes* (1932), an exercise for the closet, he employed the Greeks, jazzed to our capacity by the uses of the music hall. The speedy rhythms, vulgar diction, and hypnotic repetition add horror to an American theme, a bathtub murder, and to those typical Yankees Sweeney, Doris, Krumpacker, and Klipstein. This fragment, which remains Eliot's best play, approaches his ideal of the many-leveled play with plot for the simple, character and conflict for the more complex, words for the literate, rhythm for the musical, and a meaning, gradually unfolded, for men of sensibility.

Murder in the Cathedral unites good poetry and good theater. From the Greeks came mumbling chorus and the sense of doom, from the morality play the expressionistic tempters, and from the advanced little theater the enlargement from Ibsen's peepholed chamber. Always dramatic

---

[7] Cf. Anne Ridler: *The Nine Bright Shiners* (1943), *The Shadow Factory, a Nativity Play* (1946). Ruth Pitter: *A Mad Lady's Garland* (1935), *A Trophy of Arms* (1936), *The Spirit Watches* (1940).

in his poetry, Eliot had transferred his talent to the stage. In *The Family Reunion* (1939) or Æschylus in modern dress the Eumenides, now working for the Church of England, embody not only the need of expiation but all the evils of family and society that had been suggested in *The Waste Land* and "The Hollow Men." The ultimate integration of Harry, their victim, must be applauded by psychoanalyst and theologian alike. Remarkable verse, combining the flatness of conversation with the relaxed intensity of the *Quartets,* maintains the actual and elevation above it. Too subtle perhaps for the public stage where it was presented and too interior in its climax, the play is redeemed for the vulgar by rhythm, mounting terror, and the reality of the victims. Not least among these attractions is the chorus of aunts and uncles.[8]

With *The Cocktail* Party (1949) Eliot turned to comedy, and if this play suggests Noel Coward at times it is Noel Coward transfigured. Dr. Harcourt-Reilly with his gin and water commends two ways of salvation: that of sanctity on anthills and that of worldly adjustment at home. As the secular action suggests these responses, so the unobtrusive verse suggests poetry. It seems a pity that Eliot, who created Sweeney and Prufrock, was unable to create memorable characters here and in his subsequent play; but even without them, these plays, as objective organizations of rhythm and image, are adequate correlatives for the more liberal piety of his later years, and, judging by popular appeal, for the cultural if not the religious aspirations of his audience. No less secular in appearance, *The Confidential Clerk* (1953) employs the archetypal theme of hunting a father. Collecting pots and playing the organ become shadows of ecstasy—as Charles Williams would put it.

The relationship between Eliot and Charles Williams was close. This high Anglican produced novel after novel

---

[8] In *The Quest for Salvation in an Ancient and a Modern Play* (1941), Maud Bodkin compares Eliot with Æschylus. Eliot's essays on the poetic play: *Selected Essays* (1932), *The Sacred Wood* (1920), *Poetry and Drama* (1951), *Religious Drama* (1954). Leo Hamalian is the principal authority on the plays.

in which he also advanced holiness by secular indirection.[9] Taking his pattern from George MacDonald and maybe Chesterton's *Man Who Was Thursday,* Williams combined the thriller with theosophical melodrama and the occult concerns of Eliphas Lévi. The furniture of Williams's novels (black magic, the Holy Grail, ghosts, Tarot cards, Hermes Trismegistus, archetypal beasts, and the Ineffable Name) is there to distinguish pseudo-religion from the power of love. Maybe the Tarot cards of *The Greater Trumps* (1932) owe something to Eliot's Mme Sosostris; certainly Peter Stanhope of *Descent Into Hell* (1937) is a portrait of Eliot. Peter Stanhope (Rock, Hope of the Rock) is a successful poetic playwright, a master of "unobtrusive verse," who, having returned to the house of his ancestors, makes poetry profitable. Eliot, who is Williams's publisher, wrote a preface to *All Hallows' Eve* (1945). It is probable that Williams encouraged Eliot in the use of the grotesque and the secular for pious ends. Plainly Dr. Harcourt-Reilly is a character who would feel at home in Williams's novels, and so is Sir Claude Mulhammer of *The Confidential Clerk.*

More plainly under the spell of Williams, C. S. Lewis became another leading apologist for highest Anglicanism. After a career of brilliant scholarship, he began to deliver lectures and to write tracts, distinguished by logic, wit, and ease, on the case for Christianity. In *The Screwtape Letters* (1942), his cleverest book, one devil advises another upon the promotion of impiety. In his three interplanetary fantasies Lewis uses the frame of H. G. Wells and the manners of Kafka and Michael Innes to dramatize the war of good and evil, matter and spirit. *That Hideous Strength* (1945), the last of these transcendental thrillers, does for our time what John Bunyan did for his.[1]

Since his retreat to America, Auden, who admires

[9] War in Heaven (1930), Shadows of Ecstasy (1933), Many Dimensions (1931), The Place of the Lion (1931). Poems: Taliessin Through Logres (1938), The Region of the Summer Stars (1944). Arthurian Torso (1948) with a commentary by C. S. Lewis. N. C. Star: King Arthur Today (1954).

[1] Out of the Silent Planet (1938), Perelandra (1943). Beyond Personality (1944). Surprised by Joy (1955), autobiography.

C. S. Lewis, has professed something which, although called Anglicanism, seems more like Calvinism. For the Marxist determinism of his youth, Auden has substituted predestination and salvation by grace; Lawrence and Freud have yielded to Kierkegaard, Paul Tillich, and other Protestant theologians. Like Kierkegaard's Absurd or Wholly Other, Auden's present God bestows His favors for no good reason, and all the "lucky" or elected believer can do is sit still, awaiting the gift. But elected loquacity, which has replaced the good works of Auden's political days, demands preliminary commitment. Faced in his progress with a crossroads, the pilgrim must have chosen the better road, which, avoiding sterilities of abstract desert on the one hand and the sensualities of the sea on the other, leads to the holy city. This arduous journey or quest furnishes imagery for "The Sea and the Mirror," "The Quest," *The Age of Anxiety* (1947), and all those other recent allegories of choice and fate. Calvinist or not, *For the Time Being* (1944), a Christmas Oratorio, recalls Eliot. In *Nones* (1951) and *The Shield of Achilles* (1955) Auden, celebrating the canonical hours discursively, proves again that, like Eliot before him, he has become what Joyce called a "gracehoper."

It is curious that Joyce, the writer in our time most deeply penetrated by Christianity, was converted from, not to, it. As Cranly observes in *A Portrait of the Artist,* the mind of Stephen Dedalus is saturated with a religion in which he no longer believes. The hero of *Stephen Hero* confirms this observation. "I am," he says, "a product of Catholicism." Even Eliot, hunting heretics, found Joyce orthodox.

The detachment from religion that Joyce thought necessary for art was never so complete as he desired. A tradition that Eliot painfully pursued and almost caught remained Joyce's heritage. His art is good because it is traditional and detached, and difficult for the same reasons. His detachment sometimes amounts to privacy, and his traditionalism is beyond those outside his traditions. *Finnegans Wake,* for example, is permeated with Catholicism. The fall of man and his redemption, sin and repentance, the obsessive presence of Lawrence O'Toole and the other saints, the canonical hours, litanies, prayers, and the formulas of the sacraments compose a private nightmare.

Ulysses provides a symbol as potent for our time as *The Waste Land*. The hunt of Telemachus for Odysseus, repeated by Stephen Dedalus, who has lost both earthly and heavenly father, reflects our longing for support. That his hunt for a father should result in Mr. Bloom may seem unfortunate. But wiser than most literary men or able to walk alone, Stephen, having drunk his cocoa and having received his substitute father in that communion, departs, a father now himself.

CHAPTER SEVEN: *The Stream of Consciousness*

*A*MONG the most fruitful of new countries to be opened up by romantic explorers and surveyed with wonder is the conscious mind. What, its explorers asked, is the nature of experience and what the nature of self? Is reality to be found without the mind, as naturalists had thought, or within it? Is consciousness simple or complex, discrete or continuous? Does it proceed on one or many planes? What part does memory play, or time? Romantics of our time were not the first to ask these questions, but they were among the first to use novels for the answers.

There were other motives for introspection. For some it was an escape from the outer world, increasingly awful, to an inner refuge—an escape, sometimes, from one chaos to another. For others, despairing of external certainty, faced with the apparent impotence of action and intellect, the inner chaos, however relative, became an absolute. Reality had moved from brothel and slum to the lonely head. Explorer and refugee alike, attempting a greater reality than realists had known, belong with transcendentalist and symbolist to the great rebellion against the external, the material, the logical, and other impediments to truth.

Entering new lands ahead of English novelists, philosophers surveyed the interior and determined its economy. William James and Henri Bergson, the chief among these romantics, made explicit what others could feel and directed future feeling by map and guide. In "The Stream of Thought," a chapter of his *Principles of Psychology* (1890), William James, commencing the "study of the mind from within," found constant change and a "teeming multiplicity of objects and relations." Science, reducing life to simplicity, had tried to make consciousness clear and logical, said James; but looking within, he could see only the fringes and penumbras that surround, obscure, and give significance to images. Far from being discrete, consciousness proved on introspection to be continuous flow. "A 'river' or a 'stream' are the metaphors by which it is most naturally described. In talking of it hereafter, let us call it the stream of thought, of consciousness, or of subjective life." Having given novelists a place to float in and a name for it, James passed to the consequent problem of identity. We are not one self, as scientists and novelists had thought, but many selves; in fact, a flux of identities without determinate outlines. Novelists soon found themselves wondering if they were James or Virginia or Marcel and if their characters were characters or streams of experience or waves.

Simultaneously in France, Henri Bergson was also rebelling against scientific externality and mathematical abstraction. By intuition or intellectual sympathy he discovered reality in "the indivisible flux" of consciousness, which he called "duration." Made continuous by memory, which charges each moment with its past, duration involves a present that, like Gertrude Stein's, is "always beginning again." The trouble with science, logic, and clocks, said Bergson, is their imposition of concept upon flowing reality. Logical and scientific novelists, he continued, had distorted and simplified reality. Ticketing characters, they had drawn outlines around them and framed their thoughts. He advised novelists to get inside their heroes by intuition and, forgetting logic, clock, and all the traditions of character, to flow.

Long before James or Bergson, Turgenyev had evolved a subjective technique for *Smoke* and other novels, and Chekhov, discarding logic, outline, and plot, had devoted his short stories to small situations that reveal the depths of personality and release those vapors of mood in which reality seems to float. Dostoyevsky, looking within himself, had discovered, if not the stream of consciousness, the problem of identity. Raskolnikov in *Crime and Punishment* has two identities, one projected as Svidrigailov. The characters of *Notes from Underground* and of other novels suffer from split, contradictory, and multiple personalities. "Do you know," says Versilov in *A Raw Youth,* "I feel as though I were split in two? . . . It's just as though one's second self were standing beside one; one is sensible and rational oneself, but the other self is impelled to do something perfectly senseless. . . ." According to André Gide, his disciple, Dostoyevsky explored vast regions of the soul, revealing the baffling complexity that earlier novelists had tried to make logical and consistent. His novels, translated into English during the eighties, found English novelists unready to make use of his discoveries. But the translations by Constance Garnett, coming after 1912 upon the heels of Bergson and Freud, found them ready and willing.

Bergson was right in seeing himself and James as parts of a tendency much larger than themselves. Over in France, Édouard Dujardin had discovered the stream of consciousness before William James wrote about it, and in *Les Lauriers sont coupés* (1888) had invented a technique with which to present it. In England writers of fantasy had discovered multiple personality before their more serious compatriots. Stevenson's Dr. Jekyll and Beerbohm's happy hypocrite are as divided as Gertrude Stein's Teresa, who is one self indoors and another out.

The effects of this pioneering by philosopher and novelist were not immediately evident in England except in the works of Henry James, Conrad, and, to some extent, George Moore. But after 1916 the course of English fiction for many years was determined by these explorations and by those of the psychoanalysts. Seen from within, the characters of this new fiction lack definite outline and, often, connections with things external to themselves. Their selves are multiple; their conduct is not infrequently irrational. Mysterious organisms, not mechanisms, they have souls. The novels in which these fluid creatures move are sometimes as deficient in outline as the fluid creatures themselves. Looking back at the "typical" novels of this period—*Ulysses* and *The Waves*—William Butler Yeats found them deluges of experience "breaking over us and within us, melting limits whether of line or tint," and their people swimmers or "the waves themselves." Noting this "self-dissolving introspection, the generally heightened awareness of the goings on of our own minds, merely as goings on," I. A. Richards found Joyce his best and most sensitive example. The inner world of Stephen Dedalus is "composed of images which shift and flow and merge with an intricacy" beyond the power of intellect to follow.

Among the first in England to adjust his technique to the demands of flux was George Moore, who had commenced his career as novelist in the objective tradition of Zola. But, as we have seen, Moore gradually turned away from the scientific and the external. This reaction was assisted by *Les Lauriers sont coupés* of his friend Édouard Dujardin and by the example of Turgenyev, whom Moore distantly imitated in the short stories of *The Untilled Field* (1903). *The Lake* (1905), an expansion of one of the stories in this volume, is the first unmistakable sign of Moore's new narrative method, which, although not a stream of consciousness in the later sense of that term, achieves a kind of flow in which objective and subjective dissolve and merge. By rhythms and imperceptible transitions the reader is washed along sometimes within the hero, sometimes without. This method was brought to perfection in *The Brook Kerith* (1916), a book with currents so insidious and palpable that the reader is put to it to penetrate the surface or, sometimes, to stay awake. By a triumph of style, which maintains a melodious flow of its own above the matter it is intended to carry, Moore obtained effects that other writers were obtaining by point of view. For his autobiographical sketches, commencing with *Memoirs of My Dead Life* (1906), he contrived a method that, though not dissimilar, proved more successful because perhaps his matter fascinated him. *Hail and Farewell* (1911–14), the outstanding memoir of our times, is an extended stream of memories, proceeding capriciously by free association, and revealing by nuance and tone not so much the people of the story as the selves of its creator.

Henry James, who went further than Moore toward a suitable method, was also in revolt against naturalism. An admirer of Turgenyev, whom he knew in Paris, and brother to the philosopher of the stream, James hunted ways of presenting the mind in moral and social situations. It appears from his prefaces, however, that his methods owe less to Turgenyev and William James than to the necessities of art. For the sake of unity, drama, irony, and suspense he employed for his subjective purposes narrative in first person and the more penetrating technique of impressionism.

He found the first person singular of use for presenting delusions that the narrator cherished in his mind and projected upon external reality. In *The Turn of the Screw* (1898) James, an expert in the unmentionable, used all his arts of indirection. The story is told in first person by the governess not only because the ambiguities must not be injured by intervention of the author but because, an apparent neurotic, she must be allowed to expose the workings of her mind, upon which in the end our interest must center. In *The Sacred Fount* (1901), another study of delusion, the narrator is permitted to display himself. His week-end at a country house is made fascinating by his hypothesis about the relationship, the worse the better, of two couples. He snoops, interprets, and dodges around corners to corroborate his ingenious obsession, until, tiring of the metaphysical game, Mrs. Brissenden confronts him with the facts. " 'I think you're crazy,' " she observes. "It naturally struck me. 'Crazy'? I remember just wondering if perhaps I mightn't be."

In the technique of "impressionism" James found a better method for presenting more normal processes of mind. His impressionism, which must not be confused with impressionism in painting, is a method whereby an observer's mind is the stage upon which all action occurs. But the impressions of the observer are recorded in the third person by the author, peering through a window in the observer's head. Since the author tells what is occurring on this subjective stage, he can limit the narrative by selecting what he thinks relevant or suitable and maintain an artist's control over the flow of experience. The most objective of subjective novelists, an extrovert compared with Virginia Woolf, James generally limited the flow to levels of polite intercourse and to things external to the observer, who looked out as James looked in.

This method, which James first used in *The Spoils of Poynton* (1897), was brought to perfection in *What Maisie Knew* (1897), a tale of divorce, adultery, and the consequent difficulties of Maisie, a child. Because she occupies the center of this situation, James chose Maisie's consciousness as his stage. "The one presented register of the whole complexity," he says in his preface, "would be the play of the child's confused and obscure notation of it." That it should be presented through a child's awareness of it was required by convenience, economy, art, and above all by the fact that it afforded a "most delightful difficulty." For though the female young have "no end of sensibility," no child of six or eight could know all that the observer must know. Looking into her head, James told what she saw and did not know, expressed what she could only feel, and, by judicious interference assisted the reader through her perplexities. As we look through Maisie's eyes and feel what she feels and listen to the helpful asides of James, we discover in what might have been a common domestic tragedy the mystery, drama, and suspense that for some of us surround our own affairs.

James's method is as dramatic as exploratory; but many readers used to find the results impalpable or dull. Remarking the "copious emptiness" of these novels, H. G. Wells in *Boon* (1915) compared them to a church "without congregation to distract you, with every light and line focused on the high altar. And on the altar, very reverently placed, intensely there, is a dead kitten, an egg-shell, a bit of string. . . ." But Conrad, Dorothy Richardson, and Ford Madox Ford hailed James as master, and, with his example before them, embarked upon further explorations of the inner world. And it is clear today that James anticipated Proust not only in the analysis of a decaying society but to some extent in method. Associations of *The Middle Years* (1917), an autobiography, expand in rings from a nuclear memory as in Proust, and as in Proust each ring is subjected, as it expands, to analysis and qualification in expanding sentences.

James's earliest disciple, Joseph Conrad, who has been justly considered a nautical variety of his master, saw James in *Notes on Life and Letters* (1921) as a great artist with a "conscience troubled by the nice discrimination of shades of conduct." This describes Conrad better than James. To settle doubts of human values, to support faith in man lost in a careless universe, Conrad created Marlow, a kind of detective of conscience, whose consciousness is the scene of several important stories and novels.

In his prefaces and here and there in the novels Conrad speaks of the inner truth, the real meaning of life, and of the difficulty of getting at it. The technique of impressionism, which he learned from James and suitably modified for his own purposes, provided a way. Marlow became the observer and in his own words "went gravely about trying to account . . . for a lot of things no one would care to bother one's head about." Marlow is a many-sided character, a union of sentiment, morality, cynicism, and curiosity. His impressions of reality distort it before passing it on to the reader, and before Marlow receives it, it has been distorted by the temperaments and memories of those who report to him. As in *Lord Jim* (1900) Marlow usually works upon impressions at several removes from the facts. Interested in Jim's honor, he questions those who have seen Jim or who have talked to those who have seen him. Sometimes the facts have passed through the refracting media of three or four minds, augmented, distorted, and changing color at each passage, before Marlow in turn can impose his share and focus the result. The story, therefore, is less the story of Jim and his search for honor than the passage of this story through minds of which Marlow's is the point of interest. In his passion for truth Marlow discards chronological sequence and tells the story in fragments as he received it.

Jim's personality, in so far as we can disengage it

from Marlow's contributions, is complex, and his motives are obscure. If Jim has any depths below the moral or heights above it, however, they are not explored. Flora de Barral, the heroine of *Chance* (1914), on the other hand, is far more than a moral problem for Marlow: she is a tortured soul whose obsessions seem Freudian, or at least Russian. Innocent of Freud, and indifferent to Dostoyevsky, whom he liked far less than Turgenyev, Conrad seems to have drawn this study of father-daughter relationship and of psychological trauma, as Hardy drew Sue Bridehead, from his own observation. Marlow is fascinated; and as he pieces the story of Flora together from many reports, he illustrates again the arts of impressionism and obliquity.

Conrad used Jamesian impressionism to penetrate solitary regions that James preferred to hint at and conceal. Conrad used obliquity of structure, as James used the device of expanding awareness, to give reality its due. But subjecting reality to a longer sojourn in the mind, Conrad made more use of memory and took advantage of its nature. *Youth* (1902) is the reflection by mature memory of youthful illusion, and *Victory* (1915) brings memories of many observers to bear upon man in an exotic corner of the alien universe. James never brooded about the universe. The heaviness by which Conrad distorted what was already distorted makes his work seem profounder than James's elegant webs of colloquialism, qualification, and astonishing metaphor. But except for occasional excursions both of them pursued reality in the same area, that of conscious experience.

Dorothy Richardson admired James and Conrad. On commencing to imitate them she discovered, however, that their technique was too remote from what she thought reality. From their impressionism she independently developed a technique in which the flow of experience is conveyed not by the analysis of observer or author but by letting experience flow. Far more realistic than impressionism, her stream of consciousness is an attempt to record the contents of the mind without that selection by which James maintained the canons of art and the demands of decorum. Thoughts, feeling, images from the senses, and the endless, inexplicable irrelevancies that constitute waking life and complicate it by pursuing several simultaneous courses—in short, the buzzing, blooming confusion described by Bergson and William James as our immediate reality—became her material, and fidelity to this rich confusion provided her technique. Placing herself inside the head of Miriam, she recorded in flowing sentences or at times in disjointed fragments the flow of Miriam's mind. This flow, which began with *Pointed Roofs* (1915) and continued through nine other novels, was collected in *Pilgrimage*.

If Dorothy Richardson had attempted to record every moment of Miriam's life, she would have required more than ten volumes, but she contented herself with selecting short periods of tedium or intensity. Within these selected periods there is no selection. But the necessities of truth and silence imposed upon the novelist by the nature of the stream were fatal to structure. Held together only by continuity of person, such as it is, *Pilgrimage* falls into separate fragments. Plot and action have virtually disappeared, character has lost its elegance of shape, and personality has been all but replaced by a series of reactions; for the interest is no longer centered upon what occurs without, but upon what flows within. That we may know what Miriam looks like, Richardson has her sit before a mirror. If we can trust her own impression, Miriam is plain. It is not surprising that almost nothing happens to her. Following her heroine as she teaches school, takes tea, walks on an Alp, or enjoys a botanical rapture, the novelist bores from within. It is difficult to quarrel with Frank Swinnerton, who, while recognizing Dorothy Richardson's development of technique, wishes that Miriam had died young.[1]

Rebellion against old-fashioned fixity of character and against the imposition of plot led Dorothy Richardson in pursuit of an internal reality undistorted by concept to a

[1] Frank Swinnerton: *The Georgian Scene* (1934). W. L. Myers: *The Later Realism* (1927). May Sinclair: Introduction to *Pointed Roofs* (1919 edition). J. C. Powys: *Dorothy M. Richardson* (1931). Leon Edel: *The Psychological Novel, 1900–1950* (1955). Robert Humphrey: *Stream of Consciousness in the Modern Novel* (1954). Melvin Friedman: *Stream of Consciousness* (1955).

formlessness that is realistic enough, but monotonous and æsthetically unsatisfying. James Joyce, her contemporary and fellow explorer, showed that the new fluidity could be reconciled with form. In place of the string of sausages into which Miriam's selected and interrupted experience falls, Joyce provided symphonic structure, which, while satisfying the requirements of beauty, is closer to reality and to a greater area of reality. In place of the adequate but uninteresting prose of Miriam's stream, Joyce brought all the resources of poetry to bear upon the illustration of consciousness. Suggestion, symbol, rhythm, dramatic changes of tone, texture of language, conceits, and neologisms express the richness of experience. A virtuoso of language, reminding one in turn of Shakespeare, Flaubert, and the symbolists, Joyce could command rhythm and sound for such effects as this: "Grossbooted draymen rolled barrels dullthudding out of Prince's stores and bumped them up on the brewery float."

The obliquities and unresolved situations of the first three stories of *Dubliners* (1914) are impressionistic. In "An Encounter" the presentation of adult depravity through the childish consciousness repeats the triumph of *What Maisie Knew*. In "Clay," Joyce turned the objective method of the naturalists to the implication of inner and general barrenness. "A Painful Case," "Grace," and "The Dead," suggesting by trivial incident and mood more than they contain, reveal in the manner of Chekhov, the depths of personality and of human relationship. These cold and masterly stories of frustration are among the first and best of those we recognize as "modern."

A Portrait of the Artist as a Young Man (1916) is impressionistic autobiography. Selecting, like Dorothy Richardson, the moments of importance, Joyce penetrated below and above the decencies among which James, Conrad, and Richardson moved. At the beginning, by selection, memory, and suitable incoherence he presented the quality of the infant stream of consciousness, if not the stream itself, and later he presented from within the feelings, emotions, and intellectual life of a hero at once more emotional and more intellectual than anyone in James or Conrad.

The refusal of English and Irish publishers to accept this book reveals the extent to which Joyce, departing from convention, had enlarged the scope of the novel. The method with which he experimented in the *Portrait* was perfected in *Ulysses* (1922).[2]

The third chapter of this great comedy concerns Stephen's walk along the beach at Sandymount. In this section (Proteus in the Homeric parallel) Joyce presented change and flux by the waves, the dissolving and rebuilding of the shore, and the flow of thought through Stephen's mind. Adapting Dujardin's technique, Joyce made Stephen's stream of consciousness a bright parade of thoughts, memories, sensations, and feelings linked by free association. Isolated words and phrases or formulated sentences express the intricate, many-leveled flow of experience, verbalized sometimes by Stephen, sometimes by Joyce. The mental tone is alert, for he always suited means to purpose, and Stephen serves as his embodiment of intellect and imagination. In the fourth chapter, the Calypso episode, we enter the mind of Mr. Bloom and flow with his stream of consciousness as he visits Dlugacz's butcher shop, cooks breakfast, feeds cat and wife, and meditates in the jakes. Although Mr. Bloom's stream also consists of fragments and sentences and also reveals the total contents of his mind, it has a quality and rhythm of its own, opposite to Stephen's; for Mr. Bloom is the average man, the citizen of cities, the indifferent audience that men like Stephen fled. Mrs. Bloom's interior monologue, which we encounter in the last chapter, is different from both of these. Without the interference of intellect, her confusion of desire, feeling, and memory moves in a long gush, from which, in order to indicate its cowlike character, Joyce

[2] Frank Budgen: *James Joyce and the Making of* Ulysses (1934). Stuart Gilbert: *James Joyce's* Ulysses (1930). M. L. Hanley: *Word Index to* Ulysses (1937). Richard Kain: *Fabulous Voyager* (1947). Edouard Dujardin: *Le Monologue intérieur, son apparition, ses origines, sa place dans l'œuvre de James Joyce* (1931). Cf. Dujardin's preface to the 1924 edition of *Les Lauriers sont coupés.* Joyce's influence is plain in Samuel Beckett: *More Pricks than Kicks* (1934), *Murphy* (1938), *Molloy* (1951). Flann O'Brien: *At Swim-Two-Birds* (1939). Flann O'Brien is Brian Nolan, who, under the name of Myles Na gCopaleen, conducts a column in the *Irish Times.*

omitted all marks of punctuation. In one of her aspects Mrs. Bloom represents the flesh, and her final word is suitably affirmative.

Far from dissolving the limits of character, Joyce's streams establish them. The effect of *Ulysses* is not liquefaction, but a curious solidity and, despite subjective flow, immobility. One wonders why Yeats chose *Ulysses* and *The Waves* as his examples of contemporary dissolution, for though they are both subjective, no two books could be less alike. Joyce's solid, brilliant reconstruction of Dublin, a symbol of the modern world and his private obsession, corresponds to nothing in *The Waves,* which have washed external things away. Though Joyce created external solidity, he shied away from external action, deterred perhaps by a conviction of its unimportance or perhaps by his inability to deal with it. His interest, moreover, was not action but being or "whatness" and psychological readjustment.

Part of Joyce's solidity comes from his use of other means to supplement the stream. Mr. Bloom is the most fully realized character in recent fiction because we see him from within and without by the aid of many arts. He is as definite as sculpture. Yet we know his interior, the regions of his mind both conscious and unconscious, and, apart from these, his actions and his effect upon others through whose minds his image passes. To achieve this triumph of characterization Joyce used every known point of view and invented others. About one third of the book consists of parody, which he made an instrument for displaying or examining human nature. For another third he used drama, objective question and answer, musical development, and even traditional narrative.

Each of these methods carries many meanings, and each episode, whatever its method, is linked to the others by common themes and mazes of allusion. This labyrinthine structure is epitomized in the central chapter (the Wandering Rocks), in which eighteen brief episodes, some subjective, some objective, are elaborately tied by theme and reference to each other and to the rest of the book. If this chapter is the epitome of the book, it follows that the book itself is a labyrinth; and it is not for nothing that Joyce named his hero after that famous carpenter who assisted Pasiphaë in her strange amours. By the creation of his labyrinth, which reflects the confusion of our world while imposing order upon it, Joyce was able to control his fluid materials. The discipline imposed upon his youth by the Jesuits gave the mature artist the detachment and control required to bring intricate form to flow and chaos. Joyce's interior monologues, however unselected and realistic they appear to be, are as thoroughly controlled for the ends of art as the impressions of the observer in Henry James.

Jesuitical Stephen Dedalus, who brought "to tavern and to brothel the mind of witty Aristotle," distrusted, says Joyce, "aquacities of thought and language." Virginia Woolf adored them, and her novels, far more representative than *Ulysses* of Bergson's ideal and that of William James, mark the ultimate in deliquescence. But there can be virtue in deliquescence. Unimpeded by witty Aristotle, Virginia Woolf became an artist of the stream of consciousness, of which her works provide the most perfect examples.[3]

In "Modern Fiction" Mrs. Woolf speaks of reading *Ulysses,* which was appearing in the *Little Review.* By his subjective approach, his spirituality and sincerity, she says, Joyce reveals the "flickerings of that innermost flame which flashes its messages through the brain" and brings us face to face with life itself. He sheds light on the dark places of the mind, which for moderns are the one consuming interest, but his light is too brilliant, its focus too precise. He has shown by his technique the way to interior truth, but, she fears, there is something hard and narrow about him, a kind of intellectual angularity, inhuman and sterile. He deals in flow, to be sure, but he lays

[3] There are studies of Virginia Woolf by David Daiches (1942), Winifred Holtby (1932), Floris Delattre (1932), E. M. Forster (1942), Joan Bennett (1945), Bernard Blackstone (1949), and James Hafley (1954). Aileen Pippett: *The Moth and the Star* (1955), biography. Herbert J. Muller: *Modern Fiction* (1937); J. W. Beach: *The Twentieth Century Novel* (1932); Edward Wagenknecht: *Cavalcade of the English Novel* (1943). In *A Writer's Diary* (1953) Virginia Woolf tells of the pains and joys of composition.

pipes for it. Avoiding the plumbing, she will make use of his stream.

"Modern Fiction," which repudiates the objective methods of Bennett, Wells, and Galsworthy, is the manifesto of this streaming art. Her account of what she proposes to do with Joycean method purged of Joyce is the best description of the stream of consciousness:

> Life is not a series of gig lamps symmetrically arranged; but a luminous halo, a semi-transparent envelope surrounding us from the beginning of consciousness to the end. Is it not the task of the novelist to convey this varying, this unknown and uncircumscribed spirit, whatever aberration or complexity it may display, with as little mixture of the alien and external as possible? . . . Let us record the atoms as they fall upon the mind in the order in which they fall, let us trace the pattern, however disconnected and incoherent in appearance, which each sight or incident scores upon the consciousness.[4]

The Voyage Out (1915), in the manner of Forster, and *Night and Day* (1919), approaching the manner of Dostoyevsky (as a borrowed passage from *The Idiot* suggests), were promising. With "The Mark on the Wall" (1919), a short sketch reprinted in *Monday or Tuesday* (1921), she entered her new domain and fulfilled at once the promise of her early novels and of her manifesto. This sketch, which epitomizes her work, is the reverie of a woman who allows an unidentified mark on the wall to provoke a train of free associations. From the mark her mind wanders to thoughts on the uncertainty of life, to Shakespeare, to tables of precedence at court, to remains of the past, and back to the mark. The external world is represented by the mark, which turns out to be a snail. But no matter: the point is not the nature of the mark, but the flow of consciousness, and the interest lies in the workings of the mind for their own sake.

Snails were at home in the world of Virginia Woolf, but

[4] "Modern Fiction," written April 1919, was reprinted in *The Common Reader* (1925). Cf. *Mr. Bennett and Mrs. Brown* (1924).

not so much as fish, which became her favorite metaphor for illustrating the progress of the soul through the waves of consciousness. The reader, swimming her waves, becomes a fish, and, if he is not careful, he loses shape, like the soluble fish of André Breton, and becomes a wave. And why not? If flow is our reality, and if the aim of the realist is immersion of self and reader in the flow, if life has no meaning except the sense of immersion and flow (and she seems to hold these truths to be self-evident), by all means let us dissolve, admiring the arts by which we are transformed. It was not accidental that Virginia Woolf, a symbolist to the end, cast herself into the river Ouse and drowned.

Casting herself, before this, into the stream of her heroine's consciousness, Mrs. Woolf abandoned herself in novel after novel to her idea of ultimate reality. In *To the Lighthouse* (1927) she flows with Mrs. Ramsay, who sits on the terrace reading a story to her little boy. The words of the story occupy part of her consciousness, but she is also aware of her husband striding up and down; simultaneously she thinks of Mr. Carmichael and the rumor that he was addicted to drugs, and she thinks of the marriages of friends. Across this section of an ordinary mind on an ordinary day leaps the thought: "the bill for the greenhouse would be fifty pounds."

But Virginia Woolf was not, as this would seem to imply, a recorder of the stream; she is its poet, suggesting immersion and the quality of thought, often below the level of consciousness, by means of rhythm and image. Novels should generalize, not analyze, says she in "Notes on an Elizabethan Play," and, implying the object, should occupy a plane above reality while expressing it.

No doubt James, Conrad, Dorothy Richardson, Chekhov, and Dostoyevsky helped to confirm Virginia Woolf in her subjective ways; for she read everything, including Laurence Sterne, who, in his rebellion against eighteenth-century rationalism, had provided her with a model of free association, subjective vagary, and freedom from plot. But *Mrs. Dalloway* (1925), her first important work, is indebted primarily to Joyce. His three complementary characters, Bloom, Mrs. Bloom, and Stephen, are matched by her Septimus and Mrs. Dalloway. His episode of the Wandering Rocks, in which several minds are linked by the passage through Dublin of the viceregal cavalcade, is matched by the scene in the park in which she links several minds by a sky-writing airplane.

To Winifred Holtby, Virginia Woolf remarked that she had not read Bergson, with whom Floris Delattre associates her. But she lived in Bloomsbury, where Bergson was a fad. Her sister-in-law, Karin Stephen, published a study of Bergson in 1922, and ten minutes with a Bergsonist would be enough. Whether or not Mrs. Woolf read Bergson, she seems to have been familiar with him. Her novels reflect his hostility to concept, logic, character, and external time, and his fidelity to flux.

In the early twenties it was the fashion of intellectuals to be anti-intellectual. Inspired by Bergson, Freud, and Dostoyevsky, they exploited the possibilities of the irrational. To Virginia Woolf, intellect appeared to be the enemy of fluid life. Sir William Bradshaw and Miss Kilman in *Mrs. Dalloway* represent this enmity, especially Miss Kilman, whose raincoat, inimical to waters, symbolizes her condition. Mr. Ramsay in *To the Lighthouse* shows by his pursuit of Q and R the limitations of Sir Leslie Stephen's Victorian intellect.[5] Lily sees him as one who neglects flamingo sunsets for "angular essences" in the shape of kitchen tables "when you're not there." Mrs. Woolf's work abounds in similar symbols and in direct attacks upon concept. Her characters who, discarding intellect, abandon themselves to the mysterious flow of life are good, the others defective. Those who flow possess their souls; for however secular she appeared to be, Virginia Woolf was not without transcendental impulses. In the absence of religious instruction, public or private, she confused the soul with the flow of consciousness, evil with intellect, and spiritual exercise with the subjective method.

As Mrs. Woolf's novels seem to illustrate Bergson's ro-

[5] Noel Gilroy Annan: *Leslie Stephen* (1952). J. K. Johnstone: *The Bloomsbury Group* (1954). David Garnett: *The Golden Echo* (1953). Forthcoming study by W. V. O'Connor.

mantic fluidity and transcendentalism, so they seem to
illustrate his ideas of time.[6] The duration or inner time of
Bergson flows in her stream of consciousness. Outer time
intrudes with the striking of Big Ben, whose leaden circles, punctuating the reverie of Mrs. Dalloway, mark the
disparity between real and mechanical time. Parts one and
three of *To the Lighthouse* are duration or time lived
through, but the middle section, called "Time Passes," is
external time in which the decay of the empty house takes
the place of the clock. In *The Waves* the interludes of
wave, sun, snail, and vegetable represent external time,
while the rest of the book records the more elastic progress of duration. In *Orlando* Mrs. Woolf plays with Bergson's times. Born in the age of Elizabeth, Orlando is thirty-
six years old in October 1928. Three hundred years and
thirty-six represent inner time and outer time or vice versa.
And time is complicated by memory, through which several times, says Mrs. Woolf, may proceed simultaneously.
The expansion or contraction of inner time with the intensity of experience is discussed in the little essays on
clock time and inner time that she inserted to perplex the
unphilosophical reader.[7]

Bergson had advised novelists to discard the hard old
outlines with which they had identified, solidified, and
distorted their characters. In her subjective novels from
Jacob's Room (1922) to *The Waves* (1931) Mrs. Woolf
dissolved away the limits of character until nothing was
left but duration. Unlike Joyce, who dramatically modified the flow to suit the character, Virginia Woolf presented one flow, which may be identified with her own.
Her works are as free from characters as from external
action. Indistinguishable flow has taken the place of both.
In *The Waves,* one of the central expressions of our time,
we flow by turns within six consciousnesses at selected
periods of their lives. As each delivers the dramatic mono-

[6] For the general interest in time see: J. W. Dunne: *An Experiment with Time* (1927); Hans Meyerhoff: *Time in Literature* (1955).
[7] Orlando's home is Knole, home of the Sackvilles. See V. Sackville-West: *Knole and the Sackvilles* (1922); *The Land* (1926); *The
Edwardians* (1930); *All Passion Spent* (1931).

logue that takes the place of the stream of consciousness and performs the same service, it is hard to tell who is there. This is not surprising, for in his final monologue on Monday or Tuesday and the uncertainty of life Bernard finds himself merging, all boundaries gone, with others. Is he Bernard, he wonders, or Susan or Neville; is he male or female? He is but a wave rising from and lapsing into a common sea with which he mystically unites himself, differing from earlier mystics in uniting himself with time instead of eternity. The liquidation of Bernard met its antithesis in "Solid Objects," a story in *The Haunted House* (1944). Walking along the flowing beach one day, the hero of this story finds a piece of glass. He is so pleased by its character that he neglects career and friends in the pursuit of other solidities. It is unfortunate for the cause of solidity that this man is mad.

This madman and Septimus in *Mrs. Dalloway* owe their condition to Virginia Woolf's interest in abnormality, but her interest was directed and increased by Dostoyevsky. Septimus and Mrs. Dalloway, who think in similar images, are halves of a split and projected personality like Raskolnikov and Svidrigailov. The multiple personalities that Orlando finds in herself, however, seem to owe more to William James.

Virginia Woolf did not substitute chaos for plot as her adherence to the doctrine of dissolution might lead one to expect. In place of conventional structure imposed from without, she developed flexible organic forms from within. For *Jacob's Room* she created a ring of minds around an absent center. *Mrs. Dalloway* is kept from formlessness by unity of time and by the device of complementary persons; the division of *To the Lighthouse* into three parts is æsthetically satisfying; the sequences of interlude and monologue in *The Waves* are rhythmic and suitable. *The Years* (1937), which deals with external time, is more nearly conventional in form.

Virginia Woolf was a novelist of distinction and an artist who, whatever her dependence upon tradition, had something original to say and who surpassed most of her contemporaries in sensitive fidelity to the most evanescent movements of consciousness. Her defects are obvious and pardonable. It matters little that her novels are without action and character in the customary sense. One goes to them for other things. It matters more perhaps that her sensitivity was limited to people of her own class, that she misunderstood those who had not attended a public school or belonged by birth to those who had. Far from being a snob, however, she extended her compassion to the unfortunates who are so ill at ease in Mrs. Dalloway's garden. But flow is flow even within superior people, and we go to her novels for the sense of it. Her achievement is a style, a style of wit and intelligence, of odd conjunctions of particular with general, of rhythms, of exclamations and parentheses, that made her, as she was aware, a Bloomsbury equivalent of Laurence Sterne.

Meanwhile Eliot's Tiresias sat fishing in his dull canal; and it is fitting to recall that "Prufrock" and *The Waste Land,* in one sense at least, are personal streams of consciousness, interrupted by selection, progressing by images, linked by the free association that symbolists substituted for logic. Eliot's Laforguian stream, identical with Dujardin's, points to the common source of Eliot and Joyce. Although neither owed much to the English novelists, "Portrait of a Lady" proves Eliot an admirer of Henry James.

Of lesser writers, Ford Madox Ford was closest to midstream. In one of his autobiographies, *Return to Yesterday* (1931), he tells of friendship with James and of collaboration with Conrad, at whose knees he learned the technique of impressionism, which James and Conrad had learned, he says, from Turgenyev. Basing his method on that of *What Maisie Knew,* with hints from Conrad, Proust, and others, Ford wrote a tetralogy of Tietjens, whose troubles in love and war provide the theme.[8] His stream of consciousness, unselected, complicated by the

---

[8] *Some Do Not* (1924), *No More Parades* (1925), *A Man Could Stand Up* (1926), *The Last Post* (1928). Ford, who changed his name from Hueffer, wrote a memoir of Conrad (1924) and a study of James (1913). Autobiographies: *Ancient Lights* (1911), *Thus to Revisit* (1921). In *Myrtle* (1925) and other novels Stephen Hudson, who translated part of Proust, experimented with the subjective technique.

simultaneous flow of sensation, thought, and memory, seems more immediate, though less excellent, than James's decorous selections. From Conrad, Ford took structural obliquity and the technique of memory flash-backs, which permit past to jostle present in the flow of consciousness. In *It Was the Nightingale* (1933) Ford pauses on the curb at the beginning of the book with one foot in the air. Memory intervenes, and the foot descends in the last chapter.

Katherine Mansfield used the short story to surprise inner truth behind conventional façades. Equaling Virginia Woolf in sensitivity, surpassing her in common humanity, she was prevented by circumstance from using her gifts as she might have done. What she did do, though as delicate as anything of Virginia Woolf's, appears to come from a more limited talent.

Miss Mansfield learned her individual art from many masters. From "dull turgid" James she received an occasional "sweet shock." But like J. Middleton Murry, her husband, D. H. Lawrence, her friend, and the other Bloomsbury literates, she received more from the Russians. She read Dostoyevsky and Turgenyev, and, her husband informs us, Chekhov, whose art seems to have had the profoundest effect upon her. Her stories, like many of Joyce's, belong to Chekhov's tradition. She discarded plot and action for mood or situation, conventionally important moments for moments of hidden intensity, and—slicing life thin—peered through the sections. Like the symbolist poets, she often worked by indirection, allowing overtones, hints, and silences to suggest more than the situation seems to hold. As she said in her *Journal,* she wanted to write stories "with a radiance, an afterglow . . . I want to write poetry. I feel always trembling on the brink of poetry." Whether she employed an objective technique or worked obliquely by hints and symbols or used impressionism or the stream of consciousness—and she used all these devices—her aim was always the penetration of surfaces.

From 1916 to 1920, driven in upon herself by the death of her brother and by the war, Katherine Mansfield turned to memories of her New Zealand childhood. "Prelude," "At the Bay," "The Doll's House," and "The Garden Party," which embody these memories, are among her best. The first two are fragments, parts of a projected novel, but their very shapelessness allowed her talents an appropriate liberty. Getting by turns into each member of the Burnell family, from young Kezia to Aunt Beryl, as they pursue their blameless day, she makes each incident imply its significance and each moment a life. The other two stories, beneath their pleasant exteriors, are terrible disclosures of caste, but they are more than that. After the dancing and the sandwiches and the death of the young man in the neighboring slum, Laura exclaims: " 'Isn't life . . . isn't life—' But what life was she couldn't explain. . . . 'Isn't it, darling?' said Laurie."

Katherine Mansfield's aim was truth. She always feared that in rounding her stories she had distorted truth or had become artificial, sophisticated, or too clever. None of her work, when she reviewed it in her *Journal,* seemed quite good enough to her. She was never satisfied in her endeavor "to be simple as one would be simple before God." It was partly to purge her soul of affectation and her style of preciousness that she entered the spiritual retreat at Fontainebleau, where she died of other troubles. She was too severe a critic of her own sincerity and of her slight, sensitive accomplishment.[9]

Look at All Those Roses (1941) by Elizabeth Bowen contains stories that are even less conclusive and direct than those of Katherine Mansfield, and no less excellent. In "A Love Story" several maladjusted lives are implied in the glimpses we are given of guests at an Irish hotel. "Look at All Those Roses" is a fragment of experience in which possibilities are left unpursued. As maddening and suggestive as a symbolist poem, this story also resembles a classical tragedy in which, though everything happens offstage, there are no messengers or chorus. "The Apple-Tree" concerns traumatic hallucination; and the nameless sorrow of the little weeper in "Tears, Idle Tears" seems to

[9] *Journal* (1927). *Letters* (1928). *In a German Pension* (1911). *Bliss* (1920). *The Garden Party* (1922). *The Short Stories* (1937).

imply the sorrow of the world and all the mystery of human nature. Elizabeth Bowen's stories, which employ irrational actions, unnatural children, adhesive mistresses, and summer hotels, preferably deserted or open out of season, as subject and symbol, are at once elegant and sinister. The stories of wartime England known in England as *The Demon Lover* (1945) and, more felicitously, in America as *Ivy Gripped the Steps* suggest by small terrors a general state of mind made more harrowing by impingement upon it of an equally terrible past. Of these symbolic interludes of neurosis, hallucination, and decay, the two that provide the titles of the English and American collections are at once the most gruesome and the most delicate. The elliptical, inconclusive form of these stories, though reflecting Mansfield and Chekhov, no doubt, is an additional commentary on the times.[1]

Innocence disconcerting civilization, the theme of *What Maisie Knew,* is the theme of Elizabeth Bowen's *Death of the Heart* (1939), one of the best and bitterest novels of recent years. The heart of Portia, sixteen, orphaned, seeking heart in the heartlessness of upper middle-class society, finds only betrayal and death. This moving story, which implies the death of more hearts than hers, is subjective but analytic in method. Character sketches in the grand manner and sententious reflections upon life are made to carry the tone of experience if not its details. The similarity to James is more evident in *The House in Paris* (1935), an impressionistic account of neurotic adults and even more distressing children. The most Jamesian of Miss Bowen's books, however, is *Friends and Relations* (1931), a charming novel in which tenuity of theme is supported

[1] *Encounters* (1923). *Joining Charles* (1929). *The Hotel* (1927). *The Last September* (1929). *To the North* (1932). *The Heat of the Day* (1949). *Bowen's Court* (1942). *Collected Impressions* (1950). *The Shelbourne* (1951).

Subtlety is popularized in Rumer Godden's *Take Three Tenses* (1945) and in Rosamond Lehmann's *The Ballad and the Source* (1945). Philip Toynbee's *Tea with Mrs. Goodman* (1947, in America *Prothalamium*) and his *The Garden to the Sea* (1954), "an experimental novel," mark the climax of subjective complexity or its decadence.

by an elaborate preciousness of manner and by characters who maintain an empty reticence by implication.

Such explorations of the mind remade the novel, providing new conceptions of personality and form, new centers of interest, and new methods. Tight imposed plots almost disappeared. Conventional narrative, though still in use, was often supplemented by interludes of impression or stream. Character was often replaced by many-sided or sideless personality, and personality by the experience of the moment. The old fictional character, says Aldous Huxley, was like the victim of one of Ben Jonson's humors, neatly circumscribed; the new is as uncircumscribed as Hamlet.

But even in the twenties, at the high-water mark of the stream of consciousness, critics found the subjective novel wanting in shape. Herbert Read, discussing the modern novel in *Reason and Romanticism* (1926), objected to the decay of structure, the decline of action, and the increasing emphasis upon temperament and duration in the work of Conrad, Joyce, and Proust, in whom he found a "terrible fluidity." But from these strictures Read exempted James, who mastered flux with analysis. In *Time and Western Man* (1927) Wyndham Lewis, supporting classical outline and sculptural solidity, attacked Joyce, whom he also misunderstood, and the followers of Bergson, who were menacing Western culture by their indecent abandonment to time, disintegration, and flow. The stream of consciousness reminded Lewis of nothing so much as the conversation of Mr. Jingle. In Lewis's *Childermass* (1928), intended as a satire upon the cult of time, figures representing Joyce and Gertrude Stein wander about in a limbo of relativity and flux, the world of Bergson, Alexander, and Einstein. Although recognizing the advancement in sensitivity achieved by the subjective novelists, I. A. Richards, in *Coleridge on Imagination* (1935), saw the need of better form, not the old external form advocated by classicists, but a new one evolving from new sensitivity. And Yeats, joining the classicists in *Fighting the Waves* (1934), looked with alarm at symbolic waves engulfing Cuchulain or human integrity. Over in France, Julien Benda, the champion of clarity, order, and detachment, devoted *Belphégor* (1918) to the feminine fluidities of those who had betrayed art itself for a mystical union with their materials.

To these rebukes C. P. Snow added his. The "mindless and unreadable" novels of Joyce, Woolf, and Dorothy Richardson, he says,[2] have baffled all but readers of the *avant-garde,* who fail to see that their favorites, lost in "the most hopeless cul-de-sac in the novel's history," are "as dead as cold potatoes." What we need, continues this partisan of fact, is more science. It may be that science drove the novel of sensibility up its blind, vegetable alley and into abominable privacies, but only with the aid of science can the novel emerge. What Snow proposes is objective and moral examination of "the ecology of man." His own novels adorn this social area. *The Masters* (1951) and *The New Men* (1954) are studies of moral relationships within groups—of professors in the first and atombombers in the second. Another sign of hope, says he, is John Wyllie, whose *Goodly Seed* (1953) presents moral tensions among a group of prisoners in a Japanese concentration camp.

What Snow and maybe many readers want is a return to the simple, old-fashioned novel, the persistence of which is proved by the works of Joyce Cary. This popular novelist, whose trilogies baffle nobody, has recovered something of Dickensian spaciousness and bravura. *Herself Surprised* (1941), *The Horse's Mouth* (1944), and *To Be a Pilgrim* (1949) repeat the same story from three points of view and with three admirable flavors. The heart of these novels, as of all good ones, is created character.[3]

As William Empson adapted criticism to the condemned complexities of the twenties, so F. R. Leavis, whose interests are moral, is adapting criticism to the novel of Snow's delight and Cary's practice. In *Scrutiny,*

[2] *New York Times Book Review*, January 30, 1955.
[3] *Prisoner of Grace* (1952). *Except the Lord* (1953). *Not Honour More* (1955). *The Moonlight* (1946).

his private magazine,[4] Leavis displayed the acuteness, the pugnacity, and the lack of taste and judgment that distinguish *The Great Tradition* (1948), his most considerable work. Here, dismissing Joyce as a "dead end," he praises George Eliot and *Hard Times,* the most meager novel of Dickens; and a misunderstanding of Marlow allows praise of Conrad. It is not surprising that both Cary and Leavis prefer John Bunyan to other writers. By morality, the only value (and one left undefined), Leavis seems to mean what Matthew Arnold meant in his essay on Wordsworth: "Whatever bears upon the question, 'how to live,' comes under it." Filled with "moral enthusiasm" or indignation, seeking signs of "adult responsibility," confusing form with matter, Leavis tirelessly illustrates the importance of being earnest.

Not earnestness but circumstance at last discouraged the subjective novelists. Economic, political, and spiritual problems, increasingly pressing, were beyond the capacity of the interior monologue. When more sensitive men of our turbulent times prospected rivers of the interior, they preferred descent to deeper pools, which symbols alone could fathom and irrational conduct illustrate. For such descents the familiar reaches of the stream of consciousness were far too shallow.

[4] Eric Bentley, editor: *The Importance of* Scrutiny, *Selections from* Scrutiny, *1932–1948* (1948). Leavis: *The Common Pursuit* (1952), essays from Scrutiny. L. C. Knights: *Explorations* (1946). Cf. D. S. Savage: *The Withered Branch* (1950).

*F*REUD'S invention in the nineties and his ceaseless publication of the news in the early years of this century slowly altered man's values, his idea of his own nature, and his notions of morality and art. Unsettling a
world unsettled by Darwin, Planck, and Einstein, Freud
brought order to settle it again and light to country that
Rimbaud, Dostoyevsky, and many more had ignorantly
explored.

It will be enough perhaps to recall that Freud found
the unconscious, man's deepest being, to be sexual, primitive, and childish, hence abhorrent to the civil ego and
carefully suppressed. He found that little children are in-
cestuous or narcissistic by nature and that unless during
puberty they are able to direct their affections to a suitable
object, they suffer the fate of Œdipus or, retreating in
other ways to childhood, become neurotics, perverts, artists, or madmen. For Freud our most trivial acts—washing
the hands, slips of the tongue, or falling downstairs—
acquire significance. Dreams, too, may lead to the center
of man's labyrinth; but dreams require interpretation, for
their manifest content has been distorted and condensed
by the censorship of the ego. But symbols of dream are
universal, constantly recurring in the night of every man
and in the myths, literature, and popular sayings of his
ancestors. This fortunate arrangement gave Freud a clue
and artists a method.

His early works, *The Interpretation of Dreams*
(1900) and *Three Contributions to the Theory of Sex,*
translated in 1910, became the favorites of literary men.
Poets, novelists, and critics, convinced again that they had

keys to meaning and creation, found in Freud's account of the dream-work new ways of expressing the self or understanding it. Novelists, attracted most by infant sexuality and family relationships, adopted repression, complex, and neurosis as the mechanics or substance of their art. Taking what they wanted, loosely using what they took, ignoring Freud's later discoveries (save for the death-wish and the id), they became Freudian in the most general sense. But their heroes in the grip of the unconscious became more abnormal and irrational than Dostoyevsky's. From 1910, when Freud's doctrines were first received in England, new conceptions of the personality and of the motives of conduct, new ideas of good and evil, gave the novel a character that filled the conservative with discomfort and sometimes alarm. The battle of novelists against conventional moralists surged with Freud's help almost to victory, for belated Victorians, fearing as they fought that the good are indeed the repressed and the wicked the uninhibited, fought no longer with the strength of ten. Their feeble cries went unheeded while the young of the postwar period illustrated the new morality in their conduct as their immediate elders had done in the novel. Biographers, though somewhat less affected, found a new approach to the understanding of man in Freud's case histories or in his analysis of Œdipus and Hamlet. In these analyses and in the book of dreams, critics, becoming conscious of what lies below the form and rhythm of art, found clues to value and meaning. Poets were slower to respond, but during the thirties they consciously exploited the unconscious, using dream and hallucination as Rimbaud had done before them to reach man's central reality, and brought to symbols a new awareness of significance. From the syntax, the ambiguities, the condensation of dreams they took madness for method. The symbolist tradition, renewed with the aid of Freud, flowered into surrealism.[1]

[1] Frederick J. Hoffman: *Freudianism and the Literary Mind* (1945). Lionel Trilling: *The Liberal Imagination* (1950). E. M. Forster: *The Development of English Prose between 1918 and 1939* (1945).

Enamored of unity and order, Freud was led by his loves to extravagance and, some say, error. His dissenting disciples, Jung and Adler, objected to sex as the solitary inhabitant of the labyrinth; and others, seeing other motives than wish-fulfillment in their dreams, accused him of substituting dialectics for evidence. Correcting the master, as Darwin's disciples corrected Darwin, but without undervaluing his real achievement or altering the faith in it of literary men, Adler gave them the inferiority complex and Jung the theories of introversion and the collective unconscious with its archetypes.

The sexual pathologists, who were investigating one of Freud's themes before he had started, provided case histories for the use of writers. Krafft-Ebing, Havelock Ellis, Edward Carpenter, and many others made useful studies of perversion, which, with the aid of Freud, gave literature for some years a pathological coloring. These matters were by no means new in literature, but Freud and the pathologists gave scientific assurance to the romantic exploitation of the perverse.

Romantics, yearning ever for the mysterious and the perverse, welcomed the unconscious and its effects. Although Freud was brilliantly intellectual and a follower of scientific method, his field was so inscrutable as to prove attractive to enemies of science and lovers of mystery. And to the romantic enemies of reason the dethroning of reason by Freud gave encouragement. But the exploratory and more admirable romantics owed him a greater debt.

Of exploratory critics Robert Graves was first. Shellshocked during the war, he was treated in 1918 by psychoanalysts, in whom, especially W. H. R. Rivers, he became interested. Rivers, one of Freud's followers, and like most of them a dissenter in some things, made the conflict of unconscious personalities his theme. *On English Poetry* (1922) adopts it as the clue to poetry's nature. Here Graves defines poetry, both controlled and uncontrolled, distinguishing classic from romantic, real from fake. Real or romantic poetry is the expression of a conflict in the unconscious. When the conflict is finally resolved, the poetry—that of Wordsworth, for example—dries up. But however useful to the critic, says Graves, psychoanalysis must be supplemented by historical scholarship and æsthetic analysis. In *The Meaning of Dreams* (1924), where Graves, reviewing the theories of Freud and Jung, discusses dream and poetry, the analysis of "La Belle Dame" by Keats and "The Gnat" by Graves is psychoanalytic. *Poetic Unreason* (1925), a sequel to these, repeats them. This work is valuable, however, for the more elaborate distinction between good and bad poetry—the good from the unconscious, serving needs of poet and reader, the bad from the consciousness, serving no need at all. "As in dreams," he concludes, "so also in poetry."

While Graves was soberly applying denatured Freud, Roger Fry was austerely rejecting him. In *The Artist and Psycho-Analysis* (1924) he asserts that Freud's theory of art as wish-fulfillment defines bad art alone, the cinema or the calendar or the popular novel. The sexual basis of art fails to explain its value, and nothing, Fry says, can be more contrary to good art than dream or symbol. Good art, the formal relation of part to part, is elevated above dream, symbol, and desire to regions where only the pure may follow it. This seems to be, but is probably not, the last gasp of art for Whistler's sake.

As Herbert Read tirelessly decided between romanticism and classicism or reconciled them, he called upon Jung and Freud for help, drawing character from ego, personality from id when favoring Freud or filling the void between introversion and extroversion by fantasy when favoring Jung. When feeling superior, he called upon Adler. With their aid, the eclectic hoped to commend or to express the whole personality. In "Psycho-analysis and Criticism," an essay in *Reason and Romanticism* (1926), he proposes the improvement of criticism by psychoanalysis. Although it is concerned with the process of creation and criticism, with the product's value, psychoanalysis, he says, can do more for critics than find art neurotic or trace the complexes of artists. It can test the value of their symbols, helping to distinguish between the "real" and the neurotic, the collective and the eccentric. What is more, it can solve the old dispute between classicism and romanticism as easily as it solved the problem of Hamlet.[2] In practice, as in the essay on the Brontës in this volume or the one on Bagehot in *The Sense of Glory* (1929), Read's psychoanalysis was allusive or trivial until he encountered the problem of Wordsworth, which tested his instruments. *Wordsworth* (1930) is devoted to an analysis of the poet's childhood, his relations with women, and the inhibitions and sublimations that might explain his exuberance and his decline. By this analysis Read solved a literary problem that had baffled, and will baffle, others. *In Defence of Shelley and Other Essays* (1936) defends the psychotic poet. Tracing his images back to prenatal experience, Read explains their character. As he had hoped, psychoanalysis, increasingly eclectic, permitted him to explain creation and judge it. In *Form in Modern Poetry* (1932), still preoccupied with romanticism and classicism, character and personality, he goes for aid to Freud's id. Deciding again in favor of personality, Read surveys poetry and, noting value here or there, dismisses Joyce and Hopkins as characters. Hopkins is discovered and pardoned in *The True Voice of Feeling* (1953), another romantic manifesto, that praises organic form as symbol or as mediator between matter and spirit, the unconscious and the conscious.

As knowledge of psychoanalysis increased, other critics made use of it, though Richards and Eliot remained aloof, the one adhering to another school, the other filled with scruples. But their liberal followers followed Freud or felt his influence. William Empson, for example, brought Freud's idea of dream-condensation to bear upon the seventh type of ambiguity, and the Freudian analysis of *Alice in Wonderland* in *Some Versions of Pastoral* (1935) is exemplary.[3]

Bound as a Marxist to quarrel with Freud, Marx's op-

---

[2] Dr. Ernest Jones: "A Psycho-analytic Study of Hamlet," *Essays in Applied Psychoanalysis* (1923). Henry Treece, editor: *Herbert Read, an Introduction to His Work* (1944).

[3] F. L. Lucas in *The Decline and Fall of the Romantic Ideal* (1936) uses Freud to define romanticism as "a liberation of the less conscious levels of the mind." In *Archetypal Patterns in Poetry* (1934) Maud Bodkin finds Jung's archetypes behind the imaginative appeal of great literature from the Greeks to Eliot and Lawrence.

posite in diagnosis and cure, Christopher Caudwell, while
denouncing Freud, made better use of him than other
English critics because, perhaps, he was more brilliant
than others. In *Illusion and Reality* (1937) he compares
poetry with dream, and though he finds Freud's dream
private and bourgeois, he finds Freud, reinterpreted by
Marx, to be the clearest guide to poetry's nature. Poetry is
dream with manifest and latent levels, and creation is allied to dreaming, but poetry is public or inverted dream
with Marx manifest, Freud latent.

Of exploratory biographers Sir Harold Nicolson is
among the more eminent. In *The Development of English
Biography* (1927) he sees two courses open for biographers, the fictional and the scientific, the latter following
Freud, Havelock Ellis, the students of glands, and the
economists. Nicolson's *Tennyson* (1922), like his *Swinburne* (1926), took the latter course. Peering with the aid
of psychoanalysis beneath Tennyson's Victorian façade to
discover sex, the fear of it, and maladjustment, the biogra-
pher finds the laureate repressed by circumstance, but
capable of sublimation. Enid Starkie in her *Baudelaire*
(1933), after noting the nonsense written about that
poet's Œdipus complex, implicitly follows Freud in her
account of it. In *Son of Woman* (1931) J. Middleton
Murry performs the same service for D. H. Lawrence, his
friend. These samples indicate a trend that became so general that Lytton Strachey himself descended from his
classical eminence to imply the sexual difficulties of the
Virgin Queen. *Elizabeth and Essex* (1928) was injured by
a science for which Strachey had no talent.[4]

Two writers who approached Freud's province without his help call for notice before we notice the Freudian
novelists. It is curious to find Shaw one of these. Discussing sex like a sociologist, he alludes to Havelock Ellis in
the preface to *Getting Married* (1908), and, discussing
family relationships in the preface to *Misalliance* (1910),
he describes what seems the mother complex. In *Pygmalion* (1914) it leaves preface for play. Eliza rejects the

[4] Cf. J. C. Powys: *Autobiography* (1938). Other autobiographers
indebted to Freud are Stephen Spender and Edwin Muir.

ineffectual advances of Higgins, as Shaw explains in a note, because she considers his mother "an irresistible rival." While it is possible that Shaw had heard of Freud by this time, he usually followed the latest thing after an interval of ten years, and it is likelier that, for Higgins, Shaw had consulted his own experience. Some years later, however, we know he knew of Freud. In the preface to *Saint Joan* (1923) he compares psychoanalysts with Christian Scientists and laughs at the "Edipus complex." No less afraid of love, Conrad devoted *Chance* (1914) to a study of father complex, Lesbianism, and psychic trauma. He noted his dreams, spoke in his letters of his unconscious, and tried, by drawing upon it, to give his stories a dreamlike quality.

Under the spell of Shaw and Wells, May Sinclair had written many novels on the self-fulfillment of women before *Three Sisters* (1914), in which she put Freud to service in the feminist cause. This novel, based loosely upon the situation of the Brontës, concerns, like *The Way of All Flesh,* a country vicarage, a proper place for the study of repression. The vicar gets his satisfaction by keeping his daughters from theirs. Unaware of the meaning and causes of his acts, he seems to himself "the image of righteousness." This familiar anti-Victorian theme is given depth and new significance by Freud, who provides two areas, conscious and unconscious, and drama in the conflict between them. Deprived at last of his only satisfaction by the revolt of his daughters, the vicar solves his problem by suffering a stroke and defense amnesia, which enable him to enslave Gwenda. She remains sane, however, for although a victim of self-sacrifice, she manages to sublimate her desires. Mary, under the guise of womanliness, refuses to admit to "the lighted front" of her mind the unscrupulous sexual needs that compel her. Alice, driven to hysteria and almost to insanity, blindly seeks the marriage that her unconscious knows will relieve her. But she fears the bestiality of the only available man. "Expert in disguises, in subterfuges," her mind substitutes a lesser fear in place of the fear that would prevent her fulfillment, and once it has served its purpose, this substitute fear is gone.

These creatures with their hidden selves and apparent motives are many-sided and convincing, but, though the materials of tragedy are there, curiously wanting in tragic significance. Too clear and intellectual to be moving, defining the irrational motives of her people too well, May Sinclair has the air of penetrating mysterious recesses with a guide book in her reticule.

Mary Olivier (1919), which owes its subjective method to Joyce and Dorothy Richardson and its pattern to Samuel Butler, is May Sinclair's best and most Freudian novel. Mary and her brother Mark have a mother and father. This is sinister. Mark, in love with his mother, becomes incapable of marriage. His exemplary case history is surpassed in pathos by that of Aunt Charlotte, who suffers delusions of approaching marriage, plays, to the scandal of her family, with naked dolls, and departs at last for the asylum. Mr. Olivier, jealous of Mark, his son, takes refuge from his domestic sorrows in drink, then apoplexy. But Mary, translating Euripides, writing verses, and enjoying mystical raptures while she sacrifices normal fulfillment and feminist career to the mother who has thwarted her, can sublimate.

The brilliant light of science in the hands of May Sinclair, dissipating one mystery, created another, and careful selection cleared away what might obscure the understanding. *Mary Olivier* is less mechanical in effect, however, than this would make it seem. Her subjective approach, permitting, if not the feminine penetration of Woolf or Mansfield, at least an intellectual approximation of it, permits Mary to take her place beside Dorothy Richardson's Miriam. The girls who serve the female novelists of this period as heroines are a little gruesome.[5]

Katherine Mansfield's employment of the Œdipus complex in *"Je ne parle pas français"* is among the more successful. Treating it indirectly, she makes it the center of a small tragedy. It is likely, however, that the idea for this story came from her friend D. H. Lawrence, not di-

---

[5] Rebecca West: *The Return of the Soldier* (1918), *The Judge* (1922). Mary Butts: *Armed with Madness* (1928). May Sinclair: *Life and Death of Harriett Frean* (1922).

rectly from Freud. And Virginia Woolf, publisher of Freud, owes him much. What is the meaning of the waves and of the window and what of the lighthouse? Many of her stories occupy a region midway between reverie and dream, but although a minor theme of *To the Lighthouse* is James's Œdipus complex and its resolution, and although Septimus in *Mrs. Dalloway* is an ideal madman, Virginia Woolf seems to have been less attracted to theories of the unconscious than to those of conscious duration.

Never a confirmed Freudian, Aldous Huxley treated Freud facetiously at first, then casually, before rejecting him. "The Farcical History of Richard Greenow," a grotesque story in *Limbo* (1920), follows the case of Richard from split personality to madhouse. Mary, the advanced young person of *Crome Yellow* (1921), knows her Freud. Having dreamed of ladders and wells, she seeks love as cure for her repressions. She is a figure of fun. But Spandrell, the diabolist of *Point Counter Point* (1928), is almost tragical. His life, based on Baudelaire's, is a splendid case history of the Œdipus complex.

While Mann, Proust, and Gide were following the possibilities of perversion, English novelists, lagging as usual a little behind, were not altogether indifferent.[6] Christopher Isherwood's novels of Berlin, *Mr. Norris Changes Trains* (1935) and *Goodbye to Berlin* (1939), deal with people whose sexual aberrations complicate their social complexity. Sally Bowles is a nymphomaniac of the most abandoned sort, and Mr. Norris, like Proust's Charlus, is a masochist whose perversion is dispassionately presented as an element of a many-sided personality. These eccentrics also serve as symbols of the decadent society that produced the Nazis. In *Prater Violet* (1945), a slighter novel on a similar theme, while Isherwood's hero reveals his amours, the sex of that hero's lovers is elaborately concealed. In *Maiden Voyage* (1943) and *In Youth Is Pleasure* (1945) Denton Welch's hero invites Krafft-Ebing. After dreaming of lying in open wounds, this

<hr>

[6] Radclyffe Hall: *The Well of Loneliness* (1928). Compton Mackenzie: *Extraordinary Women* (1928).

adolescent lashes himself, shuts himself in closets, dresses as a girl, or chains himself to lawn-rollers.[7]

Liam O'Flaherty and Graham Greene, Isherwood's cousin, entered the field of the psychoanalysts and pathologists in those powerful accounts of tortured souls which seem compounded of equal parts of Freud, Dostoyevsky, the thriller, and the movies. *The Black Soul* (1924), *Mr. Gilhooley* (1926), and *The Assassin* (1928), by O'Flaherty, depict violent souls, possibly mad, certainly neurotic. The black soul in the novel of that name is a returned soldier, tortured by convictions of futility, pursued by delusions, who finally composes his psychic chaos through the love of a woman and the murder of her lunatic husband. The elementary violence of this story of the Aran Islands is repeated in the story of Mr. Gilhooley, an equally neurotic Dubliner. And in *The Assassin* McDara's anarchistic ideal reflects the anarchy within his split, maniacal personality.

The atmosphere of the thriller, strong in O'Flaherty, is stronger in Graham Greene. *Brighton Rock* (1938) and *The Power and the Glory* (1940) are studies of morbid psychology. A Catholic, Greene specializes in the minds of bad Catholics. As the Mexican priest of *The Power and the Glory* flees political persecution through the hallucinatory forests, his fatigued, haunted mind is the theater of a sickness at once mental and spiritual. But at last, becoming priest again and victim, he experiences something of the passion of Christ. The character of Pinkie, the adolescent gangster of *Brighton Rock,* owes more to Freud. While but a lad in his native slum, he observed on Saturday nights the loves of his parents. The consequent trauma makes him incapable of love or of any human feeling except fear and the desire to inflict pain. The little monster, abandoning church and slum and all that reminds him of the past, in

[7] Denton Welch: *Journals* (1952). Stephen Spender: *Burning Cactus* (1936). Angus Wilson: *Hemlock and After* (1952). In *Earl Lavender* (1895) John Davidson had used masochism and sadism for theme. Hugh Walpole: *Mr. Perrin and Mr. Traill* (1911) is a good non-Freudian study of morbid psychology.

which he is fixed, becomes the leader of a small gang "protecting" bookies. He murders, and endures for a time the disgust of marriage to close the mouth of a witness. Plotting the death of his wife, he is apprehended in the nick of time by relentless Ida, the amateur sleuth. It is to hell, constantly in his bad Catholic thought together with fragments of remembered liturgy, that his soul descends. This mixture of detective story, melodrama, case history, and moral theology, one of the impressive novels of recent times, rebukes their disorder.

From D. H. Lawrence, a greater writer than these, we get a more immediate sense of the unconscious. As the achievement of Virginia Woolf is the feeling of immersion in conscious flow, so an achievement of Lawrence is the feeling of immersion in the unconscious. But before he began these mysterious descents he devoted a novel to the conscious symptoms of the unconscious. *Sons and Lovers* (1913) is the best novel about the Œdipus complex. Unlike the ladies who studied it in the works of Freud, Lawrence, like the authors of *Hamlet* and *Œdipus Rex* before him, looked into his heart and wrote. Escaping case history for this reason among others, Lawrence wrote a novel of all but first importance, a novel that if inferior to *Ulysses,* is comparable in value to *Jude the Obscure.*

Sons and Lovers reveals the partly conscious enslavement of Paul Morel to his mother. Thrown into her embrace by her hatred of his father and by the death or departure of his brothers, Paul is incapable of other love. Not even the death of his mother can set him free. This subject, treated with the passion that Lawrence brings to it, is of universal appeal, for it is something that, in less exaggerated form, is part of every man's unconscious. Although written in a plain, adequate, and sometimes rhapsodic style, though filled with honest observation and a Hardyesque feeling for suburban nature, and though the father and some other characters maintain intense, separate lives, the book is nevertheless a little morbid because Lawrence was unable to detach himself from the mother whom he celebrates as heroine or to achieve the impersonality that the most personal art requires. He wrote the book in order, by expressing his trouble, to understand and cure it. But the reader, like the reader of *Jude the Obscure,* moved by pity alone, is half appeased.

This great disturbing book was written in 1911 and 1912. Lawrence did not know of Freud until April 1912, when, at his first meeting with Frieda, who was filled with the new theories, the conversation turned to the Œdipus complex. It is possible that Frieda helped Lawrence to point up the second draft of the book and to shape experience by theory. But such assistance was unnecessary; for, as E. T., the real Miriam, assures us in her memoir, he had been able to determine the nature of his love. Later, after Frieda had more or less released him from his mother, Lawrence read Freud with considerable horror.

In *Psychoanalysis and the Unconscious* (1921) and *Fantasia of the Unconscious* (1922) Lawrence blames Freud for exaggerating sex, especially incest, and making it the sole inhabitant of the unconscious. Freud is immoral, intellectual, scientific, and, what is worse, ignorant of "the flux of sap-consciousness." Lawrence will attend to that. Claiming direct intuition, a faculty denied to Freud, he announces that the true unconscious, unlike Freud's nasty repository of repressed incest, is the soul or life itself. Fulfillment comes from responsiveness to the unconscious, evil from its repression. The great repressive devices, like Freud's, are intellect and civilization. The problem therefore is how to suspend intellect and destroy civilization that the unconscious may make us whole, relating us to others and the universe. Consigning Jung to Freud's limbo, Lawrence considers the relationship of mother and child, lover and lover. With Theosophy and yoga as his guides, he was in a better position than Freud or Jung to understand the unconscious.

Lawrence disliked Freud and Jung, who taught him much, because he disliked his teachers. He read Dostoyevsky, admitted some indebtedness, and condemned him as too mental. He read and dismissed Proust and Gide. And Joyce, whose *Work in Progress* Lawrence looked at in 1928, seemed "putrid." Even the anthropologists, who more or less confirmed Jung's ideas about the unconscious of primitive man, seemed intellectual. Lawrence alone was the master of the unconscious.

It is time, Lawrence announced in 1913, for a revolt against Shaw and Galsworthy, "the rule and measure mathematical folk." These intellectuals, ignorant of the unconscious, seemed worse than Freud or Dostoyevsky, who misunderstood it. It is true of course that Shaw's creatures or most of them are destitute of bowels. Sometimes, however, their disembodied minds become aware of darker regions. Aubrey in *Too True to Be Good,* for example, speaking of the higher centers, from which all great literature and all conversation come, admits that there are also lower centers, "a sort of guilty secret with every one of us." When these centers begin to speak, the shock is terrible. Pursuing conversation and the literature of the higher centers, Shaw commonly repressed these terrible shocks. He took for his province everything from the neck up. Lawrence, declaring his revolt, took for his everything from the neck down.

His settled opinion, Lawrence continued, was that the body, blood, soul, and all the dark centers of the unconscious are wiser than intellect and will. After finishing *Sons and Lovers* he devoted his novels to illustrating this point. His villains are intellectuals or men of goodwill, his heroes and heroines unconscious lovers. He intended his novels to improve the relationship between man and man, man and woman, and to explore upon the æsthetic plane the fulfillment that was denied him. As much of a preacher as Shaw, he devoted his antithetical arts to the salvation of mankind.

Since Birkin, the hero of *Women in Love* (1920), is always around, recommending the irrational, the novel, like Shaw's plays, is too rational to be good. But Lawrence's intention is clear. And when Birkin becomes silent, the unconscious shows itself in irrational conduct, in trances, paroxysms, and transports to which all continually succumb, and in sudden intuitions of the darkness under their necks. Ursula, "that strange, unconscious bud of powerful womanhood," swooning over the little red pistils of the flowers, is almost immediately "gone into the ultimate darkness of her own soul." Gudrun dances, for no reason, before cows. They understand. Even Hermione, that intellectual, has her moments. In voluptuous consummation with violence, she hits Birkin on the head with her paperweight. He goes off to lie among the flowers and, on returning to full consciousness, approves of her momentary triumph over repression. Flowers and paperweights will do the trick, but the easiest way to enter the unconscious is making love. As Birkin and Ursula make love, and they are always making it, "deeper, further in mystery than the phallic source, came the floods of ineffable darkness and ineffable riches."

In *Lady Chatterley's Lover* (1928), another sermon against civilization and intellect, Lady Chatterley is rescued from these impediments by her lover. The plot is simple: they make love. It is unfortunately easy to make fun of this novel, for if it is taken as a realistic account of love, the reader, after some natural awe, must laugh. But that is not the way to take it. Lawrence is not showing what love is or ever was, but what it ought to be. The love of Lady Chatterley is the extravagance of a disappointed man. Its value lies in those beautiful, pathetic descriptions of making love, which have the unnatural brilliance of superior fantasy.

In 1914 Lawrence said in a letter that he was using "true instinctive or dream symbolism" in his poems. This statement, which probably marks his first reading of Freud, may refer to the apples, flames, doors, houses, ships, and seas that occur in the poems he wrote at this time. There is no doubt, however, about the Freudian character of *Birds, Beasts and Flowers* (1923). The symbols of "Peach" and "Figs," for example, give these poems universality and a richness absent from the earlier verses. The novels, too, abound in such symbols: Gerald and the horse in *Women in Love,* Aaron's rod in *Aaron's Rod* (1922), and here and elsewhere all the flowers.

In 1925 Lawrence complained: "Those unconscious things of mine hardly sell at all." The prosperity of their author was prevented, perhaps, by the oddness of his characters, who are of two principal kinds. A desire to improve the world led him to the creation of characters with hard outlines and clear labels like those of allegories. The bad people—intellectuals, mineowners, or horse-haters —are generally of this kind. On the other hand a desire to descend into the unconscious led him to characters of such extreme fluidity that they have no outlines at all and no qualities whereby one may be distinguished from another. When they are unconscious, even the labeled characters are undifferentiated; for in the unconscious all men are similar. On his deeper plane he achieved the death of character that Virginia Woolf and Dorothy Richardson achieved on theirs. "One can never know," he said, "and never-never understand. One can but swim, like a trout in a quick stream."

The technique that Lawrence used to convey a sense of immersion in the unconscious belongs more to poetry than to prose. By a kind of incantation, using rhythm and hypnotically repeating the words "dark" and "deep," Lawrence suggests what, because it is unconscious, cannot be felt or expressed. This incantatory prose, as indirect as the poetry of symbolism, is called upon in every novel for all characters alike to intimate, while they are making love or worshipping the gods, their absence of mind.

Of Lawrence's fiction, *The Plumed Serpent* is the most brilliant. This novel, evoking the landscape of dream or hallucination, burns with a strange inner fire. In exotic splendor it is unlike anything else in English literature, and in the literature of other lands comparable only to *Salammbô. Sons and Lovers*, also excellent, is preferred by many for pathos and British solidity. Although *The Rainbow, Women in Love, Kangaroo,* and *Lady Chatterley* have moments of great beauty and more than feminine penetration, they are not first-rate novels, for their beauties are lost among the sermons. Lawrence's fault in these novels is the intellectuality he always abhorred. The short and longer stories, from "Love among the Haystacks" to "The Man Who Died," show Lawrence at his best, and he was at his best when most unconscious. "I am almost a lunatic," he once remarked. This condition assured him

of richness and depth and, along with Blake, Lautréamont, and Rimbaud, of a place in our hearts.

James Joyce, too intellectual for Lawrence and Virginia Woolf, descended into the regions of the unconscious
in the Circe episode of *Ulysses* (1922). This chapter presents the minds of Stephen and Bloom when, disturbed by
drink and fatigue, they are no longer able to distinguish
between inner and outer reality. Under the spell of Bella
Cohen, their Circe, they turn into swine as their unconscious minds assume control. It is difficult to tell what is
hallucination, unconscious phantasmagoria, dream or objective reality. Mr. Bloom's unconscious produces most of
the objects, fears, hopes, and desires of his day, sometimes
personified or distorted, in a typical dream of guilt. His
hidden abnormalities, mostly masochistic, appear. Condemned by a jury of experts, he is compelled to prostrate
himself before the cruelty of Mrs. Cohen. The ancestors
who people his unconscious accuse him and disappear or
change to someone else. Everything shifts, changes, blurs.

This dream fantasy is not presented as a stream of
consciousness but in dramatic form, with speech tags, stage
directions, and occasional descriptions in the manner of
Shaw. The dramatization of the unconscious mind was not
new when Joyce adopted it. Under the name of expressionism it had appeared on the Continent in the theater, the
novel, and painting. Although he may have been encouraged by Flaubert's *Temptation of St. Anthony* or even
Faust, the likeliest suggestion came from Strindberg's
Dream Play (1902). It was his aim, says Strindberg:

> to imitate the disconnected but seemingly logical
> form of the dream. Anything may happen; everything
> is possible and probable. Time and space do not exist.
> On an insignificant background of reality, imagination
> designs and embroiders novel patterns: a medley of
> memories, experiences, free fancies, absurdities, and
> improvisations. The characters split, double, multiply,
> vanish, solidify, blur, clarify. But one consciousness
> reigns above them all—that of the dreamer; and be-
> fore it there are no secrets, no incongruities, no
> scruples, no laws.

Strindberg was pre-Freudian. Joyce's position is less clear. Having lived in Zurich during the stormy years of psychoanalysis, Joyce was aware of it. He makes Stephen, discussing Hamlet, refer in passing to the "new Viennese school." And he makes the relationship of Stephen to father and mother central in his book. Although Stephen has the symptoms of Freud's favorite complex and although in one sense its resolution is the climax of the book, it is probable that Joyce, like Lawrence in *Sons and Lovers,* unassisted by theory, had himself in mind. Dream in the Circe episode proceeds without the intervention of censorship. Mr. Bloom, of course, may be uninhibited, but it is more likely that his dream is innocent of Freud. For the abnormalities of his hero Joyce had read not only the pathologists but, while in Zurich, a collection of letters from sexual eccentrics.

During the seventeen years Joyce worked at his next great work, he called it *Work in Progress.* When in 1939 he got what he was doing done, he called it *Finnegans Wake.* This novel, the principal literary exploration of the unconscious mind, deals with dream.[8]

From the beginning of the book to the end, 628 pages distant, and then to the beginning again, the reader, like an earwig, inhabits the sleeping consciousness of H. C. Earwicker, who is an earwig in the reader's consciousness. Earwicker's sleep, unbroken except for a restless interval in the sixteenth chapter, is light, heavy, profound, and light again, and correspondingly easy or difficult to follow, as his night wears on. To furnish the mind of his sleeper and express it, Joyce used the theories of Freud, Jung, Bruno, and Vico. By their aid and that of many others he created a dream to suit his individual hero, yet so ideal,

[8] Joseph Campbell and Henry Morton Robinson: A *Skeleton Key to Finnegans Wake* (1944). Adaline Glasheen: A *Census of Finnegans Wake* (1956). Edmund Wilson: *The Wound and the Bow* (1941). Samuel Beckett, Frank Budgen, Stuart Gilbert, Eugene Jolas, Thomas McGreevy, *et al.*: *Our Exagmination Round His Factification* (1929). Seon Givens, editor: *James Joyce, Two Decades of Criticism* (1948). L. A. G. Strong: *The Sacred River* (1950). Harry Levin: *James Joyce* (1941). W. Y. Tindall: *James Joyce* (1950). Nathan Halper is the principal authority on *Finnegans Wake.*

general, and long that it would do very nicely for the Seven Sleepers.

As in all dreams, according to Freud, the censor is at work in Earwicker's dream, disguising things, condensing, combining, and distorting them, and making symbols. His wife, Anna, and his daughter, Isabel, become at times the river Liffey, a cloud, and the sea. Earwicker himself becomes the hill of Howth. His twin sons become Shem and Shaun, projections of his own selves, and all conflicting opposites, the fox and the grapes, Napoleon and Wellington, Mutt and Jeff. During the night one of those subtle changes in family relationships that fascinated Joyce occurs, and Earwicker's interest is transferred from wife to children. To disguise this hint of incest from itself, the censor makes Isabel a niece, Iseult, and other women. Earwicker's sleep is troubled by some sin or misdemeanor he has committed in the park, but censorship disguises this so well that we never know what it is. Disguised, it appears as a harmless encounter with a cad who asks the time or an encounter with soldiers. Like Mr. Bloom, Earwicker suffers from guilt, is tried by a jury (the customers in his pub), and is plagued by gossip, especially that of the two washerwomen who wash his dirty linen in public. During the course of his dream the images are those identified by Freud: the ascent of the ladder and the fall, the Tower of Babel, Lipoleum's hat, the ride in a jaunting-car, and all the rest. Even the letter, disinterred from the dump, is given a psychoanalytic interpretation by a professor who cites *Studium Sexophonologistic Schizophrenesis*. Referring in another place to the softnosed peruser of the letter, who "might mayhem take it up erogenously" if a girl should somersault off her "bisexycle," the voice of sleep cheerfully continues: "but we grisly old Sykos have done our unsmiling bit on 'alices, when they were yung and easily freudened."

From Jung, who became a friend, Joyce took many things, especially the theory of the collective unconscious. Following Freud, Jung held that dreams are regressions to the infantile and primitive, that ancient myths and modern dreams are identical and common to the sleeping consciousness of all men. Jung's theory of myth and dream accords with the theory of Giambattista Vico, who held that myths and heroes are projections of man's deepest life and that through them we may discover the nature of their projectors. Joyce combined Jung and Vico, making *Finnegans Wake* a compendium of all the myths, heroes, and fables of the world, and Earwicker's consciousness not only that of an individual, but that of all men at all times. Since his dream is everyman's, Earwicker dreams of much that he does not know in languages he has never heard. But almost always the universal has a personal application. He dreams of Tristan and Iseult because he lives in Chapelizod, where Iseult was born, because his daughter is Isabel, and because Tristan is tree-stone, the tree and stone beside the Liffey. Earwicker dreams of Adam because his room has an Adam fireplace, of Vico because Dalkey has a Vico Road, of death and resurrection because of Dublin's Phoenix Park and the Irish-American ballad of Finnegan's Wake, sung in pubs. He dreams of Swift, Goldsmith, and Wellington because they were Irish, of the conflict of opposites because his twin sons are rivals. "And so wider."

The language of this dream is a dream language based upon the theories of Freud and upon the explication by Humpty Dumpty of "Jabberwocky." There are as many references to Lewis Carroll in *Finnegans Wake* as to Freud. The portmanteau word into which several meanings are telescoped is efficient, amusing, and witty. In his essay on wit Freud makes it plain that wit is the product of the unconscious, and in his book of dreams he gives many examples of verbal distortions, puns, and double talk. The puns and distortions of Freud's exemplary dreams occur singly, often one to a dream. But the pun is mightier than the word; knowing this, Joyce took the hint from Freud and Dodgson, elaborated it, and made of double talk, if one may take these words literally, his vehicle. This rich language, sometimes melting like Dali's watch, sometimes combining four or five meanings in a word, is at once beautiful and complicated. "Distorted mirage, aloofliest of the plain," mutters the voice of sleep, echoing Goldsmith, or, falling asleep in sleep: "him jawr war hoo hleepy hor halk urthing hurther," or, remembering glory: "be British . . . to your bellybone and chuck a chum a chance." Often the language is distorted by the Freudian censor into the familiar symbols, "sex-caliber hrosspower," for example, an ingenious combination of gun, sword, car, and horse.

However light and gay, this book is difficult. Its subject is what is most important: man, woman, love, and children, death and resurrection, sin and repentance, sleeping and waking, and the preoccupations of modern man, time, space, relativity, flux, and the unconscious. The subject, though important, does not, of course, guarantee the importance of the book. But if read aloud as it should be read, it becomes a triumph of rhythm, sound, image, suggestion, of poetry in fact; and it is plain that here is one of the most amusing of novels. It is not realistic; for, as Freud assures us, dreams are not elaborate but condensed. Upon an intellectual frame Joyce composed an ersatz dream. Not quite dream, but summarizing all dreams, it leads through man's recesses.

Yeats, as we have seen, had preceded Joyce into these recesses. Ignorant of Freud, and ascribing all to the occult, which permitted suspension of intellect, Yeats seems, even in the nineties, to have guessed the meaning of what he brought to the surface. Later he discovered that what he had called Anima Mundi is what doctors of medicine were beginning to call "the subconscious," and that dream is but our unfulfilled desire, distorted by the conscience. In the preface to *Fighting the Waves* he remarked that a German psychoanalyst had traced the " 'mother complex' back to our mother the sea." The holidays from intellect that he had so carefully managed, the dreams he had provoked, enjoyed, and used as materials for poetry, had led him, he was now aware, to his deepest self. Undiscouraged by this discovery, he continued to use the materials from Anima Mundi under the new name or the old, content that the symbols he employed were rich and many-sided.

Part of what we call excellence in poetry is the response by our unconscious to the unconscious of the poet, and part our unconscious response to his conscious art. More than any other poet of our time Yeats drew upon his hidden self, and above all others had power to control and shape his dark materials. When his friend A. E. said in *The Living Torch* (1937) that poetry comes from man's sleeping consciousness, he had his own poetry in mind. Its failure is the failure of his waking consciousness to use what it received.

Walter de la Mare, fixing dreams by craft, is closer to Yeats. In *Behold, This Dreamer!* (1939), where he discusses imagination and dream, de la Mare tells of dreams he has had of climbing stairs, opening doors, or flying. All poetry of any value, he says, is based upon such materials. As for Freud's interpretation, he rejects it vehemently, saying that if Freud is right, it is better to ignore him and enjoy the dream. De la Mare's best poetry, so haunting and mysterious, is the manifest content of his dreams. Critics have called him an escapist, but a poet who, however careless of Freud and the world of politics, confronts his unconscious cannot be said to escape reality.

Although Eliot the critic was careless of Freud, Eliot the poet gave to the central parts of *Ash Wednesday* the air of a surrealist hallucination, and to *Family Reunion* a psychoanalytic complexion. Like Lawrence, Robert Graves and W. J. Turner sometimes used dream symbols in their poems. In general, however, the poets of Eliot's generation were as reluctant to profit by Freud's discoveries as later poets were eager.

Edwin Muir is an exception. *The Story & the Fable* (1940), one of the most sensitive and fascinating of autobiographies, takes its best materials from childhood memories, myth, and dream: "I have always been fascinated by a part of us of which we know less than our remote ancestors did." From dreams that seem images of "something I can faintly guess at, but to which I can give no name," Muir makes his excellent poems—with some assistance from Freud, Jung, and the English metaphysicals. Though his archetypal poems, lamenting Time, are among the finest of the Eliot period, they lacked general applause;

for Muir belongs to no faction. It was only upon the appearance of his *Collected Poems* (1953) that he won the
laurels he had long deserved.

The climate of Auden was heavy with Freud, Lawrence, and Marx. To these incompatibles the poet added
Georg Groddeck, an authority on the unconscious, and
Homer Lane, an obscure prophetical healer, who laid the
blame for disease on mind and undertook the cure of
neural itches. Undertaking in his turn the diagnosis and
cure of social neurosis, Auden tried to heal the split between ego and id, individual and society, by poetry, politics, and religion. At their worst his poems are case-books
and at their best integrating myths. Two of the most interesting poems, the first and thirtieth of *Poems* (1930),
the one an exhortation, the other a prayer, are based on
Homer Lane. But the effect of Freud is more pervasive. In
the Prologue to *The Orators* (1932), that queer mixture of
oratory and journal, of Freudian regression and political
fantasy, Freud's symbols acquire poetic and social values.
"Adolescence," one of Auden's best early poems, appears
to concern the Œdipus complex. The ballad of Miss Gee,
a Freudian case history in Auden's most off-hand rhythm,
is a desolating commentary upon our world. The social
plays Auden wrote with Isherwood are more Freudian
than Marxist. Few of these plays and poems are quite
successful, for, dealing consciously with the unconscious,
Auden generally wrote from the top of his head. Social
purpose and a good education made him deliberate, didactic, and allegorical. But sometimes, evading intellect, he descended for a holiday to the unconscious he so often had
in mind.[9]

C. Day Lewis, who was driven by a political purpose
more orthodox than Auden's to produce verse in greater
quantities, admits in *Revolution in Writing* (1935) that
poetry has power of survival only when it talks to the

[9] Cf. "In Memory of Sigmund Freud," *Collected Poetry* (1945).
In *The Destructive Element* (1935) Spender discusses the "clinical"
imagery Auden took from Freud and fused with Marx to present the
problem of the individual in society. Francis Scarfe: *Auden and After*
(1942). Lawrence Durrell: *Key to Modern Poetry* (1952) on Freud,
Groddeck, and Jung.

"deep unconscious levels within us" as fables do and myths. Although recognizing Freud's importance in this domain, Day Lewis felt compelled to reject him and his domain as individualistic and liberal. Our times, says Day Lewis, force upon every writer a hard decision, whether to serve the revolutionary masses or man's individual unconscious. Literature must follow the way of Marx or the way of Freud: toward satire, allegory, and semireligious drama on one hand, or on the other toward music, subtlety, complex association, and the deeper areas of man. This dilemma, so excellently stated, was that which confronted his generation, and the verses, allegorical plays, and satires that followed their choice show what it was. Spender, a better poet than Day Lewis, allowed himself as he walked beside the party line an occasional deviation. But it was left for other younger men to deviate into nonsense.

With the aid of surrealism the young explored Freud's underworld of dream and madness. Breaking the barriers between dream and reality, between the mad and the sane, surrealism is the climax of the romantic movement or its final decay. More specifically it is the climax of the symbolist tradition of Rimbaud, who, with Freud to help him, became again an agreeable ancestor. Surrealism is a product of France, and, though increasingly international in its development, it retains in other lands the character of an import.

The immediate ancestors of the surrealists were Jarry, Apollinaire, who gave it its name, and the Dadaists. Dada, a nihilistic group expressing the futility of the war, was founded by Tristan Tzara in Zurich on February 8, 1916, at six p.m. Convinced of the uselessness of literature and of all things, the Dadaists illustrated the uselessness of all things by their conduct and their art. They issued foolish poems, painted outrageous pictures, held exhibits, and at their public meetings in Paris threw tomatoes, which the audience returned. At the Dada exhibition of paintings in Cologne the public was supplied with hatchets to destroy the exhibits. Louis Aragon's poem *"Suicide"* consists of the letters of the alphabet in their normal order. Pasting bus tickets on paper, Tzara called the arrangement *"Dou-*

leur en cage." To compose a poem, said Tzara, one should cut words from a newspaper, shake them carefully in a bag, draw out the words. "The poem will be like you." Achieving what Verlaine had dreamed, Dada destroyed literature. At this point, André Breton observed: "The only way for Dada to continue is for it to cease to exist." Therefore he founded surrealism.

Breton was a disciple of Freud, from whom he had learned the importance of the unconscious and the technique of analysis by uncritical monologue. Impressed by the destruction of literature, he decided to rebuild it from the depths of the mind, to avoid the errors of realism and logic, and to affirm the mysterious and the wonderful. One night while he was falling asleep, the image of a man vertically cut in two by a window emerged from his unconscious. This image could be used, he thought, in a poem he was composing. To get other images he tried the technique of rapid monologue, by which the patients of psychoanalysts are persuaded to expose themselves. With Philippe Soupault, Breton commenced automatic writing. The results were destitute of structure, but full of buffoonery and useful images. Naming the results surrealism in honor of Apollinaire, they published their automatic texts as *Les Champs magnétiques* in 1921, and in 1924 Breton issued the first surrealist manifesto. Here he defined surrealism as psychic automatism by which, in the absence of rational control and of all æsthetic or moral preoccupations, reality is expressed. We believe, he announced, in the superior reality of dream and in childhood recaptured. As predecessors he named Lautréamont, Rimbaud, St.-J. Perse, Monk Lewis, the Delphic oracle, and many others. As addicts of "the new vice," which affects them like opium, he named Aragon, Crevel, Desnos, Péret, and Éluard. To this manifesto he added as exemplary text his own *"Poisson soluble."* "The flora and fauna of surrealism," he observed, "are shameful."

Éluard quickly emerged as the best poet of the group. Max Ernst, Picasso, Chirico, Yves Tanguy, and later, Salvador Dali became its painters. Magazines, *La Révolution surréaliste* and *Le Surréalisme au service de la révolution,* spread the new faith and announced in 1925 the conversion of the surrealists to dialectical materialism. While other reds improved the outer man, they would improve the inner. But their refusal to write proletarian literature or propaganda or to abandon Freud caused the orthodox to regard them as little better than bourgeois anarchists. Aragon left his friends for the Communist Party. Breton's second manifesto (1930), reaffirming Freud, insists upon Marx. The other major development of surrealism was provided in 1929 by Dali, who, inventing the technique of paranoia, began to find in the external world corroboration of his obsessions. "The only difference between myself and a madman," he said, "is that I am not mad."

The dreams recorded in pictures, poems, narratives, and texts by the surrealists differ from *Finnegans Wake,* which Joyce was composing in Paris during the development of surrealism. Although Joyce's intricate arrangement presents the unconscious, it is conscious. The surrealists, however, half-approving of Joyce, published him in *transition* together with photographs of some "objects" that, to display his paranoia, he had discovered near his home.

In England, as we have seen, the thirties were divided into two overlapping times, the first the time of Auden, the second that of Dylan Thomas. Auden's generation, inclining toward Marx, more or less accepted Freud. Thomas's, inclining toward Freud, accepted Marx less and less. Both generations were influenced by the surrealists, who had achieved a confusion of Marx with Freud. Orthodox surrealism in England was of little value perhaps, but its peripheral effects helped to shape and color some of the best writing of our time—the poems of Dylan Thomas and Lawrence Durrell, for example, and their prose.

Softly penetrating English literature for several years, affecting even T. S. Eliot, surrealism emerged at last in London at the exhibition in the New Burlington Galleries in June 1936. Breton attended the opening with Mme Breton, who had blue hair. Sheila Legge's face was smothered in red roses. The principal address, delivered by Dali from within a diver's helmet, was inaudible.

To improve this occasion, Herbert Read, a member of

the committee, edited *Surrealism* (1936), the "definitive manifesto" of the British group. His introduction, dismissing mockery and sneers, hails surrealism as Marxist and romantic. It will liquidate classicism and capitalism alike. The poetry by which this will be accomplished is identical with dream. In 1935, he continues, he had a dream that he made into a poem with as little conscious control as possible. As printed here, this poem, though faithful to its "myth," misses poetry. But as example the poem and its analysis by the author served an excellent cause. To this manifesto André Breton contributed an essay in praise of Freud, Marx, and the Gothic novel. Hugh Sykes Davies announced in his essay that if the surrealists are the tail of romanticism, this tail is prehensile.

David Gascoyne quickly became the leading surrealist. In 1935 he anticipated Read by issuing *A Short Survey of Surrealism,* an excellent historical account, illustrated with reproductions and translations. In 1936 he published *Man's Life Is This Meat,* a collection of poems many of which seem to be imitations in words of surrealistic paintings. Dedicating his poems to Yves Tanguy, Dali, and others, he celebrates "the last head with its fingers plaited in curls," a "tightrope covered with moths," and "perfumed lenses." His prose poems recall Rimbaud's, his images are those of Freudian dreams, but his poems are too consciously contrived to be as overwhelming as he desired. England needed surrealistic poetry. He carefully provided it.

The face of the precipice is black with lovers,

he sang, and, in another poem:

An arrow with lips of cheese was caught by a floating hair.

Since logical connections are foreign to the unconscious, and in his poetry other connections are uncommon, single lines will do to illustrate the new world of imagery.[1]

Petron (1935) by Hugh Sykes Davies, a prose narra-

---

[1] Gascoyne translated Breton's *What is Surrealism?* (1936) and Dali's *Conquest of the Irrational* (1935). Cf. Gascoyne: *Hölderlin's Madness* (1938), *Poems 1937–42* (1943). George Reavy, editor: *Thorns of Thunder* (1936), translations of Éluard.

tive with overtones of Monk Lewis, Shelley's *Alastor,* and Salvador Dali, is orthodox surrealism. Setting out on his terrible journey, Petron encounters a man who cuts his fingers into hands, then each of the resulting fingers into smaller hands until he has thousands of them. Then, passing a string through his head from ear to ear, he pulls a loop through his nostril, and swallows it. Petron flees, howling, only to meet a man whose jaw hangs between his knees, a crab disemboweling himself, and other marvels. If the reader wonders about the size of these adventures, says Davies, he should hire a cow, tie her at the foot of a cliff, and jump off the cliff, observing the size of the cow as he falls. "That is exactly the scale on which we are working."

That mixture of buffoonery and wonder which Breton prized is also illustrated in the magazine *Contemporary Poetry and Prose,* ten issues of which appeared in 1936 and 1937 under the editorship of Roger Roughton. Although he denied that his magazine was the official organ of the "loosely-constituted" group, it is the nearest approach in England to the French official magazines. About half the contributions are surrealistic.

In this periodical the best and maddest stories are those of Dylan Thomas, who, though not a member of the group, dealt with their materials. Among the strangest of his excursions into hallucination and madness is "The Mouse and the Woman," whose hero dreams in his asylum of men with mouse-nests in their beards. "The Map of Love" explores dream's topography.[2]

At first glance Thomas's poems seem mad.[3] The images are those of surrealist texts or, sometimes, of Rimbaud. "The sea-legged deck" is a picture by Dali. But on closer inspection the chaos of images assumes a kind of order and it becomes apparent that under the mad surfaces the poems are deliberate arrangements. What is more, they

[2] *The Map of Love* (1939). *The World I Breathe* (1939). *Selected Writings* (1946). *The Doctor and the Devils* (1953). *Adventures in the Skin Trade* (1955), collected stories.

[3] *18 Poems* (1934). *Twenty-Five Poems* (1936). *New Poems* (1943). *Deaths and Entrances* (1946). *Twenty-Six Poems* (1949). *In Country Sleep* (1952). *Collected Poems* (1952).

make sense at last or seem on the edge of making it. Differing in this respect from the surrealists, Thomas resembles them because, inspired by Freud, he also uses the imagery of dream and madness, which, however, he subjects to further distortion according to the example of Hopkins and Joyce, and his own ingenuity. Led to myth by Freud, he makes the Bible his myth.

The poems of Thomas present the underworld of sex in the familiar symbols.

> *When, like a running grave, time tracks you down,*
> *Your calm and cuddled is a scythe of hairs. . . .*

Here the "running grave" and the "scythe of hairs," so baffling at first glance, are Freudian symbols, mixed for the occasion with the idea of death in order to imply that love is death. "Running" in association with "tracks" presents an image of pursuit and, by its immediate context, of liquid corruption. Medieval horror is intensified by the nature of time's scythe, which cuts hairs or, since we are mammals, is itself of hair. By these rich interconnections and suggestions Thomas has expressed in two lines the central preoccupation of every man. In most of his early poems he is preoccupied with love, death, the gestation of the fetus, and the four seasons. For these universal themes he created a special language by separating, according to the practice of Mallarmé, ordinary words from ordinary contexts and usages and, by ingeniously combining or displacing them, renewing them for poetry.

Applying Hegelian dialectic to imagery, Thomas pairs incompatibles to create a new synthesis of entrances and deaths. And as if for William Empson, to whom he addressed ironic homage, Thomas arranges ambiguities and startling interconnections. In the poem on the "man aged one hundred" the word "lock" has literal, metaphysical, and sexual levels, and in other poems the word "tree" combines religion and sex. "Man be my metaphor," said Thomas, but he meant parts and functions of man. Man's physiology and his dreams are the metaphor by which Thomas expresses man. The point is not metaphor or theme, however attractive, but the poetry they help create. At its worst exploratory and cathartic, this poetry at its best is almost of the first order.

In answer to questions asked by the editor of *New Verse* (October 1934), Thomas described his poetry as "a formally watertight compartment of words," and, confessing his debt to Freud, said:

> Poetry, recording the stripping of the individual darkness, must, inevitably, cast light upon what has been hidden for too long, and, by so doing, make clean the naked exposure. Benefiting by the sight of the light and the knowledge of the hidden nakedness, poetry must drag further into the clean nakedness of light more even of the hidden causes than Freud could realise.

The debt to Freud is greater than the debts to Hegel and Empson, for what Thomas does is create by artificial dream-work artificial dreams. Their surfaces are perplexing, their ambiguities and condensations those of censorship. These poems can be enjoyed like dreams for manifest wonders, but to be understood they must be subjected not only to æsthetic analysis, but to Freudian as well.

"Where once the waters of your face" is the logical elaboration of a Freudian metaphor. Intricate in design, triumphant in rhythm, it presents the scenery of love, death, and birth again. The "bags of blood," the "bushy jaws," the hair and milk of "When once the twilight locks no longer," convey a dream of birth and a dream of corruption and guilt within this dream. Father, mother, and child at once, the dreamer is freed by dream of his obsessions and, as the air brightens, awakes. The elegy for Ann Jones and "Altarwise by owl-light," the mythical sonnet sequence that mixes Freud and the Bible, though closer to the light of day, are no less wonderful.

In "Ballad of the Long-Legged Bait" strict quatrains deliberately roughened, orderly progression, and organic cross-references appear to carry some great significance. Though a boy's progress from adolescence to manhood seems intended, details remain unclear like those of some portentous dream. It becomes plain, however, that the godlike fisherman, having put out to sea for pleasure, catches a home instead and, a catcher caught by his own bait, reconciles himself to being landed. Except for paired opposites and distortions, the images appear spontaneous; some, like those of dream, seem equally effectual in three or four senses. In its context, for example, "windows of waves," a descriptive image, dissolves into widows of waves and windows of wives. Such ambiguities, composing the substance, not the decoration of the poem, make it too private for general intrusion. But that, like Donne, Thomas can make such conceits express his passion is proved in another poem by his cry "Deliver me . . . from maid and head." Caught by the pun, we may miss the meanings and the anguish, fail to see that in these allusions to birth, love, and intellect he is calling for release from the cycle.

One may ask what happens to a poem when the poet, knowing Freud, consciously uses the unconscious. Does secondary elaboration rob the poem of power? Or can the unconscious, deprived of its common symbols, express itself without them, in new symbols perhaps or by rhythm or tone? If the poem seems magical, as Thomas's poems do, the unconscious has found another way, deviously affecting us while we are occupied with what used to be its symbols.[4]

The work of Thomas falls into three periods, an academic division to which he cheerfully agreed. In his early poems of womb and tomb, as we have noticed, a dazzling process of imagery from Freud and the Bible, carrying definite meanings, quarrels with an indefinite surface. "From limbs that had the measure of the worm," a line from an early poem, has an immediate though perplexing effect. The analyzed *worm* yields the serpent of Eden, the grave, and love's instrument, while *had*, equally ambivalent,

[4] Marshall W. Stearns: "Unsex the Skeleton," *Sewanee Review,* LII (July 1944). Elizabeth Drew and John Sweeney: *Directions in Modern Poetry* (1940). Francis Scarfe: *Auden and After* (1942). Henry Treece: *Dylan Thomas* (1949). Elder Olson: *The Poetry of Dylan Thomas, With a Bibliography by William H. Huff* (1954). Derek Stanford: *Dylan Thomas* (1954). John Malcolm Brinnin: *Dylan Thomas in America* (1955).

means "took the measure" or "had the size of." Little wonder that the reader is dazzled; for the line implies birth, death, fall, redemption, erection, and resurrection.

Thomas emerged from these cellars during the war. "Ceremony After a Fire Raid," a ritualistic celebration of renewal, is not only typical but best of the second period. The third, his reluctant acceptance of marriage, fatherhood, and growing older may be called the period of humanity. "In Country Sleep" reveals by images from fairy tales and echoes of Hopkins a father's concern for his daughter. "In the White Giant's Thigh" combines the Rabelaisian exuberance of "butter fat goosegirls" bouncing in "a gambo bed" with Vergilian tears of things. The "Lament" of the "old ram rod" suggests Joyce's "ramrod the meaty hunter," but it is safer to say that Joyce and Thomas are alike in humor, art, and love of mankind. This is most evident in his best and final period, but all three reveal what he called "burning and crested" song.

Under Milk Wood (1954), the only recent poetic play (aside from some of Yeats's) that is written in unmistakable poetry, is another vision of Llareggub, the backward and mythical center of Wales. With command of language comparable to Joyce's Thomas evokes a spring day from dreams to dawn and through the cobbled, cockled noon to night again and bridesbeds in the gooseberried wood.

George Barker[5] and Henry Treece, poets of Thomas's generation who drew images for their early poems from Freud and the Bible, are neo-Thomist. Their lyrics, like those of Thomas, owe some of their strangeness and charm to vestigial traces of surrealism. By 1938, because of its Marxist pretensions perhaps, surrealism, after flashing so bravely in the pan, had lost some of its power to move the imaginations of the young, but its dark light had been so

---

[5] One of the most brilliant poets of the Thomas generation, Barker is distinguished by extravagance of imagery and technical dexterity: *Poems* (1935), *Calamiterror* (1937), *Lament and Triumph* (1940), *Selected Poems* (1941), *Sacred and Secular Elegies* (1943), *Eros in Dogma* (1944). *News of the World* (1950), *A Vision of Beasts and Gods* (1954). Cf. Francis Scarfe: *Inscapes* (1940). Charles Madge: *The Father Found* (1941). Nicholas Moore: *The Island and the Cattle* (1941), W. S. Graham: *Cage Without Grievance* (1942).

intense that typical images and atmospheres remained to decorate the poems of Charles Madge, Peter Yates, and many others.

As surrealism declined, a group known as the New Apocalypse, midway between surrealism and sanity, emerged. In *The New Apocalypse* (1939) and *The White Horseman* (1941), manifestoes and anthologies, G. F. Hendry and G. S. Fraser, the spokesman and, to some extent, poets of the group, made principles of Thomas's practice, paid their respects to Freud and Lawrence, and dissociated themselves from Auden and the surrealists alike. Auden was too external and social. The surrealists were too mad. The Apocalyptics, new romantics, proposed, like their romantic predecessors, dream, myth, fantasy, and "obscure terrible desires," controlled, however, by sanity so that the complete man and not his depths alone might be expressed. Uniting the conscious with the unconscious, they proposed to penetrate by selected images the "psychic landscape." One might expect in Apocalyptic poetry something like that union of Housman and Thomas achieved by Henry Treece, who was, as a matter of fact, the principal poet of the group.[6]

Most of the many poets who have appeared since the decay of Apocalypse are described as "neo-romantics," a term as good as any to indicate anxious concern with feeling, personality, religion, myth, and the uncertainties of the postwar world. They constitute no group. Vernon Watkins, who began earlier, has continued to write his excellent ballads. James Kirkup is neo-Auden and W. R. Rodgers is neo-Hopkins. Terence Tiller often approximates the manner of Edwin Muir, who, along with Robert Graves and Herbert Read, invites neo-romantic song. The poems of Laurie Lee are excellent, but the two best lyrics of the postwar period, outside those of Dylan Thomas, are "Lent" by W. R. Rodgers and "Cokkils" by Sydney Goodsir Smith.[7]

---

[6] Treece: *Collected Poems* (1946).

[7] Bonamy Dobrée: "English Poets Today," *Sewanee Review*, LXII (Autumn 1954). Anthologies: John Heath-Stubbs, editor: *Images of Tomorrow* (1953); G. S. Fraser and Iain Fletcher, editors: *Springtime*

The works of Franz Kafka were being translated into English during the thirties by Edwin and Willa Muir. Exactly suited to the anxieties, guilt, and horror of this period, his stories helped reinforce the effect of the surrealists, of whom he may be regarded as a predecessor. But while they dealt in madness, he dealt in dream.

Kafka's stories of the neurotic mole, of the clerk who awakens one morning to find himself an enormous bedbug, of the clerk who is arrested and tried on an incomprehensible charge, of the surveyor who attempts, with two curious assistants, to penetrate the unknowable castle—these stories are bad dreams. Their effect of grotesque humor depends upon the attitude of the heroes, who, attempting to adjust themselves to the circumstances of nightmare, display the common sense of Alice and the sweet reasonableness of Spinoza. It is true that these stories may be read as parables of social and religious adjustment, but it is less painful to enjoy their manifest content as a dreamer, innocent of Freud, may enjoy his dream. This, however, was not the way of Kafka's English admirers.

Auden and Isherwood, their tendency toward fantastic social allegory increased by their admiration of Kafka, owe him the dreamlike quality of *The Ascent of F6*. But the member of the Auden group whose admiration produced the most significant results is Rex Warner.[8]

The short stories in William Sansom's *Fireman Flower* (1944) are the closest approximations to Kafka. These

---

(1953); Kenneth Rexroth, editor: *The New British Poets* (1949).
    W. R. Rodgers: *Awake!* (1941), *Europa and the Bull* (1952). Terence Tiller: *The Inward Animal* (1943), *Unarm, Eros* (1947). James Kirkup: *The Submerged Village* (1951), *A Correct Compassion* (1952). Vernon Watkins: *Ballad of the Mari Lwyd* (1941), *The Death Bell* (1954). Kathleen Raine: *Stone and Flower* (1943). Lynette Roberts: *Poems* (1944). Laurie Lee: *The Sun My Monument* (1944), *My Many-coated Man* (1955).

[8] Warner: *The Wild Goose Chase* (1937), *The Professor* (1938), *The Aerodrome* (1941). Edward Upward: *Journey to the Border* (1938). Two novels of the thirties also occupy a region somewhat this side surrealism: *The Black Book* (1938) by Lawrence Durrell and *The Amaranthers* (1936) by Jack B. Yeats. *The Body* (1949) by William Sansom is an account of a paranoid delusion by its victim. Samuel Beckett's *Waiting for Godot* (1952), the finest play of recent times, owes much to Kafka.

delirious visions of firemen in the intricate warehouse, of maze, potting-shed, and their occupants, and of the leg-roasting beauty seem portentous allegories but, like dreams, remain unclear. Fear is the principal emotion, the machinery is Freud's, and the manner is persuasively matter-of-fact. The stories in Sansom's *Something Terrible, Something Lovely* (1954) are even more sinister. "The Vertical Ladder" and "From the Water Junction," among the best of these, project the horrors of madmen or dreamers.

CHAPTER NINE: *The Forest of Symbols*

*I*N HIS SONNET *"Correspondances"*, Baudelaire speaks of the forest of symbols. It is this forest that the most enterprising poets and novelists have been prospecting ever since; and from it they have returned with the best as well as the most inscrutable records of our time. Among the French pioneers were Rimbaud, Verlaine, and Mallarmé, whose poems guided Valéry, Apollinaire, and the surrealists. Spreading across the Channel in the nineties, symbolism gave the more advanced English writers a new manner and new substance and, after 1910, new method. Oscar Wilde, Arthur Symons, James Joyce, T. S. Eliot, Edith Sitwell, Henry Green, and Dylan Thomas learned much of their art from the symbolists of France.[1] Yeats is in a parallel tradition; for symbolism was not confined to France—as the works of Blake, Melville, and Ibsen prove. To understand the English poets and novelists of our time it is necessary to know something of these traditions.

Baudelaire, the father of the symbolist movement in France was a decadent, a transcendentalist, and maybe, as Eliot says, the greatest poet of the nineteenth century. On

---

[1] Marcel Raymond: *De Baudelaire au surréalisme* (1934). Pierre Martino: *Parnasse et symbolisme* (1925). André Barre: *Le Symbolisme* (1911). Peter Quennell: *Baudelaire and the Symbolists* (1929). Enid Starkie: *Baudelaire* (1933), *Arthur Rimbaud* (1938). Albert Thibaudet: *La Poésie de Stéphane Mallarmé* (1929). A. G. Lehmann: *The Symbolist Æsthetic in France* (1950).

first looking into *Fleurs du Mal* (1857), one is struck by
the strangeness and morbidity of the poems. The "hypocritical reader" was disturbed; Baudelaire was prosecuted
and compelled by the judgment of Paris to remove several
of the more offensive poems. But later on it became apparent that, far from being depraved, Baudelaire was an
idealist who, like Swift, liked to torture himself with what
revolted him, who found in ugliness a sort of back door
to beauty. Verlaine saw only the "ineffable delicacy" of
Baudelaire's poem about the decomposing horse and his
"inconsolable nostalgia for the ideal." Later critics have
seen a moral and almost Christian Baudelaire. *"Voyage
à Cythère,"* which at first sight seems merely disgusting,
is medieval allegory. The evil flowers of his title appear to
have been the seven deadly sins. Filled with two conflicting
sentiments, the horror and the ecstasy of life, looking at
life with the fresh senses of the perpetual convalescent or
the child, Baudelaire extracted beauty from horror and
eternity from time.

Among Baudelaire's most disturbing poems are the
"Tableaux Parisiens." Here, with horror, compassion, and
equanimity, he presents the sad, swarming streets of Paris,
the garbage carts, rags, sewers, mud, the monstrous old
men and women. Similar images fill the prose poems of
Le Spleen de Paris (1869), where, he says, the growth
of enormous cities has given him the "obsessive ideal" of
presenting in selected images their "desolating suggestions."
The "depraved phantasmagoria" of stone, fog, and gaslight
composes "the great desert of men." It is plain that to him,
as to a later idealist, this desert and this hell represented
sin and death. Baudelaire differs from Eliot, however, in
contemplating the desert and its creatures with charity.

Baudelaire was not a naturalist presenting catalogues
of the infernal metropolis. Far from copying nature, the
artist, he says, must select significant images, heighten
them, and use them to project his vision. "In certain almost supernatural states of soul," he says in *Journaux
intimes,* "the depth of life is revealed in ordinary everyday
happenings. Ordinary life then becomes the Symbol."
Swedenborg had seen a web of "correspondences" between

the worlds of matter and spirit. Following Swedenborg, Baudelaire believed that the symbolic images of his poems accosted the ineffable. But proceeding beyond Swedenborg, he maintained that images from the external world corresponded to his own inner life, so that his poems about Paris were also portraits of himself, formulas for expressing his mind and soul. The meaning of these poems is not their ostensible themes, but the interaction between the symbol and the spiritual or subjective state symbolized. Proceeding still further, Baudelaire maintained in *"Correspondances"* that the senses correspond to one another in such a way that it is possible to hear color and see sound.

The confusion of nature became order, and matter acquired significance. Baudelaire the transcendentalist was appeased and Baudelaire the poet provided with a system of meanings and images that enabled him to employ what he detested and to remain in and out of the world at once. The visible world was only a store of images and signs to which his imagination through the "evocative magic" of words gave place and value. To glorify the cult of images, he says in *Journaux intimes,* became his passion. He was not alone, he felt, for there were Delacroix, whose paintings could be heard, and Wagner, whose music evoked color and color idea.

When correspondences proved insufficient, Baudelaire found relief from the natural in the unnatural. Opium permitted visits to an "artificial paradise." In the landscape of *"Rêve Parisien,"* the record of one of these holidays from nature, no animal or vegetable life injures arrangements of water and mineral, fountains, flights of stairs, and gigantic colonnades. To the disgust of his fellow romantics, he announced in *"Éloge de maquillage"* a preference for artifice. By unnecessary rouge, natural woman becomes supernatural, and by dandyism man can follow her. The dandy, whose outer elegance is the symbol of an inner perfection, is the last champion of human pride against the encroachments of nature and the commonplace.

A dandy in verse as well, Baudelaire was a perfectionist and a craftsman. His contrived effect lies in the con-

trast between the classical, impeccable, final surface and
the romantic interior, between his imperturbable aloofness
and his matter. Verlaine, seeing him as the unmoved
mover, calls attention to the masterly change of pace and
mood in *"Les Petites Vieilles,"* where, after seeming moved
for once, the poet deflates himself with a casual *"Avez-
vous observé . . .?"* and follows this with the "phleg-
matic impertinence" of *"méditant sur la géometrie."* Only
an artist in full control of his material could have managed
such effects, and only a man of profound humanity and
imagination could have produced the situation upon which
the effects depend. Although his ideas, his feelings, his
stately rhythms, his images with their reverberating overtones move the reader, it is the control of the artist that
gives his poems their inexplicable glory.

Baudelaire subscribed to the tenets of Théophile Gautier to the extent of praising art for art's sake; and though
he did not perfectly illustrate that doctrine in his poems,
which are very moral, Baudelaire was acceptable on the
whole to the Parnassians, whose longing for "impassibility," plastic and sculptural façades, and pagan themes
found no offense in his surface and manner. Paul Verlaine,
also on the ultimate slopes of Parnassus, was among the
earliest admirers of Baudelaire, from whom he had learned
the art of the melancholy evocative landscape and the
Parisian nocturne. Into *Fêtes galantes* (1869) Verlaine
put tender, gay, and bizarre poems about an imaginary
Versailles. *"Colloque sentimental"* is elegantly sad, *"Les
Ingénus"* is pure Watteau, and *"Fantoches"* resembles the
early poems of Wallace Stevens because perhaps early
Wallace Stevens had read this poem with profit.

Later, under the influence of Rimbaud, "his infernal
spouse," Verlaine abandoned the Parnassians and, recapturing the simplicity of ancient songs, bent his efforts toward verbal music and the liberation of metrics from the
rules to which Baudelaire and Gautier had remained more
or less faithful. *"Art poétique,"* a poetic exposition of liberated metrics, tells of his devotion to music, nuance, tenuous sensation, and to that marriage of the vague and the
precise which is suggestive of one knows not what. Illus-

trating his new rhythms, undulating and broken, *"Il pleure dans mon cœur"* and the other melancholy landscapes of *Romances sans paroles* (1874) are not descriptions of the objective Parnassian world, but internal landscapes, projecting his moods. Although the poems of *Sagesse,* written after his conversion to Catholicism, have a fresh childlike quality, they have proved less interesting than some of the later poems, *"Je suis l'Empire à la fin de la décadence,"* for example, and the celebrated *"Parsifal."*

To the young of the 1880's and '90's, Verlaine was first of all a legendary bohemian who by his life illustrated disregard of middle-class convention. For a time he attracted the young symbolists, who found his sadness and his interior landscapes congenial. Chiefly, however, they hailed him as a liberator of metrics until, learning of his debt to the more considerable liberties of Rimbaud, they transferred their praises to the makers of free verse. What made Verlaine great, his original pure lyric gift, was inimitable and for this reason comparatively ignored by the followers of schools.

Commencing as poet in 1870 at the age of fifteen, Rimbaud wrote at first in the Parnassian manner, then in the manner of Baudelaire, then in the manner of Rimbaud. His early poems, filled with outrageous comparisons, grotesque rhymes, sudden shifts in tone, are the poems, as Marcel Raymond says, of a bad boy, but, it is clear, one of a superior kind of badness. *"Comédie en trois baisers"* (1870), with its magical phrase *"les grands arbres indiscrets,"* and *"Mes petites amoureuses"* (1871), with its strange technical and colloquial words, prove that his rebellion was also directed at poetic proprieties. By 1871 he had reached maturity. *"Le Cœur volé,"* which appears to be a frivolous romp among neologisms and slang (*"ithyphallique et pioupiesque"*), is regarded by Enid Starkie as the terrible record of a terrible experience with the amorous soldiers of France. If her interpretation is right, this poem anticipates by its indirection the symbolist ideal of the eighties. *"Les Chercheuses de poux,"* another poem of the same year, is even more complex. The elegant lousehunt, the suave, malign tone of the poet, the ambiguous atmosphere, all serve to produce a portrait of young Rimbaud and a comment upon society so delicate that it could not be stated.

These ironies were not impalpable enough to detain Rimbaud for long. Hungry for experiences, he became, like Baudelaire, a *"voyant"* or visionary. By magical correspondence and incantation he proposed to cheat his senses and rise above them. Not Swedenborg but Eliphas Lévi, the Christian cabbalist, the magus who was to lead so many tired Frenchmen and Englishmen to more spiritual places, led Rimbaud not only to the idea of correspondence but to the idea of salvation. By occult, Eastern power he hoped to restore the materialistic West to its primitive glory.

A letter of May 15, 1871 is Rimbaud's manifesto. "The poet," he says, "makes himself a visionary through a long, immense and reasoned derangement of all the senses." With the discipline of an ascetic, subjecting himself to every form of degradation, he must confound his senses until in their confusion they can surprise the unknown. In a special language "of the soul and for the soul, summing up all, perfumes, sounds, colors," he will suggest his visions or state their formulas. The result of this transcendental plan is great poetry.

In the sonnet on the vowels, a playful, serious poem, Rimbaud uses infant memories of a colored alphabet for Lévi's incantation. Correspondences of color and sound bring him face to face with worlds, angels, and violet eyes. Under the symbolism of a voyage on, above, and under the sea, *"Bateau ivre"* expresses romantic impatience with limits and almost mystical desire. Baudelaire's *"Voyage"* approaches the "unknown."

Illuminations, written in 1872 and 1873, is a deeper voyage into the unknown. The title suggests fireworks or mystical raptures. Rimbaud was not a mystic, however, but a magus, a disciple of Lévi, who used incantation to compel what mystics are given. Like the poems of A. E., those of Rimbaud are sometimes descriptions of what he saw; but more often they are formulas, like the words of a magician, to create what he could see. The incoherent flood if images that his method released is like nothing previously recorded save for the Apocalypse, perhaps, or the records of literate madmen.

The poems in verse, though simple in appearance, are enigmatic. The poems in prose are even more ambiguous and more interesting. Some years earlier Baudelaire had invented a poetic prose, which he described as "musical without rhythm or rhyme, supple and bold enough to adapt itself to the lyric movements of the soul, to the undulations of reverie, to the somersaults of the consciousness." Some of his prose poems record his opium dreams, but Rimbaud's go further. His prose poems present hallucinations, dreams, infant memories, and all the rich nonsense of the unconscious. In one of his nightmares Mme X "established a piano on the Alps." *Une Saison en Enfer* (1873), his spiritual autobiography, explains her conduct:

> I discovered the color of the vowels. . . . I discovered a poetic language available to all the senses. I reserved the rights of translation. . . . I noted the inexpressible. . . . I accustomed myself to hallucination: I saw a mosque in the place of a factory, a set of drums played by angels . . . a parlor at the bottom of a lake. . . . Then I explained my magical sophistries with the hallucination of words.

Convinced of failure, Rimbaud abandoned poetry. Stéphane Mallarmé, also plagued with a sense of failure, persisted. Although impressed by the discrepancy between his ideal and its poetic realization, he resigned himself to "the grief of the inexplicable Penultimate." The famous poem of the swan in ice symbolizes his frustration. He need not have worried. *"Hérodiade"* and *"L'Après-midi d'un faune,"* symphonies of indirections, exceed the Penultimate. To Mallarmé a poem was a means of communicating between matter and idea, exhausting matter, image, and word in the process until only idea was left. Unaware of verbal alchemy, the reader might take the poem at its face value as if it were about a faun or Salomé. The later poems, however, have small face value to mistake. In place of palpable subject *"Prose (pour des Esseintes),"* for example, offers impalpable vibrations.

To do their transcendental job, words had to be relieved of their normal meanings, removed from their familiar contexts, until, purified, they could provoke reveries, resonances, ineffable suggestions. Poems built by meticulous craft from words deprived of syntax could suggest things too fugitive for expression and meanings at once precise and multiple. Poems built in this way were absolute. Free from meaning in the usual sense, they were also free from time, chance, life, passion, and matter. A symphonic relationship among the parts of the poem took the place of comprehensible relationships with external things. The poem, said Mallarmé, "is a mystery to which the reader must hunt the key." Abandoning the hope of a single interpretation, he must discover the main images, observe the effect upon them of the peripheral images, and guess the idea generated by their interaction. Mallarmé explained these matters to his disciples on Tuesday evenings.

For many years Mallarmé, Verlaine, and Rimbaud remained relatively unknown. But in 1884 their fame began. Turning away from naturalism in *A rebours,* Huysmans discovered Mallarmé; and Verlaine in *Poètes maudits,* advertised Rimbaud, Corbière, Villiers, and Verlaine. These poets immediately became the idols of the Decadents, a self-conscious group, who published the magazine *Le Décadent.* In *La Revue Wagnérienne* others began to advance the cult of Wagner and of poetry as music.[2]

But their idols were individuals, hardly representing a tendency, still less a school. That would never do. The younger poets founded a school, elected themselves and their elders to membership, and, after a few unsuccessful tries, named one another symbolists. The name was not inappropriate for Baudelaire, Mallarmé, and Rimbaud, who held the doctrine of correspondence in common; it was almost appropriate for Verlaine; and it served to cover youth with a glamour so thick that the middle class was

[2] *Les Déliquescences d'Adoré Floupette* (1885), parodies of Mallarmé, Verlaine, and Laforgue by Vicaire and Beauclair.

baffled again. Defining symbolism in his manifesto of September 18, 1886, Jean Moréas followed Mallarmé:

> Enemy of explanation, of declamation, of false sensibility, of objective description, symbolist poetry tries to clothe the Idea in a palpable form, which, nevertheless, is not an end in itself, but which, while serving to express the Idea, remains subject to it. The Idea in its turn does not let itself be seen without sumptuous trains of exterior analogies; for the essential character of symbolic art consists in never going to the conception of the Idea in itself. Thus in this art, pictures of nature, actions of men, concrete phenomena are not there for their own sake, but as simple appearances destined to represent their esoteric affinities with primordial Ideas.

"It is true," observed Anatole France, "that M. Moréas explains symbolism, but it is also true that his explanation is not easy to follow." [3]

Moréas, René Ghil, Stuart Merrill, Gustave Kahn, and the others praised and wrote "symbolist" poems. Sometimes the symbol was an image, like Mallarmé's swan, or a system of images; sometimes it was a suggestive rhythm or combination of sounds; and sometimes it was a whole poem, a symphony of sounds, images, rhythms approximating the condition of music. To be symbolist was to be subjective, oblique, bizarre, difficult, transcendental, Wagnerian, or *"anglais."*

With the help of the English tradition the symbolists, going further than earlier French romantics, freed themselves from the domination of the rules. But except for a poem here or there, the symbolists do not resemble the Englishmen and Americans who assisted them toward liberty; for coming after the climax of their tradition, they transformed what they took from their predecessors. The decadence and individuality of the symbolists permitted later Englishmen to come to them with a sense of discovery for aid in remaking the English tradition or escaping it.

[3] Moréas: *Les Premières Armes du Symbolisme* (1889).

The example of Walt Whitman and rebellion against the rules led the symbolists to free verse, which may be defined as rhythm responsive to mood, or the attempt to give words their musical value, or what is left after the rules of prosody have been abolished. Rimbaud appears to have been the first to use it. Verlaine less adventurously followed him, but Mallarmé, like Baudelaire before him, remained technically conservative until near the end of his life when in *"Un Coup de dés"* he anticipated the vagaries of E. E. Cummings. Laforgue, Kahn, Dujardin, and Whitmanesque Verhaeren all availed themselves of metrical liberty. Gustave Kahn, their theoretician, defined and justified the new poetic instrument.

With Maeterlinck and Villiers, symbolism entered the theater. New little magazines published new little poets. By 1895, however, there was some falling away from the symbolist ideal. Moréas turned to classicism. Verhaeren, after following Baudelaire through "hallucinated countrysides" and nightmare cities, began to celebrate factories, railways, and power. By 1900 symbolism was pronounced dead, but despite repeated pronouncements by the best authorities it maintained a hidden vitality and made appearances. Paul Valéry emerged as Mallarmé's most faithful disciple, as mysterious as his master and as great a poet. Guillaume Apollinaire revived the most bizarre excesses of the Decadents and invented the word "surrealism." In the twenties surrealists rediscovered the tradition of Rimbaud and Lautréamont. Exploring the unconscious, André Breton and Paul Éluard returned with metaphors.

II

The poets of England who followed the symbolists took from them what their times, their circumstances, and their capacities permitted. From the 1870's some English poets were aware, and later more were aware, that the way to revive their exhausted tradition was the way of the French. During the nineties the English knew something of all the symbolists.[4] Not all, however, had news for Englishmen; for some Frenchmen, further advanced in method, manner, and decadence, were beyond the comprehension of their Victorian admirers. The English saw part at least of what Baudelaire meant and profited by what they saw. They admired, misunderstood, and translated Mallarmé. They translated and imitated Verlaine. Some knew of Rimbaud, Laforgue, Verhaeren, and Merrill. And to some Maeterlinck seemed what the world of Darwin required. From each they took what they could in response to their needs, and English poetry or some of it became exotic, decadent, and new.

To the *Spectator* in 1862 Swinburne contributed the first review in English of Baudelaire's poems. Sadistic, Lesbian "Dolores" and "Anactoria," which seem to owe something to Baudelaire's *"Femmes damnées,"* are so successfully transposed into the lilies and languors of Swinburne that the debt is not immediately apparent. *"Ave atque Vale,"* an elegy on Baudelaire, expresses Swinburne's mistaken conviction that Baudelaire was a kindred spirit.[5]

Late in the seventies George Moore, who had fled the English Philistines for the bohemians of Montmartre, met Villiers and, through him, Mallarmé. Moore was fascinated with *Fleurs du Mal*. His *Flowers of Passion* (1878) were plucked, as the title confesses, from Baudelaire's wicked garden. "These bloomless blossoms," Moore announces, are "symbol flowers." But it is hard for a reader today to detect either symbolism or Baudelaire in the boyish imitations of Swinburne that compose the volume.

In *Confessions of a Young Man* (1888) Moore tells what Baudelaire's "poisonous blossoms" meant to him. "The children of the nineteenth century go to you, O Baudelaire, and having tasted of your deadly delight, all hope of repentance is vain. Flowers, beautiful in your sublime decay, I press you to my lips." That is not what Baudelaire meant, but what Moore needed and what he found; and it pleased him to think that Baudelaire disbe-

---

[4] Ruth Temple: *The Critic's Alchemy* (1953).
[5] Georges Lafourcade: *Swinburne* (1932).

lieved in goodness, truth, and life itself. It is not surprising
that a reviewer of *Flowers of Passion* called Moore "a
bestial bard." With the publication of *Pagan Poems*
(1881) his imitations of Baudelaire fortunately ceased, but
not his interest in the symbolists.

   Moore tells in *Confessions of a Young Man* of his
acquaintance with René Ghil and Gustave Kahn, of his
admiration of Kahn's "strange, abnormal, and unhealthy"
poems, two of which he quotes, and of the decadent charm
of Verlaine's *Fêtes galantes*. He quotes the sonnet on Parsifal. Moore had enjoyed the talk at Mallarmé's on Tuesday evenings, but he confesses that he never enjoyed the
master's poems. *"L'Après-midi"* seemed absurdly obscure,
though lucid in comparison with the "brain-curdling enig-
mas" of the later poems. He knew that these poems were
symbolist. "What is symbolism?" he asks. "Vulgarly speaking, saying the opposite to what you mean." And he proceeds to give an account of the making of a symbolist
poem in which each unexplained image stands for an idea.
This pedestrian, gay, and all too literal interpretation of
Mallarmé's method is balanced by Moore's translation of
two of Mallarmé's prose poems, which are interpreted as
"aberrations of a refined mind, distorted with hatred of the
commonplace." Longing for decadence as an antidote to
the commonplace or as irritant to the "hypocritical
reader," Moore saw only the decadence of the decadent
French.

   It was probably from his friend René Ghil and from
Baudelaire's *"Correspondances"* that Moore learned that
confusion of the senses which gives an inappropriately
symbolist air to *A Drama in Muslin* (1886), his novel
about the superior daughters of Ireland, whose dancing
at the Shelbourne Hotel seems an "allegro movement of
odours . . . interrupted suddenly by the garlicky an-
dante, deep as the pedal notes of an organ, that the perspiring armpits of a fat chaperon exhaled slowly." As
Moore had been the first in England with a volume of
Baudelairian poems, so he was the first in England with
French synesthesia. He was the first to read and praise

Huysmans's *A rebours* and to imitate it; and he was the first to write critical essays on Verlaine, Rimbaud, and Laforgue.[6] Moore is important less for what he said about symbolism or for what he did with it in his novels and poems than for his services in making it known to literate Englishmen.

Moore's guide and adviser in Paris was Édouard Dujardin, editor of the *Revue Wagnérienne,* pioneer in free verse, and author of *Les Lauriers sont coupés.* With Dujardin, Moore visited Verlaine the day he wrote *"Parsifal,"* and with Dujardin he shared an admiration for Laforgue's *Moralités légendaires.* Dujardin led Moore through the mazes of the symbolist reviews, told him about Wagner, and later on, out of his considerable Biblical scholarship, provided Moore with material for *The Brook Kerith* (1916). In *Conversations in Ebury Street* (1924), expressing his debt to his friend, Moore celebrates their wanderings through symbolist Paris.[7]

Oscar Wilde knew of the French almost as soon as Moore. While still an undergraduate at Oxford in the late seventies, he incurred the loathing of honest men by talking of Baudelaire and the beauty of evil. *Poems* (1881), though generally in the English romantic tradition, shows some traces of Baudelaire, especially *"Impression du Matin."* "The Harlot's House," written during the eighties, combines the macabre, the urban, and the grotesque with a sudden, disconcerting prettiness, more horrible than what preceded it. Wilde had captured the externals of Baudelaire, and he was no less successful in "The Sphinx" (1894). Taking theme and images from Flaubert, Huysmans, and Baudelaire, he devoted his exotic verbalism and imagery to an evocation of theatrical evil. But his purple corridors (rhyming with moaning mandragores), his basilisks, nenuphars, gilded galiots, and monstrous hippopotami somehow escape absurdity; for though one may smile, one is impressed against all judgment by the density of the atmosphere surrounding his "lovely seneschal . . . half

[6] *Impressions and Opinions* (1891).
[7] Moore's letters to Dujardin, 1886–1922, were published in 1929. Malcolm Brown: George Moore (1955).

woman and half animal." That such an air can be exhaled by the stanza of *In Memoriam* deepens one's impression.

To Wilde, Baudelaire, a symbol of sin, sensuousness, and exoticism, meant beauty separated from morality. A portent to frighten Philistines, he is paraded through *Intentions* (1891). To Baudelaire *Dorian Gray* (1891) owes the dandyism of Lord Henry, the opium, and the Wagnerian music. But it is, of course, to Huysmans's *A rebours,* Lord Henry's favorite book, that Dorian owes his symphonies of flowers and odors. Recognizing these origins, a reviewer described *Dorian Gray* as "a tale spawned from the leprous literature of the French decadents—a poisonous book, the atmosphere of which is heavy with the mephitic odours of moral and spiritual putrefaction."

Wilde's most thoroughly symbolist work, *Salomé,* published in 1893, is the most successful approximation of symbolism to that time in England.[8] Wilde wrote it with the advice and correction of several symbolists with whom he enjoyed a kind of friendship. Paul Fort, who was managing the symbolist Théâtre d'Art, helped him. So did Stuart Merrill, Marcel Schwob, and Adolphe Retté, a poet who was assisting Fort in his production of Maeterlinck's *Aveugles.* With such aid it is little wonder that Wilde achieved the authentic manner, nor is it surprising that after the British censor had denied Sarah Bernhardt a license to produce the play in London, it was accepted (in 1896) by Lugné-Poe for his Théâtre de l'Œuvre. This theater, founded in idealistic reaction against Antoine's naturalistic Théâtre Libre, was the citadel, if so definite a word may be used, of symbolist drama. Here Lugné-Poe had offered Maeterlinck, Hauptmann, Strindberg, and symbolical Ibsen. The sound of wild ducks, of footsteps down empty corridors, and of sunken bells surrounded this spiritual place.

Maeterlinck, who started as a symbolist poet in 1889, was the first to succeed in transporting the symbolist ideal

---

[8] Wilde wrote this one-act play in French in 1891. The English translation is by Lord Alfred Douglas. Wilde's Salomé is modeled upon Flaubert's *Salammbô,* Laforgue's Salomé in *Moralités légendaires,* and the *Hérodias* of Flaubert and of Mallarmé.

to the stage. For a long time Mallarmé had dreamed of a theater in which a union of music, poetry, and gesture could be kept from the audience by a veil. Maeterlinck's talents did not extend to music or poetry, but he did provide a sort of veil in the dreamlike atmosphere, the circumambient fears, and that uncertainty of time, place, and character which seemed to favor the infinite. Since the finite cannot depict the infinite or words express the inexpressible, Maeterlinck undertook to suggest the infinite and the inexpressible by childish words, overtones, and silences. Rebelling in his turn against external reality, he suggested interior and superior realities. Critics praised his *Intruse* (1890) for suggesting death without presenting it on the stage, and they saw in *Les Aveugles* (1890), *Les Sept Princesses* (1891), and *Pelléas et Mélisande* (1892) the ceremonies of a future religion. The symbolist theater, like a symbolist poem, concerned something else than it concerned.

Wilde studied *Les Sept Princesses* and *La Princesse Maleine* as well, but his sensuous and extravagant nature interfered with a faithful reproduction of Maeterlinck's manner. Exotic jewels, green flowers, white peacocks, mouths like "the red cries of trumpets," and the other furniture are Wilde's own or else Flaubert's, Laforgue's, or Mallarmé's. Apprehending Mallarmé's technique of making each ornament and gesture suggest more than it could, Wilde made *Salomé* as symbolist in its degree as the work of the master. Using Maeterlinck's simple dialogue with overtones and his habit of understatement, except, of course, in passages where sensuousness overcame him, Wilde evoked what was not presented, the problem of hedonism, Jesus, and man's regeneration. These moral and religious implications arise from a symphony of their opposites. Wilde's symbolism, crude compared with Mallarmé's, is not inferior to Maeterlinck's. Take, for instance, the behavior of the moon. At first merely strange, it becomes hysterical, turns red as blood, then hides behind a veil as a cold wind passes by. Observing these things, Hérode says to comfort himself: "One must not find symbols in everything one sees." But in a

symbolist play one must. Moreover, the sense of impend-
ing horror, the beating of unseen and unheard wings, and
the cistern show how well Wilde had learned the lesson of
the symbolist theater. On the whole his play has weathered
time as well as any of Maeterlinck's, though perhaps that
is not saying very much.[9]

Through the work of Arthur Symons symbolism
reached a wider public. His criticism interpreted the
French to the readers of magazines, his translations gave
some idea of the nature of symbolist poetry, and his original verses followed the French as well as they were able.
Coming closely on the heels of Moore, Symons began in
the early nineties to write his essays on French poets, most
of whom he had met.[1] He had attended Mallarmé's semi-
nar and, suitably impressed, could not wait to tell the news
to England. In "The Decadent Movement in Literature"
(1893) he says that though the literary movement of
France is variously called symbolist, impressionist, and
decadent, decadent alone suits Verlaine's "exquisite depravity of style," Mallarmé's symbols, by which the
"deeper meaning of things" is obscured, and the deliberate
singularity of Moréas.

The Symbolist Movement in Literature (1899), where
the word is symbolist, is Symons's masterpiece. Though
there is little understanding of Rimbaud, who had nothing
to say to Englishmen of the nineties, the essays on Verlaine, Huysmans, and Maeterlinck are adequate, and the
essay on Mallarmé is excellent. This and the introduction,
which remains the best English survey of French symbolism, give the book its value.

Symons's translation of the last part of *"Hérodiade"*
leaves much to be desired, but with the poems from Verlaine's *Fêtes galantes* Symons was more successful. Later
he turned to Baudelaire, and for remaking him into something out of *A rebours* deserved and received the rebuke
of Eliot.

Symons wrote little about Baudelaire during the nine-

[9] Cf. William Sharp: *Vistas* (1894), imitation Maeterlinck.
[1] *Studies in Prose and Verse* (1904), *Dramatis Personæ* (1923),
Figures of Several Centuries (1916).

ties, but he modeled his own verses on what he could assimilate from that poet. At their best they are wicked and bizarre, and at their worst sentimental. The favorite themes—opium, city landscapes, derelicts of the streets, alcoves, and morbid mistresses—are Baudelaire's. His too is that love of artifice confessed in *"Maquillage,"* a poem in praise of rouge and powder. Amid such delights he paused to taste audible odors and other confusions of the senses.

Ernest Dowson, a finer poet than Symons, was also indebted to France. The famous poem on Cynara transposes Baudelaire's *"affreuse Juive,"* and many of Dowson's most fastidious pieces reproduce the autumnal music of Verlaine. From him Dowson learned to divest his verse of moral, social, and philosophical preoccupations and by all the skills of prosody to perfect his isolated moods.[2]

Like others in the nineties, Dowson understood Verlaine because that Frenchman was the most English of the symbolists. What made his poetry novel in France made it familiar in England. Moreover, he visited England in 1893, lectured at Oxford and London, and while staying with Symons, met the English poets. Thoroughly comprehensible, he was decadent enough to be attractive, and his disreputable life was another point in his favor with those trying to forget or annoy the middle class.

John Gray's translations from Verlaine, Baudelaire, and Rimbaud show command of decadence. Even the malign early manner of Rimbaud, now first attempted, survives the process. Gray's own excellent poems in *Silverpoints* (1893) are very decadent. *"Les Demoiselles de Sauve"* combines the elegance of *Fêtes galantes* with a bizarre lusciousness. "The Barber" exceeds in preciousness all previous celebrations of artifice. After such delicate excesses it is as well, perhaps, that John Gray left his world for the priesthood.

Aubrey Beardsley's *Under the Hill* (1896) is the climax, in England at least, of decadent artifice. This prose

---

[2] *"Colloque Sentimental"* and *"Spleen"* are translations from Verlaine. *Pierrot of the Minute,* a poetic play, approaches the manner and tone of *Fêtes galantes.*

fragment, which Arthur Symons printed in the *Savoy*, presents "blond trousers," "intelligent curls," "little mutinies of ruffle and cravat," and little else. The model for this arabesque is the *Moralités légendaires* of Laforgue, whose mixture of the bizarre, the humorous, and the precious Beardsley was enabled by nature to improve.[3] Whereas Laforgue's prose sketches burlesque the legends of Salomé, Hamlet, and Lohengrin, Beardsley's improvement plays with the Wagnerian conceit of Tannhäuser and Venus.

As a critic of symbolists Edmund Gosse was second only to Symons. In 1875 Gosse had met Mallarmé at Swinburne's home in Chelsea, and from that time maintained a kind of uneasy friendship with the "eloquent and mysterious" poet, whose *"Après-midi"* he ventured to paraphrase in prose. During the nineties he composed many essays on the French. Free from any taint of decadence and thoroughly British, he condescended a little to these foreigners. In 1895, accompanied by Henry Harland, he went to Paris on a decadent-hunt and, ascending the boulevard Saint-Michel, looked into each café. There was Jean Moréas at his table and there Verlaine at his (in a clean shirt), speaking "with a veiled utterance, difficult for me to follow." Everywhere he heard verses he could not understand and could not have understood had he been a Frenchman.[4] This humor reappears in his obituary on "poor, charming Mallarmé." Although Gosse discusses Mallarmé's method with some understanding, he deplores his effect upon the young, whom he has driven to nonsense and affectation. It is to Gosse's credit, however, that in his essay on Samain he separates the Satanism of Baudelaire, which up to then had preoccupied the English, from that lofty severity which "his horrors at first

---

[3] Aside from this, Laforgue had little effect on men of the nineties, and Rimbaud was beyond the comprehension of most. But T. Sturge Moore in *The Vinedresser* (1899) made an excellent translation of "Les Charcheuses de poux." His "Response to Rimbaud's Later Manner," *Poems*, Vol. II (1931–3), is excellent parody. Moore also adapted poems of Baudelaire and Valéry. At his best Moore is an excellent poet.

[4] *French Profiles* (1905), *Questions at Issue* (1893).

concealed." It is to Gosse's credit, moreover, that he failed to confuse the symbolists with Donne.[5]

Symbolism was more cosmopolitan than most suspected. Although the English preferred him as a social critic, Ibsen, as Frenchmen knew, was also a symbolist, and so was Stefan George. Conspicuous in the field, Frenchmen attracted Englishmen first, and for years monopolized their attention. Taking quick looks and sometimes mistaking what they saw, the English poets of the nineties were content with exotic surfaces. Few if any of their poems are symbolist according to Mallarmé's ideal or the prescription of Moréas, but many of them show what Eugene Lee-Hamilton in his sonnet on Baudelaire calls "the gorgeous iridescence of decay." These are the issue of the marriage, unhappy as yet, of exhausted English romanticism with French romantic decadence.

The French to whom the English aspired were great poets and the aspirers small. Unable to write great poems, they succeeded, however, in spreading a novel conception of the poem as a self-contained, harmonic system, remote from society, philosophy, and politics. They expanded the themes of poetry to include the ugly, the disgusting, and the bizarre. They used theme and tone as weapons against the Philistines. But the Philistines, turning at last, used the exposure of Oscar Wilde, whose association with France was notorious, to disparage the symbolist tradition. Whether or not social pressure succeeded, symbolism or its externals, so carefully fostered in England for more than a decade, expired around 1900, to be resurrected only after ten years of triumphant convention. But the minor poets and the critics of the nineties had done their work, and it was on foundations they established that poets and critics of greater capacity were to build. The generation of 1910, desiring in turn to remake the romantic tradition, captured what had eluded the grasp of the nineties.

The portrait of Enoch Soames in Max Beerbohm's *Seven Men* (1919) provided an epitaph for this decade.

[5] Gosse's life of Donne (1899) had almost as much to do as Grierson's edition (1912) with the vogue of metaphysical poetry in our time.

Taking his absinthe at the Café Royal, Soames wrote a
book of incomprehensible essays called *Negations* in imitation perhaps of Mallarmé's *Divagations. Fungoids,* the
strange poems Soames wrote in imitation of the French,
were generally neglected. In pity for this symbolist, Beerbohm quotes several poems from *Fungoids,* among them:

> *Pale tunes irresolute*
> *And traceries of old sounds*
> *Blown from a rotted flute*
> *Mingle with noise of cymbals rouged with rust,*
> *Nor not strange forms and epicene*
> *Lie bleeding in the dust. . . .*

"Nor not," that exquisite violation of grammar, reminded
him of Mallarmé.

III

When Arthur Symons, dedicating his *Symbolist Movement in Literature* to William Butler Yeats, called his
Irish friend "the chief representative of that movement in
our country," he meant a general European movement of
which the French were leaders. Later critics have been
less precise. C. M. Bowra in his *Heritage of Symbolism*
(1943) assumes that Yeats is heir to the French. Joseph
Hone, also accepting Yeats as heir to the French, asserts
in his *Life of W. B. Yeats* (1943) that Yeats was familiar
with the *"Hérodiade"* of Villiers de l'Isle Adam, an assertion that would carry more weight if Mallarmé had not
written it and if Yeats had been familiar with it. These
critics, whose confusions suggest only that the matter is
confusing, may be forgiven for their desire to impose
cause, effect, and order upon something that seems to
deny these satisfactions.

That Yeats was a symbolist is clear. But it is also
clear that his knowledge of French was so slight that he
was unable to read the difficult poems to which he is
supposed to be indebted. His French, which he picked up
here and there without much benefit of schooling, was
adequate for adapting Ronsard's sonnet "When You Are

Old" unless, of course, he had found an English version.

The case for *Axël* by Villiers de l'Isle Adam is stronger. Probably between 1890 and 1892 Yeats read this play slowly and laboriously, for, as he says, his French was very poor. "That play seemed all the more profound," he adds in the preface he wrote for an English translation of *Axël* in 1925, "because I was never quite certain that I had read a page correctly." On February 26, 1894 he went to Paris to see the production of *Axël* at the Théâtre Montparnasse, in company with Maud Gonne, who assisted his memory by explaining the words of the actors. She or another helped him through the almost surrealist obscurities of Jarry's *Ubu roi* at the symbolist Théâtre de l'Œuvre in 1896. On his return from Paris in 1894, Yeats reviewed *Axël* in the April *Bookman* as part of the spiritual reaction of his time against science, externality, and realism; and his symbolic play *The Shadowy Waters* (1900) is a translation of *Axël* into nautical terms.

Aside from *Axël* and a number of treatises on the occult, there is no available evidence that Yeats read anything in French. But he was acquainted with the plays of Maeterlinck in English translation. Although he was less enthusiastic about Maeterlinck's plays and essays than about *Axël,* he regarded them as significant protests against the external, and he was fascinated with Maeterlinck's repeated symbols of mysterious intruders, lighthouses, and wells in the woods.

Yeats managed to supplement these inconsiderable contacts with France during the late nineties through his friendship with Arthur Symons, who, as he finished them, read Yeats his translations from Verlaine and Mallarmé. Yeats was impressed, he tells in his *Autobiography,* with Symons's selection from Mallarmé's *"Hérodiade,"* which increased his own inclination toward an art separated from circumstance, character, and "everything heterogeneous and casual," toward a poetry as unlike that of the Victorians as possible, but like the self-contained, socially isolated, and integrated poetry of Mallarmé. These translations, Yeats continues, "may have given elaborate form" to his *Wind among the Reeds* (1899); and he will never know, he adds, how much his theory and practice owe them. It is possible, as Yeats suggests, that the verses of Symons had these effects. It must be remembered, however, that Symons's translation from *"Hérodiade"* is not a good one and that any elaborateness communicated by it is from Symons, not Mallarmé. But the case for theory is a stronger one; for it must be supposed that Symons, who understood the theories of Mallarmé, talked as much as he read, and that Yeats must have acquired some knowledge at second hand of symbolist intentions. Moreover, Yeats read *The Symbolist Movement in Literature* when it appeared in 1899 and based his essay "The Symbolism of Poetry" (1900) partly upon what he had learned. "When sound, and colour, and form are in a musical relation . . . to one another," Yeats says in this essay, "they become as it were one sound, one colour, one form, and evoke an emotion that is made out of their distinct evocations and yet is one emotion." This is Mallarmé by way of Symons. That phrase about the trembling of the veil of the temple which Yeats was continually quoting comes from the *Divagations* (1897) of Mallarmé. Since this book, if not this phrase, is difficult, Yeats received it, no doubt, from Symons, who had sat on Tuesdays at the feet of the master.

A man who cannot read Mallarmé cannot be affected by Mallarmé. But it is unnecessary to look to him or to any Frenchman for the symbolism of Yeats, who was a symbolist long before he had heard of the French. He based his symbolism upon the poetry of Blake, Shelley, and Rossetti and, above all these, upon the occult. In 1886, as we know, Yeats joined the Dublin Lodge of the Theosophical Society, and two or three years later the Order of the Golden Dawn. From the works of Mme Blavatsky, Yeats learned that Anima Mundi, a reservoir of all that has touched mankind, may be evoked by symbols. From Swedenborg he received the doctrine of correspondences, from Eliphas Lévi the doctrine of magical incantations and symbols that have power over spiritual and material reality, and from Boehme the similar doctrine of signatures. The Emerald Tablet of Hermes Trismegistus informed him that things below are as things above. And the symbolic ritual of the Rosicrucians confirmed these ideas. A rebel against the world of matter, Yeats learned that all material things correspond to ideas in the world of spirit and that through the use of material objects as magical symbols the adept may call down disembodied powers. The essay "Magic" (1901) expresses his conviction that the great memory of nature "can be evoked by symbols." Like Baudelaire, who had read Swedenborg before him, Yeats became a poetic visionary, and like Rimbaud, who had followed Eliphas Lévi, Yeats became a magus, a master of magic, who through poetic symbols and trances could surprise reality. Although he had not heard of Baudelaire or Rimbaud when he read Lévi and Swedenborg, Yeats belonged, with these poets, to the great transcendental movement of the nineteenth century and turned naturally to the same supernatural sources. Material reality became for him as for them a chaos of symbols through which a poet could discover spiritual order. The example of Blake, also an occultist, taught Yeats the use in poetry of magical symbols; and the poems of Shelley, which he carefully analyzed, confirmed his symbolic system. Like Blake, Baudelaire, and Rimbaud, Yeats saw the poet as magus and priest, but as poet before magus and priest. Knowing what he was about, he went to the occult in the first place to discover, if he could, the laws of the imagination, to find ways of inducing trance and vision through which he could confront the inner and higher realities he needed and to find symbols for his poetry.

By 1890, before Yeats knew about the French symbolists, he had been writing symbolic poems for several years, and when Symons and others told him about the French poets, he welcomed them as fellow travelers on the road he was following, as fellow transcendentalists and occultists who had, like Blake and Shelley, hit upon symbolism as the only possible way to express what they had experienced. Maeterlinck was a kind of theosophist. Villiers was a student of Eliphas Lévi and of the Rosicrucians. Occult considerations led Yeats to the laborious reading of *Axël,* and it was probably MacGregor Mathers, the Rosicrucian, who introduced him to this congenial play.

The symbols of Yeats's early poems, like those of Villiers and of Lévi, are occult in character. Aware that Anima Mundi or the great memory of nature may be evoked by symbols drawn from Irish legends, Yeats used the symbolic characters of Oisin or Aengus, for example, the hound with one red ear, the white deer with no horns, and the island in the western sea. But equally characteristic are his arbitrary occult symbols of rose, cross, lily, bird, water, tree, moon, and sun, which he could find in the cabbalistic, Theosophical, and other profound works that constituted the greater part of his reading. The two trees in his poem of that name are the Sephirotic tree of the cabbala and the tree of knowledge. The "Powers" of his poem "The Poet Pleads with the Elemental Powers" are Mme Blavatsky's elemental spirits, the "Immortal Rose" is Rosicrucian, and the "Seven Lights" are the seven planets of Theosophy. The "Ineffable Name" of "To Some I Have Talked with by the Fire" is the cabbalistical *Shem Hamphorasch* or Jehovah, whose unspeakable four-lettered name in Hebrew characters admits of seventy-two combinations, as Yeats, practicing with the cabbalists in Paris, knew by experience. These symbols differ from those ordinarily employed by the French in being traditional, systematic, more arbitrary and definite in outline. But though they are first of all magical symbols, hence impersonal, as used by Yeats they become as personal, reverberating, and mysterious as the symbols of the less systematic French.

Most of the rose poems were written in his first enthusiasm after reading *Axël* with its Rosicrucian roses. But as a member of the Order of the Golden Dawn Yeats had no need to pilfer *Axël,* for the symbolic ritual of his society centered in the rose and cross. The society, of course, was secret; but Aleister Crowley, a member, violating dreadful vows, exposed its ritual at great length in the September 1909 and March 1910 numbers of the *Equinox,* a magazine he edited. This ritual does much to make Yeats's poetic symbolism plain.[6] But the rose in Yeats's poems and stories is even more complex than this ritual would imply, for Yeats was personal as well as occult and he used the rose to mean more than Father Christian Rosy Cross or MacGregor Mathers intended: earthly love as well as spirit in the battle of spirit against matter. The rose in "To the Rose upon the Rood of Time," as the title of the poem implies, is the Rosicrucian rose, but it is also the power of the creative imagination and occult philosophy too, which, Yeats fears, may remove him so completely from the present world that he will cease to be a poet. A similar fear plagues the hero of the story "Rosa Alchemica," an adventure in spiritual alchemy in which the rose as in Eliphas Lévi means the "Great Work" of transmuting matter into spirit. Taken to the headquarters of the Order of the Alchemical Rose, where adepts ceremoniously dance with spirits, the hero joins the dance. On the dancing-floor is a great cross and on the ceiling a greater rose.

More and more Yeats feared the isolation of spirit from matter, as he had feared the isolation of matter from spirit, and with these fears the rose came to mean what he called "unity of being" or the harmony of self, world, and spirit. These meanings are present in the rose or around it, but they are not all that it suggests because from each context come reverberations enriching the symbol as it in turn enriches its context. The value of a symbol, said Yeats, is this richness or indefiniteness of reference, which makes it far more mysterious and potent than allegory with its single meaning. A hundred men, he continued, would advance a hundred different meanings for the same symbol; for "no symbol tells all its meaning" to any man.[7]

The Wind among the Reeds (1899) gives "dumb

[6] Richard Ellmann: *Yeats, the Man and the Mask* (1948). Virginia Moore: *The Unicorn* (1954).

[7] For his observations on symbolism see his edition of Blake's *Prophetic Books* (1893), his essays on Shelley, the essays called "The Symbolism of Poetry," "Symbolism in Painting," and "The Autumn of the Body," and his introduction to *A Book of Images* (1898) by W. T. Horton, a fellow adept.

things voices, and bodiless things bodies." Reviewing this book, Arthur Symons hailed it as a triumph of symbolist indirection. Through the swooning diction, the musical, individual rhythms, the harmonies and overtones, and the interaction of many traditional but mysterious images each poem becomes the symbol of an unstated idea or mood. Although Yeats employed description and statement more lavishly than the French were accustomed to do, this book is closer in feeling and method to the works of the symbolists than any other that appeared in England during the nineties. It resembles these works not because it is their debtor but because, coming from the same revolt against matter and surface, it is their parallel.

Some of Yeats's plays resemble those of the symbolist stage not only because they are also transcendental reactions against the realistic stage, but because he had Villiers and Maeterlinck in mind when he wrote them. The debt of *The Shadowy Waters* to Villiers is clear. *The Countess Cathleen* (1892), however, which has all the atmosphere of Maeterlinck, was written before Yeats knew of him. It is difficult to say what part of Yeats's other plays comes from the French and what from the so-called Celtic twilight or the English romantic tradition.

The poems of *The Wind among the Reeds* and the earlier poems owe part of their richness and depth to something apart from the conscious use of occult symbols and wavering rhythms. Like Rimbaud, Yeats had discovered a way to evade the interference of his intellect and to explore his unconscious in search of symbols. Rimbaud had done this by a systematic derangement of the senses through drugs, fatigue, and depravity. Yeats, who was too prudent for such excesses, found in the occult a way of doing the same thing. Inclined by nature to waking visions and trances in which he saw wonderful things, he found that through the use of ritual and hypnotic symbols he could enjoy deeper and more effectual trances in which new images swam before his eyes. Magic, by putting his active intellect to sleep, permitted him to secure for his poems the wealth of his unconscious. Naturally he tried to give these floating images an occult value, but this did not prevent them from carrying with them to his poems, whatever his conscious intention, the richness of man's deepest reality. Like Rimbaud, then, and with the aid of Rimbaud's tutor, Eliphas Lévi, Yeats discovered a poetic country that had been neglected in England except by occasional madmen since the time of Blake. Yeats differs from Rimbaud, however, in the formal, conscious pattern he forced upon his images.

In the second part of *The Wanderings of Oisin* (1889) he tells of his hero's battle on an island in the sea with an elderly demon who keeps a lady in a cave. This episode, Yeats told Katharine Tynan, came to him in a kind of vision, which plagued him night and day and left him in a state of collapse. "Under the guise of symbolism," he told her, "I have said several things to which I only have the key." The story, he continued, was for the common reader who would remain unaware of the symbolism, yet "the whole poem is full of symbols." Aware that these unconscious symbols would bear neither an occult nor a legendary explanation, Yeats seems in this letter to Katharine Tynan, written long before Freud commenced his study of such symbols, to apprehend some part of their significance.

From his interest in semiconscious vision, Yeats was led by his occult interests to examine his dreams. "The Cap and Bells" (1899), as he assures us, is a dream recorded exactly as he dreamed it. In a note Yeats says that this poem meant much to him, but, as with all symbolic poems, its meaning was never twice the same. The first two stanzas of "The Song of Wandering Aengus" are plainly another dream or legend, which is rationalized in the third stanza.

After 1900 Yeats's poetry became colder, plainer, and more classical until in its "lofty severe quality" it came to resemble the poetry of Baudelaire. Feeling left the surface and vibrated beneath it. Far from following Baudelaire, still farther from following Moréas, who had turned to a kind of hardness before him, Yeats was responding bitterly to circumstance and self.

After 1917 Yeats returned more or less to romantic

symbolism, retaining nobility of tone and classical surface, and with this return came greater obscurity. Dissatisfied with the Golden Dawn, he announced in 1925 a system of his own. One of the demons who had dictated it to Mrs. Yeats informed her husband of its purpose: "We have come," he said, "to give you metaphors for poetry." Yeats used them in many of the poems he wrote between 1917 and 1935. "Leda and the Swan," which springs from the system, is symbolist in the sense that the manifest level is there to suggest unstated themes, the union of matter and spirit, of god and man, of Dove and Virgin, and all the cycles of history that begin with these unnatural conjunctions. In like manner "The Saint and the Hunchback," which has a dramatic, comprehensible level, implies three attitudes toward life symbolized by the saint, the hunchback, and Alcibiades, the last of whom stands for that aristocratic wholeness toward which Yeats aspired. "The Delphic Oracle upon Plotinus," a gay, preposterous poem, filled with mysterious overtones, concerns the philosopher Plotinus, swimming through turbulent waves toward a shore where Plato, Minos, Pythagoras, and Rhadamanthus await him with all the choir of love. This poem seems to be more surrealist than symbolist. As the title suggests, however, the author is not Yeats but the Delphic Oracle, who composed the poem in Greek long ago. By suppressing much and by selecting such beauties as the "golden race" and the "choir of love," Yeats made of her indifferent stuff, the stuff of poetry. As for its meaning, the Delphic Oracle, according to Porphyry, intended her symbols to imply the journey of Plotinus through the chaos of time and death to the Elysian Fields. Her symbols of sea and island attracted Yeats whose unconscious had persistently offered them to him. Like Milton, moreover, he was unable to resist the richness of names, especially those of Pythagoras and Plotinus, who were among his favorite adepts. No doubt the swimming of Plotinus toward his shore had a very personal significance to Yeats, not unlike that of the voyage to Byzantium, to the island of Innisfree, or to the Land of Youth.

These symbolic poems, which seem at first so French,

owe little or nothing to the French. But many of the later poems, "Among School Children" or "Sailing to Byzantium," have a tight logical structure and a dependence upon statement rarely found in French symbolist verse. Until the end, where the symbols of chestnut tree and dancer represent unity of being, "Among School Children" is more classical in method than symbolist, and its difficulties are those of any compressed, coherent whole of thought and feeling.

Whatever the occult bearing of Yeats's poems, they are also personal and worldly. In his most dramatic poems, those on Aengus or on the saint and hunchback for instance, Yeats had his own problems in mind. Whatever his romantic contempt of the world, it was never as thorough as that of Mallarmé, who saw the world merely as a store of symbols for something else. Even in his Rosicrucian days Yeats wanted to reconcile world and spirit and to integrate himself with world and spirit. His symbols, like his mask, gave him a way to do this. By their triple reference to self, world, and spirit they achieve on the æsthetic plane a unity of being impossible in life.[8]

IV

Between 1900 and 1910, when Yeats became satiric and more or less objective, such poetry as England produced, though not eminently Victorian perhaps, was thoroughly British. When symbolism resumed its course after this uninteresting decade, the poetry inspired by Frenchmen was better than that of the nineties because better poets with greater understanding now found the French congenial.

The Georgian poets, who undertook the revival of English poetry in 1912, were not of this kind, but the imagists, contemporaries of the Georgians, used the French to better purpose. Imagism is unusual among Eng-

[8] A more elaborate version of my account of Yeats's symbolism is included in James Hall and Martin Steinmann, editors: *The Permanence of Yeats* (1950).

lish poetic movements for having commenced with theory. In 1908 T. E. Hulme, the Bergsonist philosopher, founded a club with the object of restoring poetry to England. Looking at the declining Victorian tradition, he dismissed it as Wordsworth had dismissed the declining tradition of Alexander Pope, proposed a return to nature, to the language of common speech, and, going beyond Wordsworth, to a more natural rhythm. Late Victorian poetry seemed abstract, rhetorical, and vague. To remedy these evils Hulme advised brevity and precision, free verse, and concrete images. Some idea of the advice he gave at the sessions of his poets may be had from his "Notes on Language and Style." [9] True to the anti-intellectual position of Bergson, Hulme says in this essay that the poet must escape the limits that perception imposes upon the flow of experience. Evading logical statement, he must try to embody his feelings and sensations in precise physical analogies. Such metaphors and similes may convey the inexpressible, but any suggestions surrounding them must be controlled by the poet in order to avoid vagueness of reference. The reader of this imagistic, illogical poetry, with its limited suggestions and its economy, must work as he reads and share the task of creation. Hulme was no poet; but he carefully composed five poems to illustrate free verse, economy, and the image.[1]

Although Hulme based his theories on Bergson, who was reacting like the symbolists against externality and logic, he seems to have known little of French poetry until told of it by his young disciple F. S. Flint, who joined the second of Hulme's conventicles in a Soho restaurant in 1909. Flint had been reading the free verse of Fort, Jammes, Claudel, Gourmont, Régnier, and Verhaeren. Combining Hulme's theories with his own knowledge of the French, Flint became their chief interpreter. It was he who told Richard Aldington and Ezra Pound, new

[9] *Criterion*, July 1925. Cf. Emeric Fiser: *La Théorie du symbole littéraire et Marcel Proust* (1941), on Bergson and symbolism.

[1] Printed by Ezra Pound in *Ripostes* (1912) and in *Speculations* (1924).

members of Hulme's circle, about the French. Pound's subsequent articles about them confuse the ideas of Flint and Hulme.

Flint and Aldington were the principal English poets of the group. Aldington's early poetry, inspired by the Greeks, the Song of Solomon, and Whitman, was unaffected by the poetry of France. In *Cadences* (1915) Flint published imagistic poems that distantly reflect Verhaeren, his favorite. Poems by Aldington and Flint appear in *Des Imagistes* (1914), edited by Pound, the first imagist anthology. Although the rather French verse of Flint is even less memorable than the rather Middle Eastern verse of Aldington, Flint's poem on the swan in *Des Imagistes* is a more instructive example of imagism than any of Aldington's because it can be compared with an earlier and a later version. As it first appeared in 1909 the poem explains the feelings of the poet; but in *Des Imagistes* the feelings are presented by an image with a briefer explanation, and the last version, in *Otherworld* (1920), thoroughly objective, allows the image to speak for itself.

However Parnassian their themes or transcendental their implications, imagist poems never attained the impassibility of Parnasse or the indefinite suggestiveness of symbolism. The classical pretensions of the imagists, which seem odd in poets who, like Aldington, wanted to be petals or who could weep at the color of a tile, come less from their Parnassian antecedents than from the classical pretensions of T. E. Hulme. No poets, however, have been less classical in feeling, and few have been so trivial.[2]

The importance of the imagists is greater than the slightness of their poems would suggest; for by their example of brevity and precision they destroyed the vestiges of Victorian expansiveness. By making concrete pictures do the work of statement, they made poetry dramatic. By their rhythms they liberated verse. But having cleared a

[2] Glenn Hughes: *Imagism and the Imagists* (1931). Stanley K. Coffman: *Imagism* (1951). René Taupin: *L'Influence du symbolisme français sur la poésie américaine de 1910 à 1920* (1929). Introductions by Hughes and Ford Madox Ford to the *Imagist Anthology* (1930). Richard Aldington: *Life for Life's Sake* (1941). Herbert Read: *Annals of Innocence and Experience* (1940).

way, they found themselves unable to take it. Their failure may be explained in part by their incapacity and in part by their indifference to intellect.

The difference between imagism and French symbolism becomes evident when Flint's final image of the swan is compared with Mallarmé's image of the swan in *"Le vierge, le vivace et le bel aujourd'hui."* Mallarmé's image is surrounded with suggestions, feelings, and ideas about his position, his poetic ideals and failures, and art, society, matter, and spirit. The image, there to create its ghostly surroundings, is lost in what it creates. Flint's image, on the other hand, is relatively simple. It is there not to create but to represent the sensation and feeling of the poet at a particular moment. It takes the place of statement by dramatizing what a statement could do, whereas Mallarmé's image does more than a statement could do. An image as understood by the imagists is direct and representative; a symbol as understood by the French is indefinitely evocative. An image is a denuded and limited symbol or else a symbolic part. This difference, which owes something to a difference in poetic theory, owes more, perhaps, to a difference between poets; for Mallarmé, a great poet, had much to offer, and Flint, a small one, had little.

Of the Englishmen who went on from where the imagists left off, T. S. Eliot is the most important. While at college in America, he discovered the French through Arthur Symons's *Symbolist Movement in Literature.* To his admiration of Webster and Donne he added an even greater admiration of Baudelaire and Laforgue, especially the latter. Between 1907 and 1910 Eliot contributed several Laforguian poems to the *Harvard Advocate,* and while still at college he wrote his "Portrait of a Lady" (1909) and "The Love Song of J. Alfred Prufrock" (1910) in the manners of Webster and Laforgue.

The essays of Jules Laforgue tell almost as much about him as his verse. Inflated at first with transcendental yearning, he was deflated, he says, by Darwin. Hence the inflation and deflation of the poet's metaphors and the painful joy of punctured sentiments. But in Hartmann's theory of the unconscious Laforgue found peace and a literary method. It was the job of a poet, he felt, to follow the vagaries of the life force beyond limits, categories, and reason. "The wind of the unconscious blows where it will," he exclaims. "Let it blow." Meanwhile the poet's face assumed the expression of the clown, the *"fumiste,"* and the man about town. Slang of the boulevards, images from botany and zoology, and impressions of the suburb conceal a bleeding heart. In his prose poems, while men lean vacantly from windows, there are smells of frying, and all the "quotidian" ennuis of restaurants, pianos, and advertisements. The poems in free verse are streams of consciousness in which images of middle-class life float by in free association. To this procession the flippancy or nonchalance of the poet gives a disconcerting movement. In a letter to one of the mature women who attracted him he said: "Life is sad, history a nightmare," and I, like Pierrot, am "dilettante, virtuoso, guitarist. . . . Do you still find me young?"

Laforguian "Prufrock" is a dramatic monologue of that living dead man who, in "The Hollow Men" and other poems, was to become Eliot's specialty. Suffering from emotional anemia, repression, and weakness of will, J. Alfred owes part of his character to Henry James, more to Laforgue. But through the convenient mask of Laforgue, Eliot spoke with his own voice of his own condition, dramatizing it by images of coffee spoons, bald spots, and "lonely men in shirt-sleeves." Raised by these desolating particulars from the personal, the poem as a whole becomes a symbol of our condition and our world. It is for this value that "Prufrock" has undone so many. But this value, depending upon more than images, is a conspiracy of these with rhythm, structure, and tone to compose the symbol. The inflation and deflation, the vagaries of free association, pleasing while they perplex, are of course Laforgue's. The masterly rhythms, however much they owe to Laforgue and Webster, are Eliot's.

Wherever one looks in Laforgue there are similarities: *"Oh, qu'ils sont pittoresques les trains manqués."* It is unnecessary to multiply such lines or to cite the lines and images that Eliot lifted from his master; for they have been cited [3] and he has justified his habit. A poor poet imitates, he observed; a good one steals, and improves what he takes by making it part of a new system of thought and feeling. Taking what he needed from Laforgue, Eliot made arrangements, like the "Portrait of a Lady," which are better than anything by his master. But the dead geranium, which preceded the rose in Eliot's favor, is from the window-box of Jules Laforgue.

While enamored of him, Eliot also fancied Donne and Marvell, whose fusion of sense and intellect, according to "The Metaphysical Poets" (1921), was recaptured by Laforgue. This attractive confusion of logical Donne with illogical Laforgue, while pleasing to the sensibility, has done much to obscure the nature of Laforgue, who as a disciple of Hartmann did his best to suppress his intellect. Eliot's resemblance to logical Donne is far less than his resemblance to illogical Laforgue. In *The Waste Land* logical progress has been replaced by Laforguian sequences of feeling.

For the autobiographical poem *"Mélange Adultère de Tout"* Eliot took not only his title but his manner from Tristan Corbière, a jaunty and more virile predecessor of Laforgue. *"Le Directeur,"* also in French and one of Eliot's most fascinating poems, seems to owe its strangeness to Guillaume Apollinaire. "The Hippopotamus," as René Taupin shows by parallel columns, is a reproduction of Gautier's Parnassian *"Hippopotame."* These instances, which serve to show Eliot's reverence for tradition, make the originality of his poems appear more wonderful.

While at college Eliot also discovered Baudelaire, who proved to be almost as useful as Laforgue. In "Baudelaire in Our Time," an essay reprinted in *For Lancelot Andrewes* (1928), Eliot reviews the translation by Arthur Symons, who, says Eliot, made Baudelaire a poet of the

[3] By Edmund Wilson, in *Axel's Castle,* and by René Taupin. In his preface to Pound's *Selected Poems* (1928) Eliot says that the form in which he began to write was based upon Laforgue and the later Elizabethan drama. For resemblances to Henry James see F. O. Matthiessen: *The Achievement of T. S. Eliot* (1935). Warren Ramsey: *Jules Laforgue and the Ironic Inheritance* (1953).

nineties. More childish than Huysmans, Symons saw only the evil, the romantic unhealthiness, and the perversity of a poet who is almost as classical as Racine and "essentially Christian." After thinking these matters over for a while, Eliot softened his conclusions in another essay.[4] Classical only in tendency, Baudelaire is not so Christian as Eliot had thought, though Christian in tendency.

This essay is of value for comments upon Baudelaire's imagery, which explain Eliot's. Baudelaire had a romantic stock of images: "mulattoes, Jewesses, serpents, cats, corpses," pleasing to Symons and Wilde, perhaps, but displeasing to men of sensibility. On the other hand, says Eliot, Baudelaire used images of modern city life. Taking a suitable image from café, street, or gutter, Baudelaire presented reality as it was, yet, making it present something more than itself, raised it to "first intensity." Through his discovery of desolating city images he gave later poets expression for themselves and their world. It is difficult to distinguish Laforgue's city images from those of Baudelaire, his master, but it is probable that the "sawdust restaurants" of "Prufrock," the rusty springs in vacant lots, the cigar butts, the rancid butter in the gutter, the female smells, and all the other horrors of Eliot's early poetry are from Baudelaire's stock by way of *Bubu de Montparnasse*. The "unreal city" of *The Waste Land* is sufficiently identified by quotations from Baudelaire and Dante as Baudelaire's city and our hell. Eliot found his disgusting images in Baudelaire, but he missed as completely as Symons had the compassion behind disgust. He had gone to Baudelaire and Laforgue, however, not to improve his nature, but to find ways of expressing it.

When Eliot met the followers of Hulme in 1915, he was already an imagist of sorts, and, finding the followers of Hulme congenial, he became one of their number, succeeding Aldington as assistant editor of the *Egoist,* the principal organ of imagism. Eliot adopted the theories of Hulme, which clarified his own practices; and, like his friends, he conceived a moderate passion for Rémy de

---

[4] In *Selected Essays.* An introduction to Christopher Isherwood's translation of *Journaux intimes* (1930).

Gourmont's *"Litanies de la Rose,"* which he imitated years later in the second part of *Ash Wednesday*. "Preludes" and "Rhapsody on a Windy Night" are imagist poems, not of petals, however, but of vacant lots. With the aid of Baudelaire, Eliot made imagism more masculine and, with the aid of Laforgue, more complex. For the single image of most imagist verse he substituted long sequences of images; and for verse he substituted poetry. Though he soon turned with Pound to the quatrain of Gautier, Eliot remained a Laforguian imagist for many years. The first part of "Gerontion" is imagistic, and *The Waste Land* is a subtle suite of images.

However customary it is to class young Eliot with the symbolists, he was closer to the imagists. The particularities of his cold youth bear little resemblance in method or effect to the work of Mallarmé or Rimbaud or to the principles of Moréas. The images of these early poems are dramatizations of definite feelings about self or society, not evocations of the inexpressible. Finite, not infinite, they have little mystery about them; and their overtones, narrowly beamed by the poet, lack the expanding rings of the symbol. His cigar butt is far more precise in meaning than the smoke-rings of Mallarmé's cigar. From Baudelaire Eliot took, not the theory of correspondences, but a stock of images for less metaphysical purposes. Laforgue, from whom he took more, is more properly classed with the Decadents than with the symbolists, with whom he has little in common. The ceaseless praise of objectivity and impersonality that fills Eliot's essays reflects Gautier, the Parnassians, and the imagists. His ideal of the "objective correlative," something outside the poet that embodies something inside him, is Hulme's ideal of the image. And that fine definition of poetry (from the essay on metaphysical poets) as the "verbal equivalent for states of mind and feeling" is another reflection of Hulme and Flint, not of transcendental Baudelaire, Rimbaud, and Mallarmé. Limiting himself to the psychological and social levels of symbolism, Eliot, content to project himself, was careless of eternity.

As Eliot approached Christianity in his later poems,

he approached the symbolists. Abandoning Laforgue's manner as he approached them, he began to state his case. It is true that the symbolists had substituted indirection for statement; but, making statement musical, Eliot made it do the work of indirection. By this method, which first appears in the Sweeney poems and the latter part of "Gerontion" and reappears in "The Hollow Men," *Ash Wednesday,* and *Four Quartets,* he evokes idea and feeling less by images than by rhythm, by prosaic statements that say less than they mean, and by incantation with fragments of thought. The images within these incantations, the broken column of "The Hollow Men," or the window and winding stair of *Ash Wednesday,* or the roses of the *Quartets,* differ from the earlier images in being clear and mysterious, precise and imprecise.[5]

The theme of "East Coker," the second of the *Quartets,* is time and eternity or humanism as represented by Sir Thomas Elyot, and piety as represented by Mr. Thomas Eliot. Elegant allusions to Heraclitus, St. John of the Cross, Milton's *Samson,* and *The Hound of the Baskervilles* show need of death before rebirth; and masterly changes of pace support the references. The structure, indicated by the general title, is musical. These poems, which belong with *Point Counter Point,* the fugue of *Ulysses,* and the poems of Mallarmé, those earlier attempts to make words do what music can, are no less successful.

Edith Sitwell, Eliot's contemporary, discovered the symbolists independently during an attack of measles in 1912. She read Arthur Symons, Baudelaire, Verlaine, Rimbaud, and, after reading Eliot, Laforgue. *The Mother* (1915), her first volume of poetry, contains imitations of Baudelaire and Rimbaud that she excluded from her *Col-*

[5] Elizabeth Drew and John Sweeney: *Directions in Modern Poetry* (1940). Raymond Preston: *"Four Quartets" Rehearsed* (1946). Richard March and Tambimuttu, editors: *T. S. Eliot, a Symposium* (1948). B. Rajan, editor: *T. S. Eliot, a Study of His Writings* (1947). Leonard Unger, editor: *T. S. Eliot, a Selected Critique* (1948). R. H. Robbins: *The T. S. Eliot Myth* (1951). Elizabeth Drew: *T. S. Eliot, the Design of His Poetry* (1949). D. E. S. Maxwell: *The Poetry of T. S. Eliot* (1952). George Williamson: *A Reader's Guide to T. S. Eliot* (1953). Grover Smith: *T. S. Eliot's Poetry* (1956). Donald Gallup: *T. S. Eliot, a Bibliography* (1952).

lected Poems (1930) as too derivative. Excluded by her French demeanor from the conservative Georgian anthology and by her strangeness from the pretty collections of the imagists, she established *Wheels* (1916–21), an annual anthology of her own.

Poetry and Criticism (1925) is Dame Edith Sitwell's manifesto. It was her purpose, she says, to renew the exhausted romantic tradition. By "rag-time rhythms," grotesque words, and abstract patterns, like those of Picasso, Stein, and Stravinsky, by nonsense, synesthesia, and flippancy she composes antidotes to Wordsworth. In one of the series of articles she wrote for the *New Age* in 1922, she says that, spiritual and elegant like Villiers de l'Isle Adam, she too is plagued by the middle class. "Lullaby for Jumbo," "Trio for Two Cats and a Trombone," and the other poems of *Façade* (1922), at once fantastic and sensuous, were admirably calculated to astonish this class.

These ninetyish poems were inspired by France. From Baudelaire Dame Edith took dandyism and the exotic artificiality of *"Rêve Parisien."* Proceeding with his aid to transform Wordsworth's nature, she put bustles on the cherry trees. If a simple cherry tree is romantic, a cherry tree with a bustle on it, though no less romantic, is also decadent.

Elegant artifice was a refuge from the terror of the world. Retreat to childhood was another. In this Dame Edith was encouraged by the example of Rimbaud, who had ransacked his unconscious for infant memories. "Pleasure Gardens," a section of *Troy Park,* which celebrates her infancy, owes epigraph, atmosphere, and theme to Rimbaud. The synesthesia that she cultivated more systematically than any other English poet was inspired by Rimbaud's *"Voyelles"* and Baudelaire's *"Correspondances."* Welcoming Rimbaud's derangement of the senses, she heard colors and smelt sounds. That she thoroughly understood Rimbaud, however, is questionable; for in one of her articles in the *New Age* she says she liked him because he is decorative, exquisite, and formal. But in her introduction to Helen Rootham's translation of *Prose Poems from the Illuminations of Rimbaud* (1932) she is more orthodox. Here what she likes about Rimbaud, besides his irrational incantation, is his recovery of childhood, his abandonment to the unconscious, and his freedom from meaning.

In her preface to *Children's Tales from the Russian Ballet* (1920) she finds Laforgue's "terrible gaiety," like Petrouchka's, another refuge from the post-war world. Her poems on clowns are terribly gay. At the feet of Eliot's master she learned the arts of free association, mannered disillusionment, and verbalism. Equal admiration of Verlaine's *Fêtes galantes* is apparent in the nostalgic eighteenth-century elegance that interrupts the terrible gaiety. She learned her lessons well. Her early poems are generally agreeable, often good. Fresh impressions from startled senses, original patterns, and the resonances that assure her a place in the symbolist tradition make her poems richer than they seem.

That, like Yeats and Eliot, Edith Sitwell could develop is shown by *Street Songs* (1942) and *Green Song* (1944). As the first World War had made her rococo, so the second made her human. Retaining her virtuosity, her elegance of rhythm and texture, she used bones, apes, and carrion birds for general despair, which she expressed more movingly than most of her juniors. Age led her to the weathers and all the common things she had missed.[6] Taste, judgment, and kindliness made her single young poets out for praise—Dylan Thomas, for example, and Sydney Goodsir Smith.

In *Do What You Will* (1929) Aldous Huxley attacks Baudelaire as a nasty Satanist whose present cult among the English is explained by their hunt for what expresses them. In *Point Counter Point,* a year earlier, Huxley had modeled Spandrell's disgusting career upon Baudelaire's. But the Laurentian Huxley of the late twenties was forgetting earlier benefits. He too had found congenial expres-

[6] For her admiration of Symons, Verlaine, Baudelaire, and Rimbaud see *A Poet's Notebook* (1943). In *Street Songs* she turned to Éluard. *The Canticle of the Rose* (1949). *Gardeners and Astronomers* (1953). *Collected Poems* (1954). An account of the production of *Façade* appears in Osbert Sitwell: *Laughter in the Next Room* (1948).

sion through Baudelaire. Commencing as a disciple of
Edith Sitwell, Huxley had contributed to *Wheels,* and his
early volumes of verse maintained on their level a course
parallel with hers. Convinced like her of the emptiness of
all things, he had followed her not only to Baudelaire, but
to Laforgue and Rimbaud. Many poems and the portrait
of Denis in *Crome Yellow* (1921) present Laforgue's Pru-
frockian hero. From Laforgue, Huxley also acquired his
habit of using scientific terms in startling contexts and a
keener taste for exotic prose. Whereas Eliot improved Laforgue, Huxley reproduced him.[7]

Rimbaud gave intellectual Huxley a refuge from too
much intellect. Incapable of imaginative holidays when
well, he found that when fever was upon him his intellect softened. Under these conditions, he could approximate that derangement of the senses which permits the
combination of unrelated objects.

Huxley's translations of Rimbaud's *"Chercheuses de
poux"* and of Mallarmé's *"L'Après-midi,"* generally considered the best that have been made, express, like the
best of his original poems, the decadence rather than the
illuminations of the French tradition. A decadent young
man of great talent and great intellect, he went with the
help of the symbolists as far as talent and intellect allowed.

What cannot be expressed discursively can be presented nondiscursively. Of the poets who learned this lesson
under French masters, none learned it better than some
of the poets of the late thirties. At this time Baudelaire and
Laforgue, who had served poets as masters, were succeeded
by Rimbaud and, sometimes, Mallarmé. Although recalling
Rimbaud's *"Bateau ivre,"* Dylan Thomas's "Ballad of the
Long-Legged Bait" is an original poem of the same kind.
Poems of Lawrence Durrell and Peter Yeats, no less indebted to the French tradition, are no less original.

In Durrell's *A Private Country* (1943) arrangements

[7] For Huxley's Baudelairian and Laforguian poems see *Leda*
(1920), *The Defeat of Youth* (1918), *Selected Poems* (1925). In
Music at Night (1931) Huxley commends Laforgue's ironic juxtaposi-
tions of the scientific and the sentimental.

of thought and feeling, inseparable from their odd fastidious expression, bring Wallace Stevens to mind. And in line
behind him the shades of Rimbaud, Mallarmé, and Apollinaire fix Durrell in the symbolist tradition at its most
bizarre. His songs and elegies of Greece use the Ægean
past not so much as refuge from the unmentionable present but as medium through which to pass it. Prismatic
refractions compose his country and its climate. Dandyism,
the adjustment of ruffle and cravat in a vacant lot, gives an
air to "The Sonnet of Hamlet" and "The Death of General
Uncebunke," his most elaborate sequences. An amorist of
parts, he is not unlike Don Giovanni, that fortunate man,
who kept a private orchestra to play him *Figaro*.

Yates, a philosophical poet, thinks in symbols about
man's condition. His chiseled poems, seeming lucid, are
difficult, but, like poems of Valéry on another, parallel
plane, yield when the clue is found. On second reading,
the repeated symbols of mirror, bone, and pole communicate, and the reader discovers that *The Expanding Mirror*
(1942) reflects horror of life. Confined within "the cube
of now," the poet seeks a formula for time, space, and
prisoner. But every formula, while bringing magic and
elegance to shape, adds pressure to the "is of this." His
second collection, *The Motionless Dancer* (1943), promises escape. The dancer is a statue, surrounded by river,
love, and falling leaf, immune to change. Out of nature,
he becomes a symbol of timeless perfection, of living
death, like Yeats's golden bird, Eliot's Chinese jar, or
Huxley's Heard.[8]

Whether Thomas, Durrell, Yates, or the other poets of
their generation drew directly or indirectly upon the French
is unimportant. What matters is that English poetry, inflamed by France and freed at last from all Victorians but
Hopkins, had been renewed.

[8] Durrell: *Cities, Plains and People* (1946); *On Seeming to Pre-
sume* (1953); *Sappho* (1950), a poetic play; *The Tree of Idleness*
(1955). Yates: *Light and Dark* (1951).

V

Symbolist novels are the outstanding literary development of our time. Although the nineteenth century produced a few (*Moby Dick, Madame Bovary,* and *Alice in Wonderland*) and although Dickens, Meredith, Zola, and Hardy used images to present matters beyond analysis, it was not until the twentieth century that this form became central. Not only Flaubert and the poets but occultists, anthropologists, and psychoanalysts provided example and method. A symbolist novel is one in which the burden is carried not by narrative or discourse as tradition demands but by image, pattern, and rhythm, devices once peculiar to poetry or music. At once poetic and nondiscursive, such novels, presenting more than their apparent theme, are indefinitely suggestive. Sometimes they are centered in narrative or character, sometimes in an image surrounded by assistants, and sometimes in a concert of reflexive concretions. Details of actuality, no longer there for their own sake or to serve a sociological point, carry meaning outside the limits to which they seem confined. The greater works of Conrad, Joyce, Forster, Woolf, Lawrence, Henry Green, and L. P. Hartley grace this emergent design. As Bergson is the philosopher of the stream of consciousness so Ernst Cassirer is the philosopher of those embodiments by which we make and know our realities.[9]

Though in "Heart of Darkness" (1902) Conrad seems to depend upon adventure, ideas of imperialism, and moral analysis, these matters are there to distract the simple or earnest reader while the form offers ideas and feelings beyond moral or imperial capacity. The heart of Conrad's darkness is presented in the forest, which, assisted by peripheral devices, embodies suggestions of our unconscious and primitive selves, of all that Kurtz succumbs to and

[9] Cassirer: *An Essay on Man* (1944). Susanne K. Langer: *Philosophy in a New Key* (1942), *Feeling and Form* (1953). Philip Wheelwright: *The Burning Fountain* (1954). W. Y. Tindall: *The Literary Symbol* (1955).

responsible Marlow rejects. In this great image, at once limited and expanded by its context of smaller images, discourse, character, and action, Conrad has gathered all that man adores and fears. The nightmarish city of *The Secret Agent* (1907), the silver mine and the unguided ship of *Nostromo* (1904), and the double who projects the captain's hidden nature in "The Secret Sharer" are no less symbolic of man's condition. In *Victory* (1915) the island, the volcano, the hopeless pier, the paternal portrait, and the three intruders support the nature of Heyst by affirming the condition of all exiles. Not Marlow's discourse or Conrad's equally moral concern but such embodiments, springing from and including our deepest reality, account for the esteem in which we hold Conrad today. Essentially inexplicable, his vision of what confronts us gives us a way of apprehending it.

Joyce wrote the stories of *Dubliners* shortly after the publication of "Heart of Darkness." Shaped by Flaubert and *Chamber Music,* a first attempt at adequate symbolism,[1] the apparently naturalistic surface of these stories suggests Irish paralysis. As the dead priest of "The Sisters," the first story of Joyce's book, embodies the missing father, who is hunted in the second story, so snow, the central image of "The Dead," the last and greatest of this sequence, embodies death, but not death alone; for frozen water promises thaw, and the hero, obsessed not only by the cap of snow on the Wellington monument but by that obelisk itself, may find renewal in these contradictory intimations. These stories, not to be denuded by such accounts, allow (as Baudelaire, accounting for his swan, observed) *"bien d'autres encore."*

As, on second or third reading, particulars of Joyce's city ascend to symbols of spiritual, moral, or psychological states, so narrative and character in *A Portrait of the Artist,* which seems at first no more than a simple story of adolescence, ascend by the aid of image and pattern to meanings outside the ordinary limits of such stories. "The Dead" and "Heart of Darkness" are organized around cen-

[1] See introduction to *Chamber Music* (1954), edited by W. Y. Tindall.

tral images; *A Portrait of the Artist,* revealing another
structure, supports narrative and character by attendant
images that enrich or modify simplicities. The first two
pages, serving as a kind of thematic index, display those
images of road, water, and bird that, musically recurring,
will give and take in each new context until the structure
they help to compose seems less logical than symphonic.
To apprehend the thing as a whole we must put everyday
thinking aside, replacing it, as in the presence of a symphony or poem, by a kind of alert surrender. Not even this
approach, however suitable, will exhaust the possibilities
of the great arrangement.

The meanings of *Ulysses,* a greater example of the
same kind, reside in and come from a concert of plot,
character, tone, and image. Without the thematic imagery,
weaving in and out, acquiring new loads as it transmits
the old, story and character would remain unclear—or,
at least, less clear than they become at seventh or eighth
reading. The man in the brown macintosh, who pops
mysteriously up throughout the book, the parallel of Moses,
Plumtree's Potted Meat, Mr. Bloom's disappointed quest
for tea, and the other analogies that enlarge the meanings
of the simple plot gradually insinuate themselves and, rebuking narrow interpretation, help create the meaning for
which the work itself is the only adequate analogy. Maybe
the opening image of stately, plump Buck Mulligan is the
plainest clue to that meaning. A mock priest, he mocks
the Eucharist; but if we recall that the business of a Mass
is making God from bread and wine and that in Joyce's
economy God and artist are one, we may guess with some
assurance that Buck Mulligan's impious ceremony announces a major theme. But recurrent images of wine,
generally in the secular guise of ale, coffee, or cocoa, enlarge this meaning by implying that communion with mankind upon which the artist depends. Having received his
cocoa (*Theobroma* or God-food) Stephen becomes the
creator whose creation Buck Mulligan has celebrated.[2]

[2] For the *Portrait* see Hugh Kenner's essay in Seon Givens: *James
Joyce, Two Decades of Criticism* and W. Y. Tindall: *The Literary
Symbol,* which also includes analyses of most of the other symbolist
novels.

Meanwhile in Germany Thomas Mann, having found the hint for thematic elaboration in Wagner's leitmotiv, composed "Tonio Kröger" (1903) and *Death in Venice* (1911) of woven images so important that without them there is almost nothing there. *The Magic Mountain* (1924) is as "Hermetic" as the works of Joyce—if, as both Mann and Joyce did, we take Hermes Trismegistus as god of correspondences, not only magical and alchemical but literary. Analogies of above and below, of inner and outer, or of here and there that once fascinated Baudelaire and Mallarmé, also help to account for Kafka's castle, a central image which, although limited and expanded by K.'s disappointments, resists definition while embodying the nature of things. The spires of Martinville that invite and baffle Marcel seem at last to shadow forth *Remembrance of Things Past,* the book he wrote to replace a slight prose poem as analogy for his experience.[3] Recurring themes, such as the phrase from Vinteuil's sonata, assure a concert of smaller correspondences, the female orchid, for example, that the Duchess puts out in the absurd hope of fertilization from a possible male by a Parisian bee. This strange and hopeless flower, ironically embodying the affair of Charlus and Jupien, brings both Marcel and the reader a more immediate understanding than discourse could. Proust, Mann, and Kafka found worthy rival in Faulkner, but English developments of the form are our concern.

For *Howards End* (1910), abandoning the method of sociologists, E. M. Forster took that of symbolists for his sociological preoccupations. Images of house, elm, vine, and motor car conspire with the repeated image of hay to establish his theme and all the riches it suggests. But in *A Passage to India* (1924), his greatest novel and one of the greatest of the symbolist movement, he realized the promise of this experiment. What seems more important, though less clear, than the theme that secures our earliest notice is the central image of the Marabar caves which, reducing all to nothing, introduces ancient night. These primitive enclosures provide Miss Quested with her

[3] Arnaud Dandieu: *Marcel Proust* (1930).

hallucination, Dr. Aziz with his trouble, and Mrs. Moore with horror. As enigmatic Mrs. Moore does little and says less yet stirs the native heart and the symbolic imagination, her caves and their intricate environment of character, action, and subsidiary image demand Freudian, philosophical, or anthropological tickets; but, evading these, sink below them. Upon such nameless depths as those caves suggest, the white man and his burden seem negligible. This irony was part of Forster's plan. His distinction is to have suggested more than he said and, exceeding the lateral extensions of Kipling, to have made the Empire bottomless.[4]

That Virginia Woolf, disciple of Forster, Joyce, and Proust, was also a symbolist is plain from her lighthouse —to take the most conspicuous example. What this stark erection embodies, as we might expect by now, is far from simple. Suggesting God, death, eternity, any absolute, and the goal of all endeavors, this solitary tower amid the flux provokes, without altogether satisfying, our curiosity as it informs us. Though no less puzzling, the tower's surroundings of sea, flower, window, character, and quest promise meanings that we and the Ramsays all but grasp. Not discourse on reality but reality itself is what we are faced with in all its mysterious immediacy. Somewhat more intimate, *Between the Acts* (1941) is nevertheless a vision of time and permanence, diversity and unity, and England's past. Miss La Trobe, an artist like Lily Briscoe and Virginia Woolf, writes and directs the pageant that attempts these matters. Her sense of failure, the confusion of the audience on the lawn, and the attempt by a clergyman to reduce her vision to sermon demonstrate imperfection, isolation, and incommunicability, our portion as men and our plague as writers and readers. This account of the literary symbol and of the difficulties that surround it occupied the last moments of one who was obsessed, like earlier symbolists, with the penultimate.

In his later years Lawrence joined the great company

[4] Forster: *Aspects of the Novel* (1927). E. K. Brown: *Rhythm in the Novel* (1950).

of those who, attempting to exceed the limits of discourse, found their penultimates in rhythm, image, and form. *Women in Love,* a curious quarrel of sermon with image, was followed and surpassed by *The Plumed Serpent* (1926), a great harmony of hypnotic ritual and archetypal image that creates far better than preaching Birkin could a vision of reality.[5] *Under the Volcano* (1947) by Malcolm Lowry, another attempt to evoke vision from Mexican landscape, is one of the most successful symbolist novels of recent years, surpassed in subtlety, however, by Elizabeth Bowen's *A World of Love* (1955). This fine arrangement of indirections and concretions, that claims its place with the best of her novels, presents Anglo-Irish decay and renewal through love. From the obelisk in the yard to the airplane at Shannon airport images support and complicate the interactions of character and event. Differing in method from most of the earlier novels of Miss Bowen, *A World of Love* recalls Henry Green's *Loving* in theme, setting, technique, and title. That is far from odd; for she admires Green, who, along with her and L. P. Hartley, occupies the place of highest distinction among surviving symbolists.

In *Loving* (1945), as Green observes in another connection, "there is only a hint of what is going on" and the reader, "lost in a void of unmentionables," is "all at sea."[6] From this conspiracy of insinuations, however, something emerges that, although hard to state, is securely established by images of castle, dovecote, peacock, lost ring, and broken weathervane or rather by their reflexive relationship. Not central image as in "Heart of Darkness" or attendant image as in *A Portrait of the Artist* but a multitude of glancing reflections assures the unity and effect of this form, a third among symbolic kinds. *Party Going* (1939), a similar association of hints, seems to project by images of frustration and enclosure the plight of a social

[5] For Lawrence as symbolist see introductions to *The Plumed Serpent* (Knopf, 1951) and *The Later D. H. Lawrence* (1952), edited by W. Y. Tindall.

[6] *Pack My Bag* (1940), autobiography. Henry Green is pseudonym for Henry Yorke.

class and, beyond that, of mankind in our time. The black fog, the crowd trapped in the terminal, the rich and elegant trapped in the railway hotel, and the dead pigeon suggest this reading, which, of course, cannot be final.

Birds, which figure mysteriously here and in most of Green's works, are an important element of *Living* (1929), his compassionate novel of a foundry and its workers. Lacking certain meaning, Green's birds—whether flying free, posturing on lawns, amorously occupied, or dead and wrapped in brown paper—carry possibilities that elude statement. Though the roses of *Back* (1946), his story of a returning veteran, are agents of unity and bearers of traditional associations, Green's usual images—the increasingly amputated leg in *Nothing* (1950), for example— seem there to tease us by promising, without providing, import. In spite of title, *Concluding* (1948), is the least conclusive of novels. This nightmare of the welfare state differs from Orwell's traditionally discursive version in being composed of maddening suggestions and loose ends, which, nevertheless, are functional. Two girls are missing from the institution; one is found but where is the other? What of the missing and reappearing pig, goose, and cat? We must guess the inexplicable situation as we go; but the whole, like many of Green's works, occupies Kafka's country or at least its borders. Inconclusiveness becomes a form for attempted conclusions or for the very feeling of life and our ideas of it.

Elegance, economy, aloof compassion, and these "ambiguous undulations," as Wallace Stevens would put it, may be the virtues of Green; but that inconclusiveness and indeterminateness are not virtues in themselves is proved by the novels of L. P. Hartley. Although it is easy enough to assign meanings to the images and themes that embody his moral and psychological disclosures, his forms are brilliantly successful. His interest lies in the sensitive child, all the troubles of growing up, and ultimate defeat. *The Shrimp and the Anemone* (1944, entitled *The West Window* in America) and its two sequels, *The Sixth Heaven* (1946) and *Eustace and Hilda* (1947) concern the victimi-

zation of a boy by an older sister, who, as budding matri-
arch or like the White Goddess herself, makes all his best
rebellions vain.[7] A shrimp and an anemone in a tidal pool
introduce, include, and conclude the strange relationship
of brother and sister—and maybe that of most men and
women. At the beginning of the first volume the two children try to separate victim from beautiful diner, but as they
pull the half-consumed shrimp from her mouth, her en-
trails follow it. At the end of the third volume, after his
final defeat, Eustace returns to the pool and, finding an
anemone without a shrimp, sticks his finger in her mouth:
"The water was bitterly cold; but colder still were the lips
of the anemone." However obvious, this terrible image
is haunting. Supported by subsidiary images—the tide,
the bathtub, the lustral waters of Venice, the watches, the
wheel chair, and the west window with which Eustace
identifies himself in an ecstasy and agony of petrifaction—
this central image is the story's epitome. The three-legged
race suggested by Hilda at the end of the first volume is
one of the most painful imagistic supporters. As she ties
their legs together, Eustace asks: " 'Won't it come undone?' " " 'Not if I tie it,' " says Hilda, and away they go
over a patch of rough ground, mined with splinters: "it
looked as if they were sure to come to grief" before getting home.

The Go-Between (1953), reminiscent by turns of
James, Proust, and Lawrence, is the story of another adolescent victim of woman, this time an older one who
knows what she is about. This moral study of expanding
awareness, of innocence and childish magic yielding to
fact, is founded upon image, not analysis. The zodiac as
occasion for Proustian recall, as parallel to the characters,
and as the representative of imagination yields to bella-

[7] The White Wand (1954) contains another story of Eustace and
Hilda. A Perfect Woman (1955). Though not basically symbolist, William Plomer's Museum Pieces (1952) is raised by a final image above
the elegant decline it celebrates. Cf. the images of closet, subway, and
half-cooked chicken in William Sansom's A Bed of Roses (1954).
Rumer Godden's Black Narcissus (1938) and The River (1946) are
at once popular and symbolist.

dona, the deadly nightshade in its roofless shed. It is not accidental that when Leo, who is fascinated by this monstrous plant, pulls it up, he falls, covered with dirt, and the Virgo of a Laurentian zodiac tumbles from his sky. Hartley's great anemone has found herself another shrimp.

CIVILIZATION, to Freud in one sense, to Marx in another, the cause of all our ills, showed other curers other cures. Sometimes, however, these cures appear less cure than flight. Victorian ideas of progress had generally yielded to the conviction that we are not progressing, and that if we were, it would be bad. Although some, like Wells, remained progressive, others sought to improve themselves by return to flowers, peasants, and savages. Some lost and found themselves in myths, and some, in Joycean circles, mounted their bisexycles and were off. Such improvements or escapes had helped compose romantics from the start. Under the influence of anthropology, improvement or escape took old directions and a fresh disguise.

Peasants and primroses of Wordsworth, myths of Blake and Shelley, and noble savages provided a natural background for anthropologists, archæologists, and Mme Blavatsky. Under their direction the noble savage of earlier romantics became ignoble though no less instructive. Darwin had proved Wordsworth's nature cruel. But cruel indifferent primroses offered fiercer delight and, compared with vacant lots, were lovable.

Among the first of modern anthropologists, Sir Edward Tylor, using the comparative method, devoted *Primitive Culture* (1871) to the study of animism. Sir James Frazer followed with *The Golden Bough,* published in

1890 and expanded to its present dimensions between 1911 and 1915. However crowded with facts, the tremendous book is readable. It is to this that Frazer owes part of his appeal to the literate mind, but part he owes to disclosures for which that mind was waiting. The recurring tragedy of the priest of Nemi led Frazer to seek explanatory parallels in taboo, magic, and the dying and resurrected god. Returning to Nemi, his convenient center, with this freight, he hung it on the Golden Bough. His own piety seemed proof against disclosures that made religion myth and myth a clue to modern minds, peasant, savage, and civilized alike. The accumulation of facts begun by Frazer was increased by Bronislaw Malinowski, whose researches into savage customs appeared in the twenties, and by others, American, German or, like Malinowski, British. Inflamed by Frazer, the literary mind was ready for these, who seemed, like Freud and Jung, providers for romantic needs.

For many readers Freud, Jung, and Frazer were the most congenial people in the world. Nor was this odd, for Freud, following Frazer on taboo, found among savages the substance of childhood and our dreams. The waking mind of primitive man is the unconscious mind of modern man, who is at once far more and no less primitive than he dreams.

These disclosures were accompanied by those of the archæologists. Following Schliemann of Mycenæ, Sir William Petrie dug up Egypt and Sir Arthur Evans Crete. Their excavations provided furniture for dreams of a fabulous past. The Palace of Minos with its elegant plumbing and intricate corridors called to mind an occupant who, obsessing Joyce, Picasso, and all surrealists, has become our favorite animal.

Such a symbol, though proper to that time and to ours, may seem a little precious. The Minoan verses and the amphitheater of Aldous Huxley's story "Eupompus Gave Splendour to Art by Numbers" cannot altogether escape this reproach. But others used the new learning more soberly. Christopher Caudwell used anthropology to establish the communal character of poetry, Gerald Heard used it to establish the trouble with man, and even Shaw, who refers to Frazer in the preface to *Androcles* (1913), appears to have used him to interpret Christianity in that extravagant play. Others, innocent of Frazer and Jung, or with their help, returned to peasant, soil, and child. Some were simple Wordsworthians (too long in city pent), some romantic primitivists of other varieties, and some explorers exploring with new instruments. The only one who had everything was D. H. Lawrence.

Lawrence was Wordsworthian, but there was nothing simple about him. He loved nature and saw in it the remedy for what ails us, but having read Darwin, he loved something hostile or indifferent with which he had to struggle for success. The heroine of *St. Mawr* (1925) finds peace in nature's malevolence as she establishes polarity with tree, flower, earth, and horse. To these she has been led by a horse-rubber, a man, like the gamekeepers, gypsies, and redskins of Lawrence's other stories, close to nature. The hero of *Kangaroo* (1923) finds consolation in a farmer of Cornwall, and Lawrence himself in *Sea and Sardinia* (1921), one of the best of his glowing travel books, pursues peasants. The function of these natural men was to save him and his heroines from civilization. This is primitivism. It is only when civilization is overripe, as in Augustan Rome, Gibbon's England, or the age of Mr. Bloom, that men attempt to cure the time by past or peasant.

Frazer had found the past vestigial in peasant and barbarian. Lawrence turned from peasants to men of Ceylon, Australia, and Tahiti, but, disappointed, found the closest approximation to the noble savage in the Indians of New Mexico. Degenerate perhaps, they nevertheless retained in their drums and dances something of the noble past. Lawrence described their dances in the bright hypnotic prose of *Mornings in Mexico* (1927) and told their meaning in *Reflections on the Death of a Porcupine* (1925) and the other essays of this period. What he wanted, not to be found in practice, must be created again from such vestiges. What he wanted, however, was to be found in books. Among anthropologists he had read Frazer, Tylor, Jane

Harrison, and Frobenius, among archæologists Petrie. Some of these he loved, some, like Frazer, he despised as intellectual and corrected by intuition, but all were useful, supplying him with hints upon which to improve. His heroes are always speaking of Egyptians, Chaldeans, or darkest Africans. Birkin of *Women in Love* (1920) adores the mystic sensualism of African sculpture, and the hero of "The Ladybird" adores the scarab. Lawrence looked at Indian dances through Tylor's eyes and Jane Harrison's spectacles. These authorities showed him how to interpret vestiges and through them to recapture man's ancient relationship with earth, trees, cows, and serpents. And Mme Blavatsky showed him how to interpret these authorities.

In *The Plumed Serpent* (1926) they conspire with Mexican archæologists like Zelia Nuttall and Lawrence's genius to produce one of the most wonderful novels of our time. Its theme is the recovery by myth and symbol not only of Mme Blavatsky's Atlantis, but of Tylor's animistic past. Through the myth of Quetzalcoatl the antediluvian is recovered and civilization destroyed. There is compulsory dancing in the streets. Inspired by one myth, this novel creates another. Its intensity comes from archetypal patterns of rebirth that Lawrence, pursuing the childish, the primitive, and the unconscious, improved by his hypnotic arts. In the preface to *Fantasia of the Unconscious* (1922) he had recognized the value of myth and symbol for recapturing the past; and elsewhere he found them lying "too deep in the blood and soul" for intellect to follow. The frames of other novels come from myth, that of *The Trespasser* (1912) from Wagner's *Ring,* that of *The Boy in the Bush* (1924) from Genesis. Part of their attractiveness comes from these frames and part from that evocation of place for which he is famous.[1]

[1] Memoirs of Lawrence: Catherine Carswell: *The Savage Pilgrimage* (1932); Mabel Dodge Luhan: *Lorenzo in Taos* (1932); Dorothy Brett: *Lawrence and Brett* (1933); Frieda Lawrence: *"Not I, but the Wind . . ."* (1934); Knud Merrild: *A Poet and Two Painters* (1938); Witter Bynner: *Journey with Genius* (1951).
Frederick J. Hoffman and Harry T. Moore, editors: *The Achievement of D. H. Lawrence* (1953). Harry T. Moore: *The Iintelligent Heart* (1955). Mark Spilka: *The Love Ethic of D. H. Lawrence* (1955). F. R. Leavis: *D. H. Lawrence: Novelist* (1955).

Back in Italy, Lawrence exhumed with the help of archæologists the lost Etruscans. Their meaning for the modern world, as presented in *Etruscan Places* (1932), is that of Egyptians or Indians. And in his last illness he turned to Christian mythology. That fine new myth of Jesus *The Man Who Died* is based upon Frazer's pattern of dying and resurrected gods. *Apocalypse* (1931), exposes symbolic dragon, horses, and numbers to the lights of anthropology and Theosophy.

At first blush E. M. Forster might be taken for a lesser Lawrence. In each of Forster's early novels an oaf is used as a foil to the civilized. The animal vitality of Carella in *Where Angels Fear to Tread* (1905) quarrels with the deadness of the British suburb. The "rustic strength" of Wonham in *The Longest Journey* (1907) counteracts the unreality of the public scholars. The Indians and low-caste Englishmen of the other novels are similar. But unlike those of Lawrence, these oafs are not ideal. Carella is the son of a village dentist, and, what is worse, he is conventional and cruel. Wonham is less the natural man than what man has made of natural man. Although these imperfect instruments uncover the nature of society by contrast and resemblance, they are no better, on the whole, than the society they uncover.

In "The Story of a Panic," the most Laurentian of all Forster's stories, the respectable Englishmen are immune to Pan, but Gennaro, the Italian primitive of whom one expects much, is untrue to him for gold. This defection is compensated for, however, by the conduct of Eustace, an oaf, who, inflamed by Pan, picks flowers and goes shouting down the valleys in his nightie.[2]

The savages of W. H. Hudson are nobler. Like Hudson himself they succumb to "strange rushes or bursts of feeling" at the sight of bird or flower. As a lad on the pampas, drawn to nature by nature, he increased its pull by reading Wordsworth's poems and Gilbert White's *Natural History of Selborne*. Hudson's subsequent work as a field

[2] *The Celestial Omnibus* (1911). *The Eternal Moment* (1928). *The Collected Tales of E. M. Forster* (1947).

naturalist, consisting in descriptions of plants and beasts, together with anecdotes of their behavior, is amateur. In his opinion scientific biologists were too sedentary, too intent upon reasons and causes. To Darwin, whose natural selection seemed mechanical and cruel, Hudson preferred Lamarck and Samuel Butler, who were on familiar terms with the life force. Nature, like Wordsworth's primrose, was not only natural but something more. Like Wordsworth and Thoreau, Hudson became a mystical pantheist, thrilling to the noise of birds or the look of plants. A scientist would classify bird and plant; a rationalist might think it rational to eat them; but Hudson felt wonder alone as he botanized on Wordsworth's grave.

In *The Naturalist in La Plata* (1892) Hudson recorded his loving observations of flora and fauna, imperiled, and for this more dear, by encroaching civilization. In *A Shepherd's Life* (1910) and *A Hind in Richmond Park* (1922) he looked through England for what was still unspoilt by fences and motor cars. Lamenting the natural past before their incursions, he chose from what was left the smaller and gentler "beasties," leaving the bolder animals to Darwin. Gentle nature and her people were antidotes to cities and theirs.

Although barbarous, the gauchos of the pampas were "nature's noblemen," and in England farmers and shepherds were their more nearly perfect, because British, equivalents. Hudson differed from Lawrence, whom he abhorred, in disliking gamekeepers. He differed from Lawrence in making little use of anthropologists. Although Hudson had read them and was sufficiently impressed to refer to his own religion as animism, he saw little use in their studies of remote peoples when Salisbury Plain afforded such exemplary specimens of natural man.

The hero of *Green Mansions* (1904) flees the city and his artificial lady for the jungle. This Venezuelan refuge is to be compared only to that jungle of improbable apes devouring improbable blossoms under improbable trees which Henri Rousseau arranged. A man of the pampas who had never seen a jungle, Hudson allowed his fancy to decree a place where natural beauty is unimpaired by nature. Sheltered by the superior foliage of this Utopia lives Rima, an ambiguous thing, half woman and half bird. This child of this nature is a creation not of Hudson the naturalist but of Hudson the transcendentalist. The real children of nature, the Indians who inhabit the edge of Hudson's jungle, throwing poisoned darts as if they had been reading Darwin, are too natural to please. Although supernatural nature is successfully created in this romance, the loves of Rima and her refugee are incredible.

Hudson's memorable works are those in which his feelings were centered upon the actual, his field observations, where sentimentality is less intrusive, some of the less imaginative sketches of *El Ombú* (1902), and his autobiography, *Far Away and Long Ago* (1918), which, in its degree, is as enchanting as Proust's recovery of times past. The style of these nostalgic works is suitable to its purpose. The words, placing no barrier between reader and writer, are lucid and fastidiously chosen, the rhythms easy and natural. It is a style so nearly perfect that it cannot be thought of apart from his matter, the youth of a continent and the age of a countryside.

The dying countryside, victim of Darwin and civilization, was Hardy's concern and the background for tragedy or melodrama. *The Poor Man and the Lady,* his first novel, written in 1868, shows Hardy a nature-lover. His first poems show him a Darwinist. In the later novels the pastoral descriptions and the rustics are the result of a quarrel between Wordsworth and Darwin, the first knowing nature beneficent, the second knowing it malign. Landscapes and rustics, not decorations but parts of the story, provide source, parallel, or relief for the protagonists whose earthy drama needs chorus and setting. But this quarreling accompaniment is so intense that often, as in *The Woodlanders* (1887), it remains alone in memory. Uneasy in cities, Hardy found imperfect refuge in re-creating the past, for the countryside of which he wrote was at its best vestigial. This knowledge, the cause of intensity, was another cause of gloom.[3]

Writers of Hardy's school, apportioning the counties among them, endlessly described the landscapes in which they set their melodramas. These middle-class refugees from what their class had done to nature found or created vestiges of a more natural past. Torn like their master between Wordsworth and Darwin, and almost aware that in turning their backs upon cities they were rejecting the important reality of their class, they became morbid. And so did their peasants, trees, and flowers.[4]

Young Lawrence was the most eminent disciple. *The White Peacock* (1911), *Sons and Lovers* (1913), *The Rainbow* (1915), and "Love among the Haystacks," written in 1912, are filled with Hardyesque descriptions of the woods and pastures near Nottingham and of haymakers, milkmen, and gamekeepers. It was Hardy who turned Lawrence's eyes from the mines and towns, which constituted his reality, to pastures. As the attractive repulsiveness of these vestiges became with Mme Blavatsky's help the positive and negative polarity of his later novels, Lawrence abandoned Hardy's rural primitivism for a more exotic kind. But he returned to Hardy's countryside in *Lady Chatterley's Lover*.[5]

The novels of Mary Webb are well-made melodramas. Stating her theme, the title of *Gone to Earth* (1917) refers specifically to death and foxes. Hazel, the fox-loving heroine, is a child of nature. Most notable among Mary Webb's stories of the Welsh marches (Shropshire is her province) is *Precious Bane* (1924). This romance of long ago, told

---

[3] The substance of *The Poor Man and the Lady* is to be found in *An Indiscretion in the Life of an Heiress* (1935), edited by Carl Weber. *Far from the Madding Crowd* (1874) set the pattern for Hardy's followers.

[4] The Hardy tradition: Eden Phillpotts: *The Secret Woman* (1905); Sheila Kaye-Smith: *Sussex Gorse* (1916), *Joanna Godden* (1921); H. E. Bates: *Cut and Come Again* (1935), *The Poacher* (1935); Stella Gibbons: *Cold Comfort Farm* (1932), a parody of that tradition.

[5] For Lawrence's essay on Hardy see *Phoenix* (1936). *Rings on Her Fingers* (1930) by Rhys Davies is in the Lawrence tradition.

by the hare-shotten heroine, who possesses the beauties of language, reveals her love and the fatal ambition of her farming brother. The rustic hero, kind to sufferers, rescues Prue from bull-baiting rustics in the nick of time and carries her off on a horse. There are magicians about, but the magic of harvest and country winters is a greater magic than theirs.

John Cowper Powys, who calls himself Wordsworthian in his Rousseauistic *Autobiography* (1934), became Hardy's friend and disciple. His most ambitious novel is *Wolf Solent* (1929). Although the neurotic hero has ecstasies over the natural beauties of Dorset, for which he has abandoned the city, he is aware that the "blowflies of dissolution" are at work. He turns up stones to find hidden abominations or visits neighbors. Most of them are corrupt, sinister, or daft. Adoring bodies apart from souls and souls apart from bodies, Wolf learns to endure horrors less horrible than those of machine or town.

Meanwhile dramatists and poets had been returning to the countryside and its people. The peasant plays of Synge, Lady Gregory, Colum, Lennox Robinson, George Shiels, and other Irishmen seem less unreal than their English counterparts because Ireland is more pastoral than England, but even these Irish plays represent the nostalgia of the sophisticated. The Aran Islands and the farms of Limerick or Cork, dear to Irish novelists as well, were rapidly assuming the character of the Land of Youth. In England dramatists were less rustic, but two of the best plays of the higher drama belong to this tradition. The well-born heroine of Granville-Barker's *Marrying of Ann Leete* (1901) runs off with her father's gardener as if she were Lady Chatterley herself. John Masefield's *Tragedy of Nan,* produced by Granville-Barker in 1908, is less primitivistic than elemental. The symbolic tide, the many-sidedness of Nan, and that "delighted brooding on excessive, terrible things" that Masefield commends in his preface make the play, despite austerity of dialect, comparable to the work of Synge, his friend and undoubtedly his model.

Masefield's *Everlasting Mercy* (1911), a long narrative poem in colloquial diction and doggerel octosyllabics,

uncovers the excesses of a village. His other verse was inspired in part by A. E. Housman's Shropshire ballads,
which, representing the frustrations of the civilized by
plowmen, trees, and lads hanging around, did as much as
Hardy's verse to countrify the Georgian muse. Departing
at last with laurels from the general view, Masefield devoted his sonnets to the worship of Beauty with a Platonic
B. More elegant, T. Sturge Moore revived the idyll of
Theocritus, himself a refugee from civilization. W. H.
Davies at his best is somewhat more natural. Having read
Wordsworth, Davies became a hobo as he confesses in *The
Autobiography of a Super-Tramp* (1908), a work of astonishing simplicity, and in the latter stages of his wandering
carried Wordsworth with him. The lyrics of this artful
innocent have a childlike quality and at their best freshness and charm. This lyrical Hudson was Hudson's friend
and the friend, of course, of Edward Thomas, whose
Wordsworthian descriptions excited Robert Frost. Farmers,
barns, flowers, the open road attracted Thomas's accurate
eye, inspiring quiet verses, better than most in this kind.[6]
The technique is as old-fashioned as the accurate eye. But
as with the verses of Davies, the rural monotony of these
is sometimes redeemed by freshness or by an imaginative
turn.

Although less contemptible than recently supposed
and less bucolic, the Georgian poets are sometimes contemptible and commonly bucolic. They withdrew from
reality, not to an ivory tower, but to an oast-house. Dis-
heartened even in their happy time by its disorder and its
noise, they sought peace among loud cattle and neglected
gardens. The consequences of this withdrawal are apparent
in their verse. It is sterile on the whole, derivative in substance and technique, and at its best suburban.

The Georgians were less a group than an idea in the
head of Edward Marsh, by turns secretary to Joseph
Chamberlain and to Winston Churchill. In 1911 this gentleman decided to become what Swinnerton called "wet
nurse" to the muse. King Edward had died in 1910, the

[6] *The Poems of W. H. Davies* (1940). Edward Thomas: *Collected Poems* (1936).

Georgian era had begun, the time looked right for poetry's revival. That this was possible was shown by *The Everlasting Mercy,* a fitting expression of new times. Calling for poets, Marsh conferred. The result was *Georgian Poetry,* a biennial anthology to create or advertise a poetic renaissance. The first volume appeared in 1912, the last of five volumes in 1922. Edward Marsh was editor, Harold Monro publisher. Georgian poetry, or what they published, is that part of contemporary poetry which appealed to the taste of Edward Marsh. As might be supposed, this taste was conservative. Interesting poets, thought radical, were carefully excluded as those were who, face to face with reality, found rhythms for it and suitable metaphors. Intended to mean up-to-date, "Georgian" came to mean reactionary.

Being up-to-date meant accepting the frames of Wordsworth and Tennyson and the rhetoric of Keats, purged of richness and strength, however, in order to achieve the condition of Housman. The purge was sometimes incomplete, as in the verses of John Drinkwater, Robert Nichols, or Francis Brett Young, which seem composed of the words of Keats, and sometimes too complete, as in J. C. Squire's "To a Bull Dog," bare and flat to the point of banality. The more bucolic Georgians were these, together with Gordon Bottomley, Edmund Blunden, John Freeman, and D. H. Lawrence. Most were trying to achieve not only the condition of Housman but that of Joyce Kilmer at the moment of "Trees." D. H. Lawrence was included because of his pastoral interests, but his growing tendency toward free verse and exotic imagery must have caused uneasiness. From the ranks of older nature-lovers Marsh picked Davies, Masefield, de la Mare, and T. Sturge Moore. These gave the anthology its reputation.[7]

But the leading Georgians were far less botanical.

[7] Sir Edward Marsh: *A Number of People* (1939). James Elroy Flecker: *Collected Prose* (1922). Harold Monro: *Some Contemporary Poets* (1920). Masefield: *Reynard the Fox* (1919). Edmund Blunden: *Poems* (1930). Charlotte Mew: *Collected Poems* (1953) is less than Georgian though of the period. "The Bull" by Ralph Hodgson was generally admired.

Lascelles Abercrombie contributed quantities of academic blank verse. Before contributing his nature poems, W. W. Gibson had written *Daily Bread* (1910), short blank-verse dialogues on the poor, submitting to operations, dying in mines, or falling into furnaces. But the rhythms and images are too antiquated for these modern occasions. Rupert Brooke was more effectual. Instead of following the lead of these belated Victorians, he turned for the technique of some of his best poems to Webster, Marvell, and Donne. "Heaven" and "Dust" are witty, odd, and elaborately conceited in the manner of the seventeenth century. Brooke was the most talented of the Georgians, and had he lived he might have developed along the lines of T. S. Eliot, finding in the wit of Donne a vehicle suited to our divided times.[8]

D. H. Lawrence was also one of the imagists. These poets, otherwise barred from *Georgian Poetry* by their free verse, their clear images, their hatred of diffuse description and shop-worn rhetoric, were little less botanical than the Georgians, and Lawrence could feel as much at home with them as they with him. It took T. S. Eliot with his dead geraniums to change all that. Emerging from among the imagists, he finished them and the Georgians too, and lost himself in the unnatural past.

Others seeking the past lost themselves in childhood and history. With the aid of psychoanalysts the meaning of Wordsworth, Rimbaud, and Proust became evident, and childhood was recaptured. History, that preoccupation of romantics, was recaptured with the aid of archæologists and anthropologists. Unlike the Georgians, who sought the past in nature, some of those who sought it in childhood and history were explorers. Their intention was not to escape the present but to enrich it.

In spite of Wordsworth's "Ode," Victorians commonly thought children small adults who differed from large adults in providing better opportunities for sentiment or escape. Peter Pan's refusal of adult responsibility, though reflecting a social pattern, owes its undeniable

[8] *Poems* (1932). *John Webster and the Elizabethan Drama* (1916).

vividness to symbols provided by Barrie's unconscious. The maternal cave, the lagoon, and the intruders, whether pirate, crocodile, or ticking clock, give the fantasy a richness beyond intention. Making these symbols conscious, Freud also changed the child from small adult to child, without always improving, however, the literary result. *The Green Child* (1935) by romantic Herbert Read is another *Peter and Wendy*.

But "The Innocent Eye," a part of *Annals of Innocence and Experience* (1940), is not escapist but exploratory. In this autobiography Read recovers childhood by the method of Proust. Smelling smells, hearing the notes of violins, Read follows associations through widening circles of memory until the forgotten past is there again, the sights and sounds of a "virgin sensibility" and the pulsing of its "green heart." To Read, childhood is the unconscious, imagination, ecstasy, and nature itself, and art the recovery of the childish eye. These Wordsworthian and Freudian musings may owe something to Rimbaud, with whom Read was familiar. For to Rimbaud the memory of childhood was equivalent to vision and madness, as to psychoanalysts it is the equivalent of the unconscious and the primitive.

Dylan Thomas, invoking in one of his inverted sonnets a memory of the "black stairs," shared these convictions. "Fern Hill," all green and golden, is an even better evocation by rhythm, image, and sound of how it feels to have been young than the excellent recoveries of childhood in *Quite Early One Morning* (1954). "In Country Sleep," a father's view of the same province, is no less magical.

A High Wind in Jamaica (1929) by Richard Hughes is one of the best novels of the infant consciousness. The little victims of pirates, who are somewhat ineffectual and *démodé*, live in a world of decorum and taboo whose interpenetration of adult reality, domestic, piratical, or legal, is his theme. An adult, he says, has no more chance of "intellectual sympathy" with these animals than with an octopus, for their consciousness, differing in kind, occupies another plane. Emily's values are peculiar because like other children Emily is mad. Amnesia protects her innocence, as misunderstanding ours. Neatness, humor, and benign aloofness increase the horror of the charming story.

Since Hughes's book deals with the 1860's, it is historical, but Hughes did not use history for romantic escape as Maurice Hewlett had. In recent times the historical novel and poem, less common in England than in America, have been used in the research of lost times, a research various in kind and purpose. Some is patriotic, some amusing, and some instructive.

Once in Sussex, Rudyard Kipling sent out roots to establish himself in the present by means of the past. Some of his stories, such as "Friendly Brook" and "My Son's Wife," praise the soil, not as Hardy's followers did—because it is natural—but because it is English. When Puck of *Puck of Pook's Hill* (1906) discloses Saxons, Normans, and Romans of the Thirtieth Legion, his disclosures are filled with British tenderness. The intention of Charles Doughty was similar, but his audience is more doubtful. *The Dawn in Britain* (1906), an epic in six volumes, is composed in blank verse as uncouth as his prose, but less attractive. Archaic diction, neologisms, inversions, astonishing ellipses, do what they can to suit and to conceal the doughty deeds of "what antique wights dwelled ere in this sweet soil." Asked to recover this matter from the "vast abysm of buried ages," the Muse comes up with Britomart.

The British past also obsessed Arthur Machen, who, walking Welsh forests or rummaging *grimoires,* had taken "all obsolescence to be his province." Lucian, the hero of *The Hill of Dreams* (1907), of whom Machen spoke these words, exaggerates the concerns and feelings of his creator. As he walks the forests, Lucian feels that awe of nature which seems to have been the primitive emotion. Recapturing it like Lawrence, he centers it in the ruins of a Roman fort, where, like Forster's people, he submits to panic. In *Far Off Things* (1922), the first part of his autobiography, Machen confesses that in his effort to translate natural awe into words it became horror. But the glamour of *The Hill of Dreams* is located between these feelings.

Maybe the best historical novelist of recent years is Robert Graves.[9] *I, Claudius* (1934), a fictive autobiography of the least astonishing of the twelve Cæsars, is notable for his character and for the portraits of his abominable contemporaries. Their time, worse if possible than ours, is of use in making ours more bearable. After this success Graves turned to anthropologists and archæologists for help in further explorations. With Frazer's help, Graves retold the story of the Argonauts in *The Golden Fleece* (1944) and made myth history. Centaurs are not monsters but glyphs of a totemistic fraternity, the apples of the Hesperides are oranges, the harpies birds. As for the Symplegades, they are not there. Voyaging soberly among facts, Jason and his crew illustrate the war between the partisans of the Great Mother and of patriarchal Zeus. That war also provides background for *Homer's Daughter* (1955), which is indebted to Samuel Butler for the idea that Nausicaa wrote the *Odyssey*. Making myth commonplace and pseudo-historical, however, is only the lesser part of Graves's plan. His true interest lies in devotion to the overwhelming female figure that Baudelaire calls the giantess, that Jung calls the anima, and that Joyce calls Mrs. Bloom or Anna Livia Plurabelle, though Graves seems ignorant of these. Working under British lights, Graves calls her the white or triple goddess. Her identity would have been harder to establish had he "not known most of the answers beforehand by poetic intuition."

In *The White Goddess* (1948), his attempt at "a historical grammar of the language of poetic myth," it matters little that the historical method is that of Mme Blavatsky; for the value of this tedious discourse is supporting the rebellion of romantic imagination against fact. Graves's matriarchal moon goddess, displaced by Jove, is the poet's Muse. Incarnated now and again as Isis, Diana, the vampire, *la belle dame,* or Queen Elizabeth, this awful figure

[9] Historical novels: Naomi Mitchison: *Cloud Cuckoo Land* (1925), *The Corn King and the Spring Queen* (1931). L. H. Myers: *The Root and the Flower* (1935). Graves: *Claudius the God* (1934), *Sergeant Lamb's America* (1940), *King Jesus* (1946). Evelyn Waugh: *Helena* (1950). H. F. M. Prescott: *The Man on a Donkey* (1952). George Millar: *Orellana* (in America A *Crossbowman's Story*, 1954).

presides over all true poets, whose work, celebrating her, must employ her rites and her images of life or death. The trouble with patriarchal or Apollonian poetry is reason and sterility. It is not surprising that the "neo-romantic" poets of the neo-Elizabethan era have found as much encouragement in this "queer" document as in the works of Herbert Read and D. H. Lawrence.[1]

Explaining myth away had little place in the romantic plan. While euhemeristic Graves found actual bulls in the palace of Evans, others led by Freud, Jung, and Frazer threaded a labyrinth to find at its center man's nature and its past. The clue of Ariadne led to dream. Preserving mystery while threading it, the clue allowed pursuit of reason, if not to an *altitudo,* to that central place. Such considerations led Lawrence to Quetzalcoatl and the beasts of Revelation, led Dylan Thomas to make the Testaments, New and Old, his myth, led Edwin Muir, Vernon Watkins, and the Apocalyptics to praise, invent, or use the fabulous. For their art these matters provided theme or structure, and for their readers a meaning plainly there, but never plain.

There is little agreement about the nature of myth —though more about its function. Whereas to Freud and his followers myth is the dream of the race and dream the myth of the individual and whereas it is archetypal pattern to Jung, to Cassirer it is symbol and to anthropologists it may be celebration of vegetables or sanction for social customs. All agree, however, on myth's importance. Whether myth is this or that, it seems in the words of Erich Fromm to be a message from ourselves to ourselves by treating inner as if outer event. The embodiment of primitive wisdom, it may serve to enlighten us about our deepest motives or to express them. Rarely used nowadays for decoration as it was in the eighteenth century, myth appeals to romantics as an instrument of exploration, not only of our hearts but of our worlds. It helps make the private public and the particular general, provides richness and another dimension for our immediate concerns, gives meaning and value to a society almost without them, and serves imagination in its war with fact. In union with

[1] Graves: *The Greek Myths* (1955).

fact it may help us approach Eliot's unified sensibility and Yeats's unity of being. Myth seems to hold clues to a reality that philosophers, psychologists, historians, and theologians approach but never master through discursive reason. In short, if we take symbol according to its roots as putting together or according to usage as showing forth, myth is symbol.[2]

Some of those recovering this "forgotten language" retell ancient myth with baroque improvements. Aldous Huxley's "Leda," Thomas Blackburn's "Pasiphaë," and W. R. Rodgers's "Europa and the Bull," one of the most florid of postwar poems, are good examples. Some while retelling myth have reinterpreted it in the light of their interests. Not only the later novels of Graves but Sartre's *Flies* and Gide's *Theseus* illustrate this kind. More, resorting to what Mann calls "parody," have used myth as parallel to modern story. Sometimes ironic, sometimes comic, and sometimes serious, such works include Mann's "Tristan" and "The Blood of the Walsungs," Eugene O'Neill's *Mourning Becomes Electra*, Shaw's *Man and Superman* and *Pygmalion*, Lawrence Durrell's *Cefalu* (1947), and Christopher Fry's *Venus Observed* (1950), a comedy that starts bravely out from an ancient dilemma before straying up the garden path. As for allusions, they are everywhere as we may gather from Agamemnon and his Sweeney. In spite of Quetzalcoatl and Cuchulain, classical myth, having been shaped by the literary imagination, remains most congenial to it.[3]

[2] On myth: Erich Fromm: *The Forgotten Language* (1951); Ernst Cassirer: *Language and Myth* (1946); Bronislaw Malinowski: *Myth in Primitive Psychology* (1926). Cf. W. H. Auden: *The Enchafed Flood* (1950); Ross Nichols: *The Cosmic Shape* (1946).

[3] The following have some connection with myth: Stella Benson: *Tobit Transplanted* (1931); Denis Johnston: *A Bride for the Unicorn* (1933); James Bridie: *Jonah and the Whale* (1932), *Susannah and the Elders* (1937); Louis Golding: *Miracle Boy* (1927); Vernon Watkins: *Ballad of the Mari Lwyd* (1941); W. S. Graham: *The Seven Journeys* (1944); Ronald Duncan: *The Mongrel* (1950); E. M. Forster: "The Road from Colonus," *Collected Tales* (1947); W. R. Rodgers: *Europa and the Bull* (1952); Edwin Muir: *The Story & the Fable* (1940); Philip Toynbee: *Prothalamium, a Cycle of the Holy Graal* (1947), *The Garden to the Sea* (1954); Charles Williams: *War in Heaven* (1930).

Joyce, who named his creature Dedalus and built him a maze, used myth as analogy. The Homeric parallel of *Ulysses,* imposing past grandeur upon present confusion, may complicate the narrative it supports, but as Eliot says in "Ulysses, Order and Myth," the value exceeds the cost. In a time so shapeless as our own, he continues, something must be imported from the past to give our matter shape; but what Eliot says applies to himself rather than to Joyce, for whom there were other reasons than this for myth. Joyce's trick of imposing Homer's speed upon static situation is intentionally grotesque, as when, emerging from the verbal trance, the Cyclops-Citizen rises at last to throw his biscuit tin. Joyce's purpose was also ironic. His vision of unheroic Bloom in heroic posture is Swiftian, and Homer, like Gulliver's giant, pygmy, or horse, becomes an instrument for man's dissection. Since Bloom is also everyman, Odysseus, his symbol, gives Bloom a stature greater than his own. Victor Bérard's theory of the Semitic origins of the *Odyssey* provides connections with Bloom's other mythical counterparts, Jesus, Sinbad the Sailor, and the Wandering Jew. As Graves made myth modern, so Joyce with Homer's aid made the modern mythical, gave permanence to the impermanent, value and meaning to the trivial, and to the trivial the intensity of dream.

Although *Finnegans Wake* takes its frame from philosophy rather than from myth, the work is filled with fabulous matters. According to Vico and Jung, Joyce's guides, these matters, filling the collective unconscious, are its expression. Joyce found his furniture among anthropologists and archæologists as well. With Jung's aid, they gave him primitive man, vestigial in our sleep. The first section of *Finnegan,* with its giants, barrows, and middens, is "antediluvious" on the whole, as "he who runes may rede." Mutt and Jute, who talk of Clontarf, are not only local historians, Irishman and Dane, and creatures of modern myth, but creatures "astoneaged," less articulate contemporaries of that other ancient Mrs. Bloom, the Great Mother. Responsive to period, Earwicker becomes Uru-Wukru, which, because of the syllable "Ur" sounds "arboriginal." References in later chapters to remote periods such as the Aurignacian bring archæology to mind, and the voice of sleep, introducing the Mookse and the Gripes, feels he need not "anthropologize" for quarreling with Lévy-Bruhl. If Graves were acquainted with *Finnegans Wake,* he would find his triple goddess in the three girls of the river Liffey.

Commending myth, T. S. Eliot used it for *The Waste Land,* which appeared in the year of *Ulysses.* The notes express indebtedness to Frazer's *Golden Bough,* which has "influenced our generation profoundly," especially the volume on Attis, Osiris, and Adonis, and to Jessie Weston's *From Ritual to Romance* (1920), an application to medieval legend of Frazer and Harrison. From these Eliot took a frame on which to hang the dubious present and show it up, not a narrative frame as of *Ulysses* but a thematic and symbolic frame. Impressed with the fertility ceremonies that might have kept a greater or a lesser man from church, and with all the dying and reborn gods, Eliot adopted those symbols (also used by Lawrence) of desert, drought, and rain which expressed for a generation, as I. A. Richards remarked, its conviction of disillusionment. The Fisher King, the ruined chapel, Parsifal, Tiresias, and Tristan, less universal and hypnotic perhaps, but no less mythical, embody Eliot's hopes or advance his themes. The brilliance of this poem comes as much from these objective correlatives as from the rhythms and the tone. His later poems, *Ash Wednesday* and *Four Quartets,* which use the myth of the dying and resurrected god for decent worship, pleased another generation. Taking over the *Oresteia* of Æschylus for *The Family Reunion* (1939), the *Alcestis* of Euripides for *The Cocktail Party* (1949) and his *Ion* for *The Confidential Clerk* (1953), as we are told in *Poetry and Drama* (1951), Eliot found not only hint and sanction in these mythical matters but tradition for his individual talent.

By myth Yeats thought he could arrest the long decline from Homer's day and begin the difficult ascent to simplicity and heroism. He used Cuchulain, Fergus, and the two Cathleens of more recent origin to express country, self, and, more than these, the inexpressible. Weapon, vehicle, and metaphor, myth was an instrument of integration. In earlier romantics, Blake and Shelley in particular, he found example and encouragement. The synthetic myth that Yeats constructed on Blake's design, though far more geometrical than his, was intended as a frame for older myths. To fill the waiting structure of *A Vision* he read. the ancients and from Frazer learned the meaning of what he learned. Yeats's Leda receives the Swan without the help of Frazer, but Mary, her parallel in "Two Songs from a Play," acts a part in the myth of dying and resurrected gods. The reference to holy Dionysus in these poems and the substance of *The Resurrection* (1934), the play from which they come, show Frazer's hand.[4] It is not surprising, therefore, that in Byzantium, a mythical concretion within this convenient frame, the unnatural bard sat singing on a golden bough.

Each cycle of Yeats's system begins with a mythical conjunction of flesh and spirit. Leda and the Swan and Dove and Virgin began the cycle before ours and our own, and the next, announced in "The Second Coming," will shortly begin with one knows not what bestial intrusion. This comforting system, which explains confusion and prepares for worse before the better comes, is not original. A reference to Magnus Annus in "Two Songs from a Play" shows that Yeats had the Platonic year in mind; but —and this is more relevant—he knew Vergil and Shelley. "Two Songs from a Play" repeats the images and phrases of Shelley's chorus from *Hellas;* and another Argo and another Troy are also to be found in Vergil's Messianic eclogue. Yeats and Shelley, with Dryden too, were employing a common tradition.

The doctrine of cycles to which Yeats gave the best expression is suitable for those who, loving the past, reject all notion of rectilinear progress. That this dream of modern times, dear to some Victorians and some of us, is fading is shown by the appearance among the better roman-

---

[4] Yeats was one of the first literary men to use Frazer. In 1899 he cites *The Golden Bough;* and in *The King of the Great Clock Tower* (1934) he explains his fantasy in terms of Frazer's mother goddess and the slain god.

tics, especially those of recent times, of cyclical pattern and of that conflict of opposites which seems to go with it. Joyce, who had learned from Vico that history repeats itself, made *Finnegan* circular. The last sentence meets the first and epicycles intricately revolve upon the Viconian ring to the clashing of Bruno's opposites. As the line of progress turned upon itself to become a circle, Lawrence, familiar with the early Greek philosophers and the Theosophists, thought at times of cycles and always of opposites. And even Eliot, esteeming Heraclitus though preferring fixity to movement, and movement within fixity to fixity, observes in "Burnt Norton" the circling boarhound and the boar, and in "East Coker," like Earwicker and Mary Queen of Scots, confuses his end with his beginning.

INDEX

A.E., see Russell, George
Abbey Theatre, 66–74, 81
Abercrombie, Lascelles, 307
Action française, 86, 90
Adler, Alfred, 213, 215
Adolescence, novel of, 145–50
Æschylus, 137, 183, 314
Æstheticism, 5–17, 18, 23, 162, 249
Aldington, Richard, 24, 58 n., 98–9, 181 n., 275, 276, 280
Alexander, Samuel, 209
Allen, Charles, 24 n.
Allen, Grant, 32
Allgood, Sara, 66
Alvarez, A., 119
Amis, Kingsley, 107, 119
Anarchism, 27, 45, 49 n., 236
Anglo-Catholicism, 90, 175, 181, 181 n., 183–5
Annan, Noel Gilroy, 202 n.
Anthropology, 44, 171, 223–4, 296–9, 300, 301, 307, 310–15
Antoine, André, 31, 259
Apocalyptics, see New Apocalypse
Apollinaire, Guillaume, 235, 246, 255, 279, 286
Aquinas, St. Thomas, 12, 86
Aragon, Louis, 234, 235, 236
Archæology, 297–9, 300, 307, 310, 311, 313, 314
Archer, William, 30
Aristotle, 15, 199
Arlen, Michael, 103, 104, 105, 112

Arliss, George, 38, 42
Armitage, Flora, 58 n.
Armstrong, Terence, 88 n.
Arnold, Matthew, 3, 211
Art for art's sake, see Æstheticism
Atkins, John, 50 n.
Auden, W. H., 23, 26, 27, 43, 45, 46–7, 48, 49, 50, 98, 119, 175, 178 n., 236, 243, 312 n.; social awareness, 46–7, 49, 244; plays, 46–7, 73, 233, 244; religion, 50, 184–5; use of the unconscious, 233
Augustine, St., 23
Austen, Jane, 107, 128

Babbitt, Irving, 78, 86, 91
Bach, Johann Sebastian, 103
Bacon, Francis, 154, 157
Bagehot, Walter, 216
Balzac, Honoré de, 121, 122, 124, 126, 128, 129
Barbusse, Henri, 97
Barker, George, 178 n., 242
Baron, Alexander, 97, 148 n.
Baroque, revival of, 100, 102, 177–8, 179 n.
Barre, André, 246 n.
Barrie, J. M., 80, 117, 307–8
Basic English, 26
Bates, H. E., 303 n.
Bates, Ralph, 49
Baudelaire, Charles, 3, 5, 6, 7, 11, 18, 19, 20, 21, 217, 220,

Baudelaire, Charles (*continued*)
246–9, 250, 251, 252, 253, 255,
256, 257, 258, 259, 261–2,
263, 268, 272, 277, 279, 280,
281, 282, 283, 285, 288, 290,
310
Beach, J. W., 199 n.
Beardsley, Aubrey, 11, 17, 24,
102, 104, 115, 179; *Under the
Hill*, 104, 262–3
Beauclair, 253 n.
Beckett, Samuel, 197 n., 228 n.,
224 n.
Beddoes, Thomas, 118
Beerbohm, Max, 6, 24, 110 n.,
189; *Zuleika Dobson*, 115; on
æstheticism, 6–7, 11; drama
criticism, 34, 162; on symbol-
ism, 264–5
Bell, Clive, 15, 15 n.
Bell, Julian, 48
Benda, Julien, 86, 88, 91, 210
Bennett, Arnold, 4, 24, 132, 136,
144, 200; *Anna of the Five
Towns*, 133, 134–5; *Buried
Alive*, 133–4; *Clayhanger*, 135,
147–8; *The Grand Babylon
Hotel*, 133, 135; *A Great Man*,
4 n., 133–4; *Imperial Palace*,
135–6; *Journals*, 4, 132; *Leo-
nora*, 133; *A Man from the
North*, 133; *The Old Wives'
Tale*, 134, 135; *Riceyman
Steps*, 135; *The Truth about an
Author*, 4
Bennett, Joan, 199 n.
Benson, Stella, 312 n.
Bentley, Eric, 28 n., 160 n., 211 n.
Beowulf, 58
Bérard, Victor, 313
Beresford, J. D., 148 n.
Bergson, Henri, 86, 88, 89, 161,
187, 188, 189, 195, 202, 209,
275, 287
Bernard, Claude, 120, 122
Bernhardt, Sarah, 259
Besant, Annie, 32
Besant, Walter, 17
Betjeman, John, 119
Black and Tans, 70, 74, 76, 81
Blackburn, Thomas, 312
Blackstone, Bernard, 199 n.

Blake, William, 11, 76, 154, 164,
226, 246, 267, 268, 270 n., 296,
315
Blast, 87
Blavatsky, Mme H. P., 84, 164,
168, 169, 170, 171, 180, 267,
269, 296, 298, 303, 310
Bloomsbury, see Cambridge-
Bloomsbury set
Bloomsday celebration, 82
Blunden, Edmund, 98, 306, 306 n.
Blunt, Anthony, 44
Boas, Guy, 110 n.
Bodkin, Maud, 183 n., 216 n.
Boehme, Jacob, 267
Boer War, 55, 57, 59
Bohr, Niels, 152
Bookman, The, 8, 266
Bosanquet, Bernard, 52
Bottomley, Gordon, 306
Bourgeois, Maurice, 68 n.
Bowen, Elizabeth, 207; *Death of
the Heart*, 208; *Friends and
Relations*, 208–9; *The House
in Paris*, 208; *Ivy Gripped the
Steps*, 208; *Look at All Those
Roses*, 207; *A World of Love*,
292
Bowra, C. M., 265
Boyd, Ernest, 63 n.
Bradbook, M. C., 140 n.
Brancusi, Constantin, 149
Brander, Lawrence, 50 n.
Brémond, Abbé, 9
Breton, André, 201, 235, 236,
237, 238, 255
Brett, Dorothy, 299 n.
Bridges, Robert, 18, 84-6, 177
Bridie, James, 312 n.
Brinnin, John Malcolm, 241 n.
Brontë sisters, 216, 218
Brooke, Rupert, 47, 57, 98, 307
Brown, E. K., 291 n.
Brown, Hilton, 53 n.
Brown, John Mason, 29
Brown, Malcolm, 258 n.
Bruno, Giordano, 228, 316
Buckley, Jerome, 57 n.
Budgen, Frank, 197 n., 288 n.
Bunyan, John, 35, 159, 160, 162,
184, 211
Burdett, Osbert, 10 n.

Burns, Robert, 12, 45
Butler, Samuel, 34, 148, 149, 155, 160, 173, 219, 301, 310; *Erewhon*, 156–7; *Erewhon Revisited*, 157, 160; *Fair Haven*, 157; *A First Year in the Canterbury Settlement*, 156 n.; *Narcissus*, 158–9; *The Note-Books*, 147; *The Way of All Flesh*, 146–7, 218; effect upon Shaw, 34, 147, 159, 160, 161, 162; and Darwinism, 146, 156, 157–8; tracts, 156, 158–9; religion, 157–8, 163; poems, 158–9
Butts, Mary, 219 n.
Bynner, Witter, 299 n.
Byrne, J. F., 150 n.
Byrne, Patrick, 6 n.
Byron, Lord, 3

Cahoon, Herbert, 150 n.
Calder-Marshall, Arthur, 49 n.
Cambridge-Bloomsbury set, 88, 96, 108, 206
Campbell, Joseph, 228 n.
Campbell, Mrs. Patrick, 34
Campbell, Roy, 89–90
Cannon, Gilbert, 148 n.
Carlyle, Thomas, 3
Carpenter, Edward, 214
Carrington, C. E., 53 n.
Carroll, Lewis, 216, 230, 244, 287
Carroll, Paul Vincent, 72, 73, 74
Carswell, Catherine, 66 n., 299 n.
Carte, D'Oyly, 6
Cary, Joyce, 61 n., 210, 211
Casement, Roger, 74
Cassirer, Ernst, 287, 311, 312
Catholicism, Roman, 64, 66, 78, 89, 90, 104, 140, 175–6, 177–80, 181 n., 221–2, 250
Caudwell, Christopher, 43, 44, 45, 47, 48, 216–17, 297
Cazamian, M. L., 126 n.
Cecil, David, 110, 140 n.
Chamberlain, Houston, 52
Chamberlain, Joseph, 53, 305
Chamberlain, Neville, 89–90
Chekhov, Anton, 36, 80, 81, 196, 201, 206, 208

Cheshire Cheese, The, 9
Chesterton, G. K., 29, 139, 180, 184
Childhood, recovery of, 88, 166, 247, 251, 283, 284, 297, 307–8
Chirico, Giorgio, 85, 235
Churchill, Winston, 59, 305
Classicism, see Neoclassicism
Claudel, Paul, 275
Coffman, Stanley K., 276 n.
Colenso, John, 136
Coleridge, S. T., 25–6
Collier, John, 114 n.
Collingwood, R. G., 155 n.
Collins, Wilkie, 137
Colum, Padraic, 70 n., 79, 304
Comfort, Alex, 98 n.
Common, Jack, 148 n.
Communism, 43–51, 71–2, 80, 235–6
Communist Party, 42, 45, 48, 236
Compton-Burnett, Ivy, 107–8; *Bullivant and the Lambs*, 108
Comte, Auguste, 120, 124, 163
Congreve, William, 110
Connolly, Cyril, 24, 25, 100 n., 104 n.
Connolly, James, 51, 73, 74, 75, 80
Conrad, Joseph, 22 n., 59, 144, 189, 192, 196, 211; *Almayer's Folly*, 60; *Chance*, 194, 218; "The End of the Tether," 60; "Heart of Darkness," 60, 61, 105, 141, 287–8, 288–9, 292; *Lord Jim*, 61, 141, 142, 193–4; *The Nigger of the Narcissus*, 141, 142 n.; *Nostromo*, 61, 288; *Notes on Life and Letters*, 193; *An Outcast of the Islands*, 60; "An Outpost of Progress," 60; *The Rescue*, 141, 142; *The Secret Agent*, 59, 288; "The Secret Sharer," 288; *The Shadow Line*, 141; *Tales of Unrest*, 142 n.; *Typhoon*, 141; *Under Western Eyes*, 59; *Victory*, 22 n., 141, 142, 194, 288; *Youth*, 105, 194; stories of empire, 59–61; determinism, 140–1; idea of nature, 141; im-

Conrad, Joseph (*continued*)
  pressionism, 193–4, 201, 205,
  209; symbolism, 287–9
Contemporary Poetry and Prose,
  238
Copernicus, Nikolaus, 154
Coppard, A. E., 114 n.
Corbière, Tristan, 253, 279
Cork realists, 70, 80
Corkery, Daniel, 68 n., 78 n.
Cornford, John, 46, 48–9
Corvo, Baron, see Rolfe, Frederick
Cosgrave, William, 78
Court Theatre, 34
Coward, Noel, 43, 110, 112–14,
  183
Crackanthorpe, Herbert, 131 n.
Crashaw, Richard, 178, 179 n.
Crevel, René, 235
Criterion, The, 24, 90, 139, 169,
  181 n., 275 n.
Cromwell, Oliver, 78
Cros, Charles, 351 n.
Crowley, Aleister, 269
Cummings, E. E., 255
Cycles: belief in cyclical pattern,
  315–16

D., H. (Doolittle, Hilda), 99
Dada, 234–5
Daiches, David, 26 n., 82 n.,
  174 n., 199 n.
Daily Mail, The, 24, 53, 57
Daily Worker, 48
Dali, Salvador, 235, 236, 237, 238
Dandieu, Arnaud, 290 n.
Dante, 167, 181, 280
D'Arcy, Martin, 176 n.
Darwin, Charles, 39, 46, 52–3,
  120, 124, 131 n., 136, 137,
  138, 139, 146, 151, 155, 156,
  157–8, 161, 173, 212, 214,
  256, 277, 296, 298, 300, 301,
  302, 303
Darwin, Erasmus, 16
Daudet, Léon, 89
Davidson, Donald, 10 n.
Davidson, John, 10 n., 221 n.
Davie, Donald, 119, 119 n.
Davies, Hugh Sykes, 237–8
Davies, Rhys, 303 n.

Davies, W. H., 305, 306
Davis, Thomas, 65, 165
Day Lewis, Cecil, 44, 45, 46, 48,
  98, 178 n., 233–4
Decadence, 15–17, 24, 179, 247,
  250, 253, 256–65, 285
Décadent, Le, 253
Decadents, the, 253, 255, 281
Delacroix, Ferdinand, 248
De la Mare, Walter, 6 n., 117–18,
  232, 306
Delattre, Floris, 199 n., 252
Delphic oracle, 235, 273
Dennis, Nigel, 107 n.
Desnos, Robert, 235
Determinism, 123, 137–8, 140,
  148–9, 151–2, 156
De Valera, Eamon, 74, 78
Dickens, Charles, 129, 130, 131,
  143, 144, 145, 211, 287
Digges, Dudley, 66
Dobrée, Bonamy, 119, 243
Documentary novel, 122, 123
Dodgson, C. L., see Carroll, Lewis
Donne, John, 76, 100, 118, 154,
  179 n., 241, 264, 277, 279, 307
Dostoyevsky, Feodor, 80, 135, 138,
  152, 189, 194, 200, 201, 202,
  204, 206, 212, 213, 221, 223,
  224
Doughty, Charles M., 58, 309
Douglas, Lord Alfred, 259 n.
Douglas, George, 117
Douglas, Norman, 100–1, 102
Dowson, Ernest, 9, 179; æstheti-
  cism, 9, 10; symbolism, 9, 10,
  13, 262
Drama: "new" or "higher," 29–
  43; comedy of manners, 110–14
Drew, Elizabeth, 241 n., 282 n.
Drinkwater, John, 306
Dryden, John, 10, 15, 315
Dublin Lodge of the Theosophi-
  cal Society, 164, 169, 267
Dujardin, Édouard, 189, 197 n.,
  205, 255; friendship with
  Moore, 190, 258; effect on
  Joyce, 197
Dumas, Alexandre, *fils*, 29, 39, 40
Duncan, Ronald, 312 n.
Dunne, J. W., 203 n.
Duns Scotus, 19, 178, 179

Durrell, Lawrence, 233 n., 236, 244 n., 285, 286, 312
Duruy, Victor, 126

Eddy, Mary Baker, 46
Edel, Leon, 150 n., 195 n.
Edward VII, 305–6
Edwards, Hilton, 72
Egoist, The, 24, 99, 280
Einstein, Albert, 151, 152, 209, 212
Eliot, George, 211
Eliot, T. S., 6 n., 24, 25, 26, 45, 46, 77, 77 n., 83, 118, 139, 140, 175, 184, 185, 236, 261, 284, 286, 307; After Strange Gods, 91; Ash Wednesday, 182, 232, 281, 282, 314; "Baudelaire in Our Time," 279; The Cocktail Party, 183, 184, 314; The Confidential Clerk, 183, 184, 314; "Le Directeur," 279; Essays Ancient and Modern, 181; The Family Reunion, 183, 232, 314; For Lancelot Andrewes, 90, 279; Four Quartets, 91, 181–2, 183, 282, 314, 316; The Function of Criticism, 90; "Gerontion," 180–1, 281, 282; "The Hippopotamus," 180, 279; "The Hollow Men," 181, 183, 278, 282; The Idea of a Christian Society, 181; "The Love Song of J. Alfred Prufrock," 277, 280; "Mélange Adultère," 279; "The Metaphysical Poets," 279; Murder in the Cathedral, 182–3; Notes Towards the Definition of Culture, 181; Poetry and Drama, 314; "Portrait of a Lady," 277, 279; "Preludes," 281; Religious Dramas, 183 n.; "Rhapsody on a Windy Night," 281; The Rock, 182; The Sacred Wood, 15, 183 n.; Selected Essays, 183 n., 280 n.; Sweeney Agonistes, 282; "Tradition and the Individual Talent," 90; Ulysses, Order and Myth, 313; The Use of Poetry and the Use of Criticism, 15; The Waste Land, 86,

Eliot, T. S. (continued)
99, 105, 181, 183, 186, 205, 247, 279, 280, 281, 314; criticism, 15, 169, 181–2; imagism and symbolism, 21–2, 246, 277–82; classicism, 85, 86, 87, 90–1; satiric quatrains, 87, 99; traditionalism, 90, 279; religion, 90–1, 180–4, 185; politics, 90–1, 181; plays, 114, 182–3; stream of consciousness, 205, 278, 279; use of anthropology and myth, 312, 314, 316
Ellis, Havelock, 128, 138, 214, 217
Ellis-Fermor, Una, 66 n.
Ellmann, Richard, 65 n., 150 n., 270 n.
Éluard, Paul, 235, 237 n., 255, 284 n.
Elyot, Sir Thomas, 282
Empson, William, 25, 26 n., 152, 210, 239, 240; Seven Types of Ambiguity, 26, 216; Some Versions of Pastoral, 26, 216; The Structure of Complex Words, 26; poems, 118
English, Basic, 26
Equinox, 270
Ernst, Max, 235
Ervine, St. John, 39 n.
Evans, Sir Arthur, 297, 311
Evans, B. I., 10 n.
Evolution, idea of, 157–8; see also Darwin, Charles
Exile of artist by society, 3–4, 17–26
Existentialism, 185, 312
Expressionism, 71, 72, 73, 227

Fabian Society, 27, 30, 32, 35
Farmer, Albert J., 5 n.
Farr, Florence, 31, 66
Fascism, 46, 48, 49; Irish, 74, 78; British, 83–4, 88, 89–90; French, 86, 90; Italian, 89, 90
Faulkner, William, 290
Fay, Frank and William, 66
Feminism, 31–2, 38, 88
Ferguson, Samuel, 64, 65, 166
Fielding, Henry, 96
Firbank, Ronald, 103–4

Fiser, Emeric, 275 n.

Fitzgerald, Barry, 70, 72

Flamel, 165

Flaubert, Gustave, 5, 8, 10, 13, 120, 124, 125, 126, 129, 131, 132, 136, 142, 144, 145, 150, 176, 226, 227, 258, 259 n., 260, 288; Madame Bovary, 121, 127, 287

Flecker, James Elroy, 306 n.

Fletcher, Iain, 119 n., 243 n.

Flint, F. S., 275–7

Flower, Desmond, 10 n.

Ford, Ford Madox, 192, 205–6, 276 n.

Forster, E. M., 62, 107 n., 199 n., 200, 309; Aspects of the Novel, 291 n.; The Development of English Prose between 1918 and 1939, 213 n.; Howards End, 94–5, 290; The Longest Journey, 95, 300; A Passage to India, 62, 94, 95, 96, 290–1; A Room with a View, 95; "The Story of a Panic," 300; Where Angels Fear to Tread, 95–6, 300; symbolism, 287, 290–1; his oafs, 300; use of myth, 300; stories, 300 n; 312 n.

Fort, Paul, 259, 275

Fortnightly Review, The, 40

Fox, Ralph, 48

France, Anatole, 254

Franco, Francisco, 48, 78, 83 n., 89, 90 n.

Fraser, G. S., 119 n., 243, 243 n.

Free association, 20, 21, 152, 257, 277; see also Free verse

Free verse, 24, 255, 275, 306, 307

Freeman, John, 306

Freud, Sigmund, 20, 152, 159, 172, 173, 185, 189, 194, 202, 212–45, 291, 296, 297, 308, 311

Friedman, Melvin, 195 n.

Frierson, William C., 126 n.

Frobenius, Leo, 299

Fromm, Erich, 311, 312 n.

Frost, Robert, 305

Fry, Christopher, 114, 312

Fry, Roger, 15, 15 n., 152, 215

Fuller, Edmund, 28 n.

Fuller, Roy, 98 n.

Gaelic League, 64

Galileo, 154

Gallup, Donald, 282 n.

Galsworthy, John, 41, 136, 144, 200, 224; Forsyte Saga, 94, 145; plays, 41–2

Gardner, W. H., 177 n., 178 n.

Garnett, Constance, 189

Garnett, David, 114 n., 202 n.

Gascoyne, David, 237

Gate Theatre, 72, 73

Gaudier-Brzeska, Henri, 87

Gauguin, Paul, 62

Gaunt, William, 5 n.

Gautier, Théophile, 5, 7, 8, 87, 249, 281

George V, 295

George, Stefan, 264

Georgian Poetry, 306, 307

Georgian poets, 53, 78, 118, 274–5, 305–7; war poetry, 97–100

Germ, The, 24

Ghil, René, 128, 254, 257

Gibbon, Edward, 16, 109, 157, 298

Gibbon, Lewis Grassic, 82

Gibbons, Stella, 303 n.

Gibson, W. W., 98, 307

Gide, André, 6 n., 103, 189, 220, 223, 312

Gilbert, Stuart, 23, 197 n., 228 n.

Gilbert, W. S., 6, 7, 110

Gissing, George, 4, 129, 133, 143; New Grub Street, 4, 129, 130–1; The Nether World, 130; The Private Papers of Henry Ryecroft, 129; The Unclassed, 129–30; Workers in the Dawn, 129

Givens, Seon, 228 n., 289 n.

Gladstone, W. E., 63

Glasheen, Adaline, 228 n.

Godden, Rumer, 208 n., 294 n.

Goethe, Johann W. von, 145

Gogarty, Oliver, 150 n.

Golden Dawn, Order of the, 165, 267, 269, 273

Golding, Louis, 145 n., 312 n.

Golding, William, 50 n.

Goldsmith, Oliver, 230
Gollancz, Victor, 49 n.
Goncourt, Edmond and Jules, 14, 122, 126, 128, 131 n., 132; *Germinie Lacerteux*, 121, 122, 124
Gonne, Maud, 63, 65, 66, 69, 73, 75, 76, 166, 266
Gordan, John, 140 n.
Gore-Booth, Eva, 75, 79
Gore-Booth, Lord, 73
Gorman, Herbert, 150 n.
Gosse, Edmund, 30, 110, 128, 263–4
Gothic novel, 242
Gourmont, Rémy de, 15, 275, 280–1
Graham, Cunninghame, 59, 140
Graham, W. S., 242 n., 312 n.
Grahame, Kenneth, 114 n.
Granville-Barker, Harley, 34, 39 n., 304
Graves, Robert, 26, 99, 313, 314; criticism, 26 n., 214–15; memoirs, 97, poetry, 97–8, 232, 243; novels, 310–11, 312
Gray, John, 17, 179, 179 n., 262
Gray, Thomas, 10
Green, Henry, 49, 97 n., 292 n.; *Back*, 97 n., 293; *Blindness*, 148; *Concluding*, 293; *Doting*, 107; *Living*, 49, 293; *Loving*, 292; *Nothing*, 107, 293; *Party Going*, 292–3; symbolist novelist, 246, 287, 292–3
Green, J. T., 31
Greene, Graham, 104; *Brighton Rock*, 221–2; *The End of the Affair*, 180; *The Heart of the Matter*, 180; *The Power and the Glory*, 221; *The Quiet American*, 62 n.
Gregory, Lady Augusta, 64, 65, 66, 67, 69, 72, 75, 76; folklore, 65, 65 n.; plays, 67, 69–70, 304
Gregory, Horace, 172 n.
Grierson, H. J. C., 264 n.
Griffith, Arthur, 73, 74
Groddeck, Georg, 233, 233 n.
Guaita, Stanislas de, 165
Guedalla, Phillip, 110

Guérard, Albert, 85 n., 140 n.
Gunn, Thomas, 119
Gwynn, Dennis, 66 n.

Hafley, James, 199 n.
Halévy, Élie, 53 n.
Hall, James, 274 n.
Hall, Radclyffe, 220 n.
Halper, Nathan, 228
Hamalian, Leo, 183 n.
Hankin, St. John, 39 n.
Hanley, James, 131 n.
Hanley, M. L., 197 n.
Hardy, Evelyn, 140 n.
Hardy, Florence, 140 n.
Hardy, Thomas, 42, 58, 94, 128, 136, 151, 303 n.; *The Dynasts*, 42, 139–40, 153; *Far from the Madding Crowd*, 303 n.; *Jude the Obscure*, 137, 138, 222, 223; *The Mayor of Casterbridge*, 137; *The Poor Man and the Lady*, 302, 303 n.; *The Return of the Native*, 137; *Tess of the D'Urbervilles*, 137–8; *Two on a Tower*, 137; *The Woodlanders*, 137, 302; determinism, 136–9, 149; poems, 139–40; symbolism, 287; love of countryside, 302–3; his followers, 303–5
Harington, Sir John, 102
Harland, Henry, 24, 179, 263
Harmsworth, Alfred, 57
Harris, Frank, 6 n.
Harrison, Jane, 298–9, 314
Hart, Liddell, 58 n.
Hartley, L. P., 287, 292, 293–5
Hartmann, Karl von, 277–8, 279
Harvard Advocate, 277
Hauptmann, Gerhart, 259
Haycraft, Howard, 144 n.
Hazlitt, William, 14
Heard, Gerald, 173–4, 286, 297–8
Heath-Stubbs, John, 243 n.
Hegel, George, 239, 240
Hemans, Felicia, 12
Henderson, Archibald, 27 n.
Henderson, Philip, 44 n.
Hendry, G. F., 243
Henley, W. E., 29, 57, 59, 143
Henn, T. R., 65 n.

Heraclitus, 282, 316

Herbert, George, 180 n.

Hermes Trismegistus, 184, 267–8, 290

Hermetic Society, 164

Hewlett, Maurice, 309

Heywood, Thomas, 29

Hichens, Robert, 17 n.

Higgins, F. R., 78

Higher criticism, the, 155–6, 157, 176

Hinde, Thomas, 108 n.

Hinduism, 155, 164, 167, 169–70

History: preoccupation with, 307; historical novel, 309–11

Hitler, Adolf, 49, 83, 84, 89

Hodgson, Ralph, 306 n.

Hodgson, T. R., 98 n.

Hoffman, Frederick, 24 n., 213 n., 299 n.

Hoggart, Richard, 47 n.

Hölderlin, Johann, 118

Holland, Vyvyan, 6 n.

Hollis, Christopher, 106 n.

Holtby, Winifred, 63 n., 199 n., 202

Home Rule bill, 63

Homer, 167, 313, 314; see also Joyce, James, Homeric parallel

Hone, Joseph, 65 n., 126 n., 265

Hood, Stuart, 97 n.

Hopkins, Gerard, 18, 58, 85, 139, 172, 175–6, 180, 216, 239, 242, 286; obscurity, 18–19, 26; poems, 176–9; religion, 176–9

Horizon, 24

Horniman, Miss A. E. F., 72

Horton, W. T., 270 n.

Hough, Graham, 65 n.

Housman, A. E., 92–4, 243, 305, 306

Housman, Laurence, 94 n.

Howe, Susanne, see Nobbe, Susanne Howe

Hudson, W. H., 57–8, 305; El Ombú, 302; Far Away and Long Ago, 302; Green Mansions, 301–2; A Hind in Richmond Park, 301; The Naturalist in La Plata, 301; The Purple Land, 58; A Shepherd's Life, 301; work as a naturalist, 300–1

Huff, William H., 241 n.

Hughes, Glenn, 276 n.

Hughes, Richard, 308–9

Hulme, T. E., 83, 118–19, 280; classicism, 86–7; disciples, 86–91; imagism, 87, 275–6

Hume, David, 109

Humphrey, Robert, 195 n.

Huxley, Aldous, 92, 104, 108, 112, 113, 114, 151, 175, 176, 209; After Many a Summer, 103, 174; Antic Hay, 102, 173; Ape and Essence, 103; Beyond the Mexique Bay, 173; Brave New World, 103, 173; Crome Yellow, 102, 103, 146, 220, 285; Do What You Will, 284; Ends and Means, 173; "Eupompus Gave Splendour to Art by Numbers," 297; Eyeless in Gaza, 174; "The Farcical History of Richard Greenow," 220; The Genius and the Goddess, 103; Grey Eminence, 174 n.; Leda, 101, 312; Limbo, 220; Mortal Coils, 101–2; The Perennial Philosophy, 174 n.; Point Counter Point, 102, 173, 220, 282, 284; Science, Liberty and Peace, 174; Those Barren Leaves, 102, 173; Time Must Have a Stop, 103, 174; cynical novels, 102–3; poems, 100, 101, 284–5; stories, 101–2; religious development, 106, 173–5; relationship with Lawrence, 172–3; relationship with Heard, 173–4; relationship with Isherwood, 175; symbolism, 284–5

Huxley, Thomas, 137, 142, 158, 164

Huysmans, J. K., 8, 170, 179, 258, 261; naturalism, 124, 126, 133; symbolism, 128, 253, 258, 280; religion, 129

Hyde, Douglas, 64, 69

Hyman, S. E., 26 n.

Hynes, Sam, 86 n.

Ibsen, Henrik, 29–32, 33, 34, 35, 38, 39, 40, 42, 43, 66, 70,

Ibsen, Henrik (continued)
110, 111, 138, 147, 182, 246, 259, 264
Ibsenism, 29–34, 38–43, 66
Imagism, 24, 274–7, 281, 307–8
Imagistes, Des, 265, 276
Imperialism, 43–4, 46, 52–63
Impressionism: in criticism, 13–15; in the novel, 190 ff.
Independent Theatre, 31
Innes, Michael, 184
International Brigade, 48, 50
Irish Brigade, 78
Irish Citizen Army, 74
Irish Independent, 82
Irish literary renaissance, 12, 63–82
Irish Literary Theatre, 22, 65–6
Irish Republican Brotherhood, 63, 65, 74, 81
Irish Times, 82, 197 n.
Isherwood, Christopher, 46, 48, 50, 175, 175 n., 280 n.; plays, 46–7, 47 n., 72, 233, 244; novels, 49, 220; social and political interests, 46, 47 n., 50; religion, 50, 175

Jackson, Holbrook, 10 n.
James, Henry, 24, 55, 94, 95, 132, 144, 189, 196, 199, 206, 278, 279 n.; The Middle Years, 193; Notes on Novelists, 136; Portrait of a Lady, 205; The Sacred Fount, 191; The Spoils of Poynton, 192; The Turn of the Screw, 191; What Maisie Knew, 192, 196, 205, 208; objection to naturalism, 136, 191; impressionism, 191–3, 194, 201, 205, 206, 209, 294
James, William, 179, 187–8, 189, 191, 195, 199, 204
Jameson, Storm, 145 n.
Jammes, Francis, 275
Jarry, Alfred, 234, 266
Jean-Aubry, G., 61 n., 140 n.
Jeans, James, 151–2
Jeffares, Norman, 65 n.
Jesuits, 13, 18, 43, 148, 176, 178, 199
John of the Cross, St., 90, 282
Johnson, Lionel, 9, 10, 85, 179

Johnson, Pamela, 108 n.
Johnson, Samuel, 19, 85, 92, 163
Johnston, Charles, 164
Johnston, Denis, 72–3, 97 n., 312 n.
Johnstone, J. K., 202 n.
Jolas, Eugene, 23, 228 n.
Jones, David, 97
Jones, Ernest, 104 n., 216 n.
Jones, Henry Arthur, 39–40, 111
Jones, Henry Festing, 156 n.
Jones, P. M., 86 n.
Jones, W. P., 150 n.
Jonson, Ben, 13, 76, 209
Journalism, "new," 29
Jowett, Benjamin, 176
Joyce, James, 5, 24, 44, 45, 63, 72, 88, 170, 176, 211, 216, 242; Chamber Music, 13, 288; The Day of the Rabblement, 22; Dubliners, 80, 196, 288; Exiles, 22, 40; Finnegans Wake, 23, 152–3, 185–6, 228–31, 236, 313–14, 316; A Portrait of the Artist, 12, 22, 24, 66, 148, 149–50, 185, 196, 197, 288–9, 292; Stephen Hero, 12, 149, 185; Ulysses, 22, 24, 40, 132, 150, 186, 190, 197–9, 222, 282, 289, 313, 314; Work in Progress, 223, 228; æstheticism, 5, 12–13, 162; exile, 22–3, 81; Ibsenism, 40–1; Homeric parallel, 150, 186, 197, 227, 313; religion, 185–6; stream of consciousness, 190, 196–200, 201–2, 205, 210; symbolism, 196–200, 246, 287, 288–9, 290, 291, 297; impressionism, 190, 196, 209, 219, 239; the unconscious, 227–31; parody and other techniques, 198–9; use of myth and anthropology, 310, 313–16; use of cycles, 296, 316
Joyce, Stanislaus, 150 n.
Jung, Carl, 20, 167, 213

Kabalistic Order of the Rosy Cross, 165
Kafka, Franz, 22 n., 184, 244, 290, 293
Kahn, Gustave, 254, 255, 257

Kailyard School, the, 117
Kain, Richard, 150 n., 197 n.
Kavanagh, Peter, 66 n.
Kaye-Smith, Sheila, 303 n.
Keats, John, 5, 215, 306
Kenner, Hugh, 88 n., 150 n., 289 n.
Kenyon Critics, 178 n.
Keyes, Sidney, 98 n.
Kierkegaard, Sören, 185
Kilmer, Joyce, 306
Kipling, Rudyard, 53, 57, 59, 91, 92, 115, 131 n., 143; verse, 53–4; imperialism, 53–7, 291; short stories, 54–6, 309; novels, 56–7; children's stories, 56–7, 309
Kirkup, James, 243, 244 n.
Knight, Eric, 115 n., 211 n.
Krafft-Ebing, Richard von, 214, 220
Kronenberger, Louis, 28 n.

Labour Party, 43, 51
Laforgue, Jules, 15, 16, 21, 205, 253 n., 255, 256, 259 n., 260, 263, 277–8, 279, 280, 281, 282, 284, 285
Lafourcade, Georges, 134, 256 n.
Lahey, G. F., 176 n.
Lamarck, Jean Baptiste, 146, 158, 160, 161, 173, 300
Land League, 63
Landor, Walter, 76
Lane, Homer, 46, 233
Lane, John, 24
Langer, Susanne K., 287 n.
Larkin, James, 74
Laski, Harold, 49 n., 51
Lautréamont, Comte de, 227, 235, 255
Lawrence, D. H., 47, 94, 145, 151, 152, 154, 169, 176, 185, 206, 217, 219, 233, 243, 301, 309, 311; Aaron's Rod, 225; Apocalypse, 300; Birds, Beasts and Flowers, 172, 225; The Boy in the Bush, 299; Collected Poems, 172 n.; Etruscan Places, 300; Fantasia of the Unconscious, 171, 223, 299; Kangaroo, 84, 226, 298; Lady

Lawrence, D. H. (continued)
Chatterley's Lover, 225, 226; Last Poems, 172; "Love among the Haystacks," 226, 303; "The Man Who Died," 226, 300; Mornings in Mexico, 298; Nettles, 172 n.; Pansies, 172 n.; "Piano," 171; The Plumed Serpent, 84, 171, 226, 292, 299; Psychoanalysis and the Unconscious, 223; The Rainbow, 226, 313; Reflections on the Death of a Porcupine, 298; "St. Mawr," 298; Sea and Sardinia, 298; Sons and Lovers, 148 n., 222–3, 224, 226, 228, 303; The Trespasser, 299; "Virgin Youth," 171; The White Peacock, 303; Women in Love, 224–5, 226, 292, 299; social and political ideas, 44, 44 n., 46, 83–4; primitivism, 83–4, 88, 171–2, 298–300; occultism and Hinduism, 163, 171–2, 299, 303; influence on Huxley, 172–3; poems, 171–2, 306, 307; the unconscious, 171, 222–7, 232; symbolism, 172, 287, 291–2, 294; technique, 226; use of myth, 298–300, 311, 314, 316; debt to Hardy, 303
Lawrence, Frieda, 223, 299 n.
Lawrence, T. E., 58–9
Leavis, F. R., 210–11, 299 n.
Lee, Laurie, 243, 244 n.
Lee-Hamilton, Eugene, 264
Left Review, 44
Legge, Sheila, 236
Lehmann, A. G., 246 n.
Lehmann, John, 46, 47 n.
Lehmann, Rosamond, 208 n.
Lenin, Nikolai, 43, 45, 52
Leverson, Ada, 116 n.
Lévi, Eliphas, 165, 168, 184, 251, 267, 268, 269, 270, 272
Levin, Harry, 150 n., 228 n.
Lévy-Bruhl, Lucien, 314
Lewis, Alan, 98 n.
Lewis, C. Day, see Day Lewis, Cecil
Lewis, C. S., 184–5
Lewis, Lloyd, 7 n.

Lewis, Mark, 235, 238
Lewis, Wyndham, 24, 83, 86, 87;
  The Apes of God, 88; The Art
  of Being Ruled, 88; Childer-
  mass, 209; Hitler, 89; The
  Revenge for Love, 89; Rotting
  Hill, 89; Self Condemned, 89;
  Tarr, 88; Time and Western
  Man, 88, 209; The Wild Body,
  88
Liberal Party, 53
Liberalism, 53, 83, 181
Liddell, Robert, 108 n.
Lillo, George, 29
Lindsay, Maurice, 78 n.
Little magazines, 23-5
Little Review, The, 199
Llewellyn, Richard, 131 n.
Logical Positivists, 26
London Stage Society, 34
Longaker, Mark, 10 n., 110 n.
Longfellow, Henry, 12
Lowell, Amy, 87
Lowry, Malcolm, 292
Loyola, St. Ignatius, 176
Lucas, F. L., 216 n.
Lugné-Poe, Aurélien, 259
Luhan, Mabel Dodge, 299 n.,
  364 n.
Lully, Ramon, 165
Lynd, Helen, 27 n.

Macardle, Dorothy, 63 n.
Macaulay, Rose, 96 n.
Macaulay, Thomas, 109
MacBride, John, 74, 75
MacDiarmid, Hugh, 43, 45, 50-1,
  82, 89
MacDonagh, Thomas, 73, 74, 75
MacDonald, George, 184
McGreevy, Thomas, 228 n.
Machen, Arthur, 117, 170-1, 309
Mackenzie, Compton, 148 n.,
  220 n.
MacLean, Alistair, 97 n.
MacLiammoir, Michael, 72
MacMahon, Bryan, 81 n.
MacNeice, Louis, 48 n., 50
Madge, Charles, 242 n., 243
Maeterlinck, Maurice, 117, 255,
  256, 266, 268, 271; plays, 259-
  61

Magalaner, Marvin, 150 n.
Magazines, little, 23-5
Malinowski, Bronislaw, 297, 312
Mallarmé, Stéphane, 20, 21, 104,
  239, 246, 252-3, 254, 255, 256,
  257, 259 n., 260, 261, 263, 264,
  265, 266, 267, 274, 277, 281,
  282, 285, 286, 290
Malone, A. E., 66 n.
Mangan, James, 13, 64, 65, 166
Mann, Thomas, 220, 312; Death
  in Venice, 290; "Tonio Krö-
  ger," 22 n., 290
Manning, Frederick, 97
Mansfield, Katherine, 101, 206-7,
  208, 219-20
March, Richard, 282 n.
Maritain, Jacques, 86, 91
Markiewicz, Constance, 73-4, 75
Marsden, Dora, 24
Marsh, Edward, 97, 305-6
Marshall, Archibald, 114 n.
Marshall, Bruce, 115 n.
Martinists, 165
Martino, Pierre, 121 n., 246 n.
Martyn, Edward, 65-6, 67, 73, 79
Marvell, Andrew, 15, 26, 179 n.,
  279, 307
Marx, Eleanor, 30
Marx, Karl, 27, 35, 43, 44, 46,
  48, 233, 233 n., 234, 236, 237,
  296
Masefield, John, 97, 304-5, 306,
  306 n.
Mason, Ellsworth, 150 n.
Mathers, MacGregor, 165, 269,
  270
Matthiessen, F. O., 279 n.
Maugham, W. Somerset, 43; Ash-
  den, 62; Cakes and Ale, 140 n.;
  The Explorer, 61; Liza of Lam-
  beth, 131 n.; The Moon and
  Sixpence, 62; Of Human Bond-
  age, 148-9; The Razor's Edge,
  149, 175; The Summing Up,
  111 n., 131 n.; plays, 43, 110,
  111-12; stories, 61
Maupassant, Guy de, 54, 61, 80,
  121, 124, 125, 131, 131 n., 134,
  142, 142 n., 149, 170
Maurras, Charles, 86, 89, 90, 91
Maxwell, D. E. S., 282 n.

May, J. L., 24 n.
Meaning, science of, 25–6
Melville, Cecil, 88 n.
Melville, Herman, 246, 287
Menen, Aubrey, 107 n.; *Dead Man in the Silver Market*, 63 n.; *The Duke of Gallodoro*, 100 n.; *The Prevalence of Witches*, 100 n.
Meredith, George, 145, 287
Merrild, Knud, 299 n.
Merrill, Stuart, 254, 256, 259
Metaphysical poetry, 26, 118, 177, 179 n., 264 n., 279, 307; *see also* Donne, John, and Marvell, Andrew
Mew, Charlotte, 306 n.
Meyerhoff, Hans, 203 n.
Meynell, Alice, 180 n.
Mill, John Stuart, 32
Millar, George, 310 n.
Milne, A. A., 43, 114
Milton, John, 91, 177, 273, 282
Mitchell, Susan, 79
Mitchison, Naomi, 310 n.
Monro, Harold, 306, 306 n.
Montague, C. E., 97
Moore, George, 8, 24, 65–6, 79, 132, 136, 137, 189, 190; *Avowals*, 9 n.; *The Brook Kerith*, 9, 190, 258; *Celibates*, 129; *Confessions of a Young Man*, 8, 9, 14, 126, 128, 256–7; *Conversations in Ebury Street*, 9 n., 258; *A Drama in Muslin*, 128, 257; *Esther Waters*, 128–9; *Evelyn Innes*, 129; *Flowers of Passion*, 256–7; *Hail and Farewell*, 66 n., 190–1; *Héloïse and Abélard*, 9; *Impressions and Opinions*, 13–14, 128, 258 n.; *The Lake*, 190; *Literature at Nurse*, 127; *Memoirs of My Dead Life*, 190; *A Modern Lover*, 126; *Modern Painting*, 8, 14; *A Mummer's Wife*, 126–7, 132, 134; *Parnell and His Island*, 63; *Pagan Poems*, 257; *Pure Poetry*, 9; *Sister Teresa*, 129; *The Untilled Field*, 190; æstheticism and style, 5, 8–9; impressionism, 13–14; naturalism, 126–9,

Moore, George (*continued*) 135; symbolism, 128, 256–8, 261; later narrative method, 190–1
Moore, Harry T., 299 n.
Moore, Nicholas, 242 n.
Moore, T. Sturge, 263 n., 305, 306 n.
Moore, Thomas, 72
Moore, Virginia, 270 n.
More, Paul Elmer, 86, 91
Moréas, Jean, 20, 254, 255, 261, 263, 272, 281
Morgan, Charles, 9 n.
Morris, William, 5, 11, 27, 28
Mottram, R. H., 97 n.
Mozart, Wolfgang, 102, 107, 161, 286
Mudie's circulating library, 127
Muggeridge, Malcolm, 156 n.
Muir, Edwin, 82, 232–3, 243, 244, 311
Muir, Willa, 243
Muller, Herbert J., 199 n.
Murray, T. C., 70 n.
Murry, J. Middleton, 206, 217
Mussolini, Benito, 38, 83 n., 90
Myers, L. H., 310 n.
Myers, W. L., 195 n.
Myth, 157, 167, 169, 212, 229–30, 233, 237, 239, 243, 246 ff.

Na gCopaleen, Myles, 82, 197 n.
Nashe, Thomas, 114
National Theatre Society, *see* Abbey Theatre
National Vigilance Association, 127–8
Nationalism: English, 52–62; Irish, 63–82; Scottish, 82; Welsh, 82 n.
Naturalism: English, 24, 126–53; French, 120, 124–5; *see also* Zola, Émile
Nelson, Lord, 137, 139
Neoclassicism, 52, 76, 77, 109, 215–16; French, 18, 84, 86; English, 76, 77, 78, 84–7, 90, 109, 215–16, 280
Neo-Platonism, 85; *see also* Plato
Neo-Thomism, 86, 88, 242
Nethercot, A. H., 28 n.

Nettleship, J. T., 24
New Age, The, 283
New Apocalypse, the, 243, 311
New Burlington Galleries, 236
New Country, 56
New Critics, 26
New Signatures, 23
New Verse, 240
New Writing, 46
Newbolt, Henry, 57
Newby, P. H., 107 n.
Newman, John Henry, 176
Newton, Isaac, 132, 137, 139, 152, 154, 155, 173
Nichols, Robert, 98, 306
Nichols, Ross, 312 n.
Nicoll, Allardyce, 39 n., 42
Nicolson, Sir Harold, 110 n., 217
Nicolson, Marjorie, 155 n.
Nietzsche, Friedrich, 83, 84, 159, 160
Nikhilananda, Swami, 175
Nobbe, Susanne Howe, 61 n., 145 n.
Noh play, 67-8
Nolan, Brian, see O'Brien, Flann
Nordau, Max, 17 n.
Normal School of Science, 143
Nuttall, Zelia, 299

O'Brien, Flann, 197 n.
O'Brien, Justin, 145 n.
Obscurity, 18-23
O'Casey, Sean, 51, 70-2, 74
Occultism, 164-73, 184, 251, 267-74, 296-9, 303, 310
O'Connor, Frank, poems, 78; stories and novels, 80-1, 81 n.
O'Connor, John, 180
O'Connor, W. V., 202 n.
O'Duffy, Erin, 78
O'Faolain, Sean, 80, 81-2
O'Flaherty, Liam, political novels, 80; studies of neurotics, 221
Ogden, C. K., 25 n.
O'Grady, Standish, 64
Olcott, H. S., 164
O'Leary, John, 65
Olson, Elder, 241 n.
O'Neill, Eugene, 71, 312
O'Rahilly, Egan, 78

O'Rahilly, the, 74
Order of the Golden Dawn, 165, 267, 269, 273
Orwell, George, 43, 49-50, 53 n., 63 n., 103, 293
Osborne, E. A., 48 n.
O'Sullivan, Seumas, 79
O'Sullivan, Vincent, 6 n.
O'Toole, St. Lawrence, 186
Owen, Wilfred, 98, 100
Oxford Movement, 176

Pall Mall Gazette, 7
Papus, 165
Paracelsus, 165
Parkinson, Thomas, 65 n.
Parnassians, 249, 276, 279, 281
Parnell, Charles, 63, 64, 72, 138
Pasteur, Louis, 161
Pater, Walter, 5-6, 7, 8, 9, 10, 11, 12, 13, 14, 15, 16, 17, 128, 170, 176, 177, 179
Paterism, 5-17, 177, 179
Patrick, Arthur, 16 n.
Paul, Elliot, 23
Peace Pledge Union, 173, 174
Peacock, Thomas, 102
Pearse, Padraic, 72, 73, 74, 75, 82
Pearson, Hesketh, 6 n., 28 n.
Pease, Edward, 27 n.
People's Front, the, 48
Péret, Benjamin, 235
Perse, St.-J., 235
Personality, split or multiple, 188, 189-90, 204, 227
Peters, W. A. M., 176 n.
Petrie, Sir William, 297, 299
Phillpotts, Eden, 303 n.
Phoenix, 303
Physics since 1900: effect on literature, 20, 37, 150-3
Picasso, Pablo, 235, 283, 297
Pick, John, 176 n., 178 n.
Piers Plowman, 177
Pinero, Arthur, 38, 39, 110, 113
Pippett, Aileen, 199 n.
Pitter, Ruth, 182 n.
Planck, Max, 151, 212
Plato, 3, 163, 167, 168, 273, 305, 315
Plomer, William, 96, 107 n., 294 n.
Plotinus, 273

Plunkett, Horace, 170
Plunkett, James, 81 n.
Plunkett, Joseph, 74
Poe, Edgar, 5, 10
Pope, Alexander, 15, 86, 87, 114, 275
Porphyry, 273
Positivism, 122, 124; logical, 26
Postwar disillusionment, 92, 96–114, 284
Pound, Ezra, 10 n., 21, 24, 67, 68 n., 87, 90 n., 99, 118, 275–6, 279 n., 281
Powell, Anthony, 106–7, 148 n.
Powys, J. C., 195 n., 304
Powys, T. F., 114 n.
Prabhavananda, Swami, 175
Praz, Mario, 17 n., 83 n.
Prescott, H. F. M., 310 n.
Preston, Raymond, 282 n.
Primitivism, 83–4, 88, 171–2, 296–300, 310–11
Pritchett, V. S., 107 n.
Proust, Marcel, 44, 192–3, 205, 209, 220, 223, 275 n., 290, 291, 294, 307, 308
Psychoanalysis, 151, 212 ff., 296–7, 307, 311; effect on criticism, 213–17; effect on biography, 217; effect on the novel, 218–31, 244–5; effect on poetry, 231–43
Punch, 6
Purcell, Edmund, 108, 179
Pythagoras, 273

Quennell, Peter, 246 n.

Rabelais, François, 114
Racine, Jean, 86, 280
Raine, Kathleen, 244 n.
Rajan, B., 282 n.
Ramsey, Warren, 279 n.
Ransome, Arthur, 6 n.
Raymond, Marcel, 246 n., 250
Read, Herbert, 49 n., 311; Annals of Innocence, 276 n., 308; The Green Child, 308; Reason and Romanticism, 209; politics, 49 n., 90 n.; poems, 99, 243; criticism, 209, 215–16; surrealism, 236–7

Realism: objective, 120 ff.; subjective, 187 ff.; see also Naturalism
Reavy, George, 237 n.
Redmond, John, 73
Régnier, Henri de, 275
Reid, Forrest, 118 n., 148 n.
Religion, 83, 86–7, 155 ff., 175–86; see also Catholicism, Roman
Remarque, Erich, 97
Retté, Adolphe, 259
Révolution surréaliste, La, 235
Revue Wagnérienne, La, 253, 258
Rexroth, Kenneth, 244 n.
Reynolds, Horace, 65 n.
Rhodes, Cecil, 54
Rhymers' Club, 9–10, 11
Rhys, Ernest, 9, 10 n.
Rhys, Keidrych, 82 n.
Richards, I. A., 14, 44, 181, 190, 314; Coleridge on Imagination, 15 n., 25, 209; Practical Criticism, 25; Principles of Literary Criticism, 14–15, 25; Science and Poetry, 26, 169
Richardson, Dorothy, 192, 194–5, 201, 210, 219, 226; Pilgrimage, 195; Pointed Roofs, 195
Richardson, Henry Handel, 145 n., 148 n.
Rickword, Edgell, 44
Ridler, Anne, 182 n.
Rilke, Rainer, 45
Rimbaud, Arthur, 14, 19, 20, 21, 23, 212, 227, 234, 235, 237, 238, 246, 249, 250–2, 253, 255, 256, 261, 262, 268, 271, 272, 281, 282, 283, 285, 286, 307, 308
Rivers, W. H. R., 98, 214–15
Robbins, R. H., 282 n.
Roberts, Lynette, 244 n.
Roberts, Michael, 86 n.
Roberts, Morley, 58 n.
Robertson, T. W., 38
Robinson, Henry Morton, 228 n.
Robinson, Lennox, 70, 304
Rodgers, W. R., 150 n., 178 n., 243, 244 n., 312
Rolfe, Frederick, 179, 180
Rolland, Romain, 148 n.

Rolleston, T. W., 9, 64

Romanticism, 77, 78, 86, 91, 125, 187, 214, 215, 234, 237, 243, 264, 283, 296, 307

Rook, Alan, 98 n.

Rootham, Helen, 283

Rosenberg, Isaac, 98 n.

Rosenblatt, Louis, 5 n.

Rosicrucians, 165, 268, 269, 270

Rossetti, Christina, 14

Rossetti, Dante, 5, 6, 7, 11, 24, 267

Rothenstein, William, 10 n.

Roughton, Roger, 238

Rousseau, Henri, 301

Rousseau, Jean Jacques, 47, 86

Royalism, 86, 87, 90

Ruggles, Eleanor, 176

Russell, George (A.E.), 66, 67, 74, 79, 164, 169–70, 176; poems, 170, 232, 251

Rutland, William, 140 n.

Sackville-West, V., 203 n.

Sade, Marquis de, 103

Saga novel, 145, 145 n.

Saki (Munro, H. H.), 115–16

Salisbury, Lord, 53

Samain, Albert, 263

Samhain, 67

Sansom, William: A Bed of Roses, 294 n.; The Body, 244 n.; Fireman Flower, 244–5; Something Terrible, Something Lovely, 245

Sardou, Victorien, 29

Sartre, Jean-Paul, 312

Sassoon, Siegfried, 97–8, 98 n.

Saturday Review, The, 33, 38

Savage, D. S., 211 n.

Savoy, The, 11, 24, 263

Scarfe, Francis, 233 n., 241 n., 242 n.

Schliemann, Heinrich, 297

Schopenhauer, Arthur, 139

Schweitzer, Albert, 156 n.

Schwob, Marcel, 259

Science: effect on literature, 101, 117, 120–4, 131–2, 136–7, 142–4, 150–3; rebellion against, 152–3, 154; see also Physics

Scribe, Augustin, 29

Scrutiny, 210–11

Semantics, 15, 25–6

Shakespeare, William, 26 n., 33, 35, 44, 85, 92, 196, 200, 222

Shanks, Edward, 53 n.

Sharp, William, 261 n.

Shaw, Bernard, 6 n., 33, 44, 44 n., 57, 180, 227; Androcles and the Lion, 160 n., 298; The Apple Cart, 37; Back to Methuselah, 161; Cæsar and Cleopatra, 83; Candida, 33, 34; The Devil's Disciple, 83 n., 160; The Doctor's Dilemma, 83 n., 160; Dramatic Opinions, 28, 33, 160 n.; Everybody's Political What's What, 36; Fanny's First Play, 34–5; Geneva, 38, 83 n.; Getting Married, 34, 217; Heartbreak House, 36–7, 42; Intelligent Woman's Guide, 35; The Irrational Knot, 28–9, 30; Major Barbara, 83, 160; Man and Superman, 83, 159, 160–1, 312; The Millionairess, 37–8; Misalliance, 34, 217; On the Rocks, 37, 83, 161–2; The Philanderer, 31–2; Pygmalion, 35, 217–18; The Quintessence of Ibsenism, 30; St. Joan, 152, 161, 218; The Simpleton of the Unexpected Isles, 37; The Six of Calais, 162; Too True to Be Good, 37, 152, 224; An Unsocial Socialist, 28; Mrs. Warren's Profession, 32, 34; Widowers' Houses, 31; anarchism, 27; socialism, 27–8, 32, 35, 83, 159; political opinions, 27, 35–6, 83; music criticism, 29; Ibsenism, 29–34, 38–43; feminism, 31–3; drama criticism, 33–4, 38–9; his love of Nietzschean superman, 35–6, 83, 159–60; his debt to Butler, 34, 147, 159, 160, 161; his sadistic temper, 83; his religion, 159–63, 164; on the unconscious, 217–18

Shelley, Percy, 3, 47, 86, 139, 160, 164, 216, 238, 267, 268, 270 n., 296, 315

Sherard, Robert, 6 n.

Shiels, George, 304

Shorter, Clement, 31

Shri Purohit Swami, 169

Sigerson, George, 64

Sinclair, May, 148 n., 195 n., 218–19

Sinnett, A. P., 164, 167

Sinn Fein, 73, 74

Sitwell, Edith, 88, 285; her terrible gaiety, 98, 284; later poems, 100, 284; symbolism, 246, 282–4

Sitwell, Osbert, 88, 100, 104 n., 284 n.

Sitwell, Sacheverell, 85 n., 88; poems, 85 n.; his discovery of the baroque, 100

Slocum, John, 150 n.

Smith, Grover, 282 n.

Smith, Henry, 7 n.

Smith, Sydney Goodsir, 82, 243, 284

Smithers, Leonard, 24

Smith's circulating library, 129

Snow, C. P., 210

Social Democratic Federation, 27

Socialism, 27–8, 83, 159

Sophocles, 222

Soupault, Philippe, 235

Soutar, William, 82

Spanish-American War, 59

Spanish Civil War, 48–50, 78, 89–90, 90 n.

Spectator, 256

Spencer, Herbert, 132, 136

Spender, Stephen, 43, 45, 47–8, 50, 148 n., 221 n., 233 n., 234

Spenser, Edmund, 64

Spilka, Mark, 299 n.

Spillane, Mickey, 82

Spinoza, 244

Squire, J. C., 306

Stalin, Joseph, 38, 49, 50

Stanford, Derek, 241 n.

Starkie, Enid, 217, 246 n., 250

Stearns, Marshall W., 241

Stein, Gertrude, 188, 189, 209, 283

Steinman, Martin, 274 n.

Stendhal, 135

Stephen, Karin, 202

Stephen, Sir Leslie, 202

Stephens, James: poems, 79; prose, 79–80

Stern, G. B., 145 n.

Sterne, Laurence, 101, 201, 205

Stevens, Wallace, 249, 286, 293

Stevenson, R. L., 54, 57, 189

Stone of Scone, 82

Strachey, John, 43–4, 49 n.

Strachey, Lytton, 108–10, 217

Strauss, David, 155, 176

Stravinsky, Igor, 283

Stream of consciousness, 151–2, 187 ff., 196 ff., 278

Strindberg, August, 72, 228, 259; Dream Play, 227

Strong, L. A. G., 148 n., 228 n.

Suez Canal, 58

Surrealism, 20, 88, 93, 213, 234–6, 243, 244, 246 ff., 255, 273, 277; English, 236–45

Surréalism, 237

Surréalisme au service de la révolution, Le, 235

Swedenborg, Emmanuel, 247–8, 251, 267, 268

Sweeney, John, 241 n., 282 n.

Sweeney Todd, 39

Swift, Jonathan, 16, 50, 72, 101, 157, 247, 313

Swinburne, Algernon, 5, 6, 7, 8, 10, 11, 217, 256, 263

Swinnerton, Frank, 131 n., 144, 195, 305

Symbolism, French, 13, 18, 19–21, 86, 87, 128, 187, 196, 205, 206, 207, 235, 246 ff., 277; manifesto, 21–2, 251, 254; English imitation of, 21–2, 246, 254–95; novels, 287–95

Symonds, J. A., 76

Symons, A. J. A., 10 n., 179 n.

Symons, Arthur, 5, 24, 279–80; "The Decadent Movement in Literature," 261; The Symbolist Movement in Literature, 261, 265, 267, 277; æstheticism, 5, 9, 10–11, 13; impressionism, 14, 261; decadence, 15, 16, 179, 261; symbolism, 246, 261–3, 266–7, 268, 271, 282, 284 n.

Synesthesia, 248, 251, 257, 259, 262, 283
Synge, J. M., 63, 64, 67, 70, 71, 81; plays, 68–9, 304

T., E. (Miriam in *Sons and Lovers*), 223
Taine, Hippolyte, 120, 121, 122, 124, 132, 152
Tambimuttu, 282 n.
Tanguy, Yves, 235, 237
Taupin, René, 276 n., 279 n.
Taylor, Estella, 63 n.
Temple, Ruth, 256 n.
Tennyson, Alfred, 5, 21, 127, 177, 217, 306
Thackeray, William, 96
Théâtre d'Art, 259
Théâtre de l'Œuvre, 259, 266
Théâtre Libre, 31, 259
Théâtre Montparnasse, 260
Theocritus, 305
Theosophy, 155, 164, 170, 171, 180, 223, 267, 268, 269, 316; see also Blavatsky, Mme H. P.
Thibaudet, Albert, 246 n.
Thirkell, Angela, 116–17
Thomas, Dylan, 23, 90 n., 119, 178 n., 236, 238, 246; *Portrait of the Artist*, 148; *Quite Early One Morning*, 308; *Under Milk Wood*, 242; poems, 23, 238–43, 284, 285, 286, 308; stories, 238; use of myth, 311
Thomas, Edward, 305
Thompson, Francis, 179 n.
Thoreau, Henry, 301
Tiller, Terence, 243, 244 n.
Tillich, Paul, 185
Tillyard, E. M. W., 155 n.
Time, preoccupation with, 134, 188, 203, 204, 209
Tindall, W. Y., 150 n., 228 n., 287 n., 289 n., 292 n.
Todhunter, John, 64
Tolkien, J. R. R., 115 n.
Tomlinson, H. M., 71 n.
Tory (Conservative) Party, 53, 63, 89, 91
Toynbee, Philip, 208 n., 312 n.
Transcendentalism, 125, 155 ff., 246 ff., 202, 203, 301

transition, 23, 236
Treece, Henry, 216 n., 241 n., 242, 243
Trilling, Lionel, 96 n., 213 n.
Trollope, Anthony, 116
Turgenyev, Ivan, 70, 128, 145, 188–9, 190, 191, 194, 206
Turner, W. J., 232
Tyler, Sir Edward, 296, 299
Tynan, Katharine, 64, 168, 272
Tyndall, John, 164
Tzara, Tristan, 234–5

Ulrich, Carolyn, 24 n.
Unconscious, the, 19, 88, 212 ff., 247, 251, 271–2, 283–4, 297, 298, 299, 307–8
Unger, Leonard, 282 n.
University College, 82
University Wits, 118–19
Upward, Edward, 44, 244 n.
Ussher, Arland, 63 n.

Valéry, Paul, 246, 255, 263 n., 286
Vedanta and the West, 175
Vedanta Society, 175
Vergil, 315
Verhaeren, Émile, 255, 256, 275, 276
Verlaine, Paul, 19, 235, 246, 247, 249–50, 253, 255, 257, 258, 261, 262, 266, 282, 284
Verne, Jules, 143
Vicaire, 253 n.
Vico, Giambattista, 228, 230, 313, 316
Villiers de l'Isle Adam, Philippe, 253, 255, 256, 265, 268, 271, 283; *Axël*, 268, 269
Vitalism, 155, 158, 160
Vizetelly, Henry, 127–8
Von Hügel, Friedrich, 78
Vorticism, 87

Wade, Allan, 65 n., 77 n.
Wagenknecht, Edward, 199 n.
Wagner, Geoffrey, 82 n., 88 n.
Wagner, Richard, 29, 33, 84, 159, 160, 248, 254, 259, 263, 289, 299
Wain, John, 107 n., 119
Wales, 82 n.

Walpole, Hugh, 221 n.
Ward, Mrs. Humphrey, 156 n.
Warner, Rex, 49, 244, 244 n.
Warner, Sylvia, 114 n.
Watkins, Vernon, 243, 244 n., 311, 312 n.
Watson, William, 16
Watteau, Antoine, 249
Waugh, Arthur, 24
Waugh, Evelyn, 24, 92, 107, 107 n., 108, 113, 114, 180; *Black Mischief*, 62–3; *Brideshead Revisited*, 100; *Decline and Fall*, 105; *A Handful of Dust*, 105; *Helena*, 106 n., 310 n.; *The Loved One*, 106; *Men at Arms*, 97 n.; *Officers and Gentlemen*, 97; *Put Out More Flags*, 105–6; *Scoop*, 63 n.; *Scott-King's Modern Europe*, 106; *Tactical Exercise*, 106; *Vile Bodies*, 105; inclination toward fascism, 90 n.; Catholicism, 104, 105, 106
Weaver, Harriet, 24
Webb, Mary, 303–4
Webb, Sidney, 27 n., 83
Weber, Carl, 303 n.
Webster, H. C., 140 n.
Webster, John, 277, 278, 307
Welch, Denton, 148, 220–1
Wellek, René, 26 n.
Wellesley, Lady Dorothy, 77 n.
Wells, H. G., 24, 44, 44 n., 47, 56, 57, 136, 150, 163, 169, 180, 184, 200, 296; *Ann Veronica*, 32 n.; *Bron*, 192; *Experiment in Autobiography*, 144; *History of Mr. Polly*, 144; *The Invisible Man*, 143; *The Island of Dr. Moreau*, 143; *Kipps*, 144; *Love and Mrs. Lewisham*, 143–4; *A Modern Utopia*, 144 n.; *The New Machiavelli*, 144; *The Open Conspiracy*, 163; *The Time Machine*, 143; *This Misery of Boots*, 144 n.; *Tono-Bungay*, 144; *The War of the Worlds*, 143; *The World of William Clissold*, 163; scientific fantasies, 143; novels, 144; Fabianism, 144 n.; religion, 163

West, Alick, 44 n.
West, Geoffrey, 144 n.
West, Rebecca, 219 n.
Weston, Jessie, 314
Weyand, Norman, 176 n.
Wheels, 285
Wheelwright, Philip, 287 n.
Whistler, James, 5, 7, 8, 15
White, Gilbert, 300
White, T. H., 115 n.
Whiteing, Richard, 131 n.
Whitman, Walt, 47, 172, 177, 255, 276
Wilde, Oscar, 5, 9, 11, 24, 29, 102, 104, 116, 132, 179, 264, 280; "The Harlot's House," 258; *An Ideal Husband*, 111; *The Importance of Being Earnest*, 111; *Intentions*, 7, 13, 17, 259; *Lady Windermere's Fan*, 111; *The Picture of Dorian Gray*, 7–8, 11, 259; *Poems*, 6, 258; *Salomé*, 17, 259, 260; "The Sphinx," 258; *A Woman of No Importance*, 111; æstheticism, 5, 6–8; impressionism, 13; decadence, 16, 17, 258–9, 260–1; plays, 110–11; symbolism, 246, 258–9, 260–1
Wiley, Paul, 140 n.
Williams, Charles, 177 n., 183–4, 312 n.
Williamson, Claude, 176 n.
Williamson, George, 282 n.
Wilson, Angus, 221 n.
Wilson, Edmund, 53 n., 228 n., 279 n.
Wingfield-Stratford, Esme, 27 n.
Wintringham, Tom, 48
Wodehouse, P. G., 116
Wolfe, Thomas, 148
Wood, Grant, 85
Woolf, Virginia, 4 n., 192, 205, 210, 219; *Mr. Bennett and Mrs. Brown*, 136; *Between the Acts*, 291; *The Common Reader*, 14, 200 n.; *Mrs. Dalloway*, 201, 202, 203, 204, 220; *The Death of the Moth*, 4 n., 96 n.; *The Haunted House*, 204; *Jacob's Room*, 203, 204;

Woolf, Virginia (*continued*)
"The Mark on the Wall," 200;
"Modern Fiction," 199, 200;
Monday or Tuesday, 200; *Night
and Day*, 200; "Notes on an
Elizabethan Play," 201; *Orlando*, 32 n., 203; *A Room of
One's Own*, 32 n.; "Solid Objects," 204; *To the Lighthouse*,
201, 202, 203, 204, 220, 291;
The Voyage Out, 96 n., 200;
The Waves, 152, 190, 198,
203, 204; *A Writer's Diary*,
199 n.; *The Years*, 204; criticism, 14; feminism, 32 n.; objections to naturalism, 136, 145,
151, 200; stream of consciousness, 199–205, 220, 222, 226;
symbolism, 200–1, 287, 291;
transcendentalism, 202; anti-
intellectualism, 202, 227; concern with time, 203–4
Woman, "new," *see* Feminism
Wordsworth, William, 16, 17, 85,
137, 211, 214, 216, 275, 283,
296, 298, 300, 301, 302, 303,
305, 306, 307, 308
World War, first, reaction to, 92,
96 ff., 172, 284
World War, second, poets of,
98 n., 100, 284
Wren, Christopher, 102
Wycherley, William, 35, 112
Wyllie, John, 97 n., 210

Yates, Peter, 243, 285, 286
Yeats, Jack B., 24 n.
Yeats, John Butler, 11–12
Yeats, William Butler, 9–10, 11–
12, 13, 30, 35, 45, 53, 63, 69,
72, 79, 81, 84, 85, 93, 98,
110, 139, 169, 178, 182, 190,
198, 284, 286; "Adam's Curse,"
78; "Among School Children,"
273; *Autobiography*, 10 n., 266;
"The Cap and Bells," 272;
"Coole Parke, 1916," 75 n.;
Cathleen Ni Houlihan, 66, 67;
The Countess Cathleen, 66,
271; *Deirdre*, 67; "The Delphic
Oracle," 273; "The Double
Vision of Michael Robartes,"

Yeats, William Butler (*continued*)
167; "Easter, 1916," 75; *Es-
says*, 78 n.; "Fergus and the
Druid," 165; *Fighting the
Waves*, 78, 209–10, 231; "The
Fisherman," 76; "In Memory of
Eva Gore-Booth," 75; *The
King of the Great Clock Tower*,
78 n., 169, 315; *The King's
Threshold*, 67; *Land of Heart's
Desire*, 66, 180; *Last Poems*,
78; "Leda and the Swan," 273;
"Lines Written in Dejection," 76;
"Magic," 268; "Meditations in
Time of Civil War," 75; *Mosada*,
164; "Nineteen Hundred and
Nineteen," 75; "On a Political
Prisoner," 75; *On Baile's Strand*,
67; *The Only Jealousy of Emer*,
68; *On the Border*, 78 n.; *Ox-
ford Book of Modern Verse*,
11; *A Packet for Ezra Pound*,
166, 168–9; "The Phases of the
Moon," 166; "The Poet Pleads
with the Elemental Powers,"
269; *Purgatory*, 68; *The Resurrection*, 315; "Rosa Alchemica,"
11, 165, 270; "The Rose Tree,"
75; "Sailing to Byzantium," 77,
167, 168, 273, 315; "The Saint
and the Hunchback," 273; "The
Second Coming," 168, 315;
"September, 1913," 74; *The
Shadowy Waters*, 68, 266, 271;
"Sixteen Dead Men," 75; "The
Song of Wandering Aengus,"
272; "The Symbolism of Poetry," 267; "Three Marching
Songs," 78; "To a Friend
Whose Work Has Come to
Nothing," 76; "To Ireland in
the Coming Times," 166; "To
a Wealthy Man," 77; "To
Some I Have Talked with by
the Fire," 269; "To the Rose
upon the Rood of Time," 270;
"Two Songs from a Play," 168,
315; *A Vision*, 166, 167, 168,
169, 315; *The Wanderings of
Oisin*, 165–6, 272; "What Is
Popular Poetry?" 12; *Wheels
and Butterflies*, 78; "Who Goes

Yeats, William Butler (continued)
with Fergus?" 166; *The Wind
among the Reeds*, 266, 270,
271; *Words upon the Window
Pane*, 78 n.; nationalism, 64–8,
74–9, 166, 314; early poems,
64–5, 165–6; folklore, 64–5,
165–6, 272, 314–15; plays, 66–
8, 78, 164, 266, 271; political poems, 74–6, 78; change to
later manner, 76–9, 166–9,
272–3, 274; love of aristocracy,
76–7, 78, 273; doctrine of the
mask, 77, 93, 110, 274; occultism, 163–70, 267–70; the
Rose poems, 164, 165; symbolism, 166–8, 246, 265–74;

Yeats, William Butler (continued)
Hinduism, 169; use of the un-
conscious, 231–2, 271–2; use
of myth, 312, 314–15; doctrine
of cycles, 315–16
Yeats, Mrs. W. B., 166, 273
Yellow Book, The, 24
Young, Ella, 79
Young, Francis Brett, 306

Zola, Émile, 8, 70, 80, 86, 120,
121, 122–5, 128, 129, 130,
131, 133, 137, 140, 145 n.;
150, 151, 190, 287; *L'Assommoir*, 121, 123–4, 126, 127;
Au Bonheur des Dames, 124,
125, 136

WILLIAM YORK TINDALL was born in 1903 in Williamstown, Vermont. He went to public schools in Montpelier, Vermont, and New York City, and did both his undergraduate and graduate work at Columbia University, where he was awarded his Ph.D. in 1934. Apart from his teaching (he is a Professor of English at Columbia University), he has written several books on literary subjects.

THE TEXT of this book is set in Linotype TIMES ROMAN, designed by Stanley Morison for *The Times* (London), and first introduced by that newspaper in 1932. The book was composed, printed, and bound by THE COLONIAL PRESS INC., Clinton, Massachusetts. Paper manufactured by S. D. WARREN COMPANY, Boston, Massachusetts. Cover design by PAUL RAND.

Vintage Books

K-1	The Art of Teaching BY Gilbert Highet
K-2	The Stranger BY Albert Camus
K-3	Death in Venice & Seven Other Stories BY Thomas Mann
K-4	A Short History of Music BY Alfred Einstein
K-5A	Democracy in America BY Alexis de Tocqueville, VOL. I
K-5B	Democracy in America BY Alexis de Tocqueville, VOL. II
K-6	In Search of Theater BY Eric Bentley
K-7	Howards End BY E. M. Forster
K-8	The Immoralist BY André Gide
K-9	The American Political Tradition BY Richard Hofstadter
K-10	Stephen Crane: Stories and Tales EDITED BY R. W. Stallman
K-11	Lectures on Psychoanalytic Psychiatry BY A. A. Brill, M.D.
K-12	Poetry and the Age BY Randall Jarrell
K-13	James Joyce's Ulysses BY Stuart Gilbert
K-14	Moses and Monotheism BY Sigmund Freud
K-15	Hawthorne's Short Stories EDITED BY Newton Arvin
K-16	No Exit & Three Other Plays BY Jean-Paul Sartre
K-17	Freedom and Responsibility BY Carl Becker
K-18	The Life of Henri Brulard BY Stendhal
K-19	The Captive Mind BY Czeslaw Milosz
K-20	The Armed Vision BY Stanley Edgar Hyman
K-21	The Death of the Heart BY Elizabeth Bowen
K-22	The Law of Civilization and Decay BY Brooks Adams
K-23	The Plumed Serpent BY D. H. Lawrence
K-24	Poems and Essays BY John Crowe Ransom
K-25	The Vintage Mencken GATHERED BY Alistair Cooke
K-26	The American Democrat BY James Fenimore Cooper
K-27	Strait Is the Gate BY André Gide
K-28	Five Stories BY Willa Cather
K-29	Stories BY Frank O'Connor
K-30	The Rebel BY Albert Camus
K-31	Rendezvous with Destiny BY Eric Goldman
K-32	The Hero BY Lord Raglan
K-33A	Gide Journals EDITED BY Justin O'Brien, VOL. I (1889–1924)
K-33B	Gide Journals EDITED BY Justin O'Brien, VOL. II (1924–1949)
K-34	The Autobiography of Michel de Montaigne EDITED BY Marvin Lowenthal
K-35	Forces in Modern British Literature BY William York Tindall
K-36	Short Stories of Katherine Mansfield EDITED BY Elizabeth Bowen
K-37	The American Character BY D. W. Brogan
K-38	The Critical Performance EDITED BY Stanley Edgar Hyman
K-39	Poetics of Music BY Igor Stravinsky
K-40	The American Essays of Henry James EDITED BY Leon Edel
K-41	The Future of the Novel—Essays by Henry James EDITED BY Leon Edel